Democracy in Moderation

Montesquieu, Tocqueville, and Sustainable Liberalism

Democracy in Moderation views constitutional liberal democracy as grounded in a principle of avoiding extremes and striking the right balance among its defining principles of liberty, equality, religion, and sustainable order, thus tempering tendencies toward sectarian excess. Such moderation originally informed liberal democracy, but now is neglected. Moderation can guide us intellectually and practically about domestic and foreign policy debates, but also serve the sustainability of the constitutional, liberal republic as a whole. Our recent theory thus doesn't help our practice, given our concerns about polarization and sectarianism in ideas, policy, and politics. A rediscovery of Montesquieu and his legacy in shaping America's complex political order, including influence on Washington's practical moderation and Tocqueville's philosophical moderation, addresses these enduring theoretical and practical problems. Moderation also offers a deeper theory of leadership or statesmanship, particularly regarding religion and politics, and of foreign policy and strategy rooted in liberal democracy's first principles.

Paul O. Carrese is Professor of Political Science, United States Air Force Academy. He has been a Rhodes Scholar; Research Fellow at Harvard; Fulbright Scholar at University of Delhi; and Fellow of the James Madison Program, Princeton.

Moderation in the American founding
Constantino Brumidi's frescoed mural of 1873, showing President George Washington conferring with Thomas Jefferson and Alexander Hamilton, is located in the Senate Reception Room, room S-213 in the United States Capitol. Washington's capacity to balance and reconcile, even for a time, the opposing principles of two leading strains in American political thought embodies the political and philosophical balance that Montesquieu advocated, and Tocqueville developed.
Source: Architect of the Capitol.

Democracy in Moderation

Montesquieu, Tocqueville, and Sustainable Liberalism

PAUL O. CARRESE
United States Air Force Academy

CAMBRIDGE
UNIVERSITY PRESS

CAMBRIDGE
UNIVERSITY PRESS

University Printing House, Cambridge CB2 8BS, United Kingdom

One Liberty Plaza, 20th Floor, New York, NY 10006, USA

477 Williamstown Road, Port Melbourne, VIC 3207, Australia

4843/24, 2nd Floor, Ansari Road, Daryaganj, Delhi - 110002, India

79 Anson Road, #06-04/06, Singapore 079906

Cambridge University Press is part of the University of Cambridge.

It furthers the University's mission by disseminating knowledge in the pursuit of education, learning and research at the highest international levels of excellence.

www.cambridge.org
Information on this title: www.cambridge.org/9781107548367

First published 2016
First paperback edition 2017

A catalogue record for this publication is available from the British Library

ISBN 978-1-107-12105-8 Hardback
ISBN 978-1-107-54836-7 Paperback

For Susan
wife, mother, teacher, American and global citizen

I say it, and it seems to me I have brought forth this work only to prove it: the spirit of moderation ought to be that of the legislator; the political good, like the moral good, always is found between two limits.

Montesquieu, *On the Spirit of Laws*, Book 29, Ch. 1

This book is not precisely in anyone's camp; in writing it I did not mean either to serve or to contest any party; I undertook to see, not differently, but further than the parties; and while they are occupied with the next day, I wanted to ponder the future.

Tocqueville, *Democracy in America*, Introduction

Contents

Preface

Moderation is a philosophical as well as political and moral principle that we should take seriously in liberal, constitutional politics. We used to, we don't anymore, and we're paying the price. One price is intense polarization, a destructive kind of partisan and intellectual discourse, which now predominates in American culture and has analogues in other liberal democracies. Another consequence is America's incapacity, as leader of the alliance of liberal democracies and guarantor of a liberal order in world affairs, to sustain internal and external consensus on policies for perpetuating that alliance and the post-Cold War global order.

Into these dilemmas I propose that liberal democracy should seek its best form through moderation. Democracy in moderation would aim to strike the right balance among its several defining principles, while also tempering its endemic weaknesses or tendencies toward extremes. Moderation thus guides us about the current political contest in domestic or foreign affairs and about the manner in which to study and debate particular policies. More generally it guides, and warns, about the sustainability of the constitutional, liberal republic as a whole. Regarding America, we should consider it in one sense a democracy, as Tocqueville's famous study does. Yet to be sustainable as a free and egalitarian polity we always have been more than democratic, and Tocqueville advised us to affirm this complexity. We must connect current issues or demands, domestic or international, to the philosophical, moral, civic, and religious resources that sustain not one principle but the balance or blend of our principles – liberty as well as equality, and preserving our basic social and political capital as well as pursuing progress, to cite two examples. These deeper resources require replenishment through broad study, civil debate, and respectful recognition, not only through faithful remembrance. There is growing awareness in American higher education, and broader discourse, that our academic communities and public debates are not marked by breadth of study, but by self-selection into narrow schools, and that our academic and public debates are not civil and fruitful, but shrill and destructive. Thus there is reasonable worry about the trajectory of liberal democratic culture and politics.

Indeed theorists of liberal democracy, and thoughtful citizens, might notice that environmentalist thinking has persuaded many people to take seriously the idea of limits. This includes limits to or revisions of progress, thus the need to temper our confident quest for the new with a concern for viable patterns of consuming our resources. The moral and political analogue of this idea lies within the Preamble to the American Constitution, albeit mostly ignored. "We the People" are a sober, constitutionalized citizenry who do "ordain and establish" this legal-political order to "secure the Blessings of Liberty" – not only for "ourselves" in any generation but for "our Posterity." We should adapt the vogue currency of sustainability to help us rediscover the deeper resource of moderation. This virtue long enjoyed, after all, the status of "the golden mean." That constitutional Preamble, like the polity, encompasses a range of ends that don't easily fit together. The entire Constitution was the product of vigorous debate that required both advocacy of principle and recognition of alternative, competing principles – a capacity to modulate rhetoric and reconcile multiple views. If we cannot recover this capacity in the American polity and academy, and do so in concert with other liberal-democratic polities, we won't thrive, or perhaps even survive. If we can't rediscover intellectual and political moderation, we will have squandered our heritage and cheated our posterity.

My focus is America, but since it is the leading liberal democracy, and this is still the dominant form of politics in the world, the health and sustainability of this polity matter globally. I argue that a now nearly forgotten causal chain is crucial for us and for global affairs: the eighteenth-century French philosopher and jurist Montesquieu was the most important source of America's first political science and of the subsequent liberal global order marked by gradually expanding commerce and peace; Montesquieu elevated moderation as the central principle of his political science and of the humane policies in domestic and international realms that he sought; *The Federalist* opens and closes by invoking moderation, and the complex constitutionalism defended throughout the work is a Montesquieuan program to find balance and avoid extremes; further, the debate between Federalists, Anti-Federalists, and Democratic-Republicans that produced the Constitution, Bill of Rights, and first two decades of our constitutional politics itself embodies balance across rival principles; thus, to the extent that we have forgotten moderation as Montesquieu and the founders understood it, we do not understand ourselves, or the global order built upon these principles, whether we seek to endorse, criticize, or refine. Moreover, since Tocqueville views both Montesquieu and America through this lens, study of the sources and character of the American polity in terms of moderation is salient not only to understand America but also for global debates about "democratization" and the sustainability of liberal democracy itself. The editors of the *Journal of Democracy* declared in 2000 that "We are all

Tocquevilleans now," signaling a concern about not just extending but con-
solidating liberal constitutionalism, with Tocqueville's insights on the nexus of
political culture and institutions as a crucial resource. Americans and West-
erners should note the fact, for example, that our Asian partner India soon
will be both the world's most populous country and the world's largest liberal democracy. Given the immense complexity of principles that define modern India – equality and hierarchy, religion and secularism, nation building but
also regional and religious diversity – the ideal of balancing and reconciling
principles, while avoiding extremes, is salient.

Appreciation of moderation and its role in sustainability will require rediscovery, alas. Moderation once was understood as a central virtue of liberal
constitutionalism, but academia no longer teaches or writes much about it. Our
theory is failing our practice, since we still invoke moderation in politics and
discourse. This often occurs indirectly when criticizing the other side, in politics or thought, as extreme, single-minded, imbalanced – thus as unfair, unjust,
uncivil, or unreasonable. Or, moderation appears as a lament by ordinary folk
when wishing that leaders could tone down the rhetoric, or pull back from
hard-line stances, and just be productive. Or, we indirectly invoke it when worrying about single-mindedness or bias in ourselves or others, instead praising a
capacity to compromise not by abandoning principle but finding a higher middle ground that preserves competing, legitimate principles. The gap between
our mostly indifferent theory and these enduring practices indicates the persistence of qualities in human nature, or of a deeper culture, despite the efforts
of modernity and modern theory. This question deserves our attention, but this
would require self-criticism by modern minds. It is surprising, after all, that
moderation survives in our modern era of revolutions, radical progress, and
extremes of analytical ambition and doctrines in both thought and politics.

This is an American book in many ways, but it argues that two Frenchmen
understand our ideals and practice better than do the dominant schools in political theory today; and, as a book it first took form while teaching Tocqueville in
India. I intend no narrow-minded pride in arguing that study of America's constitutional and dispositional moderation is of global import, since our power
and influence can be used well or badly. These two spirits who teach us the
most about modern conceptions of moderation exemplify this balance of local
and global concerns; both were travelers in spirit and body to foreign lands,
and pioneering global thinkers. Montesquieu (1689–1755) is the first philosopher of a globalized, liberal commercial order; Tocqueville (1805–59) was the
first philosopher to forecast America as the predominant global power dedicated to liberty and equality, against autocracy. It nonetheless is a mark of
their philosophical moderation that they mostly studied liberal constitutionalism and social order; this was the basis for commercial and global concerns.
Their idea of moderation as a search for "the political good" begins in the dialogue between soul and city – though they don't often say this, since they seek a
hearing in the modern world – and then comprehends the broader world. The

effects are astounding: philosophical and political moderation, now neglected by elites, produced not mediocrity but the first truly global form of political, economic, and military power. It did so by reconciling and balancing principles: the Anglo-American republic, and allied liberal democracies, mixed liberty and commerce, military power and restraint, pluralism and enduring principle, continental scale and local self-government.

The American statesmen who built this new politics learned political science from Montesquieu above all, a science drawing upon Plutarch more than Hobbes, and premodern as well as modern philosophy. Tocqueville reformed this philosophy of moderation, drawing upon the study of Montesquieu and America; and, while his emphasis on Christianity is widely noted, we overlook his study of Publius in *The Federalist* and also of the life of George Washington by America's great chief Justice John Marshall. Tocqueville applied Montesquieu's balanced spirit in a transformed world. Upon considering the statesmanship and constitutionalism of the liberal democratic republic, he finds its religious principles as important as its philosophy – and finds the former in need of support. Indeed, for these philosophers and statesmen, moderation is a liberal and modern adaption of the classical and medieval ideals of political and intellectual balance in the Aristotelian tradition. One great fruit of this approach is religious liberty, which for the founders (and Montesquieu and Tocqueville) requires reasonable accommodation of the importance of religious belief for a healthy, sustainable republic rather than strict government neutrality about religion to protect individual conscience or Enlightenment rationalism. A second example explored here is the balance between justice and interest in America's first grand strategy and foreign policy, proposed and practiced by Washington; this stance is more concerned with exemplary justice than realists can abide, and more attuned to national security and interests than liberal idealists can endorse. Moreover, the structure and scope of this book tries to recover this more adequate political science – one that, through a balance and breadth of considerations, bespeaks moderation by comprehending domestic, constitutional, and international principles. This breaks with our current academic culture of single-mindedness and abstract theories in one field, ignoring connections to others.

We should rediscover voices who warned about various sorts of immoderation and the damage they do to the self-understanding, and self-governing, of a free people – voices from Montesquieu, and the statesmanlike moderation of Washington, to the moderate political science developed from these sources by Tocqueville and then revived, a century later, by scholars like Herbert Storing. Montesquieu noted that English liberty tended toward partisan conflict and free discourse, but also intellectual inwardness or narrowness: "In extremely absolute monarchies, historians betray the truth because they do not have the liberty to tell it; in extremely free states, historians betray the truth because of their very liberty, for, as it always produces divisions, every one becomes as much the slave of the prejudices of his faction as he would be of a despot"

(*The Spirit of Laws*, Book 19, Chapter 27, end). Because he also was a historian (publishing *Considerations on the Romans* a decade earlier), his warning encompasses broader intellectual activity and all such "schools." Academics are more susceptible, paradoxically, to this self-sorting and bias. Today academia often reinforces self-segregated, self-reinforcing paths of inquiry of left or right or other persuasions. Those who worry about destructive polarization in politics do not as often identify the intellectual imbalance that produces such phenomena. Tocqueville, too, sees this problem and offers a remedy. I have chosen as an epigraph his aim in *Democracy in America* "to see, not differently, but further than the parties" but I also am guided by his defense of candor: "it is because I was not an adversary of democracy that I wanted to be sincere with it. Men do not receive the truth from their enemies, and their friends scarcely offer it to them; that is why I have spoken it" (*Democracy*, Volume Two, Author's Notice).

This book is a sequel to *The Cloaking of Power: Montesquieu, Blackstone and the Rise of Judicial Activism* (University of Chicago, 2003), which addressed broad issues of liberal constitutionalism and political theory through a focus on the development of judicial power, and eventually of juridically enforced individualism that has provoked complaints about judicial activism. Concerns persist over judicial activism and the self-corroding quality of legal realism or instrumentalism, the eschewal of fixed or natural principles undergirding law and constitutionalism. While more should be said on those topics, this book shifts to a broader constitutional and philosophical moderation – from the negative aim to secure liberty through judicializing politics to the positive political virtue of moderation in constitutional balance and statesmanship. Still, constitutional law scholars and jurists might find here an argument for taking seriously Montesquieu, Blackstone, Hamilton, and Tocqueville as jurists deserving attention in their curricula and research. Their jurisprudence of moderation is a worthy alternative to the narrower schools that dominate academic and public discourse today.

Two fellowships, and two sabbaticals from the United States Air Force Academy, offered time and collegial experiences for developing and completing this book. A Fulbright Fellowship to University of Delhi in New Delhi, India, allowed me to teach political theory and a graduate seminar on *Democracy in America*, as well as to give lectures in the university and beyond about America, Tocqueville, American foreign policy, and religion and politics. I am grateful to the Fulbright Program and to my hosts, colleagues, and students in India for such extraordinary experiences. More recently, I held the Forbes Visiting Fellowship in the James Madison Program in American Ideals and Institutions, Department of Politics, Princeton University, which permitted a year of writing and conversation, during which I drafted the manuscript. I am grateful to Robby George and Brad Wilson, the other Fellows in my Madison Program class, Matt Franck of the Witherspoon Institute, the Princeton Politics Department, and the staff and supporters of the Madison Program. Amid the prevailing discourse of academia and public life, the Madison Program is a voice for moderation. I also am grateful to longtime friends and mentors Harvey Mansfield, James Stoner, Tim Fuller, and Paul Ludwig, and to new friendship with Rahul Sagar, among many other debts of gratitude to academic friends and mentors, including those who discussed these ideas with me in lectures and presentations, conferences, or as reviewers and editors. My colleagues, military and civilian, at the United States Air Force Academy across two decades have made it an honor to teach and write there about constitutionalism and the civic and intellectual virtues that sustain it.

Several of the chapters are revised versions of published journal articles or book chapters. I am grateful for permissions to reprint and revise granted from Johns Hopkins University Press, Palgrave Macmillan, Rowman & Littlefield/Lexington Books, and The Jack Miller Center and the University of Chicago Press. I have revised such essays (or parts thereof) to account for subsequent developments and as part of a coherent whole.

I am indebted to the editors of staff of Cambridge University Press for their support and professionalism and also to the keen insights provided by the external readers they procured. I am grateful to the Earhart Foundation for providing grant funds that allowed me to attend and present ideas from the book at two conferences. McDermott Library at the United States Air Force Academy, Tutt Library at Colorado College, and Firestone Memorial Library at Princeton University provided staff support and congenial places to work. The Architect of the Capitol helpfully provided an image of the fresco by Brumidi used for the cover art and frontispiece, and permission to use it.

The dedication bespeaks a gratitude beyond words to my wife and friend, the mother of our children Hannah and Dominic. All three have shown moderation and many other virtues toward me, and remind me of the larger and higher balance of life.

Prologue

The Spirit of Moderation in Constitutional Democracy

Academic and public discourse today retains a dim awareness that moderation was a political as well as moral virtue for classical and medieval political philosophy, defining the political good and justice by the avoidance of theoretical and practical extremes. This negative inquiry prepared for a principled middle ground or consensus that would best approximate justice and truth, precisely by reconciling worthy but competing principles. Broadly understood, Aristotle and Thomas Aquinas embody this twofold conception of moderation in the theory and practice of politics, as rooted in the Socratic tradition and adopted by Christianity. The inclusion of a balanced or mixed regime among the best regimes is one mark of their commitment to comprehending and balancing all the dimensions of political reality. Modern adaptations of moderation eventually produced an entirely new kind of regime and politics, an American order that reconciled principles hitherto seen as opposing extremes. Moreover, this complex polity became the model for a world order friendly to its principles and its security, with many peoples adopting its principle of moderation or balance to their particular circumstances and histories.

In the past century, however, moderation has been conceived as at best a tactic rather than a central principle of liberal-democratic theory and practice. This marks a revival of the radical Enlightenment spirit of Spinoza, Hobbes, Locke, Rousseau, and Kant among others – with some roots in Machiavelli. In this strain of modern thought, moderation was largely ignored, and sometimes vociferously criticized, as a betrayal of both truth and right (or, for Machiavelli, as ignoring reality). The modern demand for clear and novel conceptions of theory and practice, and for accelerated progress, required eschewal of the classical and medieval muddle of moderation. The singular achievement of the complex, moderate polity on the Anglo-American model was taken for granted as sustainable even while new software – single-minded and streamlined in its views of justice and progress – replaced the old. What could go wrong?

Another turn may be developing, and this demands broader academic and public attention. Recent theoretical interest in democratic deliberation and persuasion, together with contemporary concerns about destructive polarization in American politics and discourse, suggests the enduring salience of moderation as both concept and practice. The philosophical tradition that defined moderation as something more than a tactic, or mushy avoidance of conflict, or settling for third best in theory or practice, deserves rediscovery. So understood, a modern concept of moderation that incorporates elements of classical and medieval philosophy can be a central concept for inquiry, and for civic self-definition and civic education, among free peoples. Moderation conceived as avoiding theoretical and practical extremes, seeking breadth and balance among all the relevant dimensions and principles, and reconciling worthy principles in a higher middle ground can be both a guide and an aim for practical statesmen, and a benchmark for judging their character and conduct. Moderation properly understood also offers an important historical perspective on our theorizing and practice, since it has been a theme of not only liberal but also preliberal modes of politics and theory that have elevated balance, persuasion, and noncoercive legitimacy over power, conflict, and single-minded hegemony. In the current American context, the search for a path beyond polarization and beyond our incapacity to address serious public problems through long-sighted policies – social, fiscal, economic, and political – has led some public intellectuals to invoke a principle of moderation as an alternative.[1] Moreover, recent academic works have counseled not only theorists but also leaders and citizens to rediscover a principle of moderation.[2] This surge of interest in moderation among American pundits and academics is good news, for the sake of the intellectual health of our universities and public discourse and for the sustainability of a just and decent liberal politics. Nonetheless, the most important resource for recovering and investigating moderation as a political and philosophical principle still needs exploration. This is the dialogue that occurs among Montesquieu, the American Founders, and Tocqueville as it unfolds across the "Moderate Enlightenment" that spans the eighteenth and nineteenth centuries.[3]

---

[1] See David Brooks, "What Moderation Means," *The New York Times*, October 25, 2012, citing scholarship by Aurelian Craiutu (see note 2 below); Brooks's earlier "A Moderate Manifesto," *The New York Times*, March 3, 2009, provoked commentary by William Galston, "The Good, Bad, and Ugly of Brooks's 'Moderate Manifesto'," *The New Republic*, March 4, 2009.

[2] See Harry Clor, *On Moderation: Defending an Ancient Virtue in a Modern World* (Baylor University Press, 2008); Aurelian Craiutu, *A Virtue for Courageous Minds: Moderation in French Political Thought, 1748–1830* (Princeton University Press, 2012); and Peter Berkowitz, *Constitutional Conservatism: Liberty, Self-Government, and Political Moderation* (Hoover Institution Press, 2013).

[3] I adapt this from Jonathan Israel, *Radical Enlightenment: Philosophy and the Making of Modernity 1650–1750* (Oxford University Press, 2001), which distinguishes radical from moderate philosophers, to criticize the latter; see also his *A Revolution of the Mind: Radical Enlightenment and the Intellectual Origins of Modern Democracy* (Princeton University Press, 2009). Dennis

Of course, among the excellent studies of Montesquieu's philosophy, a few rightly identify moderation as the central principle of his political philosophy (as Montesquieu did). Many studies of the political thought of America's founders strive to encompass Federalists, Anti-Federalists, and Democratic-Republicans. Moreover, a resurgence of scholarly interest in Tocqueville in the past half-century has yielded many insights. What largely is missing, however, is the appreciation that philosophical and political moderation is a central concept explaining the development of both the theory and practice of moderate liberal constitutionalism from Montesquieu, through America, to Tocqueville.[4] Indeed, Tocqueville was neglected for a century in Europe and America until rediscovery in the mid-twentieth century; Montesquieu fell from being the central figure of political science to being breezily dismissed by academics such as Woodrow Wilson, on the basis of little careful study; and, while a few continue to study Montesquieu and *The Federalist* for enduring lessons about liberal constitutional democracy, they are a minor presence for most scholars and students.[5] Recent studies of Tocqueville do help to correct this larger imbalance, but these mostly lack a grounding in his serious study of Montesquieu and Publius, or in his appreciation of the statesmanship of George Washington.

The theoretical and practical threads of moderation in these works of the moderate Enlightenment were rejected by thinkers inclined toward more

Rasmussen, *The Pragmatic Enlightenment: Recovering the Liberalism of Smith, Hume, Montesquieu, and Voltaire* (Cambridge University Press, 2014) approaches Montesquieu in a similar spirit to this study (at 83–96, 149–152, 204–207), but only indirectly addresses philosophic moderation, and his stress on Berlinian pragmatism or pluralism (2, 9–10, 19–23) minimizes Montesquieu's commitment to natural right (252–58) and regard for religion (173–78) while overplaying his skepticism about right and focus on history and sentiment (58–69).

[4] Among notable exceptions, beyond Clor, Craiutu, and Berkowitz (footnote 2 above), see Anne Cohler, *Montesquieu's Comparative Politics and the Spirit of American Constitutionalism* (University Press of Kansas, 1988); other important studies connecting Montesquieu, the Americans, and Tocqueville, or otherwise emphasizing moderation, include Harvey Mansfield, *Taming The Prince: The Ambivalence of Modern Executive Power* (Free Press, 1989) and *America's Constitutional Soul* (Johns Hopkins University Press, 1991); James Ceaser, *Liberal Democracy and Political Science* (Johns Hopkins University Press, 1990), and *Designing a Polity: America's Constitution in Theory and Practice* (Rowman & Littlefield, 2011); Norma Thompson, *The Ship of State: Statecraft and Politics from Ancient Greece to Democratic America* (Yale University Press, 2001); Paul A. Rahe, *Montesquieu and the Logic of Liberty* (Yale University Press, 2009) and *Soft Despotism, Democracy's Drift: Montesquieu, Rousseau, Tocqueville, & The Modern Prospect* (Yale University Press, 2009); and Rasmussen, *The Pragmatic Enlightenment*.

[5] I discuss below some works recovering broader study of politics and thought beyond analytical liberalism; regarding Montesquieu, Alan Ryan features him as an important republican and liberal theorist in *On Politics: A History of Political Thought – Book Two: Hobbes to the Present* (W. W. Norton, 2012) 497–531, especially 518–31. Phillip Pettit references Montesquieu throughout *Republicanism: A Theory of Freedom and Government* (Oxford University Press, 1999 [1997]), on both the ideal and psychology of nondomination and the complex constitutional and legal forms for achieving it, for example, 18–21, 40–41, 106–109, 153–57, 177–80, 226–29, 251.

progressive, streamlined ideals and eager for implementing such transforma-
tive, radically just (or justly radical) ideals. The reasons that modern liberal
theory and practice eschewed moderation deserve study, but so does the quiet
persistence of this principle, including recent renewed interest. Perhaps resid-
ual awareness of the costs of immoderation in theory and practice explains the
persistence of some regard for moderation. If our immoderate age honors moderation mostly in the breach rather than the observance and indulges in brand-
ing rival ideas or groups as extremes to be shunned, we still should notice the
tribute these practices pay to virtue. Due notice also should be given to recent
theorizing about civil discourse amid disagreement, or "democratic deliberation" – and most recently, about compromise. These themes suggest a kinship
with moderation, and some of these studies of egalitarian, fair-minded deliberation and discourse might recognize the affinity. However, much of this work
adopts the premises of John Rawls and his "ideal theory" of high analytical
liberalism and understands itself as an extension thereof.[6] As discussed below,
the Rawlsian project repudiates the tradition of philosophical moderation, so
the possibility of conversation across these divergent philosophical approaches
poses a worthy challenge. A few scholars have attempted this, but the voice of
moderation needs and deserves to be more clearly articulated on its own terms
before the dialogue can advance.[7]

This book therefore investigates in Part I the Tocquevillean principle of
moderation in philosophy and constitutional founding, with chapters on Montesquieu, George Washington, and Tocqueville, and then in Part II investigates
this constitutionalism of moderation in practice – a twofold effort to exemplify
intellectual moderation, with theory paying due respect to practice. To prepare
for these theoretical and practical dimensions, a prologue should briefly survey
the roots of Western conceptions of philosophical and political moderation in
Aristotle and Aquinas and the fate of this tradition. I try to meet halfway (so to
speak) our contemporary academic spirit by offering an analytical, conceptual
outline of moderation stretching from Aristotle to American constitutionalism

---

[6] Central to this scholarship is work by Amy Gutmann and Dennis Thompson; see, for example, *Democracy and Disagreement: Why Moral Conflict Cannot Be Avoided in Politics, and
What Should Be Done About It* (Harvard University Press, 1996); *Why Deliberative Democracy?*
(Princeton University Press, 2004); and *The Spirit of Compromise: Why Governing Demands It
and Campaigning Undermines It* (Princeton University Press, 2012); for an early review of this
approach, see Robert P. George, "Law, Democracy, and Moral Disagreement," *Harvard Law
Review* 110 (1997) 1388–1406; also in George, *In Defense of Natural Law* (Oxford University
Press, 2001). In a related yet distinct vein, Alin Fumurescu undertakes a genealogy in *Compro-
mise: A Political and Philosophical History* (Cambridge University Press, 2013); he explores the
Aristotelian tradition and links between compromise and moderation, at 29–36.

[7] Two works informed (as I see it) by the tradition of moderation that engage with recent democratic deliberation and discourse theory are Sharon Krause, *Civil Passions: Moral Sentiment and
Democratic Deliberation* (Princeton University Press, 2008), and – perhaps the more moderate
of the two – Bryan Garsten, *Saving Persuasion: A Defense of Rhetoric and Judgment* (Harvard
University Press, 2006).

and Tocqueville. I then briefly encounter the predominant approach in political theory today, Rawlsian "ideal theory," and also some dissenters from that orthodoxy, to suggest why the dissenters are right but also are looking for moderation more than they might understand. The stage would be set for deeper study of Tocquevillean philosophical and constitutional moderation, including the salience of moderate views on religion, grand strategy, and a political science that redresses polarization and our current deficit of statesmanship.

Dimensions of Moderation – Philosophy, Liberal Constitutionalism, Statesmanship

A conceptual map of moderation as developed by Montesquieu and refined by the Americans and Tocqueville must recognize the root in the Aristotelian tradition. Even basic consideration of the deeper roots in Platonic philosophy, and then the principles in Aristotle's ethics and political science, would require another book. I can be suggestive only, nonetheless daring to sketch a bridge from Aristotle to Montesquieu provided, at least indirectly, by Thomas Aquinas. My focus is the modern liberal development of this classical and medieval tradition. That said, one dimension of the moderation in these modern philosophers and founders is their blending of classical, medieval, and modern ideas as best for tempering earlier modern thought.[8]

The light of the Socratic tradition that survives into modernity allows us to recognize moderation as a political and especially a moral virtue, but we can barely conceive of it as an intellectual virtue. For politics, we recognize the principle of balancing institutions or centers of power as found in separation of powers, federalism, and competing parties or interests. We faintly recall that we understand these modes of political moderation through Montesquieu's philosophy above all, since Hobbes's liberalism eschews such principles, and Locke's offers only a simple separation of powers and nothing on federalism and parties. Indeed, in our age of abundant calories and other choices, we retain some familiarity with moderation as a guide to personal morality and consumption. Our predominant view is that if moderation has any value, it is on these planes of private morality and perhaps politics. In contrast, we admire the single-mindedness we find in Hobbes and Locke – not to mention Machiavelli, Spinoza, Rousseau, Kant, Marx, or Nietzsche – as an indication of their philosophic seriousness. For Montesquieu, the charge arose in his lifetime that his works reveal not philosophical complexity but confusion, with their sprawling efforts at comprehensiveness and balance. Shouldn't a philosopher be intransigent, clear, and single-minded in the search for the truth – or, as later moderns

---

[8] Craiutu surveys classical and medieval views of moderation, from *sōphrosunē* (Greek) to *modestia* and *temperantia* (Latin), then modern adaptations and responses – ranging from Plato and Aristotle, to Polybius and Cicero, to Aquinas, Montaigne, and Hume among others – in *A Virtue for Courageous Minds*, 13–32.

might urge, in seeking the most recent revaluation of ever-changing values? A complicated case is Leo Strauss, often considered a conservative thinker, who at once praised philosophical moderation and distanced philosophy from it in his widely read essay "What is Political Philosophy?" When advocating the politic position that the philosopher should take toward nonphilosophers and a decent constitutional regime, especially after the recklessness of Heidegger's philosophizing (as an epitome of modern philosophy), Strauss argued for a pairing of philosophy and moderation. At another moment, when discussing classical political philosophy in its purest form, in Plato's *Laws*, he voices the radical purity of philosophic longing for wisdom: "For moderation is not a virtue of thought: Plato likens philosophy to madness, the very opposite of sobriety or moderation; thought must be not moderate, but fearless, not to say shameless. But moderation is a virtue controlling the philosopher's speech." In the final moment of the essay, Strauss addresses the relationship of moderation to philosophy again, arguing that a tempering of intellectual expectations opens up space for philosophy – since it must strive to be "the highest form of the mating of courage and moderation" in order to resist the charm at one extreme of reducing knowledge to mathematics or rationalism (mind over reality) but also, at the other extreme, the charm of succumbing to a simple awe that refuses to pursue knowledge.[9]

Other dimensions of Strauss's philosophy feature irreducible tensions in thought and in the cosmos that the philosopher must navigate, such as those between reason and revelation, Athens and Jerusalem, nature and culture or law, man and the city. Still, Strauss seems not to view such navigation as a virtue of intellectual moderation or path in itself to the truth; he seems instead to hold to the pure form as true philosophizing, while a qualified or Socratic acceptance of moderation counsels prudence. Aristotle and the Aristotelian tradition provide an alternate view that points toward a virtue of intellectual or philosophical moderation. As a student of Plato, Aristotle begins with the cautionary notes that Strauss later voices, but as is argued below, Aristotle develops a distinct stance. Should a philosopher be dogmatic and fanatical in pursuing his or her favored views? Should a thinker impose a degree of clarity that does not exist in the phenomena, simply to meet an abstract theoretical test of rigor or purity? The roots of philosophical moderation as understood through these cautionary queries are deep in our tradition. Ultimately they are traceable to Socratic dialectic, but they appear more substantially in the dialectical method of the *quaestio* in Aquinas – which is integral to the substantive moderation that he demonstrates in exploring the compatibility of revelation and reason. Consideration of Aquinas helps us to see that the most recognizable, developed,

---

[9] Leo Strauss, "What Is Political Philosophy?" In *What Is Political Philosophy? And Other Studies* (University of Chicago Press, 1959), 26–27, 32, 39–40. Thomas L. Pangle discusses the views of moderation in this and other Strauss essays in *Leo Strauss: An Introduction to His Thought and Intellectual Legacy* (Johns Hopkins University Press, 2006), 34, 50, 87–88, 108.

and characteristic forms of such moderation lie in the Aristotelian tradition, broadly conceived.[10]

The classic exposition of the mean as the method and principle of moral philosophy is the *Nicomachean Ethics*. Its complexity and care reveals the challenge: any analysis of ethics or politics that seeks moderation between alternatives must cogently define the extremes and the spectrum between them.[11] Aristotle proposes an ethical science of virtue, in which excellence in action, and practical wisdom or prudence in choice of actions, almost always is found in a mean between extremes. The fact that moderation (*sōphrosunē*, literally "soundness of mind") is one of the eleven virtues analyzed in the *Ethics*, as the mean regarding pleasures, complicates the story; moderation is both the philosophical approach and a particular virtue found through it.[12] This paradox is not a peculiar moment within Aristotle's philosophy of human affairs, which often uses analogous meanings to achieve understanding. His aim is not to impose meaning or artificial clarity upon reality through an ideal theory, but to discern inherent meaning.[13] A further complexity is that he defines virtue not merely as a middle point on a continuum but as an excellence that rises above opposing and false extremes, like the peak of a triangle, toward moral excellence as golden mean. Moreover, he specifies two important qualifications. The true and just point – being courageous, being magnanimous, being just, etc. – is not mathematically in the middle, but instead is farther from whichever false extreme is the graver error or danger. Further, some actions or passions allow no middle or mean and are simply wrong. Aristotle cited, as examples, adultery, theft, murder, spitefulness, shamelessness, and envy. One could not do such deeds, or indulge such passions, in a moderate way.[14]

While Aristotle does not launch the *Politics* – his sequel to the *Ethics* – by stating the method and aim of moderation, this first work of political science argues that the political good and justice are found in a mean between

---

[10] Among scholars viewing Aquinas in this moderate, dialectical vein – while differing about other points in interpreting Aquinas – are Josef Pieper, *The Silence of St. Thomas: Three Essays*, tr. John Murray and Daniel O'Connor (Pantheon, 1957); Anthony Kenny, *Aquinas* (Oxford University Press, 1980); and, John Finnis, *Aquinas: Moral, Political, and Legal Theory* (Oxford University Press, 1998).

[11] A new translation with critical resources is Aristotle, *Nicomachean Ethics*, tr. Robert C. Bartlett and Susan D. Collins (University of Chicago Press, 2011). I also consult Aristotle, *Nicomachean Ethics*, tr. Martin Ostwald (Library of the Liberal Arts, Bobbs-Merrill, 1962).

[12] Clor, *On Moderation*, 26–27, notes this paradox and explains his preference for the broader conception of moderation as the principle guiding all virtue, in contrast to the Platonic conception as one of four cardinal virtues.

[13] Thus in *Politics* Book 3 the central concept of the new political science is "the regime" (*politeia*) and yet one instance – the mixed regime comprising elements of monarchy, aristocracy, and democracy – is defined as *politeia* ("polity"). The paradox of using one word for genus and species makes sense in light of the larger political science.

[14] See Aristotle, *Nicomachean Ethics*, tr. Bartlett and Collins, Book 2, Chs. 6–9 (1106b37–1109b27, 33–41), especially at 1106b5–16 (34), 1107a9–18 (35), and 1109a1–2 (39).

intellectual and institutional extremes. The *Politics* instructs political philosophers and legislators to avoid extremes about the status of gods, beasts, and humanity; about money, communism, and private property; and about unity, divisiveness, and pluralism in Plato's ideal polis or a more reasonably best polis. Aristotle thus defends polity or the mixed regime as one of the correct regimes; arguably, he finds it one of the potential best regimes, if rightly structured.[15] Long before the claims of modern philosophers (especially the radical Enlightenment) about mathematically precise foundations for new sciences of moral philosophy and politics, Aristotle warned of rationalist extremes. The *Ethics* argues that any science of human affairs (ethics or politics) should strive to attain only "the clarity that accords with the subject matter," thus "one should not seek precision in all arguments alike." Arguments about what is just, noble, or prudent will be lost upon, or dismissed by, seekers of mathematical clarity. Thus, "it belongs to an educated person to seek out precision in each genus to the extent that the nature of the matter allows: to accept persuasive speech from a skilled mathematician appears comparable to demanding [mathematical] demonstrations from a skilled rhetorician."[16] Aristotle thus famously makes practical wisdom or prudence (*phronēsis*) a central idea of his ethical and political philosophy. There is only so much work that abstract philosophy can do, but a science of ethics can point out the respect due to, and the arena to be left for, prudence.

It often is overlooked that prudence also is a central concept for the ethics and political philosophy of Aquinas.[17] There is substantial latitude for judgment by individuals and statesmen within the frame of natural law, virtue ethics, and his preferred polity, the mixed regime.[18] Much discussion of Aquinas's

---

[15] See Aristotle, *The Politics of Aristotle*, ed. Peter Simpson (University of North Carolina Press, 1997) – in book and chapters, 1.2 (1253a26–28, 12); 1.8–11 (20–29); 2.3–5 (37–45); 3.11–13 (95–105), 3.17–18 (112–14). Interpretations supporting this view – that Aristotle doubts whether rule by a godlike one or few is political if completely excluding the many, and that polity is excellent if restricting the highest offices to the excellent – are Mary Nichols, *Citizens and Statesmen: A Study of Aristotle's Politics* (Rowman & Littlefield, 1991), and Kevin M. Cherry, "The Problem of Polity: Political Participation and Aristotle's Best Regime," *The Journal of Politics* 71 (2009), 1406–21; see also Stephen Salkever, *Finding the Mean: Theory and Practice in Aristotelian Political Philosophy* (Princeton University Press, 1990). See also Pierre Manent, *The City of Man*, tr. Marc Le Pain (Princeton University Press, 1998 [1994]), 165–69, especially on Aristotle's argument for intellectual and political moderation at p. 167.

[16] Aristotle, *Nicomachean Ethics*, tr. Bartlett and Collins, Book I, ch. 3 (1094b12–28), 3–4.

[17] Among the many topics to consider regarding Aquinas on moderation, beyond the importance of prudence as a mark of philosophical moderation, is his analysis in the *Summa Theologiae* of the cardinal virtue *temperantia* (temperance or moderation) and the affiliated virtue *modestia* (modesty, with overtones of moderation); for an overview, see Josef Pieper, *The Four Cardinal Virtues* (University of Notre Dame Press, 1966), and more specifically, on political implications of temperance and modesty as moderation, see Michael P. Foley, "Thomas Aquinas' Novel Modesty," *History of Political Thought* XXV (2004), 402–23.

[18] For a range of views on Aquinas and prudence see, for example, Jeremy Catto, "Ideas and Experience in the Political Thought of Aquinas," *Past and Present* 71 (1976), 3–21; James V.

views on politics and a best regime focuses on his letter to the king of Cyprus, *De Regno (On Kingship)*, or on his unfinished commentary on Aristotle's *Politics*. In fact the most comprehensive, if brief, analysis of the best regime occurs in his great *Summa Theologiae*, near the end of his questions on law, in *Summa* I–II, q. 105. Here Aquinas argues that "the best constitution" or regime is outlined both in the Hebrew Bible ("the Old Law") and Aristotle's *Politics*. From this blend of sources, Aquinas finds a higher balance among several elements: rule by the virtuous one and few, with elections and participation by the many.[19] Among many striking points here, Aquinas moves beyond Aristotle by using "democracy" favorably, although he knew from his close commentary that for the *Politics* democracy was unjust, with the many ruling for their advantage rather than for the common good. Aquinas underscores that while his best regime has an element of monarchy, such a singular ruler should be selected by all the people from among all the people while (in Aristotle's spirit) also assuring that the most important offices are held on the basis of virtue, to include practical wisdom.[20] If moderation means avoiding extremes in theory and practice, comprehending a balance and breadth of principles, and blending or reconciling worthy principles, then the Aristotelian tradition is the main carrier of moderation into the modern philosophical and political world. Furthermore, Aquinas clearly seeks to reconcile philosophy and faith, reason and revelation, regardless of the worthy criticisms coming from both the philosophers and the faithful that in so doing he has misunderstood, or betrayed, the purest understanding of each view of reality.[21]

Schall, "A Latitude for Statesmanship? Strauss on St. Thomas," *Review of Politics* 53 (1991), 126–45; Daniel Nelson, *The Priority of Prudence: Virtue and Natural Law in Thomas Aquinas and the Implications for Modern Ethics* (Pennsylvania State University Press, 1992); Daniel Westberg, *Right Practical Reason: Aristotle, Action, and Prudence in Aquinas* (Oxford University Press, 1994); Marc D. Guerra, "Beyond Natural Law Talk: Politics and Prudence in St. Thomas Aquinas's *On Kingship*," *Perspectives on Political Science* 31 (2002), 9–14; and Finnis, *Aquinas*, 118–31, also 79–90 (among other accounts of prudence or "practical reasonableness" therein).

[19] Diverse approaches to Thomas largely agree upon this reading of *Summa Theologiae* I–II, q. 105, a. 1; see Douglas Kries, "Thomas Aquinas and the Politics of Moses," *Review of Politics* 52 (1990), 84–104; James V. Schall, "The Right Order of Polity and Economy: Reflections on St. Thomas and the 'Old Law'," *Cultural Dynamics* 7 (1995), 427–40; Finnis, *Aquinas*, 7–8, 260–63; and Christopher Wolfe, *Natural Law Liberalism* (Cambridge University Press, 2006), 179–80. More broadly, see Ernest L. Fortin, "The Political Thought of Thomas Aquinas," in Fortin, *Classical Christianity and the Political Order: Reflections on the Theologico-Political Problem (Collected Essays,* Vol. 2), ed. Benestad (Rowman & Littlefield, 1996), 151–76.

[20] Finnis, *Aquinas*, 7–8 and 17 (note l), provides a close English translation and the Latin text.

[21] It is telling that Mary Keys occasionally addresses moderation throughout her analysis of the moral and political philosophy of Aristotle and Aquinas, which argues that Aquinas succeeds in reconciling religion, philosophy, and politics – and that she concludes considering "Thomistic and Aristotelian Moderation for the Common Good," in *Aquinas, Aristotle, and the Promise of the Common Good* (Cambridge University Press, 2006), 236–38; on Aquinas's response to Aristotle's political science, see 87–115.

It is important to note, from this brief survey, that moderation for Aristotle and Aquinas encompasses three levels: first, a *philosophical* argument that natural right or natural law, and the good in human affairs, can be specified to a limited degree in abstraction, and thus complexity of principles and the virtue of prudence must be recognized; second, a sound *political philosophy and political science* suggests a balanced constitution, since an ideal ruler or small number of rulers might be possible (virtuous monarchy or aristocracy) but a mixed regime incorporating prudence in higher offices and democratic (or republican) participation also can be best – and indeed, for Aquinas, it is the best simply; and, third, a more specific discussion follows from these levels, of how *prudence or practical wisdom* operates, and why *statesmanship* is as indispensable as the rule of law in a best political order or a decent one.

This is roughly the three-level conception of moderation employed by Montesquieu, adapted by the American founders, and refined by Tocqueville. These latter thinkers are moderns and liberals, and we should not ignore the question of whether the development of classical and medieval moderation by these moderns is a species of adaptation, or distortion, or confusion. Still, the lineage first must be noted and explored before assessed. Part I of this book argues that Montesquieu, America's founders, and Tocqueville share, first, a *philosophical* disposition for breadth and balance in inquiry, for dialectical care in canvassing alternatives, so as to avoid narrow, doctrinaire extremes. This moderated philosophy sees in human nature both reason and faith, both social and individual dimensions, thus both duties and rights. At a second level, this modern moderation guides a *political science* that points to a *moderate liberalism* and thus to the principle of *complex constitutionalism*. Montesquieu, the founders, and Tocqueville endorse a liberal politics bounded by natural right, natural rights, and the rule of law, including a basic or constitutional law structured in a complex balance of institutions and powers. This structure calls for, thus leaves space for, a general prudence in the philosopher and in the founders or legislators designing (or reforming) a constitution. According to the first level, no one abstract theory or universally right constitution exists that would do justice to, or secure natural right among, diverse peoples and circumstances. A moderate, liberal constitution will balance or reconcile, at the second level, important moral principles, to include liberty, rule of law, equality, religious belief, and the civic virtues or character needed in citizens.[22] At a third level, for citizens and their representatives or rulers, philosophical and

---

[22] A modern argument for constitutional democracy that shares (and occasionally cites) Montesquieu's argument for complexity and balance, both of moral principles and institutions, is Walter Murphy's *Constitutional Democracy: Creating and Maintaining a Just Political Order* (Johns Hopkins University Press, 2007); George Thomas emphasizes the Aristotelian and Montesquieuan dimensions of Murphy's approach in his review essay "The Tensions of Constitutional Democracy," *Constitutional Commentary* 24 (2007), 793–806.

constitutional moderation together call for *prudence* in politics, both domestic and international, especially for *statesmanship* that will vary in character according to the role or office. These capacities permit governing of oneself and the community in accord with the higher-order principles by adapting the latter to, and preserving them in, diverse circumstances. This level brings moderation closer to our concerns with civil discourse, persuasion, and compromise, which are discrete subjects of scholarship and public discussion. One distinction between moderation and these analogous concepts is that, in the philosophical tradition from Aristotle through Tocqueville, there are fundamental principles of natural right and constitutional order that provide general guidance about, and limits to, persuasion, compromise, and civility in discourse and disagreement.

Ideal Theory as Not So Ideal After All: The Case for Reconsidering Moderation

An approach that begins political analysis with current circumstances and opinions before seeking ideal understanding is a mark of philosophical moderation. Such moderation stands in contrast to the predominant conceptions of recent political theory. Foremost among these is Rawlsian "ideal theory," which draws upon Kant and points back to Rousseau and the spirit of the radical Enlightenment. Why did a long tradition of philosophical moderation, which succeeded in influencing political moderation, face such severe critics and ultimately decline? Here is not the place to rehearse this history of philosophy and political philosophy since Machiavelli. If one could consider Machiavelli as launching a revolution against classical and medieval views of natural right – as cynical ploys by the Church, princes, and philosophical elites to maintain control, and at the cost of political stagnation and civilizational weakness – then surely the philosophical and political moderation intrinsic to the Aristotelian and Thomistic traditions is a prime target. One could add that political moderation and the mixed or balanced regime did not successfully prevent either religious conflict in Europe or the rise of absolute monarchies, from the medieval to the modern eras – problems that provoked not only Machiavelli and Bacon but also Hobbes and Locke. There also is, of course, the confidence held by these four philosophers, and other moderns, regarding a new view of philosophy itself that renders man and reason as the central considerations, eschewing teleology and metaphysics in favor of immediate aims and powers. For the purposes of this study, however, a most pertinent line of consideration – articulated by Tocqueville – is that philosophical and political moderation was swept away by the idea of human equality and, paired with this, a rationalism devoted to practical achievement of egalitarian political, moral, and economic conditions. Moreover, while the liberal designs of Hobbes and Locke about individual rights and the social contract eschewed traditional

moderation, their philosophies in turn were deemed insufficiently radical, egalitarian, and progressive by Rousseau and Kant. The dominant schools of political theory in the American and European academy now draw, as does Rawls,
from this more rationalist and egalitarian eschewal of moderation. At the core
of not just Rawlsian theory but other schools is a view that theorizing must
begin from an uncompromisingly rational ideal.

Ideal theory, for Rawls, presumes that an abstract conception of one theory
(the modern social contract) should seek a "well-ordered society" that meets
complete, uncompromising standards of justice. This requires the theorist first
to articulate this ideal order, informed by only one strain of philosophy – which
elevates equality as the benchmark for justice and envisions all citizens as fully
rational, thus fully complying with its fair terms of order. Only later should
"nonideal theory" compromise with the complexities or failings of particular
societies, albeit as guided by the proper theory of justice. My point is not to
review Rawls's "theory of justice" in itself, elaborated in several works, shifting
from a universalist conception to a "political liberalism" that abandoned universal principles of right. Nor am I reviewing the range of criticisms or responses
to Rawls's theory. Rather, it is telling that Rawls himself later deemed his first
theory "unrealistic" for overlooking the basic moral and religious differences
within any modern society. Presumably because he wanted his theory to be
relevant to at least the liberal democracies, he revised it toward a more political, "constructivist" concept of justice fashioned through particular, defined
boundaries of public reason and acceptable political views.[23]

Commentators see this revision as Rawls's shift toward a "moderate" idealism. This revised ideal theory continues to dominate English-speaking theory,
and yet minority voices persist in arguing that there is little or no moderation
even as modified. One way to note this disjunction is the stark contrast between
the moderate philosophical tradition and the abstracting lens of ideal theory.
Rawlsian thought, which includes other variants of late liberalism such as theories of deliberative democracy, mostly ignores philosophers from Aristotle to
Tocqueville who exemplify moderation. For ideal theory, these figures fail to
gain clarity about politics, being too entangled with particular, historical con-
ventions or thinking. Even Rawls's later theory remains abstract by defining,
through a standard of "public reason," precisely which moral ideas are permitted to debate in a "reasonable" liberal order. In this uncompromising view, the
moderate tradition also deserves dismissal given its related moral failing – that
of obscuring the main issue of equal rights and moral autonomy by seeking
to balance ideas, or see complexities, or include empirical phenomena so as to
understand justice or a decent political order.

---

[23] See John Rawls, *A Theory of Justice* (Harvard University Press, 1971), 3–17 for the outline
of "ideal" theory; and *Political Liberalism* (Columbia University Press, 1993), xvi–xxi for the
revision toward a putatively more realistic, political conception.

The counter arguments offered by the small cohort that still study the moderate tradition recently have been joined by criticisms from a range of political theorists – grouped by one scholar under the banner of "realism" – who reject the concept of "ideal" theory.[24] These so-called realists – who are not Machiavellians, to be clear – argue that such abstraction and rationalism undermines achievement, and understanding, of the very aims of justice it seeks. Even Rawls's later shift still assumes uncompromising compliance by all citizens in an order constructed by purely rational liberals, and thus is an ideal that never could be achieved even under the most favorable conditions. Theory should not be impossible to achieve. Moreover, any actual community must develop and sustain institutions for mediating conflict and forming basic order, internally and externally, before considering ideals of justice. Politics, in this view, has some autonomy in relation to moral philosophy. In that vein, a leading scholar of the republican tradition – viewed as an alternative to both analytical liberalism and its communitarian critics – deems it "little short of scandalous" that the kind of political philosophy in Machiavelli's *Discourses on Livy*, Montesquieu's *The Spirit of Laws*, and Mill's *Considerations on Representative Government* – addressing the realities of factional bias and passions, limited resources, and the strengths and limits of institutions – "is hardly ever emulated by political philosophers today."[25] Uniting these various criticisms of ideal theory is a concern about an imbalance between theory and practice, or between moral principles and the realities of political association. This turn away from the abstract, a priori demands of recent theory is a step toward the moderate philosophical tradition. The reference to Montesquieu is telling, since his conception of moderate philosophy is the basis for a very real American constitutional order that in turn has shaped many other constitutional orders, as well as the international order of states and commerce we enjoy. Moreover, extended study of such moderate views of philosophy and politics should have a moderating effect on the demands made by theorists for political reform or transformation in politics, especially as matters of rights. This immoderation of theory is an overlooked source of polarization and acrimony in liberal democratic politics today.[26]

---

[24] One critic from within analytical liberal theory who turns away from the Rawlsian school is Colin Farrelly, "Justice in Ideal Theory: A Refutation," *Political Studies* 55 (2007), 844–64. I place greater reliance here on William Galston, "Realism in Political Theory," *European Journal of Political Theory* 9 (2010), 385–411; he features Bernard Williams, John Dunn, John Gray, William Connolly, Bonnie Honig, Judith Shklar, and Stephen Elkin among other theorists and political scientists who adopt this more realistic view.

[25] Phillip Pettit, in Galston, "Realism in Political Theory," 394; Galston also endorses generally Aristotelian and Madisonian ideas of political order in contrast to the abstractions of ideal theory. Pettit criticizes Rawlsian abstraction in *Republicanism*, arguing that political theory should pursue such practical topics as resolving conflicts and institutional design; see 2–7, 240.

[26] See also, from another direction, an early criticism of Rawls by Delba Winthrop arguing that Aristotle considered the conceit of a "theory of justice" theoretically impossible and practically harmful, for undermining genuine human associations from friendships to politics; in "Aristotle and Theories of Justice," *American Political Science Review* 72 (1978), 1201–16.

Modern Moderation, Tocqueville's "New Science of Politics," and Sustainability

Beyond the academic "realists" who would restore sober notions of theory and political science – including occasional nods to Montesquieu or Madison – there has been renewed attention to moderation itself. However, there is less consideration of Montesquieu and his legacy than one would expect among scholars who have rediscovered the central principle of his political science.[27] Even when examining ideas of moderation in *The Federalist*, or Tocqueville, these often are not traced to their near source.[28] When Montesquieu is included – most recently in studying the historical development of concepts of moderation – he is paired with politically engaged intellectuals rather than philosophers.[29] A grounding in Montesquieu is necessary, however, to grasp that moderation is not just an ancient virtue wandering, alien, in the modern world but is a distinctive and energizing component of the most successful and dominant form of modern politics – albeit a component that now is paradoxically demoted yet desired.

Of the philosophers and statesmen examined here, the one most welcome in academic discourse today is Tocqueville, but the argument here is that he is a Montesquieuan who also appreciated lessons gleaned from watching a Montesquieuan constitution in action, in America. This minority strain within modern political philosophy argues that constitutional complexity is an essential expression of moderation, to include federalism, a tripartite separation of powers, bicameralism, and plural parties or interests. Montesquieu authored this concept of "moderate government," which could take several forms in given circumstances, for example, a liberal, commercial republic or constitutional monarchy. Scholars advocating ideal theory or postmodern constructivism should weigh this fact: the great prosperity, power, security, and equality of recent centuries, so beneficial to peoples in the West and beyond (India being a prime example), were achieved not by democracy or egalitarianism, or

---

[27] The most philosophical of these is Clor's defense of "an ancient virtue in a modern world," in *On Moderation*; see, for example, 1–6. Clor studies political moderation as balancing extremes, personal moderation as taming the passions, and philosophical moderation as tempering the mind. He occasionally cites Tocqueville and Madison, but never Montesquieu, preferring a dialogue between Aristotle and Nietzsche, Montaigne and Freud, Burke and Rousseau. None of his advocates for moderation (Aristotle, Montaigne, Burke) are Biblical or Christian at core, because religion can be as much a source of fanaticism, including Clor's concerns with Islam and terrorism (e.g., 37–42). Montaigne therefore is crucial for his inquiry (4, 103–4, 109–10).

[28] Clor analyzes Publius and Tocqueville as exemplars of moderation at 21–23, 31, 33–37.

[29] See Craiutu's *A Virtue for Courageous Minds*, examining invocations of moderation before and after the cataclysm of 1789 by a set of philosophers and practitioners from Montesquieu to Constant. My review of Craiutu's rich study is in *Society* 50 (2013), 324–27. Craiutu offers one of the few analyses of Montesquieu that focuses upon moderation; nonetheless, the historical-conceptual approach gives Montesquieu equal status with statesmen and intellectuals rather than considering his contribution as original and transformational.

radical projects of transformation, but by complex, liberal constitutions guided by moderation as anchored in natural rights.[30]

This awareness of moderation's powerful legacy does not mean it is only a conservative virtue.[31] Both liberal and conservative views of political theory can be more or less doctrinaire, blind to the question of extremes in the mode or content of thought.[32] That said, a scholarly or political concern with moderation is conservative in the way environmental thinking prizes conservation. The recent scholarship on moderation is rightly worried about the perpetuation or sustainability of liberal constitutional democracy, regardless of whether a particular governing majority is liberal or conservative. That said, we still need to grasp the Montesquieuan roots of Tocqueville's great insight, in opening *Democracy in America*, that a "new political science is needed for a world altogether new" – to guide, moderate, and thus sustain the new politics.[33]

This spirit largely is missing from the dominant schools in political science and philosophy today, which leads me to a seemingly odd turn, in the final chapter, from classic sources on moderation to a twentieth-century scholar, Herbert Storing, who adapted this Tocquevillean spirit to a new era. Certainly there are sober public and academic debates in liberal democracies today about not just environmental sustainability but our deficit spending of social, fiscal, civic, moral, and political capital. Political science should consider how it might have become as much a cause of such problems as a resource. Montesquieu's approach for analyzing governments was to grasp, first, the general ways that humans could turn away from our nature as it was intended to be (according to the larger order of nature); that is the basic problem that government (thus political science) must address. He suggested, therefore, that God and then the moral philosophers precede the political philosophers and statesmen

---

[30] Craiutu explores Montesquieu's theme of moderate government in *A Virtue for Courageous Minds*, 33–68; see also the fourth of his final "theorems" about moderation, on constitutionalism's balance between pluralism and individual rights, at 242. That said, his study perhaps is led by its even-handed, historical-conceptual approach to overlook some of the moral substance to Montesquieu's moderation, including its adherence to natural right; see Chapter 1.

[31] Craiutu astutely makes this point as "theorem Eight" from his "Decalogue" of lessons on moderation, in *A Virtue for Courageous Minds*, 247.

[32] Berkowitz's *Constitutional Conservatism* invokes political moderation to counsel American conservatives after a period of national electoral losses, since a return to this principle should propel success. His theoretical point is that moderation properly understood "accommodates, balances, and calibrates to translate rival and worthy principles into practice," and that the Constitution weaves this conception throughout its structure and principles to guide a free, self-governing people (xi–xii). My review of the book appears as "Dear Prudence." *Commentary* 135 (May 2013), 41–42. Interestingly, Berkowitz chides Goldwater's proclamations at the 1964 Republican National Convention that "extremism in the defense of liberty is no vice" and "moderation in the pursuit of justice is no virtue," both because this ignores the centrality of moderation for America's founders and because this flourish ignored Goldwater's proven capacity for reconciling worthy principles and avoiding extremes (at 91).

[33] Alexis de Tocqueville, *Democracy in America*, ed. and tr. Harvey Mansfield and Delba Winthrop (University of Chicago Press, 2000), Volume 1, Introduction, 7.

in developing laws to return us to our intended condition. Thus the political philosopher must understand a primary set of divine, moral, and positive laws: the laws of religion, as God reminding us of our ultimate nature; the laws of morality, as philosophers reminding us of our human nature; and political and civil laws, as legislators reminding us of our public and private duties for living in society (*The Spirit of Laws*, Book 1, Ch. 1). Montesquieu next articulates the kinds of positive law or right that men should develop in accord with natural law, in order to secure peace and order after we have abandoned our natural state of peace. These three kinds are the right of nations that governs international affairs, political right that governs the constitutional order of rulers and ruled, and civil right which orders civil and criminal laws affecting individuals (*Spirit*, Book 1, Ch. 3). This comprehensive, double set of laws informs the complex organization of Montesquieu's masterwork, and I have adapted it to structure this book. Tocqueville guides the larger spirit of this study, however, exploring what kind of political science helps to sustain liberal constitutional democracy by understanding its philosophy, its constitutionalism, its statesmanship in domestic and foreign affairs, and its balanced incorporation of guidance from metaphysical views and religion. Democracy in moderation means finding the right balance among its high and noble principles to help it to be its best, thereby helping liberal democratic constitutionalism to avoid its characteristic extremes or weaknesses. It is incumbent upon both philosophers and statesmen to seek, and encourage, such moderation.

PART I

TOCQUEVILLEAN MODERATION IN PHILOSOPHY AND FOUNDING

These chapters argue that Montesquieu developed a philosophy of moderation, one that the American founders adapted, and that Tocqueville refined this given his somewhat different perception of human nature and his awareness that – after the trauma of the French Revolution and the more successful result of the American Revolution – both Montesquieu's philosophy and its American instantiation required moderation through recourse to deeper principles of the Western philosophical and theological tradition.

This is an unconventional journey, for the tenets of the radical Enlightenment, or developments thereof, increasingly dominate academic and elite public discourse in twenty-first-century America.[1] Montesquieu saw some of these elements of thought and practice arising in embryo, after the first wave of Enlightenment philosophy and the radical politics of liberty versus authoritarianism in England between 1640 and 1660. For American elites today, it is a paradox that our Constitution and several basic, resilient elements of our political culture – attachment to religion, to the founders of the republic, and to political moderation at least as an ideal – stem from the moderate Enlightenment. Indeed, these elements were adopted and retained in full knowledge of radical doctrines that were rejected. The legacy of moderation is frustrating and perplexing for intellectual elites who advocate the (to their minds) greater justice and reasonableness that stem from the radical Enlightenment and its predominant American progeny, the Progressive movement. These projects seek to collapse the space between theory and practice so as to achieve reform and even transformation. Yet perhaps progressive minds should be more curious about,

---

[1] Per the Prologue above, Footnote 3, Jonathan Israel propounds the "radical Enlightenment" and coined the term partly to criticize the "moderate" alternative to philosophical efforts by Spinoza and Hobbes (among others); Dennis Rasmussen's recent work defends the "pragmatic" Enlightenment philosophers, including Montesquieu.

and less frustrated by, the persistence of moderate elements in our politics and culture; after all, the radical Enlightenment held that rigorous discourse about various alternative hypotheses and views is an intellectual virtue.

Montesquieu's masterwork, *The Spirit of Laws* (1748), was praised in the latter eighteenth century as the standard of political science by nearly all the voices of Enlightenment, and especially was consulted by statesmen as well as theorists. It eventually was eclipsed by the French Revolution and its aftershocks, and by the greater weight accorded to radical Enlightenment thinkers and later developments of their projects. One reason for this fate was the consensus view that it embodied a distinctly moderate and complex philosophy, adopting elements of both Enlightenment and counter-Enlightenment thought. This characteristic also explains the greater persistence and influence of Montesquieu's philosophy in Britain and America than in his homeland, or in Europe generally.[2] Moreover, the complexity and capaciousness of Montesquieu's philosophy – characteristics he considered integral to its moderation – led to its influence upon a broad range of thinkers, from Hume, Rousseau, Blackstone, Smith, Burke, and Gibbon to Madison, Hamilton, Hegel, Constant, and Tocqueville.[3] One burden of the following chapters is to show that Montesquieu's influence is indispensable for explaining the American founders' capacity to blend liberalism and modern republicanism, as well as classical philosophy, Christianity, and the classic common law, into their liberal republic – in the Declaration of Independence as well as the Constitution.

Eventually Montesquieu's influence fell to philosophical criticism of his complicated style and also the charge – made by, among others, Jefferson in his later years – that his republicanism was antidemocratic and insufficiently progressive. Woodrow Wilson and his heirs still today criticize the complexity of a constitutional order they see as embodying gridlock, inefficiency, distance from democratic majorities and popular priorities, and impediments to rational progress. Nonetheless, Montesquieu's political philosophy still is indispensable for understanding our modern world, and not only for its influence upon America and our shaping, in turn, of liberalism and globalization. This broad influence is especially evident if we include not only *The Spirit of Laws* but

---

[2] Gertrude Himmelfarb, in *Roads to Modernity: The British, French, and American Enlightenments* (Knopf Publishing, 2004), implicitly agrees with Israel's distinctions within Enlightenment, but emphasizes national and social differences shaping philosophy, thus demarcating the French Enlightenment (more rationalist and radical) from the British (to include "Scottish") and American Enlightenments (more moderate and reformist); Montesquieu, she argues, "was more representative of the British Enlightenment than the French," but she also notes his deep influence on the American conception of political liberty; see 15, and more generally 15–18, 20–21, 51–52, 159–64, 192, 199, 202.

[3] For synopses of Montesquieu's extraordinary influence upon political thought in the eighteenth and nineteenth centuries, see David Carrithers, "Introduction," in *Montesquieu's Science of Politics*, eds. Carrithers, Mosher, and Rahe (Rowman & Littlefield, 2001), and Paul Rahe, "Introduction," in *Montesquieu and the Logic of Liberty* (Yale University Press, 2009), especially xviii–xxi.

also his other major works, the philosophical novel *Persian Letters* (1721) and the philosophical history *Considerations on the Causes of the Greatness of the Romans and Their Decline* (1734). His deliberately multifaceted approach, within each of these works and across them, once was very appealing to statesmen but is less so today. Statesmen are adept at reconciling seemingly opposed views and coping with paradoxes. Philosophers and academics now mostly prefer that reality conform to linear, logical theory, or (after the rise of Romantic and postmodernist thought) that the agony of anthropocentrism be the central, imposing element of reality. Montesquieu, in contrast, always blends concern for the practice of governing with theoretical inquiry about it.

The blend in *The Spirit of Laws* of encyclopedic breadth with discrete advice on laws, governing, and reforms especially appealed to American statesmen. The authors of *The Federalist*, Hamilton, Madison, and Jay, sought to be enlightened statesmen. Hamilton and Jay were, like Montesquieu, learned in the theory and practice of law (Madison, too, had studied it). George Washington sought all three of them to serve as counselors and trusted lieutenants. Tocqueville, the lawyer and magistrate turned philosopher and historian, admires a philosophy of moderation attentive to political practice and human nature as revealed in history. He also admires the enlightened American statesmen, informed by that philosophy, who founded their republic by blending old and new ideas. Indeed, the philosophy broadly shared by Montesquieu and Tocqueville includes an historical dimension – both wrote separate works of history – and what we now call a sociological perspective that speaks to statesmen and founders especially. Nonetheless, neither philosopher is historicist or merely sociological, since both affirm natural right, the centrality of human nature, and the religious aspiration of that nature. Their main philosophical works examined here, *The Spirit of Laws* and *Democracy in America* (1835, 1840), incorporate elements of history and particular human phenomena into their philosophical evaluations. Both philosophers would understand why Chapter 2 focuses not on *The Federalist*, or Anti-Federalist and Jeffersonian republican writings, but instead on a case study of moderation in a great statesman, Washington, who forged these ideas into an American mind. Washington was a founder as if working a foundry, forming alloys and casting them into shapes. He marshaled leaders of each of these views or schools to serve as counselors while reserving final judgment on how to balance and reconcile competing views.

To many political theorists, whether of a modern or more neoclassical bent, the complexity and moderation of our two Frenchmen disqualifies them from the ranks of philosophers. Alternately, some scholars respect their philosophical stature but labor to reduce their philosophies to one dominant principle. Montesquieu and Tocqueville might reply that they observed philosophers who were too theoretical or too wedded to one principle; this led to failure to grasp the complex realities of human nature, or of a particular situation, or of how to sustain a political order. Our two jurist–historian–philosophers instead undertook complex analyses that tested their philosophical understanding by comprehending great historical events, ideas, founders, or failed founders. Montesquieu's *Considerations on the Romans* assesses lessons for modern monarchs and republicans about Rome's decline from republic into empire and thus to self-destruction, and this clearly informs the philosophy of his masterwork. That project had begun in *Persian Letters*, precisely to help European thought and politics avoid the cycle of extremes he observed in seventeenth-century England. He saw all the same ingredients in his own era – the cycle from authoritarian rule to revolution premised on doctrines of equal rights, liberty, and wholly new orders. Tocqueville's *The Old Regime and the Revolution* (1856) similarly sought to grasp the broader implications for humanity and modernity of violent and morally fraught events, especially failed revolutions and foundings; moreover, its predecessor *Democracy in America* already had shown his decision to blend historical-philosophical analysis. Scholars of political theory today might consider that these insightful and influential analyses of modern liberal democratic life, which include their anticipation of globalization and liberal-republican hegemony in international affairs, are rooted in a distinct philosophy of moderation that avoided an emphasis on either theory or particulars.

Part I investigates what I term Tocquevillean moderation, because his conception of philosophy and of founding (thus statesmanship) offers a deeper, more comprehensive understanding of late modern politics, philosophy, and religion. Using these benchmarks to compare the statesman–founder Washington with philosophers is not inapt, yet it requires thinking by analogies. Analogical thinking is at the heart of the philosophy of moderation, from its roots in Aristotle, Plutarch, and Aquinas to its development in Montesquieu and Tocqueville. This approach permits points of reconciliation or development that a narrower reasoning would not see or permit. Tocquevillean moderation uses such thinking to refine and deepen Montesquieu's philosophy. Washington's greater appreciation for virtue and religion already had moderated Montesquieu's effort, and Tocqueville appreciates the statesman's discernment about the challenges of sustaining liberal constitutional politics. Of course, Tocqueville did not look only to Montesquieu as he developed his own philosophy; on the other hand, it is very much in Montesquieu's spirit to refine and temper one's thinking by recourse to a range of earlier sources, and to lessons of historical experience.

For Tocquevillean philosophy, democracy in moderation means not only recognition of the fundamental justice of equal rights for all under law, but also recognition that constitutional liberal democracy needs to find its internal limits in accord with its inherent or corollary principles of liberty, religion, and nature so as to be a better, and sustainable, form of democracy. All three of the modern figures examined here had witnessed efforts to repudiate, or demote within scholarly and public discourse, the views of the human and political good considered by classical and medieval philosophy and by the moderate voices in modernity. The question posed by Montesquieu, Washington, and Tocqueville in tandem is whether the philosophical and practical consequences of the more radically modern doctrines have been truer to, or better for, humankind than what has been achieved by the moderate alternative.

I

Montesquieu's Philosophy of Moderation

Natural Right, Liberalism, Constitutionalism

The central theme of Montesquieu's political philosophy is moderation, a classical and medieval ideal he imbued with a modern and humane spirit to support liberty while tempering the rationalism and individualism in earlier modern philosophy. His moderation thus embraces philosophical and political balance to discern "the political good" (*The Spirit of Laws*, 29.1). Because he identified moderation as the central principle of his philosophy and the statesmen and philosophers most shaped by him distinguish his philosophy from the radical Enlightenment, this principle should be central to debates about his philosophy and its influence. He chose as the epigraph of *The Spirit of Laws* "a child born without a mother," from the Roman poet Ovid (in *Metamorphoses*); among several implications, one is that his philosophy of moderation and liberty was an orphan in an era of extremes. These included political absolutism from extreme monarchy and established religion to despotism, but also radical Enlightenment challenges to all prior thoughts and politics. Perhaps he would not be surprised that his philosophical moderation is the ultimate orphan, since, in contrast, his political moderation of constitutionalism achieved great effect. Nonetheless, *The Spirit of Laws* has provoked continual debate on its design and meaning, and few take Montesquieu at his word: that his masterwork has a design but a complex one, that liberty is indispensable but is defined by natural right and a complex constitutionalism, and that an architectonic principle of philosophical and political moderation guides the entire work.[1]

---

[1] I note below scholars who discuss moderation as important for Montesquieu, but three recent works addressing interrelations among these themes of design, liberty, natural right, and moderation are Paul A. Rahe, *Montesquieu and the Logic of Liberty* (Yale University Press, 2009); Ana Samuel, "The Design of Montesquieu's *The Spirit of the Laws*: The Triumph of Freedom over Determinism," *American Political Science Review* 103 (2009), 305–21; and Céline Spector, "Was Montesquieu Liberal? *The Spirit of the Laws* in the History of Liberalism," in *French Liberalism from Montesquieu to the Present Day*, eds. Geenens and Rosenblatt (Cambridge

Montesquieu's is the first political philosophy to declare moderation its central principle. He thinks it best befits human nature to avoid extremes of theory that obscure the complexities of human life and affairs, and avoid despotic political and moral structures lacking the complexity and self-restraint to secure individual (and family) liberty against rulers. The constitutionalism of liberty he formulated in his two earlier works and developed in *The Spirit of Laws* laid the foundation for the commercial, globalized liberal order now dominant.[2] He declared in the Preface to *Spirit* that his philosophical labors across decades had produced a cautious accounting of what we could know about human affairs, and this was based not upon prejudices, nor any school or sect, but upon "the nature of things."[3] Near the end of the work, shortly after declaring moderation in the principle of his philosophy (Book 29, Ch. 1), he boldly indicts Plato, Aristotle, Machiavelli, Thomas More, and other philosophers as too swayed by prejudices. With 600 prior pages of capacious inquiry as warrant, Montesquieu indicates that moderation does not preclude bold judgments. Indeed, he earlier pronounced that while he admired great works by European writers, his own work signaled some "genius" (29.19, 882–83/618; Preface, 231/xlv).

In contrast to the rationalism of some Enlightenment predecessors, his philosophy sought to account for the complexities in human thoughts and deeds. Unlike the fatigue and skepticism of his late-modern or postmodern successors, he encompassed complexity while resisting moral and political relativism. This balanced approach appealed to statesmen, especially Americans, but one scholar rightly deemed Montesquieu "the father of constitutions" – seminal for all the liberal democracies struggling to be born in later centuries.[4] This philosophy ultimately was less appealing to philosophers and to academics, and even among admirers there is quite a range of interpretations. Is Montesquieu a sly disciple of Hobbes and Locke on individualist natural rights and the social contract, or the father of modern historicism and sociology, or adapting the modern natural law of Grotius, or not a philosopher but an advocate of particular political and social reforms? Perhaps this scope of readings is an indirect affirmation of the moderation or balance in his philosophy, since a given interpreter might focus upon one element in the amalgam, one note in his

University Press, 2012), 57–72. Aurelian Craiutu's study of Montesquieu integrates moderation and liberty, but not the work's design or natural right; *A Virtue for Courageous Minds: Moderation in French Political Thought*, 1748–1830 (Princeton University Press, 2012).

2 I provide an overview of his political philosophy in the Montesquieu entry in *The Encyclopedia of Political Theory*, ed. Gibbons (Wiley-Blackwell, 2014).

3 Montesquieu, *De l'Esprit des Lois*, Preface, in *Œuvres complètes*, Pléiade edition, ed. Caillois, 2 vols. (Gallimard, 1949–51), 2: 229. I have checked my translations against *The Spirit of the Laws*, eds. Cohler, Miller, and Stone (Cambridge University Press, 1989) and the translation of Thomas Nugent (Hafner, 1949 [1750]), often using a more literal, precise rendering. Subsequent references to *The Spirit of Laws* are parenthetical, citing part of the work, then pages in the Pléiade edition (Volume 2) and the Cohler translation (e.g., Preface, 229/xlii).

4 Judith Shklar, *Montesquieu* (Oxford University Press, Past Masters series, 1987), 111–26.

harmony. The analysis offered here tries to recover the spirit of Montesquieu's own moderation by seeking to understand, through a complex journey, how natural right, historical complexity, constitutionalism, and prudential judgment fit into a comprehensive political philosophy.[5] Paradoxically, this requires adopting a reverse order to the presentation in *The Spirit of Laws* – postponing analysis of the opening, compact discussions of natural law and natural rights until these are placed in the context of the work and its larger philosophy. This accords, nonetheless, with the opening plea Montesquieu made, given the awareness of the complexity of his massive work, and the likelihood that the whole or particular parts would be misinterpreted: "I ask a favor that I fear will not be granted: it is that one not judge, by a moment's reading, the labor of twenty years; that one approve or condemn the whole book, and not some few sentences" (Preface, 229/xliii).[6] His request is reasonable, given that the scope of *The Spirit of Laws* has no counterpart in earlier liberalism, not even if one tried to fuse Locke's discrete analyses of education, religion, and politics into a larger philosophy.[7]

E Pluribus Unum: Complexity, Spirit, and Balance in Montesquieu's Philosophy

The variety of Anglo-American scholars who analyzed Montesquieu's *De l'Esprit des Lois* since the mid-twentieth century were drawn to its views on human nature, constitutional politics, and liberalism, and a healthy interest continues among scholars undaunted by its reputation as complicated or convoluted.[8] It is rarer for scholars to notice that the principle of moderation through which he elaborated his philosophy of complexity and equilibrium

---

[5] Much of the remainder of this chapter draws upon, yet substantially revises, my article "Montesquieu's Complex Natural Right and Moderate Liberalism: The Roots of American Moderation," *Polity* 36 (2004), 227–50.

[6] By seeking a sense of the whole before examining Book 1, I depart from the method employed by my teacher David Lowenthal in "Book I of Montesquieu's *The Spirit of Laws*," *American Political Science Review* 53 (1959), 485–98, and from two other analyses of natural right in Montesquieu from which I have learned much: Thomas L. Pangle, *Montesquieu's Philosophy of Liberalism: A Commentary on The Spirit of the Laws* (Chicago: University of Chicago Press, 1973) and Michael Zuckert, "Natural Law, Natural Rights, and Classical Liberalism: On Montesquieu's Critique of Hobbes," *Social Philosophy and Policy* 18 (2001), 227–51. The focus on Book 1 leads to a narrow comparison with (or reduction to) radical Enlightenment theories of natural law, right, and rights, especially Hobbes and Locke; this disregards Montesquieu's plea to assess the entire work, and his statement on moderation as its architectonic principle.

[7] See Nathan Tarcov, "A 'Non-Lockean' Locke and the Character of Liberalism," in *Liberalism Reconsidered*, eds. MacLean and Mills (Rowman & Allanheld, 1983), 130–40, and Peter Berkowitz, *Virtue and the Making of Modern Liberalism* (Princeton University Press, 1999).

[8] See, for example, the works by Berlin, Oakeshott, Arendt, Aron, Pangle, Shklar, Ceaser, and Rahe cited and discussed throughout this chapter. Note also the range of scholarly views or approaches evident in two recent collections: David Carrithers, "Introduction," in *Montesquieu's Science of Politics*, eds. Carrithers, Mosher, and Rahe (and the chapters therein) and *Montesquieu and His Legacy*, ed. Rebecca Kingston (SUNY Press, 2009). See Footnote 3 in

might be the thread for navigating his labyrinthine masterwork. The complexity of *The Spirit of Laws* deliberately seeks to modify the more doctrinaire liberalism of the radical Enlightenment by capturing the multifarious reality of humanity and politics, although not by eschewing universal principles of natural justice for a mere sociology of diverse particulars. Montesquieu did think analytical simplicity had slighted the multiple dimensions of human affairs and the equilibrium – the moderation – in things. This idea obviously informs his constitutionalism of separated and balanced powers, but he also argues that moderation defines natural right. The laws of our nature balance individual preservation and interest with humane sympathy for one's fellows; moreover, prudent judgment recognizes variation in the requirements of natural right in particular political circumstances. This view blended some main philosophical alternatives of the Western tradition, sought to capture the individual and social dimensions of our nature, and tempered some of the more abstract and revolutionary claims of early liberalism.[9] Understood in this way, Montesquieu's philosophy also lends perspective on recent liberal theory and its critics, by grounding both Rawlsian and communitarian views in a broader view of human nature and politics. The deeper aims of contemporary antifoundationalist and individualist liberalism, but also of contemporary communitarian ideas of civic duty and communal moral identity, would be better served by a tradition of theory that comprehends both kinds of concerns, and which better captures the complexity of American political thought. Political science and the social sciences, too, could benefit from a model that reconciles or balances empirical analyses with theoretical or normative ones, as well as balancing narrowly specialized and more holistic studies.

Many scholars have examined Montesquieu's conception of natural right by focusing upon the discussion in Book 1, "On laws in general," but his full understanding of a complex natural right arises through themes that permeate *The Spirit of Laws*, especially the principle of moderation or balance that animates his philosophizing and advice on good government. His modern liberalism incorporates some ancient and medieval principles, and his view of natural right cannot be reduced to Hobbes, Spinoza, or Locke. We should extend recent analyses of Hume and Smith to their French predecessor, since Montesquieu's complex philosophy informed their efforts to blend Enlightenment and

the Prologue on my appreciation for Dennis Rasmussen's approach in *The Pragmatic Enlightenment: Recovering the Liberalism of Smith, Hume, Montesquieu and Voltaire* (Cambridge University Press, 2014) but also significant differences.

9 Alan Gilbert emphasizes philosophical complexity in "'Internal Restlessness': Individuality and Community in Montesquieu," *Political Theory* 22 (1994), 45–70, but he sees Hegelian synthesis and omits natural right. On complexity in Montesquieu's analysis and use of natural right, see Céline Spector, "Quelle Justice? Quelle Rationalité? La Mesure du Droit dans *L'Esprit des Lois*," in *Montesquieu en 2005*, ed. Volpilhac-Auger (Voltaire Foundation, 2005), 219–42, and Paul Rahe, "Montesquieu, Natural Law, and Natural Right," in *Natural Law, Natural Rights, and American Constitutionalism* (Witherspoon Institute). Available at: www.nlnrac.org/earlymodern/montesquieu (accessed May 2013).

counter-Enlightenment principles into a more moderate conception of Enlightenment.[10] Nonetheless, Montesquieu's philosophy of moderation and complexity, developed over thirty-one books and 605 chapters in *The Spirit of Laws*, tends to pull scholars toward either analytical simplicity – reducing the whole to one idea – or toward a more holistic view that nonetheless risks incoherence. To grasp Montesquieu's melding of individual and community, classical natural right and modern natural rights, universal truth and particular context, one must see broader dimensions to his principle of moderation. Foremost among these are the complexity inherent in his concept of a "spirit" of politics and the larger meaning in the six-part structure of the work. The frequent recourse to poetry in *Spirit*, and its blending of Newtonian dynamics with a statesman's perception of both flux and stability in politics, further reveals a principle that seeks to bring coherence to a vast landscape of observations. Montesquieu's philosophic ambitions, and his fundamental influence upon modern liberal life, can come to light only through exploration of these and other aspects of his works. Understanding his attempt at philosophical complexity also helps us to step outside our contemporary debates in political theory to test whether today's dominant modes of theorizing effectively serve their stated aims. The inward-looking, antifoundationalist stance of Rawlsian political liberalism and related theories of deliberative democracy, and the similarly skeptical stance of communitarian theories that seek civic purpose and communal meaning without recourse to natural standards of natural justice, would benefit from rediscovering a more balanced, and grounded, philosophy of liberal republicanism.

Understanding Montesquieu's political philosophy requires grasping why the complexity of *The Spirit of Laws*, in both structure and argument, is deliberate, and for more than rhetorical or aesthetic purposes. The work has been criticized as incoherent since publication, although in its first century, greater tolerance for complicated works of philosophy and letters led to its enormous influence and wide audience. D'Alembert, the encyclopedist of Enlightenment, defended *The Spirit of Laws* by noting that one "must distinguish apparent disorder from real disorder" and that "voluntary obscurity is not obscurity."[11] This adduces rhetorical reasons for esotericism, but Montesquieu

---

[10] See, for example, Charles Griswold, Jr., *Adam Smith and the Virtue of Enlightenment* (Cambridge University Press, 1999), and John Danford, *David Hume and the Problem of Reason* (Yale University Press, 1990). For a more sympathetic view of Montesquieu from a scholar of the Enlightenment, in contrast to Israel's studies, see Peter Gay, *The Enlightenment*, 2 vols. (Knopf, 1966) I, Preface, x; see also II, 325–26, 332. Andrea Radasanu, "Montesquieu on Moderation, Monarchy, and Reform," *History of Political Thought* 31 (Summer 2010), 283–307, finds only a narrow conception of moderation in Montesquieu, as neo-Machiavellian pragmatism.

[11] Jean D'Alembert, "Éloge de Montesquieu," in *Œuvres complètes de Montesquieu*, ed. Masson (Nagel, 1950–55), xvii–xviii; see Lowenthal, "Book I of *The Spirit of Laws*," 485–86; Pangle, *Montesquieu's Philosophy of Liberalism*, 11–12; and Rahe, *The Logic of Liberty*, 85–91.

himself defends his work not as esoteric but as a complex whole requiring careful reading. Those who reduce his philosophy to the radical liberalism of Hobbes and Locke by focusing on particular passages to the exclusion of others – in particular, those that address or embody his philosophical moderation – might recall that he begins the work by asking readers to "approve or condemn the whole book, and not some few phrases." He further warns that "many of the truths will not make themselves felt until after one sees the chain that links them to the others" (Preface, 229/xliii–xliv). After the famous analysis of England's constitution in the middle of the work, he signals his aim to provoke deeper or further thoughts: "one must not always so exhaust a subject that one leaves nothing for a reader to do," since readers must not only read but "think" (11.20, 430/186). A Notice he added to a revised edition is still bolder and, along with his opening appraisal of his "genius" and his later appraisal of the prejudices marring some philosophers, signals his blend of indebtedness to others and independent insights: "I have had new ideas; new words have had to be found or new meanings given to old ones."[12]

While much can be learned by contextualizing *The Spirit of Laws* in relation to eighteenth-century France or the Enlightenment, Montesquieu emphasizes that his meaning largely lies in the work itself. Moreover, his dialectical philosophy will not follow Enlightenment modes of deduction from axiomatic principles. While he insists that his genius matches that of previous philosophers, he further compares his ingenuity to that of artists – the master of metamorphoses, Ovid; the epic poet Virgil; the inventor Daedalus; and the painter Corregio (Epigraph, 227/v; Preface, 231/xlv). Montesquieu's approach to natural right or natural law in Book 1, understood as a standard of justice by which to measure politics and law, thus draws upon Montaigne's complex humanism as much as Cartesian or deductive rationalism, in the proportion he finds truest to the nature of things. His nearly interchangeable use of "natural right" and "natural law" suggests this kind of deliberate effort to blend or reconcile seemingly competing concepts or schools.[13] The Preface and Book 1 together introduce the blend of ancient and modern ideas he discerns in politics and

---

[12] *Avertissement de l'Auteur*, Author's Notice (first published in 1757), 227–28/xli. Later he noted that, in retrospect, *Persian Letters* (1721) had sought "to join philosophy, politics and morals, to a tale, and to link the whole by a chain that is secret and, in some fashion, unknown." "Some Reflections on the *Persian Letters*" [1754], in *Œuvres complètes*, 1, 129; see *The Persian Letters*, ed. and tr. George Healy (Hackett, 1999 [1964]), 3–4.

[13] Contrary to Zuckert's argument in "Montesquieu's Critique of Hobbes," Montesquieu blends these terms throughout the work, for example, the "laws of our nature" in Book 1 invoke yet modify the analyses of natural law and natural rights in Hobbes and Locke; in Book 26 he uses the terms interchangeably (Chapters 1, 3, 5, 6, 7); in 26.1 *droit naturel* is a kind of *loi* (750/494); 26.6 uses *droit naturel* in the title, but *loi naturelle* and *droit naturel* in the body (755/498, 757/499–500); natural law in 26.3 includes "natural defense" and "natural modesty" (752/496; see also 26.7), but in 10.2 and 24.6 natural defense is a right (see 377/139 and 719/464; compare 6.13).

which inform the spirit of politics, properly understood. The aim is to moderate early modern efforts to establish new foundations for political philosophy upon abstract analyses of man and right in a state of nature. Like Plato, Aristotle, and Cicero – and Tocqueville after him – Montesquieu grasps natural right through the complexity of human experience, found both in our likely primitive condition and in large, complicated societies. Many studies nonetheless reduce his philosophy to some earlier modern philosopher or school, or, at the opposite extreme, argue that he practically invented sociology and historicism, eschewing natural right.[14] The one approach overlooks his opening declaration in *The Spirit of Laws* of his philosophic originality, while the other overlooks his early pronouncement that philosophy can help man to discover "his own nature" despite erroneous philosophies that obscure it (Preface, 230/xlv; see also 29.19).

A more promising view finds Montesquieu adapting aspects of Aristotelian philosophy to modern purposes, using ancient and modern sources to forge a new science of politics.[15] This is evident in the conception of natural right he develops not only in the early contractarian analysis of Book 1 but throughout the work, a method that links natural right with complexity. His view of natural right unfolds through an epic account; this is a plausible characterization for a work that begins and ends with Virgil and grasps human affairs in a manner indebted as much to classical humanism as to Hobbes. Montesquieu also employs his knowledge as a lawyer and jurist by making crucial statements about philosophy, natural right, and moderation in the closing books of *The Spirit of Laws* on the history (and, he insists, the theory) of classical Roman and medieval French laws and constitutionalism – books that most scholars dismiss as an appendix. The hero of this massive investigation of nature and politics is the philosopher-legislator who watches over mankind by inculcating prudence about how to moderate politics and make it more humane (Preface; 1.1; 24.10; 28.38; 29.18). Moreover, Montesquieu seems to be signaling moderation in his opening declaration that his work does not employ the "striking features" (*traits saillants*) of "present-day works," which only seem persuasive because "the mind attaches itself to a single point, and forgets all others." He notes that this defect can be cured by achieving "a certain distance" (Preface, 229–30/xliv). He recapitulates this concern just after declaring English liberty as "extreme" and defending governments that have a "moderate" liberty, declaring that "the excess even of reason is not always desirable." That philosophical

---

[14] As noted below, Rousseau, Arendt, Hulliung, Manent, and Kingston find sociology, communitarianism, or antifoundationalism at the core of Montesquieu's philosophy; Lowenthal, Pangle, and Zuckert basically find Hobbes; Waddicor, Tuck, and Courtney find Grotius and modern natural law. See also Mark Waddicor, *Montesquieu and the Philosophy of Natural Law* (Martinus Nijhoff, 1970), 16–17, for another typology of views on Montesquieu.

[15] As discussed below, Aron, Cohler, Mansfield, and Gilbert see some appropriation of classical thought; Simone Goyard-Fabre argues he is "an ancient among the moderns" in *Montesquieu: la nature, les lois, la liberté* (Presses universitaires de France, 1993), 343.

statement in turn informs his empirical observation that "men almost always accommodate themselves better to middles [the medium] than to extremes" (11.6, 407/166).

As noted, while some find *The Spirit of Laws* incoherent or historicist, others reduce it to one analytical principle. There is some presence of Newton, Descartes, and Hobbes in Montesquieu's capacious philosophy, but one of its aims is to temper the rationalist excesses of earlier modern philosophy. His delay of a pronouncement on moderation until Book 29, near the end of the reader's long journey, suggests not confusion but respect for the world's complexity: "I say it, and it seems to me I have brought forth this work only to prove it: the spirit of moderation ought to be that of the legislator; the political good, like the moral good, is always found between two limits" (29.1, 865/602). He chastises both ancient and modern political philosophers shortly after – as "legislators" who educate mankind, especially rulers and founders – for succumbing to "passions and prejudices" (29.19). Throughout the work he insists upon the irreducible complexity of reality and the need for a dialectical, balanced judgment. The principle of his philosophy, moderation, thus is almost a nonprinciple, a marker for complexity.[16] These concluding maxims of *Spirit* about political and moral moderation warn about the inhumanity of reducing human phenomena to simple foundations. In Book 11 he had boldly argued that the English derived their constitution from the medieval Germans, a system of equilibrium and liberty devised "in the forests." This best government ever formed – praised for securing liberal aims of individual tranquility, liberty, and rule of law – was achieved not by philosophy but by a common-sense understanding of human needs and aspirations, and how to achieve them in given circumstances (11.6 end, 11.8). A philosophy of moderation also explains his odd use of the term "theory" in the historical Books that close the work, a journey through medieval Franco-Gothic law that redefines a "theory of laws" (titles to Books 30, 31). Montesquieu's philosophy is modern and liberal, marked by weakly teleological and nonscholastic views of nature and morals, as well as by individual rights, the rule of law, confidence in intellectual and political progress, and religious toleration. Yet his three main works – the poetic and philosophic *Persian Letters*, the historical and philosophical *Considerations on the Romans*, and his complex masterwork – comprise a single project to temper rationalism, the distortion of reality caused by artificial insistence

---

[16] On this conception of moderation in Montesquieu's philosophy, see Harvey Mansfield, *Taming The Prince: The Ambivalence of Modern Executive Power* (Free Press, 1989), 214ff; also Raymond Aron, *Les Étapes de la pensée sociologique: Montesquieu, Comte, Marx, Tocqueville, Durkheim, Pareto, Weber* (Gallimard, 1967), *Main Currents in Sociological Thought*, tr. Howard and Weaver (Penguin, 1968 [1965]), 27–35, 56–57, 60; Pangle, *Philosophy*, 271–73; Shklar, *Montesquieu*, 85, 91; Anne Cohler, *Montesquieu's Comparative Politics and the Spirit of American Constitutionalism* (University Press of Kansas, 1988), 66–97; and Rahe, *Logic of Liberty*, 214–24, also 16, 36, 46, 63, 70, 74–76, 91, 94, 122, 151–54, 194, 198, 210–11.

upon demonstrability or clarity.[17] Moreover, while it is helpful to consider that "whereas Aristotle's moderation is supported from above, by a conception of human virtue, Montesquieu's moderation is supported from below, by a conception of elemental human needs and passions," Montesquieu's vantage is not as low as it may seem.[18]

The Dialectical Design of *The Spirit of Laws*

To grasp the comprehensive, moderate philosophy of the *The Spirit of Laws*, one must move between part and whole, between the apparently rationalist account of law in Book 1 (especially Chapter 1, "On laws in their relation with the various beings") and the historical particularity and prudence emphasized thereafter. The structure of the work embodies Montesquieu's philosophy, reviving a kind of Socratic dialectic that is alert to part and whole, simplicity and complexity, universals and particulars.[19] He in fact provides three signposts for this dialectical journey through *The Spirit of Laws* – its title, its division into six Parts, and its epigraph from Ovid. In the final chapter of Book 1, "On positive laws," he summarizes the work by defining its title in terms of the various "relations" that comprise the spirit of laws, and in doing so captures the blend of principle and fact for which his political science is known (1.3). He implicitly separates this list of relations or things into four categories, by using "relate" four times, in three verbal moods. First, laws "must relate to" the "nature" and "principle" of a government. Second, laws "should be related to" the physical aspect of a country, including climate, terrain, and "the way of life of the

---

[17] Montesquieu satirizes abstract, petty thinking throughout *Persian Letters*; see nos. 45, 72, 73, 109, 128, 134–37, 145, in *Œuvres complètes*, vol. 1 (or the Healy translation). See also *Spirit*, 11.5, chastising Harrington for utopian speculation (396/156), and criticism of devising an intellectual "system" in 30.10 (891–92/627) – drawing upon Ovid for counsel to avoid extremes and find the middle. On Aristotelian prudence in Montesquieu, see Isaiah Berlin, "Montesquieu" (1955), in *Against the Current*, ed. Hardy (Viking Press, 1980), 130–61; Pangle, *Philosophy*, 260–305; Melvin Richter, *The Political Theory of Montesquieu* (Cambridge University Press, 1977), 1–19; Mansfield, *Taming the Prince*, 213–46; Simone Goyard-Fabre, *La philosophie du droit de Montesquieu* (Librarie C. Klincksieck, 1973), 53–76, and *Montesquieu*, 1–12; Michael Oakeshott, "The Investigation of the 'Character' of Modern Politics: Montesquieu," in *Morality and Politics in Modern Europe*, ed. Letwin (Yale University Press, 1993), 29–43, at 36, 41; and Diana Schaub, *Erotic Liberalism: Women and Revolution in Montesquieu's Persian Letters* (Rowman & Littlefield, 1995), 136–44.

[18] Schaub, *Erotic Liberalism*, 25.

[19] I emphasize Books 1–11 of *Spirit* here, the typical focus of scholars reducing Montesquieu's thought to some one idea; in Chapters 3 and 4 of *The Cloaking of Power: Montesquieu, Blackstone, and the Rise of Judicial Activism* (University of Chicago, 2003), I discuss Books 12–31, emphasizing the projects for prudent reform and view of prudence. I endorse recent efforts to explain *Spirit*'s dialectical design or larger logic in Rahe, *Logic of Liberty* (see 39, 85–95), and Samuel, "The Design of Montesquieu's *The Spirit of Laws*," but philosophical moderation nonetheless is the architectonic principle, which defines and justifies the work's view of liberty, to include warnings that liberty requires moderation.

peoples." Third, laws "should relate to" the "degree of liberty" a constitution can sustain and also to the religion, "inclinations," wealth, population, commerce, and mores and manners of the people. Fourth, "laws are related" to one another, their history, the "purpose of the legislator," and to "the order of things on which they are established." Laws must be considered from all these points of view: "I shall examine all these relations: all together they form what is called THE SPIRIT OF LAWS" (1.3, 238/8–9, emphasis in original).

This list of topics and relations does not neatly correspond to the six-part structure of the work, nor to the topics announced in the titles of the thirty-one books. Nevertheless, the work examines all these relations and things, a scope that suggests a new political science blending the natural science of Bacon and Newton with traditional, Aristotelian political science. The spirit of laws comprises the various elements of nature and man's nature in their relations with various laws, then the actual and theoretically optimal relations among laws themselves – thus comprehending the political, social, environmental, and theoretical phenomena affecting mankind. Politics must be understood not through one idea or condition but by grasping the actual ethos, the complex web of ideas and facts, shaping laws, constitutions, and civilizations. Unlike modern sociology, Montesquieu thinks this requires study of permanent aspects of man's being, and one framework for analysis is a Newtonian view of man's psychology and physiology, observing forces and ideas acting and reacting.[20] This natural-science element explains in part why his notions of rationality and psychology omit classical teleology, precluding traditional inquiries about the best life, or best regime. His analysis of human nature and politics thus is prescriptive, but, in comparison to classical and medieval philosophy, somewhat relativist and reductive. The new science of relations or spirit occupies a middle point between subjectivism and Socratic teleology – adopting neither the distinction between facts and values in modern social science nor the universal moral judgment of Aristotle's political science. This moderate position identifies Montesquieu as a modern with classical moments. Instead of a law of the human spirit sought by Aristotle or Aquinas, he analyzes a spirit of laws, thus preparing for, but not entailing, value-neutral social science. Still, this political science rejects the historicist notions from Rousseau or Nietzsche that human being is essentially malleable or radically self-transforming.

The concepts of "relations" and "spirit" embodied in the work's title, which suggest a newly comprehensive human science, in turn explain the division of *The Spirit of Laws* into six Parts. Scholars often dismiss this second major signpost of the work, either ignoring Montesquieu's plan or making their own.[21]

---

[20] See Lowenthal, "Book I," 497–98; I discuss Newton further, below, including in notes 23 and 28.

[21] The most recent, comprehensive arguments for the importance and logic of the Parts are, as noted, by Rahe and Samuel; earlier exceptional efforts include Schaub, *Erotic Liberalism*, 136–44; Cohler, *Montesquieu's Comparative Politics*, 11–33; and Paul A. Rahe, *Republics Ancient*

This structure reinforces complexity and moderation in his philosophy, and suggests why the understanding of natural right in Book 1 ultimately is not abstract or rationalist. Part 1 (Books 1–8) discusses laws in general and then human or political laws as derived from the "nature" or ruling structure and then "principle" or motive forces of the basic types of governments (see 2.1, 3.1). Recent political scientists would recognize this part, since it surveys traditional modes of political analysis and reformulates them. By the end of Book 3, Montesquieu indicates, however, that the crucial distinction for his political science is not between three (or four) types of government – democracy, aristocratic republic, monarchy, despotism – but between moderate and despotic governments (see 3.10, title; 8.8, 356/118; 5.14, 297/63). Thus, when propounding his own constitutionalism in Books 11 and 12, he never uses the nature or principle concepts, and Book 19 uses a new term, the "general spirit" of a nation, as a basic principle of analysis – a comprehensive predecessor to today's term "political culture" (19, title; 19.4). Montesquieu's fundamental ambition is to refound political science upon new principles, while utilizing the best of traditional and modern approaches. The structure of the government or who rules, and the defining principle or motives of the political order – which together suggest Aristotle's *politeia* or regime – are relevant, but less crucial than the effects of these and other political phenomena upon individual tranquility. He utilizes but demotes such mainstays of ancient and early modern political science as regime types, republican political liberty, or abstract natural rights, while emphasizing that liberalism must educate governments to provide for moderation in political and civil life and to avoid despotism and brutality. This blending of Montaigne's humane counsels with Newton's science of mechanics informs his kinder, gentler view that human nature and natural right seek equilibrium and tranquility – that is, moderation, both individual and communal.

These fundamental principles of spirit, moderation, and tranquility, which unfold in Part 1 of *The Spirit of Laws*, in turn inform the work as a whole. The latter books of Part 1 (Books 2–8) analyze whether the traditional governments and concepts adequately secure the moderation and tranquility essential to a humane politics. Part 2 (Books 9–13) completes this criticism of, and transition beyond, both classical political philosophy and early modern liberalism by proposing a new liberal constitutionalism in its three component parts – a federal structure and its international relations (Books 9 and 10); its national or political constitution (Book 11, with his first famous discussion of England and separation of powers); and, the dimensions of the constitution affecting individuals most directly – the criminal and civil laws (Book 12) and fiscal

& Modern, vol. 2, *New Modes and Orders in Early Modern Political Thought* (University of North Carolina, 1994), 210–14. The third edition of *Spirit* (1750) restored the six-part structure omitted by the printer in 1748: Part 1, Books 1–8; Part 2, 9–13; Part 3, 14–19; Part 4, 20–23; Part 5, 24–26; Part 6, 27–31. See also *De L'Esprit des Loix*, ed. Brethe de la Gressaye, 4 vols. (Société Les Belles-Lettres, 1950–61), 1: l–li.

or economic policy (Book 13). Since traditional analyses and forms of government fail to provide for moderation and tranquility, and having sketched a complex constitutionalism that does so, Part 3 (Books 14–19) then examines obstacles to political moderation from climate, terrain, and culture. Here Montesquieu scientifically analyzes politics and human nature in relation to nature and history, explaining the predominance of despotism and scarcity of political liberty or tranquility throughout the world and recorded history. The last book in this part investigates the general spirit of the people and launches the subtle, practical education in prudence and moderation that occupies the remainder of the work. He revisits England to examine the spirit of dynamism and faction shaped by its constitutionalism, an analysis that deeply influenced Madison and Tocqueville, among others (19.27). He launches Part 4 (Books 20–23), and the second half of the reader's journey, with emphatic praise for the civilizing and humanizing effects of commerce on politics and culture, and then addresses population growth, thereby sowing the seeds of modern political economy and "globalization." Part 5 (Books 24–26) continues to blend theory and practice by discussing laws on religion and tolerance, then by defining distinct categories of law – separating political from civil law, religious law from local custom – in order to secure both individual liberty and general order. The unduly neglected Part 6 (Books 27–31) examines the history of certain classical Roman and medieval Gothic or French laws and in doing so propounds a new historical "theory" of law, punctuated by general remarks on the spirit of law (Book 29). These final three Parts of the work (from Book 20) examine crucial aspects of a constitutionalism of moderation and tranquility. From modern commerce to medieval French law, Montesquieu inculcates a liberal prudence on reforming the laws and spirit of any particular people or government, the more subtly the better.

The third initial signpost Montesquieu provides for *The Spirit of Laws*, beyond the title and Parts, is the epigraph from the *Metamorphoses* of Ovid: *Prolem sine matre creatam*, "An offspring created without a mother."[22] Montesquieu's use of poetry is rarely discussed, but one must account for the prominence here, and in the epigraphs for Books 20 and 28 (Virgil and Ovid, respectively), of invocations to classical poetry about the nature or transformations of gods, the physical world, and men. As evident in the Preface, his "genius" seeks original approaches to both longstanding and novel human problems; his recourse to poets and artists bespeaks a reordering of given ideas or political circumstances even while wearing the mantle of things "classic." His new political science of spirit, of the complex interrelations among natural and political phenomena, marries Enlightenment natural science with earlier elements of the Western tradition. Such complexity seeks to both understand and oppose

[22] Ovid, *Metamorphoses*, Book 2, line 553, eds. Miller and Goold (Harvard University Press, 1977), I: 98–99; see Richter, *The Political Theory of Montesquieu*, 319, note 2, and the discussion of poetry at notes 27–29.

despotism, the epitome of political extremism, imbalance, and disequilibrium. His primary remedy for this threat to a humane, free life is not simply the invocation of liberty, but the moderation available in nature and human nature. This informs his most noted constitutional doctrine, separation of powers, for a principle of equilibrium guides his study of England's constitution: "So that one cannot abuse power, it is necessary that, by the disposition of things, power check power" (11.4, 395/155). Moderation also informs his other well-known concepts, such as the pluralism of parties and factions (or interests) that defines free politics, but which can yield its own kinds of extremism (19.27). Less obvious is that *The Spirit of Laws* as a whole seeks to inculcate philosophical moderation or equilibrium by drawing upon diverse modes of knowing about human nature and politics, from poetry and history to science and philosophy, blending them for a comprehensive portrait of human and political reality. Perhaps Montesquieu signaled that his work had no one mother because, by drawing upon many sources, it achieved a unique argument and approach.

The scope, complexity, and design of *The Spirit of Laws* embodies, then, Montesquieu's notion of spirit, and this idea – of the myriad interrelations among phenomena and the dialectical inquiry needed to comprehend them – points to moderation. These principles bind the many Parts, Books, and chapters of a work that claims to grasp "the infinite diversity of laws and mores" among men and "the histories of all nations" (Preface, 229/xliii). Since he ultimately announces that the spirit of laws, and of his political science, is moderation, one must grasp how this principle shapes such core ideas of his philosophy as natural right and constitutionalism – rather than analyzing particular passages in isolation or through a lens alien to his stated aims.

Moderation, Humane Letters, and a New Science of Politics

Montesquieu's concept of moderation tempers, without repudiating, moral virtue and internal ethical balance – concepts central to classical and Christian ethics – so as to comprehend the myriad ideas and actions of human life. One general formulation of moderation is "spirit" as a quasi-Newtonian equilibrium between bodies, forces, or ideas. Thus, the correct "relation between the laws and the principle" of each government "strains all the springs of the government; and the principle receives, in its turn, a new force. It is in the same way as, in physical motion, an action is always followed by a reaction" (5.1, 273/42).[23] Often, however, relations among humans and ideas cannot be

---

[23] Denis de Casabianca analyzes Montesquieu's use of Newtonian and especially Cartesian physics in "Dérèglements mécaniques et dynamiques des fluides dans L'Esprit des lois," *Revue Montesquieu* 4 (2000), 43–70, emphasizing his analogies of physical equilibrium to political moderation and of sheer mechanistic force to despotism; Montesquieu employs these to oppose Hobbes's resort to principles of physics and mechanics in constructing a Leviathan of undivided sovereignty and efficacy. See Rahe, *Logic of Liberty*, 128.

defined so starkly, and Montesquieu's recourse to poetry is one way of tempering analogies to physics. His predecessor as a counselor in the Parlement of Bordeaux, Montaigne, may inform this disposition, even though, as with Locke, he is never cited in *The Spirit of Laws*. Montaigne and Montesquieu both wrote works known for their comprehensiveness, seeming disorder, and blend of philosophy and *belles-lettres*. In the *Essays* and *The Spirit of Laws*, each jurist compares himself to a painter; each prominently cites Ovid, Virgil, Plutarch, and Lucretius; each addresses moderation, religious toleration, culture, and climate as factors in politics.[24] Both sought a humane politics, to address human timidity and fear by moderating the cruelty evident in all tyrannies, whether as sheer barbarism or as religious and moral zealotry.[25] Still, even if Montaigne is not the skeptic he seems, he never proposes a political science or philosophy that is as systematic as Montesquieu's (itself only moderately systematic).[26] Perhaps *The Spirit of Laws* gives both Montaigne and Locke the silent treatment because each reads nature in too skeptical or atomistic a mode, the one assaying provocative musings, the other treating politics, religion, education, and morals analytically, and artificially, in discrete works.

The comprehensive scope and complex design of *The Spirit of Laws* suggest that moderation serves a bold synthesis, albeit in a Socratic, not Hegelian, sense. Montesquieu moves from the humane spirit of Montaigne in the Preface, to scientific analysis in the opening chapter of Book 1 on "laws in their relation with the various beings," then quickly shifts back to a middle ground when defining the spirit of laws in the empirical terms of man-made, positive laws (1.1, 1.3). The last theoretical Book of the work echoes this synthetic approach, albeit without any reflections on the order of the universe: the spirit of moderation should guide legislators, for the political and moral good exists between extremes (29.1). Moderation thus contains physical, epistemological, and political senses, analogous meanings that correspond to the relations he saw between the natural, psychological, and social aspects of reality.[27] He

---

24 Montaigne compares himself to a painter in "*De l'amitié*," *Essais*, Book 1, ch. 28, in *Œuvres complètes*, eds. Thibaudet and Rat (Gallimard, 1962), 182; "Of friendship," in *The Complete Essays of Montaigne*, tr. Frame (Stanford University Press, 1958), 135. Montesquieu names Plato, Malebranche, Shaftesbury, and Montaigne "the four great poets" in his *Pensées*; *Œuvres complètes* 1: 1546 (no. 2095). See Alan Levine, *Sensual Philosophy: Toleration, Skepticism, and Montaigne's Politics of the Self* (Lexington Books, 2001), 16, 179, and 246, note 24.

25 See Shklar, *Montesquieu*, 15, 26–7, 114; David L. Schaefer, *The Political Philosophy of Montaigne* (Cornell University Press, 1990), 340–41, 383–84, 394; Paul A. Rahe, "Forms of Government: Structure, Principle, Object, and Aim," in *Montesquieu's Science of Politics*, eds. Carrithers, Mosher, and Rahe, 75, 84–88; and Michael Mosher, "Monarchy's Paradox: Honor in the Face of Sovereign Power," ibid., 217.

26 See Albert Sorel, *Montesquieu*, deuxième édition (Librarie Hachette, 1889), 173–74, on Montesquieu lying between Montaigne and Pascal in a "middle ground" or golden mean for knowledge, reflection, and common sense.

27 See Charles-Jacques Beyer, "Montesquieu et l'esprit cartésien," in *Actes du Congrès Montesquieu* (Imprimerie Delmas, 1956); David Lowenthal, "Montesquieu, 1689–1755" in *History*

tempers any traditional moral deposit by blending in modern elements – Cartesian or Newtonian science, and Machiavellian realism about the need to temper the moral aims of politics.[28] Although a crucial aim of his new science of politics is liberty, a distinctively modern moderation is thus both its indispensable guide and condition. His negative idea of liberty, as tranquility or freedom from fear (11.6), partly follows Hobbes in defining human nature more by aversion to insecurity than by orientation to a higher end. However, against Hobbes he argues that liberty requires political moderation, and that our nature is open to higher aims, even to the divine (1.1–2; see also 4.2, 5.12, 24.1). Proper liberty entails moderation, the avoidance of any structural imbalance of forces, since the latter signals despotism. Montesquieu will not have man suffer any forms of despotism as a patient citizen of the city of God. He condemns the brutality of ambitious princes or factious republics and the yoke of security imposed by any Leviathan. He would reform the city of man by emphasizing the natural desire for a tranquil, hospitable abode, including a weak teleology of higher aspirations for genuine honor and religious belief.[29]

Related to this new conception of moderation is the recourse to poetry throughout *The Spirit of Laws*. A subtle redefinition of moderation is but one device by which, as the Roman poet Lucretius might put it, Montesquieu coats his controversial medicine with honey. His citations to poets and artists, from the opening epigraph to a closing sentence that quotes Virgil, rarely have been studied with care.[30] His aim, in part, is to recall the Epicurean materialism of Lucretius, a doctrine more quietly present in Virgil and Ovid, since Montesquieu largely accepts the Lucretian and Newtonian challenges to the physics and metaphysics of Plato and Aristotle.[31] To replace a strong teleology of forms,

---

of Political Philosophy, eds. Strauss and Cropsey, 3rd edn. (University of Chicago Press, 1987 [1963]), 513–34, at 514, and "Montesquieu and the Classics: Republican Government in *The Spirit of the Laws*," in *Ancients and Moderns: Essays in Honor of Leo Strauss*, ed. Cropsey (Basic Books, 1964), 258–87, at 259. Goyard-Fabre sees a Newtonian blend of the empirical and theoretical, not Cartesian rationalism, in *La philosophie du droit*, 57–65.

[28] On Machiavelli and natural science see David Lowenthal, "Introduction," in *Considerations on the Causes of the Greatness of the Romans and their Decline*, ed. and tr. David Lowenthal (Hackett Publishing, 1999 [1965]), 11; on moderation, Schaub, *Erotic Liberalism*, 25. I discuss these issues in "The Machiavellian Spirit of Montesquieu's Liberal Republic," in *Machiavelli's Republican Legacy*, ed. Rahe (Cambridge University Press, 2006), 121–42.

[29] See Gilbert, "'Internal Restlessness';" Sharon Krause, "The Spirit of Separate Powers in Montesquieu," *Review of Politics* 62 (2000), 231–65; Rahe, "Forms of Government," and Sharon Krause, "Despotism in *The Spirit of Laws*," both in *Montesquieu's Science of Politics*, 69–108, 231–71. I discuss these issues further in Chapter 4, on religion and politics.

[30] See Pangle, *Philosophy*, 235–37, and Schaub, *Erotic Liberalism*, 144, 150, 175, note 13. Christopher Sparks, *Montesquieu's Vision of Uncertainty and Modernity in Political Philosophy* (Edwin Mellen, 1999), overlooks the philosophic reflection throughout *Persian Letters* and the poetry (including Montesquieu's own) throughout *Spirit*.

[31] I am indebted to Eve Adler, "Vergil on World Empire" (unpublished essay) and *Vergil's Empire: Political Thought in The Aeneid* (Rowman & Littlefield, 2003); see also James Nichols, *Epicurean Political Philosophy* (Cornell University Press, 1976), 190–98, 206.

essences, and natural ends, Montesquieu updates the ancient materialists with a Newtonian science of the structure and power of matter and its motions, guided by basic or minimal natural laws for matter as well as for humanity. However, he applies such mechanistic and minimal principles to politics in a blend with the realistic, empirical spirit of Machiavelli's factious republicanism, although this element, too, is suitably tempered. Indeed, Montesquieu invokes the cosmopolitanism and humane grandeur of Virgil more than either Epicurean or modern materialism, preferring *The Aeneid*'s praise for human emotions and attachments, and for piety, tradition, and honorable sacrifice to a larger good. He composed his own poem, an "Invocation to the Muses," for a draft of *The Spirit of Laws*, and launched his praise of commerce by recalling the tragedy of Dido and Aeneas; he then regularly praises Carthage, the counterpoint to Rome's warlike imperialism (Book 20, and epigraph).[32]

This blending of ideas from ancient poetry, modern science, and Machiavelli is in fact the basis for Montesquieu's most noted political doctrine, a constitutional politics of separated powers in a dynamic equilibrium, serving tranquility and moderate satisfaction of the passions. In this complicated, factional politics, the checking of each force by another "strains" all the springs of the governmental order, producing actions and reactions that keep the system moving and avoid the dangerous inertness of despotism (5.1, 11.13, 19.27). This new moderation blends a classical poet's perception of the passions, a modern scientist's mathematical view of motion, and a realist's eye for the dynamics of politics. His philosophy embodies this dynamic equilibrium, with each element tempering the others so as to capture the complexity of nature and politics. To temper the radical tendencies in Lucretius, Machiavelli, or modern science, Montesquieu invokes the concern for moderate reform and prudence in Aristotle and Plutarch. He is the master painter who draws upon earlier masters, just as Corregio acknowledges Raphael (a Florentine contemporary of Machiavelli), but he utilizes earlier thinkers in light of his own view of reality and human nature (Preface, 230–31/xliv–xlv). This synthetic ambition informs his complex constitutionalism, with no hint of a Hegelian dialect driving it. He thinks that a politics of moderation and complexity could take many forms in different circumstances (see 1.3, 5.14 [end], 11.6 [end], 11.20). This spirit of moderation yields a complicated work of hundreds of chapters and thousands of citations to authorities, at once synthetic and original.

One price for eschewing a strong teleology is that Montesquieu's philosophy resembles, at moments, Machiavelli's reductive realism. Unlike either the classical focus on the end(s) of man or the earlier modern focus on state-of-nature

---

[32] The "Invocation" traditionally is printed at the head of Book 20 of *Spirit*, but Catherine Volpilhac-Auger argues that Montesquieu ultimately did not intend to place it there, in "Une nouvelle 'Chaîne secrète' de *L'Esprit des lois*: L'Histoire de texte," in *Montesquieu en 2005*, ed. Volpilhac-Auger (Voltaire Foundation, 2005), 85–216 (esp. 185–94, "Que faire de Muses?"); see Rahe, *Logic of Liberty*, 154, 310–11.

origins, he emphasizes the political state most historically and geographically prevalent, despotism.[33] This suggests a foundationalism that defines man in terms of interacting forces. The lone citation of a modern authority in Book 1, the Italian jurist and poet Giovanni Gravina (1664–1718) of the modern natural law school led by Grotius, further suggests this.[34] In the third chapter, on positive laws, Montesquieu defines "POLITICAL RIGHT" (*droit*) and "CIVIL RIGHT" in seemingly relational, amoral terms: "*The union of all individual forces*, Gravina states very well, *forms what is called the* POLITICAL STATE"; "Individual forces cannot be united without all wills being united. *The union of these wills*, Gravina again states very well, *is what is called the* CIVIL STATE" (1.3, 236–37, emphasis in original). Nonetheless, he tempers any rationalism by looking to a fellow jurist and poet for these crucial terms, not to Machiavellian, Cartesian, or liberal philosophers. Moreover, these statements presuppose earlier remarks in Book 1 on divine and natural laws governing all of reality, as well as potential principles of justice and equity inherent in nature (1.1). As Book 1 closes, a jurist's distinction between political and civil spheres embodies a philosophical balance between universal laws, historical practice, and individual freedom. A political science of moderation relates natural laws of motion to psychological agency and the interactions between human wills. Montesquieu concludes that only multiple governing powers can maintain a dynamic equilibrium, preserving both individual tranquility and communal order. Indeed, the context for these remarks on the union of forces and wills is a taxonomy of three kinds of positive law that men establish to recover from the state of war that arises in society. All societies establish a "right of nations" to govern international relations and war, a "political right" to order relations of rulers and ruled in a given society, and a "civil right" to govern relations between citizens (1.3, 236/7). This is the second of two tripartite taxonomies of law that Montesquieu develops in Book 1, and both of them temper the rationalism of the modern elements in his analysis by redeploying categories from classical and medieval philosophy.

The concepts of spirit and moderation in *The Spirit of Laws* thus aim to comprehend motion as well as stability, mankind's evident political diversity as well as essential humanity, all as reflected in the natural and positive laws that reasonably govern humanity. This new human science seeks a "law" of politics to explain the diversity of political practices across time and place, moderating the ancient political science of virtue but also the early modern political science of rationalism, efficacy, and sovereignty. For Montesquieu, a quasi-Newtonian

---

[33] Schaub, *Erotic Liberalism*, 20; see also Lowenthal, "Book I," and Pangle, *Philosophy*, 20–47. Alternately, see Shklar, *Montesquieu*; Cohler, *Montesquieu's Comparative Politics*; and Goyard-Fabre, *La philosophie du droit* and *de Montesquieu*; and Rahe, *The Logic of Liberty*.

[34] See Waddicor, *Philosophy of Natural Law*, 16, 59–64, 96; Richard Tuck, *Natural Rights Theories* (Cambridge University Press, 1979), 72–81; and C. P. Courtney, "Montesquieu and Natural Law," in *Montesquieu's Science of Politics*, 41–67.

analysis of human things actually tempers the ambition for certainty in the new natural science, since a science of "man" in fact concerns an "intelligent world" that is "far from being as well governed as the physical world" (1.1). This condition is caused by man's limited nature, that he is "subject to ignorance and error" and "falls subject to a thousand passions," but this means his condition also is caused by his agency or freedom (1.1, 233–34/4–5). After citing Gravina on will and force, he declares that the political and civil laws (political and civil right) "should be so appropriate to the people for whom they are made that it is a very great accident if the laws of one nation can suit another" (1.3, 237/8). This is not mere relativism, however, since Montesquieu presupposes the first of the tripartite taxonomies of law announced in Book 1, which he develops when noting that, because humans have such a capacity for choice despite the laws of our nature – because we have the freedom to depart from those laws – we need instruction from philosophers on political and civil laws to achieve happiness by reminding us of our duties (1.1 [end]; see also the Preface). One aspect of human nature relates to the broadest generalities of a divine or ontological law governing nature, as briefly delineated in the opening passages of Book 1, and this approach leads him to compare the primordial principles of human justice and equity with *a priori* axioms about radii and circles (1.1, 233/4). This note of modern rationalism does not contradict, however, the pervasive argument of *The Spirit of Laws* that a philosophy of human affairs requires lenses beyond Cartesian or Hobbesian abstraction and certainty. Indeed, by the close of Book 1, his analysis shifts toward empirical, historical reality, taking account of man's intelligence, will, passions, and history, among other complexities of man and nature.

Montesquieu's philosophy of epistemological, moral, and political moderation thus breaks with classical philosophy but employs some of its elements to criticize his modern predecessors. As is already evident, an important topic for discerning his dialectical stance toward both ancients and moderns, and his enduring influence upon later political theory and practice, is the novel conception of natural law or natural right yielded by this philosophy of moderation. Much scholarship has examined this topic, but mostly with a focus on the brief passages in Book 1 and without attention to the broader principle of moderation that Montesquieu identifies as the architectonic aim of his analysis.

Nature, the Politics of Decent Tranquility, and Natural Law and Right

As noted, Montesquieu's capacious spirit finds him turning from the classical humanism of the Preface to launch an abstract discussion of "laws in general" in Book 1.[35] The opening lines of the opening chapter announce that "Laws, taken

---

[35] Rahe, "Montesquieu, Natural Law, and Natural Right" includes a comprehensive bibliography of excellent scholarship on this topic; see also more recently Rahe, "Montesquieu's Natural

in their most extended meaning, are the necessary relations deriving from the nature of things." More specifically, "invariable laws" govern all the five classes of beings in the world, from "the divinity" to brute matter and including "the intelligences superior to man," "the beasts," and man himself (1.1, 232/3). Even the "creator and preserver" cannot violate or alter these rules; this is a world of necessary laws, aimed at preservation. While much scholarly debate arises over whether Spinoza, Descartes, Malebranche, or another modern philosopher is the greater influence upon these extraordinary and cryptic statements, few scholars consider that we should take Montesquieu at his word – stated immediately prior in the Preface (and reinforced in the prefatory Notice or author's note) – that he admires earlier philosophers but his own genius seeks to incorporate, blend, and reconcile earlier philosophies. This may explain the rather striking citation Montesquieu actually makes as an authority for these opening statements on cosmic law, the *Moralia* of the Hellenic biographer and moralist Plutarch. Indeed, our failure to take seriously his philosophy of moderation explains why this reference to Plutarch mostly is ignored, or when discussed, is dismissed.[36]

The cited passage in Plutarch's essay "To an Uneducated Ruler" quotes the ancient Greek poet Pindar: "law is the king of all, mortal and immortal."[37] Difficulties abound with citing such an authority on the most general meaning of law, putting aside that neither Plutarch nor Pindar appear in medieval or modern philosophy as primary authorities on such matters. Pindar's poem suggests a divine and natural law dictating that might justifies right, and many Sophists, as well as Plato's Callicles in the *Gorgias* and his Athenian Stranger in the *Laws*, so interpret it.[38] The eclectic, moderate philosophy of Plutarch, however, instructs the young ruler that natural law stands above human power, counseling princes to be wise and just. Plutarch's philosophy, widely studied by the well-educated until our era, is eclectic without being vacuous, selecting

---

Rights Constitutionalism," *Social Policy and Philosophy* 29 (2012), 51–81, especially section II and the citations at note 17 therein.

[36] Pangle, who has studied more seriously than most scholars the natural theology underlying Montesquieu's philosophy of natural right, briefly mentions Plutarch in *Montesquieu's Philosophy of Liberalism*, at 25; he more extensively if still briefly discusses Plutarch, albeit in a dismissive tone, when developing his Hobbesian and Spinozist reading of Montesquieu in "The Philosophic Understandings of Human Nature Informing the Constitution," in *Confronting the Constitution*, ed. A. Bloom (AEI Press, 1990), 9–76, at 25 (see 25–35 generally); most recently, in Pangle, *The Theological Basis of Liberal Modernity in Montesquieu's Spirit of the Laws* (University of Chicago Press, 2010), he notes the Plutarch reference in a footnote, at 150, note 8, but emphasizes Montesquieu's Jansenist, hyper-Augustinian critics. I discuss these issues in Chapter 4, on religion. See also notes 37 and 38.

[37] Plutarch, "To an Uneducated Prince," *Moralia* 780c, ed. Fowler (Harvard University Press, 1936), X: 56–57. Pindar and Plutarch have "king," but Montesquieu uses "queen"; he perhaps prefers a moderating feminine spirit on this point; see *Spirit* 7.17 on female rulers.

[38] See Plato, *The Laws of Plato*, ed. Pangle (University of Chicago Press, 1988 [1980]), 690b (Book III, note 24, 522–23).

elements of the Greek and Hellenistic schools. His moral sobriety rejects materialism and hedonism, Pyrrhonic skepticism, and radical cosmopolitanism. Dryden described his philosophy as largely Platonic but also colored by the "Electic" or Eclectic school in Hellenism, "which selected from all the other sects what seemed most probable in their own opinions."[39] Moreover, tradition suggests the deep piety of both Pindar and Plutarch, in their writings and in their belief in the oracle of Apollo at Delphi, for whom Plutarch was a priest; Montesquieu also would be aware that neither held a mechanistic, rationalist conception of the cosmos that would preclude miraculous intervention by divinities. Such an ambiguous citation in the work's initial remarks on natural theology, natural law, and natural right warrants caution about finding a Spinozistic or Hobbesian doctrine here. On the other hand, there is too much sober philosophic reflection in his earlier works and throughout *The Spirit of Laws* to dismiss these opening statements as confusion or as ironical Pyrrhonism about fundamental philosophical questions. Rather, the content and manner of these lines suggest an intention to moderate the canonical views of natural law in ancient and medieval philosophy, and to temper the reductive tendency in modern philosophy, while signaling that his philosophy is not reducible to any one prior school or philosophy. Most fundamentally, in his subsequent "Defense" of *The Spirit of Laws* and his reply to criticisms of the Sorbonne theology faculty, Montesquieu insisted that these brief opening discussions were appropriate for a work of simple or mere (*pure*) politics and jurisprudence, not a work of natural or revealed theology. He also restates his self-definition as a lawyer and jurist (*jurisconsulte*); Book 25, Chapter 9 of *Spirit* had announced a distinction between political and theological analyses of such issues.[40]

Montesquieu's analysis of natural right in Book 1, and beyond, does draw upon the rationalism of Machiavelli, Hobbes, and Locke, each of whom explains reality and politics through a foundational principle – necessity, fear, or self-possession. His regard for such rationalism is limited and, moreover, wanes as *The Spirit of Laws* unfolds and deepens its emphasis on complexity, particularity, and political moderation.[41] Even in the early passages with the strongest

---

[39] In Plutarch, *Lives of the Noble Grecians and Romans*, ed. Clough, tr. Dryden, 2 vols. (Modern Library, 1992), 1: xxiv. A recent analysis of the complexity, and heft, of Plutarch's political and moral philosophy, including attention to its Aristotelian element, is Hugh Liebert, "Plutarch's Critique of Plato's Best Regime," *History of Political Thought* 30 (2009), 251–71.

[40] "Défense de *l'Esprit des Lois*" and "Réponses et explications données a la Faculté de Théologie," in *Œuvres complètes*, Pléiade edition, 2: 1121 (first Part, first section), 1130 (first Part, second section, response to third objection), 1146 (second Part, on toleration), 1148 (on celibacy), 1184 (to the Sorbonne faculty, response to thirteenth proposition). I discuss these issues in Chapter 4, on religion, particularly the controversy (still continuing today) as to whether these brief statements are compatible with Christian or biblical belief.

[41] Among the recent scholarship, Pangle's various writings and Zuckert, "Montesquieu's Critique of Hobbes" adopt the more critical or skeptical stance toward Montesquieu's analysis, effectively reducing his philosophy to the radical rationalism of Hobbes and Locke, while Rahe and Spector discern deliberate and plausible complexity in his philosophy.

imprint of earlier modern and liberal theorists, Montesquieu asserts his genius by referring his most abstract idea of law to a didactic essay by Plutarch, quoting a poet. Unlike Hobbes, Spinoza, and Locke, his philosophy is concerned not with abstract analysis but with educating statesmen through reflections on discrete problems and ideas for humane ruling and reform. Moreover, whatever the allure of Machiavellian efficacy or the certainty of modern sovereignty, all rulers are governed by a higher law. On the other hand, observation of nature and human nature cannot support the moralism or paternalism of classical and medieval natural law (to the extent – a separate issue – that Thomistic natural law is strictly paternalistic at all). In this way, Montesquieu provides the lineaments of a modern "common sense" philosophy, neither strongly teleological nor reductive, of the sort evident in the American Declaration of Independence. The American founders balanced Enlightenment doctrines with appeals to Providence, legal tradition, duty, and honor throughout that text, echoing a philosophical moderation that assimilates moderns and ancients, liberalism and classic common law.[42]

Montesquieu's moderation continues to govern throughout the first chapter of Book 1. His first general law, covering all beings other than the divinity, embodies a complex equilibrium: "Between one moving body and another moving body, it is in accord with relations of mass and velocity that all motions are received, increased, diminished, or lost; every diversity is *uniformity*, every change is *constancy*" (1.1, 232–33/4, emphasis in original). This law, with all its paradoxical import, informs the analysis of the "nature" and "principle" of the four types of government in the rest of Part 1 (Books 1–8). Amid the flux of politics, consequences necessarily follow from antecedent states: "One must see which are the laws that follow directly from this nature, and that consequently are the first fundamental laws" (2.1, 239/10). Causal mechanisms can illuminate the messiness of politics because Montesquieu finds that every uniformity includes diversity and every constancy, change. The basic principle of nature and human nature, of natural science and political science, is the necessary governance of being by laws, but these are complex laws, about motion and diversity. The interior and exterior freedom of each human exists within, and presupposes, a natural and social world in which bodies move according to uniform laws, albeit laws of dynamic interaction. This accommodation of motion and constancy, and of the diverse circumstances in which a rule applies, is Montesquieu's original, imaginative response to his predecessors in both natural and political philosophy.[43] While Montesquieu is no Thomist, his philosophy holds some analogy to Aquinas's effort to reconcile the regularity of natural law (applicable to all matter, all living creatures, and to man) with both the human capacity to depart from natural law and the human need to exercise

---

[42] James Stoner, *Common Law and Liberal Theory: Coke, Hobbes, and the Origins of American Constitutionalism* (University Press of Kansas, 1992), 179–96; and see Chapter 2.

[43] See Lowenthal, "Montesquieu," 516, 514.

prudence in discerning how the general, first principles of natural law apply, or should be respected, in diverse particular circumstances.[44]

The synthetic ambition of Montesquieu's political science finds a fundamental coherence between its citations to Ovid, Virgil, Corregio, and Plutarch (thus Pindar), and its seemingly rationalist analysis of universal laws. Poetry and natural science had met before in the Roman poet Lucretius, and more subtly in Virgil and Ovid, who toned down the materialism and Epicureanism of their predecessor. Montesquieu's first enunciation of a general law echoes the blending of materialist dynamics and human originality in Lucretius and in Ovid's poem on metamorphoses, while confirming a modern philosopher's debt to Newtonian physics. Phrases in Book 1 indeed reflect the sources that scholars often examine, whether Descartes or Hobbes, Spinoza or Malebranche or Clarke. Nonetheless, both in Book 1 and the Preface, Montesquieu embraces philosophical, phenomenological complexity rather than analytical simplicity, seeking to temper modern philosophical rigor with the humane understanding of the ancients and, more particularly, a central concern with prudence and education for founders and statesmen.[45] Like Epicurus and Hobbes, he thinks nature orients man toward individual freedom and security. However, his analysis of freely moving human bodies and wills borrows from Virgil and Montaigne to temper modern reductionism, observing that humans naturally and freely share affections, and desire peace and sociability (1.2). This synthesis supports his argument that individual security requires a political and social order free of the Hobbesian elements of a rigid basic contract, atomism, and fearsome sovereignty. Hobbes may be, as Michael Oakeshott argues, a systematic but not rationalist philosopher whose rules for order seek to open up a free private sphere, but this is not how Montesquieu read him. The one reference to Hobbes in *The Spirit of Laws* chastises the imposition of a fabricated (*composée*) idea onto natural, presocial man – the idea of empire or domination. Montesquieu terms such systematic thinking "unreasonable." This is a foretaste of criticisms of rationalist, abstract thinking made throughout *The Spirit of*

---

44 Zuckert notes a similarity between Montesquieu and Aquinas in placing natural law within a cosmic conception of law, but ultimately sees more disjunction; "Montesquieu's Critique of Hobbes," 230–31. In contrast one can note, for example, that Montesquieu would affirm Aquinas's arguments on parameters of natural law, recognizing that human law should not repress all vices because legal regulation of morals should address only basic order rather than Christian perfectionism (Thomas Aquinas, *Summa Theologiae*, 2nd edn. tr. Fathers of the English Dominican Province. Burns, Oates, and Washbourne, 1920, I–II, q. 96, a. 2); and, that judgment about proper action (in accord with natural law) requires consideration of diverse circumstances, including deliberation that only the prudent or wise can undertake (*Summa* I–II, q. 100, a. 1); Aquinas also extensively analyzes prudence in other parts of the *Summa*, for example, II–II q. 47–56. See James V. Schall, S.J., "A Latitude for Statesmanship? Strauss on St. Thomas," *Review of Politics* 53 (1991), 126–45; and Daniel Westberg, *Right Practical Reason: Aristotle, Action, and Prudence in Aquinas* (Clarendon Press, 1994), especially Chapter 16, "Law and Prudence."

45 Lowenthal, "Montesquieu and the Classics," 258–59.

Laws, whether of the utopian Harrington or of French historians of the monarchy (1.2, 235/6; 11.6, 407/166; 30.10, 891–92/627; see also 11.5, 396/156).[46]

Book 1 as a whole affirms a divine law and law of nature, but this ordered yet only weakly teleological universe yields only the moral or political guidance of general physical and psychological laws. Some moral order inheres in nature, as is indicated by the one authority cited in this brief cosmology and ontology – not the Bible or Aristotle, Newton or Spinoza, but Plutarch's *Moralia*. The mixed character of Montesquieu's political science, neither entirely subjective nor universalistic, is evident in his minimalist natural laws or prepolitical "relations of equity" that humans "have" prior to any positive laws they "have made." These indicate, for example, that "supposing that there were societies of men, it would be just to conform to their laws" or that "if there were intelligent beings that had received some benefit from another being, they ought to have gratitude" (*reconnoissance*) (1.1, 233/4).[47] These laws of equity accord with man's prepolitical nature as limned in the sequel, "On the Laws of Nature" (1.2). When read in light of the whole work, the analysis of human nature in Book 1 does not adopt earlier state of nature theories but responds to them, and transcends them. Montesquieu employs his phenomenological analysis to expose the excesses of this method of early liberalism, and recovers natural right from the extremes of Hobbesian and Lockean atomism. There is no need for the remedies these philosophers propose for their untenable situations – either sovereignty or revolution. Montesquieu finds neither the diagnoses nor the remedies accurate, or tenable. His complex argument in Book 1 begins a redefinition of natural right in the non-Hobbesian terms of our basic feelings and knowledge, such as sentiments toward family and friends, a revision confirmed by the very next reference to natural laws of human conduct after Book 1 – indeed, the first use of *droit naturel* in the work (3.10, 260/29–30).[48]

When Montesquieu's analysis of natural law and natural light is read in the broader way he recommends – to read "the entire work" and see moderation as the architectonic principle – then the closing lines of the first chapter in Book 1 need not be read as ironic, or a ruse, as scholars tend to do; indeed, most scholars simply ignore them. Having begun by grasping law in its "most extended

[46] See Michael Oakeshott, "Introduction to *Leviathan*," in *Rationalism in Politics and Other Essays*, Expanded edition (Liberty Fund, 1991 [1962]), 221–94, especially 230–32, 235–48, 264–67, 282–83.

[47] *Reconnoissance* means both acknowledgement and gratitude, suggesting that Montesquieu is an anticipation of Hegel's view that "recognition" is the basic human relationship. See *Philosophy of Right*, ed. Wood, tr. Nisbet (Cambridge University Press, 1991 [1821]), sections 57, 207. See also Mosher, "The Particulars of a Universal Politics: Hegel's Adaptation of Montesquieu's Typology," *American Political Science Review* 78 (1984), 178–88.

[48] Pangle overlooks this in *Philosophy*, 309–10, and in "The Philosophic Understandings of Human Nature," 15–18, 24–37; he briefly discusses it in *Theological Basis of Liberal Modernity*, 34, but can see only Montesquieu's antitheological subterfuge (as discussed in Chapter 4); Zuckert also omits this passage in "Montesquieu's Critique of Hobbes," 228 at note 5.

meaning," he prepares for a discussion of natural laws and positive laws in the subsequent two chapters, indeed prepares for the great emphasis on particular laws and prudence throughout the work, by delineating the first of the two tripartite taxonomies of law offered in Book 1. These laws are developed by God and man because man, as an intelligent yet embodied thus passionate being, can defy the fundamental laws of his nature, the basic natural laws:

> Such a being could, at any moment, forget his creator; God has reminded him by the laws of religion. Such a being could, at any moment, forget himself; philosophers have warned him by the laws of morality. Made for living in society, he could forget his fellows; legislators have returned him to his duties by political and civil laws. (1.1, 234/5)

A Humane Natural Right, Political Moderation, and Constitutionalism

Montesquieu sows many seeds for his redefinition of natural right in his chapter "On the Laws of Nature" (1.2), which discusses human nature or "the constitution of our being." The opening states that the natural laws guiding man in his primitive, presocial, or prepolitical condition antedate the positive laws of God, of moralists, or of legislators just noted (1.2, 235/6). It becomes clear that this is not the kind of state of nature or social contract theorizing used by either Hobbes or Locke. Montesquieu initially refers to the "law that impresses on us the idea of a creator and thereby leads us toward him." This is the first natural law "in importance" but not "in the order of these laws," and he then drops any treatment of divinity (1.2, 235/6). As Chapter 4 argues, his analysis of religion throughout the work, and especially the extensive discussion in Books 24 and 25, is more sympathetic than that of Machiavelli and other moderns. Still, it is significant that he omits here and in the first parts of the work any analysis of what he declares to be of prime importance. Montesquieu's political science treats only ambivalently a city of God that broadens the horizon of the city of man. He justifies this judgment, and deferral, by observing that "man in the state of nature" would think more of "the preservation of his being" than of his origin. This demotion does not contradict the closing reference in Chapter 1 to a providential divinity who calls man through religious or divine laws. As a modern and liberal philosopher, even a moderate one, he seeks the proper relationship between religion and politics. This complexity does not justify, however, the scholarly consensus to ignore or explain away the references to divinity and religion at the close of Chapter 1 and the opening of Chapter 2. Rather, we should consider that Montesquieu is tacking back, at least slightly, toward classical and medieval ideas of revealed and natural theology after the radical repudiation of these by earlier modern philosophy. Most scholars also ignore, or explain away, his simultaneous use of state of nature analysis and subversion of it given his conclusion that man is by nature a social being.

Montesquieu's brief sketch of human nature in Chapter 2 achieves coherence once he has recognized but postponed the religious dimension of human

nature and natural law. He focuses on four remaining natural laws that emphasize man's feelings and passions, and he readmits reason only in the last of
these laws, in a seemingly subordinate role. Natural man "at first" would "feel
only his weakness" and is marked by extreme "timidity" (1.2, 235/6). Given
that man is a passionate animal with some potential for rational, higher aims,
Montesquieu discerns that peace is "the first natural law" – first in historical
appearance – since each man "feels himself inferior" and would hardly attack
his fellows. He explicitly criticizes Hobbes for projecting such a "complex"
idea as desire for power and domination upon prepolitical man (1.2, 235/6).
The second law of nature is "nourishment," since "man would add the feeling
of his needs to the feeling of his weakness" (236). The "natural entreaty" that
men "always make to another," or man's natural sociability, is the third natural
law, although this has a complex root in fear, pleasure, and sexual charm. Man's
natural timidity and fear prompts recognition of "mutual fear," which would
"soon persuade them to approach one another." Alternately, "the pleasure one
animal feels at the approach … of its own kind" would foster sociability. This
third drive for community thus is the increase in such pleasure brought about by
"the charm that the two sexes inspire in each other by their difference" (236/6–
7). Each of these sources of the natural law of sociability – which Montesquieu
might also term, in Stoic fashion, "man's humanity toward man" – is a passion
or drive. Still, he closes by noting that beyond "sentiment" or feeling, "which
belongs to men from the outset," men eventually gain "knowledge." This is no
end in itself, but another "bond" that other animals lack, "another motive for
uniting," and thus "the desire to live in society" is the fourth natural law (236).
Man is naturally rational in that he develops this capacity through historical
experience. While a modern view, it is not Rousseau's historicist view of a basically malleable humanity, nor is it the antifoundationalist or sociological view
that Arendt, Manent, and others find.[49] Once again, his position lies between a
Thomistic view of rational and political man, a Hobbesian view of rational but
apolitical man, and a Rousseauan view of irrational and apolitical man developing toward reason and society. His complex view of human nature guides
his political science, in that reason is a dimension of our nature but passions or
sentiments – orienting us to peaceful sociability – define us more fundamentally.
This sketch in Book 1 accords with his three-part statement in the Preface that
he would be "the happiest of mortals" if his tome could educate citizens, rulers,
and indeed all of mankind to bring to politics greater reason, and less prejudice – the latter defined as "what makes one unaware of oneself," presumably
of our nature and the laws thereof (Preface, 230/xliv).

---

[49] See Hannah Arendt, *The Human Condition* (University of Chicago Press, 1958), 190–91, note
17, 202–3, and *The Life of the Mind, Volume Two: Willing* (Harcourt Brace Jovanovich, 1978),
198–202; Mark Hulliung, *Montesquieu and the Old Regime* (University of California Press,
1976), 108–72; Pierre Manent, "The Authority of History," in *The City of Man*, tr. Marc LePain
(Princeton University Press, 1998 [1994]), 11–49.

Montesquieu's portrait of the prepolitical laws of equity (1.1) and of "man in the state of nature" (1.2) conveys man as he was and is, not an abstracted, idealized projection onto man's historical reality. The political science based upon these principles steers a middle course between the strongly teleological natural right of Aristotle or natural law of Aquinas, and the minimalism of Machiavelli or Hobbes.[50] His analysis of a human nature oriented to security, sociability, and freedom holds a philosophical middle ground because both the new physics and his observations of man's nature indicate that we are neither as beleaguered nor as blessed as some have thought. The genius of politics – the spirit of laws – is to constitute laws that will best preserve our nature in all its complexity. The first use of "natural right" in the work, which occurs in Book 3, confirms this humane revision. Here natural right primarily involves neither self-preservation nor self-defense, nor even individual liberty, each of which tends to privilege the isolated, atomistic individual. Rather, it concerns "natural feelings," such as "respect for a father, tenderness for one's children and women, laws of honor, or the state of one's health." It is just such standards of "natural right" that a despot eschews, even if he might be checked by religious doctrines (3.10, 260/29–30). It is no accident that the title of this chapter connects moderation with his new idea of natural right, by signaling his intention to move beyond the typology of governments used in Books 2 and 3 – itself an echo of the Platonic and Aristotelian typology of regimes. It is in this title that Montesquieu indicates for the first time that the more important typology distinguishes "moderate governments" from "despotic governments" (3.10, title). Shortly thereafter, he also states, when discussing honor in monarchies, that men are "born to live together" and "born to please each other," and that "the soul" can achieve "virtues" of "magnanimity" and "greatness" (4.2, 263/32; 5.12, 292/58). To be sure, because he elsewhere equates monarchical honor with self-interest, he hardly makes himself a virtue theorist with these claims (see 3.7). Nevertheless, these humane dimensions to his natural right frustrate any reductionist readings of his philosophy. Further, once we consider a more moderate reading of Book 1, other such passages and themes in the work come to light.[51]

By avoiding extremes of rationalism and skepticism, Montesquieu's political science grasps the multiplicity, complexity, and diversity of phenomena affecting politics while insisting that natural right is a crucial standard for these. He ultimately deems a complex, moderate constitution the best government, both for peoples disposed to it by nature and history and for those who could gain

---

[50] Lowenthal, "Book I," 495; see also Pangle, *Philosophy*, 20–47; however, these analyses place Montesquieu much closer to Hobbes or Machiavelli than to classical and medieval philosophy.

[51] See Sharon Krause, "The Politics of Distinction and Disobedience: Honor and the Defense of Liberty in Montesquieu," *Polity* 31 (1999), 469–99, and *Liberalism With Honor* (Harvard University Press, 2002); see also Mosher, "Monarchy's Paradox."

it through gradual reforms (Book 11, Chapters 8, 11).[52] England's constitution is a possible model, but each time he examines it in *The Spirit of Laws*,
Montesquieu at once praises it and declares it extreme (11.6 end, 19.27 end).
He thus broadens – moderates, one might say – modern liberalism by insisting that its aims also are achieved by "Gothic" constitutions that are "well-
tempered" through their "true distribution," among a "free people," of legislative, executive, and judicial powers (11.8, 409/167–68; 11.11, 411/169–170).
Indeed, this Gothic regime is "the best kind of government men have been able
to contrive," although the English needn't be too chagrined, since their constitution is a cousin in the Gothic family; its initial form was found "in the
forests," as Tacitus first sketched its provenance among the ancient Germans
(11.8, 409/168; 11.6, 407/165–66). The philosophers, to include radical and
intransigent philosophers of Enlightenment reason, could observe and perhaps
modify such a government, but they did not first conceive of it based on their
new foundational theories. This is not to say that Montesquieu is a classical
or medieval philosopher oriented by the quest for the best regime. His aim
is philosophical moderation after the extremes of radical Enlightenment, not
a reactionary grasp for what he sees as the extremes of the full Aristotelian
approach.

The philosopher of moderation employs an historical and practical approach
to liberal ends and means, guided by background principles of natural right,
and this includes an examination of not only republic and monarchy but also
the enduring political phenomenon of despotism. The diverse circumstances
of human communities – from climate, economics, and history to mores and
religion – practically ensure despotism in some cases. Montesquieu distinguishes, however, the moderation of proper monarchies from the harshness of
despotism, so as to make constitutional monarchy more respectable for liberals, if not for strict republicans.[53] Montesquieu ultimately links these numerous
themes, and explicitly shifts to a new typology of moderate and immoderate
governments, in Book 5. After examining despotic severity and measures to
moderate it, he frames the essential problem of our political condition and proposes a remedy. As Book 1 indicates, we lie between divinity and brute matter,
between the liberty of intelligence and the necessity of material existence. This
middling condition is confirmed by the fact of despotism, for "despite men's
love of liberty, despite their hatred of violence, most peoples are subjected to
this type of government" (5.14, 297/63). This problem and its underlying causes

[52] This is the theme of the Montesquieu chapters in *The Cloaking of Power*, since his novel advo-
      cacy of an independent judiciary was his crucial means to achieve moderate government in
      various forms, which, in some degree, could secure individual liberty and political decency.
[53] Kenneth Minogue find Montesquieu endorsing complex monarchies as the best basis for lib-
      eralism in *Citizenship and Monarchy: A Hidden Fault Line in Our Civilisation*, The Institute
      of United States Studies (University of London, 1998), 10–22. Annelien de Dijn, "Was Mon-
      tesquieu a Liberal Republican?," *Review of Politics* 76 (2014), 21–41, astutely criticizes the
      view of Montesquieu as radically liberal but goes too far in seeing simply a liberal monarchist.

perpetually confront humane legislators like Montesquieu and the Stoic philosophers he praises, those who watch over mankind (see Preface, 24.10, 29.19). At once political philosopher, great political founder, and reformer, his solution is complexity itself:

> In order to form a moderate government, one must combine powers, regulate them, temper them, make them act; one must give one power a ballast, so to speak, to put it in a position to resist another; this is a masterwork of legislation, that chance rarely makes, and prudence rarely is allowed to produce. (5.14, 297/63)

Well before offering his constitutionalism in Books 11 and 12, Montesquieu provides the fundamental rationale for his separation of powers principle. Liberty can achieve security only if man's free motion is structured according to the dynamics of the laws of nature. Since our natural condition is not so low and desperate as Hobbes thinks, there is no *need* for the initial contract and the absolute Leviathan nor for the threat of revolution in Locke's contractarian politics. Since, however, our natural condition is not so favored as either the Bible or Aristotle indicate, there is no *warrant* for a strong moral orientation to politics and laws, a paternalism that restricts individual liberty. Man need to face neither the fearsome judgment of Leviathan, nor continual fear of revolution, nor the prospect of divine judgment or ethical censure. Nature indicates, rather, that politics be structured through multiple powers and perspectives that at once check and facilitate the free movement of political passions and energies. This humane tale of moderation and balance, which recommends devices ranging from an independent judiciary and commerce to toleration and the complexities of the medieval French constitution, constitutes the work's great theme. Moreover, as Chapter 2 argues, understanding the philosophy of moderation that informs Montesquieu's view of natural right and politics illuminates his influence on the American conception of pluralism and political balancing evident in *Federalist* Nos. 10 and 51. He is extensively discussed in the less famous essays (Nos. 9 and 47) that prepare for these more celebrated efforts by Publius. Montesquieu develops his notion of separation of powers on this basis of moderation and complexity in Parts 1 and 2 of *The Spirit of Laws* (up to Book 13), culminating in the constitutionalism of Book 11 and the protections of due process – secured by an independent judiciary protecting individual security and tranquility – endorsed in Books 6 and 12. This is the complex legacy he bequeathed to American constitutionalism, politics, and political theory, directly and through his disciple Blackstone – which in turn shaped Tocqueville, and the subsequent theory and practice of liberal constitutionalism.

2

Washington's Harmony

The Balance of Traditions in the American Founding

In 1783, as the Revolutionary War was won, a leading founder considered America's achievement and prospects. Scholars continue to debate the character of the new republic's principles and ideals, and which intellectual sources most influenced the founding. Although mostly overlooked today, this letter provides interesting evidence from an unusual source:

The foundation of our Empire was not laid in the gloomy age of Ignorance and Superstition but at an Epoch when the rights of mankind were better understood and more clearly defined than at any former period. The researches of the human mind, after social happiness, have been carried to a great extent. The Treasures of knowledge, acquired by the labors of Philosophers, Sages and Legislatures, through a long succession of years, are laid open for our use, and their collected wisdom may be happily applied in the Establishment of our forms of Government. The free cultivation of Letters, the unbounded extension of Commerce, the progressive refinement of Manners, the growing liberality of sentiment, and above all, the pure and benign light of Revelation, have had ameliorating influence on mankind and increased the blessings of Society. At this auspicious period, the United States came into existence as a Nation, and if their Citizens should not be completely free and happy, the fault will be entirely their own.

For all the Enlightenment confidence, this founder did not endorse inevitable progress. The letter proceeded to warn about the consequences of American choices and conduct:

Yet it appears to me there is an option still left to the United States of America, that it is in their choice and depends upon their conduct whether they will be respectable and prosperous, or contemptible and miserable as a Nation. This is the time of their political probation. This is the moment when the eyes of the whole World are turned upon them ... it is yet to be decided, whether the Revolution must ultimately be considered as a blessing or a curse – a blessing or a curse not to the present age alone, for with our fate will the destiny of unborn Millions be involved.

In deducing which American founder could pen such Enlightenment phrases, scholars today might consider Jefferson, or Adams, or Hamilton given the sharp edge (and preview of *Federalist* no. 1). We hardly would think of the ill-educated general who relied on leading minds but was no serious thinker himself. Perhaps, just as the British learned about his generalship, George Washington should not be underestimated in this arena, either. This in fact is the first farewell address of the man deemed, in his lifetime, the Father of his country. It is striking just for urging state leaders to fortify the Articles of Confederation government. This largely forgotten "Circular to the States" from the retiring Commander in Chief launched a constitutional reform movement that bore fruit in the 1787 Convention.[1] Moreover, the team of Hamilton and Madison who helped with his final farewell statement in 1796 did not draft this one.[2] The peroration of the Circular, a parting prayer for his nation, also tests the scholarly consensus that Washington was more of a deist than a Christian. His references to religion in his many addresses and letters are regular but broadly theistic. Here he adapts a favorite phrase from the Old Testament and makes a rare reference to Christ (discussed in Chapter 4). In sampling just these few passages from the 1783 circular, we see interrelated invocations of liberal rights, republican civic duty, and religious belief.

Two arguments from Aristotle's philosophy support analysis of a statesman to balance study of a polity's intellectual sources. First, Aristotle argues that two crucial virtues in politics, the moral virtue of magnanimity (greatness of soul) and the intellectual virtue of prudence (practical wisdom), are properly studied through a great-souled or prudent person as distinct from abstract analysis of such qualities. Indeed, on prudence, the *Nicomachean Ethics* states that it is better to analyze the person rather than abstract traits.[3] This insight extends through Plutarch and Shakespeare to the American founders, although analytical philosophy and social science now eschew it. In the *Politics* Aristotle employs this approach in comparative study of polities and their regimes, beside his typology of good and bad regimes. Moreover, for a possible best regime, the mixed regime, he argues that in actual instances (versus ideal types), one mark of a "nobly mixed" or balanced polity is that one cannot easily tell what type it is. It might seem a democracy with aristocratic elements mingled, or seem an aristocracy with a democratic admixture.[4] In debates about the sources

---

[1] "Circular to the States," June 8, 1783, in *George Washington: Writings*, ed. John Rhodehamel (Library of America/Literary Classics of the United States, 1997), 516–19; throughout this chapter I revise spelling in Washington's writings, but retain capitalization, emphases, and other features.

[2] For Washington's initiative on the Circular, see John Ray, "George Washington's Pre-Presidential Statesmanship," *Presidential Studies Quarterly* 27 (1997), 207–20, and Glenn Phelps, *George Washington and American Constitutionalism* (University Press of Kansas, 1993).

[3] *Nicomachean Ethics*, eds. and tr. Bartlett and Collins (University of Chicago Press, 2011), Book 4, Chapter 3 (1123a35ff, p. 75); Book 6, Chapter 5 (1140b24ff, p. 120).

[4] Aristotle, *Politics*, Book 4, Chapter 9 (1294a30ff, especially at 1294b13ff); see *The Politics of Aristotle*, ed. and tr. Simpson (University of North Carolina Press, 1997), 6.9 (in Simpson's

and character of America's founding principles, no one claims it is a mixed regime strictly, since it eschews monarchy and aristocracy as legitimate bases for rule. Nonetheless, we perpetually debate the character of the founding in part because its ideas are complex or diverse – leaving dissensus on whether one source or school is dominant in the mix.[5] The candidates range from modern liberalism and classical republicanism to Protestant Christianity, the Scottish Enlightenment, and Whig opposition thought.

Aristotle's insight about the limits of abstraction supports study of how the Founding Father blended intellectual traditions. Indeed, Washington's distinctive moderation, intellectual as well as ethical and political, embodied such a balance. His harmonious blending reflects an intelligent statesman's perception of the Montesquieuan spirit of intellectual and political moderation evident in the revolutionary era, a spirit dominant during the framing of the Constitution and Bill of Rights. For the postrevolutionary statesman, concerned that the first constitution was flawed, this was a question of "a young nation" with "a character to establish."[6] Montesquieu addressed this same concern by analyzing the "general spirit" of a nation (*The Spirit of Laws*, Book 19). This is an echo of Aristotle's idea that any polity is complex and cannot be a complete unity, but is "a many-voiced harmony" rather than unison, a "rhythm" rather than one beat.[7] Montesquieu's choice of *esprit* as the central concept of political science similarly embraces the complexity of human affairs, rather than seeking to reduce it. When he makes "the general spirit of a nation" a central concept, he affirms that any polity is a blend of ideas (religion, mores, laws, maxims of government), practices (history), and natural context (climate, geography). Being so does not make it a mere plethora or unstable hodgepodge.[8]

Montesquieu knew that a general spirit (or a reform to it) can be imparted to a nation by a founder or a guiding philosopher (*The Spirit of Laws*, Preface and 29.19). Regarding America, so deeply influenced by his philosophy, it is heartening that recent debates about its intellectual character include the view that its founding is neither reducible to any one school or tradition informing it (liberalism, republicanism, Christianity, Scottish common sense) nor merely a plethora of views, but instead is a unique amalgam or blend. Study of

---

reordering of the Books; 4.9 otherwise), 187–88. See the Prologue, at note 15, for contending views on whether polity is one of Aristotle's possible best regimes.

[5] A summary, mostly transparent about its leanings, is Alan Gibson, *Interpreting the Founding: Guide to the Enduring Debates over the Origins and Foundations of the American Republic* (University Press of Kansas, 2006). I return to this question in the closing section of this chapter.

[6] Letter to John Augustine Washington, June 15, 1783, in *Writings*, ed. Rhodehamel, 527; hereafter cited parenthetically in the text as W. See "Note on the Texts" (W 1076–81) about this one-volume selection and various multivolume collections. Another useful one-volume edition is *George Washington: A Collection*, ed. William B. Allen (Liberty Fund, 1988).

[7] Aristotle, *Politics*, Book 2, Chapter 5, 1263b27ff, p. 42. See also 2.2 (1261a22–31), 2.9 (1270b17–27), 3.4 (1276b35–1277a11), 3.11 (1281b21–30), and 7.14 (1332b16–31).

[8] Montesquieu, *De l'Esprit des Lois*, Book 19, Chapter 4, in *Œuvres complètes*, Pléiade edition, ed. Caillois, 2 vols. (Paris: Gallimard, 1949–51), 2: 558; in *The Spirit of the Laws*, eds. Cohler, Miller, and Stone (Cambridge University Press, 1989), 310.

Washington reinforces this view, since while there may be tensions or lumpiness in the American blend, the Founder's thought and example help it to achieve substantial harmony.

Washington's Statesmanship and Intellectual Moderation

George Washington (1732–99) is less appreciated by his countrymen today than during the first two centuries after America's founding era.[9] His declining status stems in part from our admiration in modernity for theoretical innovation and abstract concepts over practical judgment, despite the latter's obvious importance for political action. Few of the teachers of his countrymen today – professors, writers, and other opinion shapers – find him an exemplar of American political thought worthy of study. His best-known writing is his "Farewell Address" (1796), declaring to "Friends, and Fellow-Citizens" his retirement from public life. For the second time in a long career, he relinquished near-absolute power when equally ambitious yet less principled men usually have grasped for more. Such deeds, and his statements of principle about them, led his countrymen to rank him with an ancient Roman renowned for relinquishing absolute power once the threat to his country had passed: he was the American Cincinnatus. Washington used his final farewell not only to offer prayers to Heaven for continued blessings upon his country but also to "offer to your solemn contemplation, and to recommend to your frequent review" advice on union, constitution, republican government, partisanship, and foreign policy, all under the principle of America's national character ("Farewell Address," W, 962, 964). He sought a legacy in thoughts as well as deeds, so that "these counsels of an old and affectionate friend" would make a "strong and lasting impression" and yield "a wise People" (W 976, 970). This farewell, like his first one in 1783, is forged from ideals of classical republicanism, moderate liberalism, and Christianity – an American alloy that still was molten, in need of reinforcement.

We also tend to dismiss Washington's final testament because, as we all know, Madison and Hamilton really wrote it. Convinced that Washington cannot be genuine, we overlook his careful use of bright advisers, always maintaining his independent judgment. Confident, too, in our rational analyses of power and interest, we miss the central lesson of the Farewell Address about subordinating these drives to principles. Few anthologies of American political writings include even excerpts of the Farewell Address anymore.[10] We associate Washington with deeds, not thoughts; many now discount even his deeds given

---

[9] The middle of this chapter adapts parts of my "Liberty, Constitutionalism, and Moderation: The Political Thought of George Washington," in *History of American Political Thought*, eds. Frost and Sikkenga (Lexington Press, 2003); see also my essay "George Washington's Greatness and Aristotelian Virtue: Enduring Lessons for Constitutional Democracy," in *Magnanimity and Statesmanship*, ed. Holloway (Rowman & Littlefield Publishers, 2008).

[10] A welcome exception is *Leading and Leadership*, Ethics of Everyday Life series, ed. Timothy Fuller (University of Notre Dame Press, 2000), 135–36, 140–47.

their remoteness from the present – and because he owned slaves. Here, too we overlook his eventual repudiation of slavery and emancipation of his slaves; more generally, our democratic temperament doesn't appreciate this remote father-figure and martial hero, the embodiment of republican propriety.[11] Even the rare historian who now praises "the greatness" of Washington, lamenting that he "no longer seems to be first in the hearts of his countrymen," focuses upon his political character but not his ideas. It is good to hear an intellectual historian state that he "fully deserves the first place he used to hold" and "the accolades his contemporaries gave him" because "Washington was truly a great man and the greatest president we ever had."[12] Still, we further should note his intellectual effort in discerning how to forge his character and develop a constitutional order that would reflect a similar balance between ideals and practical constraints, and between rival traditions or schools.

We should rediscover the serious political thought in Washington's writings across three decades as the leading citizen of his republic, and the embodiment of moderate Enlightenment through his commitment to liberty, constitutional order, and moderation.[13] As the leader of the constitutional reform movement, he encouraged his more learned protégés such as Madison to devise a new constitution to replace the Articles. The outlines of his constitutionalism imbibed the Montesquieuan principles of institutional complexity and balance, to include space for judgment in specific offices to balance the democratic principle, and a federalism that permitted both national strength and local attention to liberty and civic character. He sought to blend classical republican ideals of civic virtue and character with liberal commitment to equal rights and government by consent, seasoned by Christian sensibility for the moral foundations and aspirations needed to temper any political ideals. Washington thus reflected but also crystallized the moderate, complex American mind shaped by the classic common law and Montesquieu – a mind that could amalgamate, even forge an alloy of, strains of Lockean liberalism and classical republicanism, Whig opposition thought and the Scottish Enlightenment, and Protestant Christianity. He concluded his First Inaugural Address in 1789 on this note of

---

[11] For Tocqueville's anticipation of the tendency in modern social science and humanities scholarship to eschew great figures and emphasize egalitarian, social, or structural forces, see *Democracy in America*, eds. and trs. Harvey Mansfield and Delba Winthrop (University of Chicago Press, 2000), "Social State of the Anglo-Americans" (vol. 1, pt. 1, Chapter 3), "On Some Tendencies Particular to Historians in Democratic Centuries" (vol. 2, pt. 1, Chapter 20), and "Why Democratic Peoples Show a More Ardent and More Lasting Love for Equality than for Freedom" (vol. 2, pt. 2, Chapter 1).

[12] Gordon Wood, "The Greatness of George Washington," in *Revolutionary Characters: What Made the Founders Different* (Penguin, 2006), 31.

[13] The boldest argument for Washington as a thinker whose blend of serious ideas and practical efficacy merits comparison with the more learned founders is Jeffry H. Morrison, *The Political Philosophy of George Washington* (Johns Hopkins University Press, 2009). Morrison's fine study emphasizes Washington's blending of traditions, although he does not discuss Montesquieu's moderate liberalism or the common law as elements of Washington's synthesis.

moderation and balance, urging America's new representatives to strive for "the enlarged views" and "temperate consultations" indispensable for "the success of the Government" (W, 734).

Washington saw these fundamental tenets of liberty, constitutionalism, and moderation as both reflecting and reinforcing his more specific principles, including subordination of military to civil authority; a complex, federal Union; the need in republics for statesmanship, especially executive power; and realistic but just foreign policies. Less obvious today is his emphasis upon religious faith in republics, and upon civility and honor. Beyond his unrivaled deeds, his importance for shaping American political thought was as great as that of more recognized thinkers of his era. This is not to deny his own concerns – as a surveyor, soldier, and farmer – that he was less educated than such advisers as George Mason, Jefferson, Madison, Hamilton, Adams, and Jay. Nonetheless, he sought to refine his thoughts, not replace them, by consulting these minds; in the process, he often refined or moderated theirs. His earliest writings, from letters and journals to his boyhood copying of "Rules of Civility and Decent Behavior in Company and in Conversation," do not reveal theoretical genius. However, copying those 110 rules of propriety, penned by French Jesuits in the sixteenth century to educate for private and political life, instilled both ethical principles and a trait of clarifying the ultimate principles to guide one in life (W, 3–10). His library at Mount Vernon held over 900 books by his death, extending beyond military and agricultural topics. During the peak of his stature he advocated a national university and national military academy; when thwarted by Congress he privately endowed schools and educational funds, and Washington and Lee University is one beneficiary of such support. The intellectual confidence he developed allowed him to consult a range of learned advisers and to rely upon one or another as he judged best. Careful study of the Farewell Address shows that he revised every argument or draft that he requested, and made it his own.[14] A perceptive analysis concludes that Washington was "a leader who sought explanations and explainers all his life, and who mastered both what he was told and those who told him."[15]

---

[14] See Matthew Spalding and Patrick Garrity, *A Sacred Union of Citizens: George Washington's Farewell Address and the American Character* (Rowman & Littlefield, 1996).

[15] Richard Brookhiser, *Founding Father: Rediscovering George Washington* (Free Press, 1996), 139; see "Morals" and "Ideas," 121–56. Throughout, I rely upon the works by Phelps, Brookhiser, Spalding and Garrity, and Morrison, and the indispensable John Marshall, *The Life of George Washington: Special Edition for Schools*, eds. Faulkner and Carrese (Liberty Fund, 2000 [1838]). I also rely upon three essays by Robert Faulkner: "Foreword," in Marshall's *Life*; "Washington and the Founding of Constitutional Democracy," in *Gladly to Learn and Gladly to Teach: Essays on Religion and Political Philosophy in Honor of Ernest L. Fortin, A. A.*, eds. Foley and Kries (Lexington Books, 2002); and "Obscuring the Truly Great: Washington and Modern Theories of Fame," in *The Case for Greatness: Honorable Ambition and Its Critics* (Yale University Press, 2007).

The scope and balance of Washington's thinking reveal a mind that blended Federalist, Anti-Federalist, and even Democratic-Republican ideas. In effect, he was a moderate Federalist, but he deplored the ferocious partisanship that undermined sobriety and civility at the close of the founding era. Hamilton was a main influence; but Washington not only consulted other counselors, he usually emphasized moderation and compromise – principles not easily attributed to his brilliant but immoderate protégé.[16] On the other hand, while Jefferson echoed Washington's spirit in stating, after his election in 1800, "[w]e are all Republicans, we are all Federalists," neither his zealous democratic theory nor his partisanship really adhered to Washington's standard.[17] There are good reasons that Washington alone was deemed the Father of his country during his lifetime. A just assessment concludes that "General and President Washington, all hagiography aside, was the linchpin that...held together a fragile Revolution and afterward a federal Union torn by domestic and foreign controversies in the 1790s."[18] Upon his death, the resolutions in the House of Representatives declaring him "first in war, first in peace, first in the hearts of his countrymen" were presented by a Federalist, John Marshall, but drafted by a Democratic-Republican and a Federalist, Henry "Light-Horse Harry" Lee and James Madison.[19]

As the forger of a distinctly American conception of intellectual moderation in service of political moderation, Washington was an intellectual linchpin as well. The lessons he bequeathed in his final farewell cap a career of pairing actions with reflection and justification; two decades earlier, in his "General Orders" of July 9, 1776, he ordered the Declaration of Independence be read to the troops so that they might understand "the grounds & reasons" of the war (W, 228). Nonetheless, some find a Machiavellian cunning in the Farewell Address and his entire career – that Washington saw the need, in a democratic republic, to resign power or pretend to eschew it so as to gain greater power or glory. However satisfying this view is to some, in reality, each principle in the Address affirms earlier deeds and statements. Such consistent dedication to liberty, constitutionalism, and moderation bespeaks a practical wisdom serving higher principles in particular circumstances. Indeed, study of Washington

[16] On the complexity of influences and advisers surrounding Washington, see Stuart Leibiger, *Founding Friendship: George Washington, James Madison, and the Creation of the American Republic* (University Press of Virginia, 1999). In retirement, Washington criticized Democratic-Republican partisanship, but also chastised Federalists for emphasizing personalities and partisanship over principles; see letters to Patrick Henry, January 15, 1799, and to Jonathan Trumbull, Jr., August 30, 1799 (W 1016–18, 1048–50).

[17] "First Inaugural Address," March 4, 1801, in *Thomas Jefferson: Writings*, ed. Merrill D. Peterson (Library of America/Literary Classics of the United States, 1984), 493.

[18] Don Higginbotham, "Introduction," in *George Washington Reconsidered*, ed. Don Higginbotham (University Press of Virginia, 2001), 6; in the same volume, see also W. W. Abbot, "An Uncommon Awareness of Self: The Papers of George Washington."

[19] Marshall, *Life of Washington: Special Edition*, 463. Subsequent references to this one-volume edition of his larger work, finished by Marshall just before death, are cited in the text as *LGW*.

challenges the Machiavellianism pervading much political analysis now, for his principled moderation made him an extraordinarily effective statesman. Such study thus is indispensable today for translating constitutional principles into sound policies, both domestic and foreign.

The "Liberty and Justice for Which We Contend": Building a Moderate Character

Washington served in Virginia's legislature from 1758, and after the tumultuous British-American politics of the 1760s, he chose to defend liberty and natural rights. The sobriety, and philosophical touchstones, of his thinking are evident in several early letters. Since "our lordly Masters in Great Britain will be satisfied with nothing less than the deprivation of American freedom," he wrote in 1765, "it seems highly necessary that something should be done to avert the stroke and maintain that liberty which we have derived from our Ancestors." Indeed, "no man should scruple, or hesitate a moment to use a–ms in defense of so valuable a blessing, on which all the good and evil of life depends." Still, he tempered his zeal for liberty; if petitions about American "rights & privileges" failed, then a trade embargo should be tried before resorting to arms (W, 130). Washington has been called a constitutional or conservative revolutionary for such moderation; he grounded the American cause both in abstract rights and in the tradition of Anglo-American common law. As early as 1765, he argued that laws enacted without the consent of the colonists' elected representatives were an "unconstitutional method of Taxation" and "a direful attack upon their Liberties" (W, 116).

By 1774, Washington put his prestige behind the cause of liberty; as the former commander of all Virginian colonial forces in the French and Indian War, he was known throughout the colonies. He voted for a congress of all the colonies; he presided over the drafting of the Fairfax County resolutions advocating the right to colonial self-government and a trade boycott against Britain; and he was a delegate to the First Continental Congress. He justified these actions by reflecting, in a 1774 letter, that "an Innate Spirit of freedom first told me" that the acts of the British administration "are repugnant to every principle of natural justice." Indeed, he linked natural right, the English constitution, and individual rights in a seeming echo of Montesquieu: the government's actions are "not only repugnant to natural Right, but Subversive of the Laws & Constitution of Great Britain itself"; the King's ministers were "trampling upon the Valuable Rights of Americans, confirmed to them by Charter, & the Constitution they themselves boast of" (W, 157). When the Second Continental Congress appointed him General and Commander in Chief of the Continental Army, his address balanced humility and pride: he was grateful for the "high Honor" being done him yet fearful for his "reputation," since his abilities and experience "may not be equal to the extensive & important Trust." He refused any pay, asking only reimbursement for official expenses (W, 167). He earlier had linked sacrifice and virtue in justifying America's actions: "the once happy and peaceful plains of America are either to be drenched with Blood, or Inhabited by Slaves. Sad alternative! But can a virtuous Man hesitate in his choice?" (W 164).

General Washington's principles of civil–military relations, foreign policy, and grand strategy deserve separate study in Chapter 5, but it is noteworthy here that his principle of military subordination to laws and civil authority reflects his broader moderation. Real liberty is ordered liberty, securing self-government and political decency under law; this requires military power, but as a carefully controlled means to a higher end. John Marshall, the great Chief Justice of the United States who served as a young officer under Washington's direct command, concluded that without the general's distinctive character, the American cause likely would have failed. Marshall marveled at the moral toughness of a commander who sustained his out-manned, under-supplied, ill-equipped army, and in a dark hour, the winter of 1776–77, conceived counterattacks at Trenton and Princeton: "Among the many valuable traits in the character of Washington, was that unyielding firmness which supported him under these accumulated circumstances of depression...To this unconquerable firmness – to this perfect self-possession under the most desperate of circumstances, is America, in a great degree, indebted for her independence" (*LGW*, 75). America and the cause of liberty in the world also are fortunate that Washington was not tempted by absolute power when prospects brightened. After the victory at Yorktown a colonel suggested in late 1781 that he should be king, and Washington – in contrast to a Caesar, Cromwell, Napoleon, or Benedict Arnold – denounced such ideas in his army as violating "constitutional" authority (W, 468–69). A more serious threat loomed in 1783, when some officers at headquarters in Newburgh, New York, thought he might support a threat of mutiny against Congress to demand the army be paid. He denounced any such idea, arguing that "the calm light of reason" and "moderation" must control "feelings and passions." To sow "the seeds of discord and separation between the Civil and Military powers" would undermine "that liberty, and...that justice for which we contend" (W, 495–500). His extraordinary speech concluded by appealing to both reason and emotion: "let me conjure you, in the name of our common Country, as you value your own sacred honor, as you respect the rights of humanity, and as you regard the Military and National character of America," to reject this plot to "overturn the liberties of our Country" through civil war. This would prove them models of "unexampled patriotism and patient virtue" and "afford occasion for Posterity to say...'had this day been wanting, the World had never seen the last stage of perfection to which human nature is capable of attaining'" (W, 498–500). This is the American alloy, forged in crisis, which now provokes wonder as to whether the republic could have survived if not for this blending of republican virtue with invocations of reason, moderation, and liberal rights – rather than, as an ancient republican general might have done, demanding that the rebellious be shamed, then killed.

Principled to the end, Washington disbanded the army once the peace treaty was official, and he resigned his commission before Congress in December of 1783. He professed "honor" at being present to "surrender into their hands the trust committed to me" and asked "the indulgence of retiring from the Service of my Country." With repeated recognition of "the interposition of Providence," which had secured America's independence, and gratitude for the support of his countrymen and trusted aides, he bade farewell: "Having now finished the work assigned me, I retire from the great theatre of Action; and bidding an Affectionate farewell to this August body under whose orders I have so long acted, I here offer my Commission, and take my leave of all the employments of public life" (W, 547–48). Jefferson soon wrote to him: "the moderation & virtue of a single character has probably prevented this revolution from being closed as most others have been, by a subversion of that liberty it was intended to establish."[20] By repeated displays of his own moderate character, Washington helped to forge that of a new republic, by establishing its standards for justice and statesmanship.

"Citizens of America:" Advocating Constitutionalism, Union, Republicanism

Washington declared ideas about Union, constitutionalism, and statesmanship years before Madison, Hamilton, or others elaborated them, as necessary for securing liberty and republicanism. Indeed, such minds could expound ideas of constitutional reform in part because Washington had paved the way; Hamilton is not the only leading mind of the era who could have said that the Founder had been an "Aegis," a shield, "very essential" to him.[21] He was a leader in the constitutional reform movement from 1783 to 1789, both in his own voice and by encouraging others. Many who became Federalists looked up to him as a defender of liberty and the Revolution who also had urged in his 1783 Circular reforms to rescue liberty from anarchy. He then risked his reputation on a plan for constitutional reform, ending his retirement to back it. Indeed, his blend in the Circular of ultimate principles with advocacy of specific policies informs the two major statements of his later career, his First Inaugural and Farewell Address.

Already by 1783 Washington quietly had supported efforts by Hamilton, Madison, and others in the Confederation Congress to augment national powers on taxation, finances, and trade. The absence of such powers, due to excessive fear of governmental authority, had nearly lost a war for liberty; he feared America might squander the peace in economic and political chaos. He used his

---

[20] Jefferson to Washington, April 16, 1784, in Jefferson, *Writings*, 791. Compare Marshall's extraordinary tribute in *LGW*, 301.

[21] Hamilton to Tobias Lear, January 2, 1800, in *Selected Writings and Speeches of Alexander Hamilton*, ed. Morton J. Frisch (AEI Press, 1985), 456.

final Circular address to governors and legislatures not only to congratulate the states on the success of the war, and to announce his retirement from public life, but also to urge support for Congressional measures to strengthen the Union. He proposed in outline the constitutionalist principles America must develop to secure and perpetuate liberty. While the Circular closes with a Biblical and even Christian prayer, it opens with a more general invocation of gratitude to Providence – considering the great "prize" at issue in the war, ultimate success despite long odds, and the "natural," "political," and "moral" blessings Americans now enjoy (W, 516–17). The "Citizens of America" should note the providential fact that "our Republic" came to freedom in an era of history providing "a fairer opportunity for political happiness" than any other. Washington's pen produces, as noted, a striking invocation of the progress achieved through rational enlightenment about rights by "Philosophers" as well as legislators, now available to guide America's institution-building. Advances in and the spread of learning, global commerce, refinement of manners, tolerance, "and above all, the pure and benign light of Revelation" have meliorated human affairs "and increased the blessings of Society" (W, 517). Some of these phrases may seem to echo the radical Enlightenment spirit of a Locke or Voltaire, but the emphases on duty, decency, and Providence, as well as on commerce, suggest the moderate Enlightenment and especially Montesquieu. Moreover, there is a higher priority for virtue here in an appeal that also blends in interest; the classical and medieval element supports his warning that without prudent judgment and virtuous effort Americans will squander their blessings – and "the fault will be entirely their own" (W 517).

The postwar crisis in domestic and foreign affairs was a trial that would show America as either "respectable and prosperous, or contemptuous and miserable." The only sure path was to establish a "national Character." After further vigorous advocacy about the proper view of liberty and its ultimate ends, Washington proposes the means for establishing a "wise and liberal government." Four "Pillars" are necessary to support "the glorious Fabric of our Independency and National Character." While affirming that "Liberty is the Basis" of any legitimate American government, nonetheless "the well-being" and even "the existence of the United States" were at risk – and so reforms are needed to strengthen the federal union:

1st. An indissoluble Union of the States under one Federal Head; 2dly. A Sacred regard to Public Justice. 3dly. The adoption of a proper Peace Establishment; and 4thly. The prevalence of that pacific and friendly Disposition, among the People of the United States, which will induce them to forget their local prejudices and policies, to make those mutual concessions which are requisite to the general prosperity, and in some instances, to sacrifice their individual advantages to the interest of the Community. (W 518–19)

Certainly the first, third, and fourth pillars reflect the Montesquieuan political science of moderation, by invoking a federalism of political balance, an adequate "peace establishment" that avoided either militarism or disarmament, and, a political character of magnanimity and comity rather than maximalism pursuing narrow views. Washington states that he will leave the last point, national comity, to "the good sense and serious consideration of those immediately concerned," but in fact his arguments for the first three pillars promote American fraternity and national spirit as the proper fruit of the Revolution. As noted in the Prologue, the moderate Enlightenment that was carried to America via Montesquieu, and also by Protestant Christian voices, itself carries echoes of an Aristotelian and Christian view that friendship, both utilitarian and charitable, is as vital to humane politics as the right institutions.[22] As to the first pillar, it was his "duty" and that of "every true Patriot" to observe that, beyond the "great question" of whether the states should "delegate a larger portion of Power to Congress or not," Congress must be allowed to exercise powers it is "undoubtedly invested with by the Constitution." Here Washington shifts American thinking away from "articles" of a super-treaty among mere confederates to a "Constitution" uniting a nation through federalism. He subtly undermines state-centered confederalism in order to bolster America's fundamental law and federal structure. Without a constitutionalism informed by "entire conformity to the Spirit of the Union," America would descend to "a state of Nature," left with "the ruins of Liberty abused to licentiousness" (W 518–20).

Washington's description of financial obligations (the second pillar) as "Public Justice" might suggest fixation with property or prosperity; in fact, his complex thought echoes Montesquieu's tempering of Lockean individualism and materialism. He indeed prized his success as a farmer and landowner, and also America's prosperity. Still, he tempered these interests with devotion to honorable and just conduct, charitable and Christian aims, and political fraternity. His broader motives for promoting internal navigation and commerce – and for emancipating his slaves at the end of his life – exemplify this complexity. He invokes the "honor," "honesty," "justice," and "feelings of humanity" that require repayment of not only creditors but of "the bravery, and the blood" of soldiers (W 520–24). This moral moderation also informs his third pillar, "placing the Militia of the Union upon a regular and respectable footing." Experience, coupled with awareness of a common good, counsel that we must sacrifice both money and local autonomy; state militias at least must be "absolutely uniform" in organization, equipment, and training (W 524). The "Circular" then closes by invoking awareness of "the immutable rules of Justice" and his civic duty to leave a "Legacy" that will be "useful to his Country." This is the template for his First Inaugural and the Farewell Address, balancing liberal principle with republican civic virtue, liberty with fraternity, human agency with belief in the transcendent. As Washington bids "adieu" to

---

[22] See Aristotle, *Nicomachean Ethics*, 8.1, 8.9–11 (1155a22–28, 1159b25–1161b10); Thomas Aquinas, *Summa Theologiae*, 2nd edn. tr. Fathers of the English Dominican Province (Burns, Oates, and Washbourne, 1920), I–II, q. 105 a. 5; II–II, q. 23, aa. 7, 8; q. 25, aa. 8, 9; q. 26, a. 8.

"public life," he suggests that the statesman's final duty is to elevate the gaze of his fellow citizens, through his striking final prayer (W, 524–26).

Washington's deeds and thoughts during the last phases of his career, as Constitution-maker and Constitution-enactor, flow from the character as statesman he established by 1783, and the aspiration for a unified nation he had publicly declared. From retirement, he supported the 1785 Alexandria Conference between Virginia and Maryland on trade and tax policies; indeed, the conference began in Alexandria but concluded at Washington's Mount Vernon. When the five states who attended the 1786 Annapolis Convention then proposed to Congress and the states a national convention for 1787, to discuss the defects of the Articles, Madison nominated Washington as a Virginia delegate. After he reluctantly accepted, he expended his unrivaled national prestige for the Convention's success. Recognizing Madison's ability to conceptualize reforms he had long promoted, Washington took the initiative to endorse bold measures to the man whose efforts would earn him the title Father of the Constitution: "a thorough reform of the present system is indispensable"; the government "wants energy and that secrecy and dispatch...which is characteristic of good Government." The precise form of a new federalism "indeed will require thought," but he gave Madison his Aegis: "my wish is, that the Convention may adopt no temporizing expedient, but probe the defects of the Constitution to the bottom, and provide radical cures; whether they are agreed to or not. A conduct like this will stamp wisdom and dignity on the proceedings and be looked to as a luminary, which sooner or later will shed its influence" (W, 647–48). In fact, Madison had been studying republican forms and had proposed the outlines of a new constitution to Jefferson. Still, a comparison of Washington and Madison as constitutionalists and chief executives would find Madison the more learned yet also more timid. Washington's early endorsement of Madison's nascent plans likely emboldened him to further develop a specific strategy for achieving reform in Philadelphia.

Washington sustained this drive for a newly ordered liberty in the crucial years ahead. His public statements at the Convention do not remotely reveal his full role in founding the new order.[23] His prudent use of overt and subtle support for a constitutional revolution was indispensable. Tocqueville's analysis of the Convention praises the delegates as including "the finest minds and noblest characters that had ever appeared in the New World," and lists "Washington, Madison, Hamilton, the two Morrises." Still, he emphasizes one above all: "George Washington presided over it."[24] The political context reveals the importance of this largely hidden hand guiding the Constitution to life. By 1786, discontent with America's affairs was rising, and the armed conflict in

---

[23] Brookhiser's chapter "Constitution" in *Founding Father* superbly remedies the oversight of most scholars about this dimension of Washington's political thought and statesmanship.

[24] Tocqueville, "History of the Federal Constitution," in *Democracy in America*, ed. and tr. Harvey Mansfield and Delba Winthrop (University of Chicago Press, 2000), vol. 1, pt. 1, Chapter 8, 107.

Massachusetts called Shays's Rebellion had sparked momentum for reform. Congress was helpless in restoring order or redressing the financial and commercial policies, or lack thereof, that fed such crises. Those later termed Anti-Federalists, for opposition to the 1787 Constitution, largely conceded these points in the ratification debate of 1787–88. Still, even after these events, Washington faced the view that the Philadelphia Convention was illegal without approval by Congress. Even when that was gained, Rhode Island's refusal to participate meant that the amendment clause of the Articles, requiring approval of all the states, would not sanction the Convention's work. Washington's imprimatur therefore was crucial, and he let it be known that he would attend nonetheless. He arrived weeks before a quorum formed and worked with his delegation to refine the opening salvo, the Virginia Plan. Only one other delegate could legitimize the Convention so much; yet it was Franklin himself who spoke of the propriety and necessity of electing Washington to preside. Both in symbolic and practical ways, he then kept the Convention and reform on track by attending every session for four months and voting on all motions; by enforcing the secrecy rule that permitted – as Madison's notes reveal – extraordinarily candid deliberations; and, finally, by signing the Constitution and serving as sole signatory of the letter transmitting it to Congress.

Washington also must be credited for restraint at the Convention. His moderate, restrained role bolstered the credibility and viability of its product. He occasionally voted against Madison's political science of efficient national sovereignty in the Virginia Plan, to accommodate concerns of opponents. He could have used his prestige to enact pet ideas, especially regarding the single executive for which he was the delegates' obvious model. Instead, his silence indicates care not to abuse his authority. When he rose on the last day for a rare intervention, Madison notes that he voiced this concern: "his situation" as presiding officer "had hitherto restrained him from offering his sentiments on questions depending in the House, and it might be thought, ought now to impose silence on him." Yet in a spirit of compromise he backed a motion to enlarge the House of Representatives: "it was much to be desired that the objections to the plan recommended might be made as few as possible," and this motion was "of so much consequence that it would give him much satisfaction to see it adopted." This idea had been defeated repeatedly in the final weeks. Now it was approved unanimously, without debate.[25] A less moderate man might have used such influence quite differently.

In the ratification debates as well Washington told associates to use his name, yet, knowing that he might be the first President, he did not openly campaign. He did arrange publication in Virginia of *The Federalist*, the New York essays of his associates Hamilton, Madison, and Jay. He subsequently wrote to Hamilton that, having read many Federalist and Anti-Federalist efforts, none was

[25] James Madison, *Notes of Debates in the Federal Convention of 1787*, ed. Adrienne Koch (W. W. Norton, 1987), 655.

better designed to "produce conviction." Indeed, his verdict on *The Federalist* is remarkably perceptive: "When the transient circumstances & fugitive performances which attended this *crisis* shall have disappeared, that work will merit the notice of Posterity; because in it are candidly and ably discussed the principles of freedom & the topics of government, which will always be interesting to mankind so long as they shall be connected in Civil Society" (*W*, 691–92). Both sides thought his public support tipped the scales toward the Constitution's narrow victory; for Marshall, "had the influence of character been removed, the intrinsic merits of the instrument would not have secured its adoption" (*LGW*, 325). James Monroe wrote to Jefferson that "his influence carried this government."[26]

Enacting the "Great Constitutional Charter:" Moderation at the Helm

Although pledged to perfecting the Union through constitutional reform, Washington reluctantly assumed the office of President. His First Inaugural Address, to "Fellow Citizens" of the Senate and House, opens by noting his "anxieties." Having been "summoned by my Country," he surrendered what had been an "immutable decision" to retire (*W*, 730).[27] Given his still greater reluctance at accepting a second term in 1792, his decisions to serve stem not only from civic duty but also from two principles he had long advocated: the executive statesmanship needed in republics, and deference to popular consent. He knew from the war, however, that effective statesmanship and popular opinion did not always harmonize. During his presidency he would hazard his happiness and reputation in balancing them as he judged best for American constitutionalism. He was a strong but moderate and faithfully constitutional executive, justifying decisions with stated principles. He sought to quell the partisanship gripping his countrymen by calling them to the enduring interests and higher ends that united them. His letters before his inauguration accurately predict how difficult the unprecedented task of chief executive would be, and how contentious the politics might become.

His First Inaugural refrained from long constitutional and policy discourses, which he initially had drafted, to emphasize principles of American republicanism. Liberal rights and mutual self-interest appear, but amid chiefly republican and Christian themes. The address begins with Providence, as in all his major texts. Having peacefully, seemingly miraculously achieved a new government, he quoted "the Great Constitutional Charter" for terms of his relations with Congress, and he urged Congress, too, to consult the Constitution for its

---

[26] Monroe to Jefferson, July 12, 1788, in *The Papers of Thomas Jefferson*, ed. Julian Boyd et al. (Princeton University Press, 1950–), 13: 352.

[27] This is not the "discarded First Inaugural," a longer address he prepared with his secretary David Humphreys but decided not to use. On this interesting text and surviving fragments, see *Washington: A Collection*, 440–42, 445–59, and W 702–16, 1116–17.

powers and agenda. He praised the "talents, the rectitude, and the patriotism which adorn the characters" of those elected, since such "honorable qualifications" should ensure that "no local prejudices" or "party animosities, will misdirect the comprehensive and equal eye which ought to watch over this great Assemblage of communities and interests." Thus, "the foundations of our national policy, will be laid in the pure and immutable principles of private morality," and such "pre-eminence" would win for free government "the respect of the world" (W, 731–32). This becomes the keynote of the address:

I dwell on this prospect with every satisfaction which an ardent love for my country can inspire: since there is no truth more thoroughly established than that there exists in the economy and course of nature an indissoluble union between virtue and happiness; between duty and advantage; between the genuine maxims of an honest and magnanimous policy and the solid rewards of public prosperity and felicity; since we ought to be no less persuaded that the propitious smiles of Heaven can never be expected on a nation that disregards the eternal rules of order and right which Heaven itself has ordained: and since the preservation of the sacred fire of liberty and the destiny of the republican model of government are justly considered, perhaps, as *deeply*, perhaps as *finally*, staked on the experiment entrusted to the hands of the American people. (W, 732–33)

Washington then endorsed the moderate, Madisonian strategy for constitutional amendments, addressing only "the characteristic rights of freemen." He reiterated his policy from the war of requesting only reimbursement for expenses in lieu of any salary. He closed with echoes of his 1783 Circular, by invoking religion while reiterating the humility, civility, and moderation befitting an American politics:

[I resort] once more to the benign Parent of the human race in humble supplication that, since he has been pleased to favor the American People with opportunities for deliberating in perfect tranquility, and dispositions for deciding with unparalleled unanimity on a form of government for the security of their union, and the advancement of their happiness, so his divine blessing may be equally *conspicuous* in the enlarged views, the temperate consultations, and the wise measures on which the success of this Government must depend. (W, 733–34)

Washington abided by this principled moderation during the tumultuous years ahead, despite any temptations to abandon it in self-defense amid ferocious partisanship and popular outrage. His deeds went far toward showing that liberty and constitutionalism require a balanced, complex mode of prudential judgment that avoids the theoretical and practical extremes to which human politics can tend. Marshall was not alone in judging that the American experiment might not have survived if not for his moderation.

Looking back upon Washington's two presidential terms from the vantage of his Farewell Address allows us to see that his parting advice to his country affirms the principles that guided him in office. The Address is indispensable reading for studies of American politics and history, and of republicanism and statesmanship more broadly. The issue of how much the ideas are Washington's,

or Madison's, or Hamilton's, evaporates upon examining his control throughout the drafting process and the clear lineage of ideas and phrases from his earlier writings.[28] More important is his direction to Hamilton that the Address
retain Madison's 1792 draft of a Farewell; he had wanted to retire then, but
pleas from all sides persuaded him to remain as the obvious choice for President again. By 1796 these two protégés were rivals. Washington wanted both
involved with his truly final statement in part to symbolize the balanced views
and shared principles eclipsed by the severe partisanship of the 1790s. This in
itself confirmed a practical wisdom and moderate sense of justice surpassing
that of any statesmen who succeeded him save Lincoln, amid dilemmas dwarf-
ing those faced by any successor save the Great Emancipator. Indeed, Jefferson
and Madison deemed the Farewell Address so important for American political
thought that they placed it and his First Inaugural on the reading list for the
University of Virginia, with the Declaration of Independence and *The Federalist*.[29] Tocqueville also elevates it above any other American state document,
praising this "admirable letter addressed to his fellow citizens, which forms the
political testament of that great man" – noting also that it still serves, decades
later, as basic charter of American foreign policy.[30]

The great, related themes of Washington's presidency were that executive
power was safe for republicanism, and that constitutional government, not populism or parties, should lead the way. These principles animated his speeches
and deeds, including his example that a republic's executive should not hold
office for life. The Constitution provided a strong keel and rudder, but the
final stage of his career proves how crucial his prudence and adherence to constitutionalism were in guiding the ship of state past storms and siren songs.
His commitment to making the Constitution work by fleshing out the powers sketched in Article II (indeed throughout) still shapes our politics today,
although his moderation was tested while protecting the republic from both
European powers and visionary creeds at home. Ideas of presidential power and
of statesmanship or leadership have changed since, but Washington's principles
remain a benchmark for evaluating whether these are improvements.[31] To him

---

[28] For some of the correspondence and drafts, see W 804–6, 938–48, 950–51, 954–56, 960–61.
Spalding and Garrity, *A Sacred Union of Citizens*, 46–57, defends in great detail Washington's
authorship; see also *Washington's Farewell Address*, ed. Victor H. Paltsits (The New York Public Library, 1935). An overview of many interpretations is Arthur A. Markowitz, "Washington's
Farewell and the Historians: A Critical Review," *Pennsylvania Magazine of History and Biography* 94 (April 1970), 173–91; further sources are discussed in Chapter 5.

[29] Madison to Jefferson, February 8, 1825, in *The Mind of the Founder: Sources of the Political Thought of James Madison*, ed. Marvin Myers. Revised edition (University Press of New
England, 1981), 350.

[30] Tocqueville, "The Manner in Which American Democracy Conducts External Affairs of State,"
in *Democracy in America*, vol. 1, pt. 1, Chapter 5, 217.

[31] See Sidney M. Milkis and Michael Nelson, *The American Presidency: Origins and Development,
1776–2011*, 6th edn. (CQ Press, 2011), and Marc Landy and Sidney M. Milkis, *Presidential
Greatness* (University Press of Kansas, 2000).

we owe not only the principle limiting a president to two terms, skirted only by Franklin Roosevelt and then entrenched in constitutional amendment. He also established that presidents should recruit the best talents and characters for offices, from a range of viewpoints, unaffected by patronage. Thus, his cabinet included Hamilton and Jefferson. His Supreme Court nominees included such leading jurists as John Jay and James Wilson. Adherence to separation of powers meant respect for the legislative dominance of Congress; instead of pushing an extensive program, a president should endorse a few measures, mostly about core Article II powers of foreign and security policy. Similarly, the executive should use the veto with care, on constitutional and not policy grounds; his one qualification was a veto over a core presidential power, the size of the army. The executive and Senate should cooperate on treaties while holding separate roles and judgments; however, he insisted the House play no role, given "the plain letter of the Constitution" and his knowledge of "the principles on which the Constitution was formed" (W, 930–32). The executive and legislature, not just the courts, should weigh the constitutional merits of policies, as he did in canvassing Hamilton and Jefferson on the Bank. Perhaps dearest to him was the principle that the president represents all the American citizenry, its regions and states, its common principles and highest ideals, and not one party or set of policies. Similarly, he balanced republican dignity and simplicity, as exemplified in the simple but formal ceremony of his inaugurations – to include augmenting the constitutional oath of office with "so help me God," sworn upon the Bible, a precedent followed by nearly all presidents since.

Washington's conduct amid the partisanship that rocked his presidency offers lessons of prudence and moderation worth pondering today as much as ever. The two great domestic disputes concerned national finances: first, opposition to the Bank and other parts of the economic plan devised by Treasury Secretary Hamilton; second, the protest in western Pennsylvania against the tax on distilled spirits. The two great foreign policy disputes involved the upheaval of the French Revolution and the radically egalitarian, antimonarchical theory France sought to impress upon Europe and America. Washington's two measures to shield America from such turbulence – his 1793 Neutrality Proclamation and 1795 treaty with Britain (the Jay Treaty) – brought bitter partisan attacks. His policies on this range of domestic and foreign issues were remarkably consistent, informed by his view that liberty is best secured by a complex constitutionalism that balances popular consent with competent offices, and also by moderation regarding the theoretical and practical extremes of politics. In domestic policy, his Annual Messages praise Congress for enacting his administration's funding and financial plans, and he reports their evident benefits for America's public credit, commerce, and prosperity. He commends sober deliberation among separated powers to discern sound policies for the republic, unaffected by short-term concerns over creeds, personalities, class conflict, or reelection. The basic outlines of Washington's financial system remain today, grounded in the principles he directed Hamilton to develop into a detailed plan.

Without dismissing criticisms raised concerning national administrative power, commercialism, and inequality, it has helped to produce more liberty, prosperity, and equality than perhaps any regime in history can boast.[32]

This complex, Montesquieuan conception of liberty also informed Washington's response to protests against both federal taxation and his policy of neutrality toward France and Britain. In western Pennsylvania, opposition to the "whiskey tax" exploded from 1791 to 1794 into a grassroots movement against the national government, peaking in armed resistance there to any federal laws. From at least his Third Annual Message in 1791, he proposed "wise moderation" in addressing reasonable concerns of the Pennsylvanians. He issued proclamations in 1792 and 1794 on his constitutional duty to enforce duly enacted laws and the duty of citizens to comply with them, and further explained his policy in his Fourth, Sixth, and Seventh Annual Messages. He ultimately readied militias from four states to suppress an armed resistance that was "subversive equally of the just authority of Government and of the rights of individuals." When this mobilization and final efforts at conciliation failed to persuade the "insurgents," he sent an overwhelming force of 15,000 troops – which he deemed an "army of the constitution" – to restore order. The Whiskey Rebellion dispersed; the leaders arrested and tried in the courts; but Washington ultimately pardoned those convicted of treason and sentenced to death. At stake had been "the fundamental principle of our constitution, which enjoins that the will of the majority should prevail." The lesson for citizens was to "persevere in their affectionate vigilance over that precious depository of American happiness, the constitution of the United States," and to ask continued protection from "the Supreme Ruler of nations" over a government dedicated to securing "human rights" (W, 789, 829, 870–73, 882–84, 887–93, 922).

Staying true to his long-held concern about demagoguery, Washington published the text of his Farewell Address in a newspaper, foregoing a ceremonial speech. It had no grand title, only "United States, September 19, 1796," addressed to "Friends, and Fellow-Citizens"; another newspaper later termed it his "Farewell Address." The harmony with earlier writings is striking: the "Address" opens by invoking republican virtue and civic duty; patriotic devotion to the common good; gratitude to Heaven for the country's blessings, and prayers for continued Providence; and the need for prudence and moderation to sustain such goods. He pledged "unceasing vows" that America and the world would enjoy five further blessings:

that Heaven may continue to you the choicest tokens of its beneficence; that your Union and brotherly affection may be perpetual; that the free constitution, which is the work of your hands, may be sacredly maintained; that its Administration in every department may be stamped with wisdom and Virtue; that, in fine, the happiness of the people of these States, under the auspices of liberty, may be made complete, by so careful a

---

[32] See "Sketch of a Plan of American Finance," October 1789, in *Washington: A Collection*, 535–37; and economic and financial issues in the "discarded First Inaugural," in W 713–15.

preservation and so prudent a use of this blessing as will acquire to them the glory of recommending it to the applause, the affection, and adoption of every nation which is yet a stranger to it. (W, 962–64)

He then cites his 1783 Circular as a precedent for offering advice as well as prayers, and proceeds to propound several lessons for the "solemn contemplation" and "frequent review" of the citizenry. The first lesson concerns liberty: that Americans are so deeply attached to it, he need say no more. This subtly implies an imbalance needing redress; the advice to follow concerns the need to order and sustain liberty. Indeed, the next two lessons reinforce two of his prayers: America must strengthen the Union and cherish the Constitution if it truly prizes liberty. These two aims were the central concerns of Washington's public service and writings from 1783, and these Montesquieuan themes of a strong federalism and a strong constitutionalism garner the bulk of the Address. On the Union: "The Unity of Government which constitutes you one people is also now dear to you. It is justly so, for it is a main Pillar in the Edifice of your real independence, the support of your tranquility at home, your peace abroad; of your safety; of your prosperity; of that very Liberty which you so highly prize ... The name of AMERICAN, which belongs to you in your national capacity, must always exalt the just pride of Patriotism more than any appellation derived from local discriminations" (W, 964–65). One of the strongest counsels of moderation in the Address follows, in his explication of constitutionalism:

To the efficacy and permanency of Your Union, a Government for the whole is indispensable ... Sensible of this momentous truth, you have improved upon your first essay, by the adoption of a Constitution of Government better calculated than your former for an intimate Union, and for the efficacious management of your common concerns. This government, the offspring of our own choice, uninfluenced and unawed, adopted upon full investigation and mature deliberation, completely free in its principles, in the distribution of its powers, uniting security with energy, and containing within itself a provision for its own amendment, has a just claim to your confidence and your support. Respect for its authority, compliance with its Laws, acquiescence in its measures, are duties enjoined by the fundamental maxims of true Liberty. The basis of our political systems is the right of the people to make and to alter their Constitutions of Government. But the Constitution which at any time exists, till changed by an explicit and authentic act of the whole People, is sacredly obligatory upon all. The very idea of the power and the right of the People to establish Government presupposes the duty of every individual to obey the established Government. (W, 967–68)

Having enjoined his fellow citizens to be a constitutionalized people, Washington turns to brief advice on four principles supporting Union and constitutionalism, all of which counsel avoidance of extremes: wariness of parties, as a "fire not to be quenched" in free politics but one that if not moderated could destroy the republic through domestic conflict or foreign intrigue that exploits factions; adherence to separation of powers and the rule of law over populism and passion; the need for religion, morality, and education so as to inform sober and just policies; and, responsible public finances. The final counsel, nearly as long as those on the Union and constitution, concerns America's independence and capacity for justice in foreign affairs (W, 969–72). Washington's maxim "to steer clear of permanent Alliances" is among the best-known points of the Address still today, along with his call to inculcate religion and morality in a self-governing citizenry (W, 975, 971). Given the importance of his enunciation of moderation through these two counsels, I address them in separate chapters.

We should be prudent in how we consult the counsels of the Address in our era, given Washington's own criticisms of the French Revolution and its effects in America – for trying to impose doctrines when knowledge of human nature and practical realities supported moderate views and the need for judgment. The Address does not easily yield answers for the problems of the twenty-first century; still, it offers more than we might think. One such is the importance of prudence itself, which he defined in classical and medieval terms of practical wisdom in service to virtuous aims of a nation and its public servants – rather than as self-interested calculation to rationalize expedient deeds. Moreover, as he had done since his First Annual Message to Congress, he endorsed liberal learning and institutions "for the general diffusion of knowledge," it being "essential that public opinion should be enlightened" (W 972, 750). The guiding spirit of the "Address" is moderation, advising that a principled prudence should guide domestic and foreign affairs, private and public life. He hoped these "counsels of an old and affectionate friend" would "control the usual current of the passions" and "moderate the fury of party spirit" (W, 976; see also 832, 851, 924). An element of Christian Aristotelianism tempers his enlightened liberalism and classical republicanism, and as Brookhiser speculates, this seems to be the mark of the "Rules of Civility" imbibed as a youth. The last of these states: "Labor to keep alive in your Breast that Little Spark of Celestial fire Called Conscience" (W 10).[33] This element explains, indeed, the basic but extraordinary reason for the Address. Brookhiser astutely notes a generous comment from an old nemesis, King George III – who said that Washington's two retirements from power "placed him in a light the most distinguished of any man living," and that he was "the greatest character of the age."[34]

Moral judgments about Washington's complicity in slavery often prevent us from appreciating his thought and character today. In fact, his thoughts and deeds on slavery are a model for any struggle to rise above historical circumstance and self-interest toward justice, a model always needed in politics. For

---

[33] See Brookhiser's chapter "Morals"; also *George Washington's Rules of Civility: Complete with the Original French Text and New French-to-English Translations*, ed. John T. Phillips, II, 2nd edn. (Goose Creek Productions, 2000), and Brookhiser, *Rules of Civility: The 110 Precepts That Guided Our First President in War and Peace* (Free Press, 1997).

[34] Brookhiser, *Founding Father*, 103.

the last three decades of his life he stated that slavery was unjust – expressing "regret" at being a master, and hoping it would not be "displeasing to the justice of the Creator" if he made his adult slaves "comfortable" while laying "a foundation to prepare the rising generation for a destiny different from that in which they were born" (W, 158, 701–2). From the early 1770s he never sold slaves, and after other temporizing measures, he resolved in his Will to emancipate all his slaves upon his wife Martha's death. He prepared them with education and skills so as to give them a reasonable chance in the world. The aged and orphans not wishing or able to be freed were to be cared for, educated, and trained in skills. He emphatically declared that these directions be "religiously fulfilled" by his heirs "without evasion, neglect or delay"; the estate spent money on pensioners until 1833 (W, 1023–24).[35] Like Lincoln, he was neither slavery apologist nor abolitionist, judging this moderate plan more humane and a model to other slave owners. He may have feared that earlier, more conspicuous antislavery statements or actions would fan civil discord between North and South more than it would help the slaves. He admitted that he had redressed the evil later than he should have, but we should consider that no other slaveholding president freed all his slaves. He inherited an evil practice and strove to help eradicate it through his example of prudence and principle.

Marshall's biography concludes, in the spirit of Aristotle and Plutarch, by linking a statesman's moral and intellectual virtue and encouraging all "candidates for political fame" to study Washington's character. Featured are his "incorruptible" integrity; "the texture" of a mind that balanced "modesty" with "dignity"; and a "sound judgment" that was "more solid than brilliant" and thus rightly prudent (*LGW* 465–69). Social science now finds such qualities, and praise of them, implausible or naive. Yet we also constantly complain of destructive partisanship and our dissatisfaction with Congress especially, but also with presidents and other institutions or leaders. Our ambivalence about ideals of statesmanship – too savvy and realistic to believe in them, yet worried or resentful when no one adheres to them – arises from our more democratic and rationalist political culture. From Jefferson and Jackson to the Progressives, we have embraced greater populism as always more legitimate; simultaneously, the Progressives taught us to demand rational projects of progress from political leaders. Marshall's final effort to sketch Washington's character and statesmanship, revised in 1833 (during Jackson's presidency), incorporates his critique of Jeffersonian and Jacksonian populism while anticipating the rationalism of the Progressives. We should hold high but moderate expectations of statesmen and politics; we rightly expect more than demagogic self-seeking, but not administrative philosopher-kings. Marshall celebrates the classical republican elements of Washington, from his "dignity" and "gracefulness" to comparison with two Roman generals celebrated by Plutarch. He was "a real republican" in political

---

[35] See Brookhiser, *Founding Father*, 177–85, and James T. Flexner, "George Washington and Slavery," in *George Washington, Anguish and Farewell* (Little, Brown, 1972), 112–25.

beliefs, but also devoted to "equal political rights" for all. He insisted, nonetheless, upon the difference between "a balanced republic" and democracy as like that "between order and chaos," or between "real liberty" under "the authority of laws" and descent to the politics of the "demagogue."[36] Christianity also graces the American alloy: "Without making ostentatious professions of religion, he was a sincere believer in the Christian faith, and a truly devout man." Moreover, while Marshall's final words on the Washingtonian-American character reflect republican and liberal principle, the elevated tone suggests a Christian source as well: his judgment ever was guided by "an unvarying sense of moral right," a "fairness of intention" that harbored no guile, and "a purity of virtue" both untainted and unimpeachable.

A final point on Washingtonian statesmanship is that its intellectual and practical moderation, its melding of different traditions and its prudence, is neither mushy compromise nor mere centrism. Moderation is not the only virtue for the philosopher or the statesman; for the latter, courage or fortitude will mark the difficult decisions. This includes war and other uses of force to defend right and law. If Washington tacks toward one side then another in his career as leading statesman, and if he seeks wide counsel before committing to policy, it is with a firm sense of moral and political principle grounded in natural right and constitutional law, British then American. His capacity for prudence, and for fortitude both in judgment and deed, is still a model for statesmanship no matter what the new issues to be faced. Indeed, Lincoln patterned his extraordinary moderation of judgment, rhetoric, and action upon the Founding Father.[37]

Moderation and the Washingtonian Alloy in America's Mixed Regime

Washington argued for, and embodied, a harmonizing of principles that could seem contradictory; it surely involves tensions. Liberty and individual rights must be balanced by the complex rule of law in the Constitution, in order to distinguish liberty from license in domestic or foreign policy. Provision for special offices and talents in government must balance ideals of equality and popular representation, to keep the republic on an even keel and steady course. A higher moral calling to Christian virtue and decency, and gratitude to

---

[36] Faulkner emphasizes the blend of liberal and classical republican (especially Ciceronian) elements in Washington, and in Marshall's account of him, in "Obscuring the Truly Great"; see also Morrison, *Political Philosophy of Washington.*

[37] Lincoln's 1838 address to the Young Men's Lyceum, "The Perpetuation of Our Political Institutions," closes by invoking Washington as well as Christianity; when the president-elect bid farewell to Springfield in February 1861, he invoked Providence for protection and noted that the "task before me" was "greater than that which rested upon Washington." In *The Collected Works of Abraham Lincoln,* ed. Basler, 9 vols. (Rutgers University Press, 1953), 1: 108–115, and 4: 190–91. See also Steven Kautz, "Abraham Lincoln: The Moderation of a Democratic Statesman," in *History of American Political Thought,* eds. Frost and Sikkenga (Lexington Press, 2003).

Providence, must guide and temper both republican and liberal ideas while also affirming religious liberty. The predominant voices in scholarship about the founding, however, demote this moderation – the balance of traditions, and avoidance of extremes – in the Founder's ideas and deeds. Washington's character is significant, but intellectually it is deemed the muddle of a busy, practical man. Scholars instead seek one element or school in the founding blend – Lockean liberalism, classical republicanism, Protestant Christianity, among others – as predominant in shaping America's political culture and institutions. Both responses avoid an obvious if complex reality. The chief statesman of the founding, who shaped and embodied its intellectual and practical character more than any other, also embodies the kind of moderation that Montesquieu's political science exemplifies. Moreover, Montesquieu was the mostly widely cited philosopher in America, and probably the most influential, during the 1780s and 1790s as the constitutional order was formed.[38] This seems more than a coincidence.

This nexus is overlooked in part because our radical Enlightenment sensibilities now dismiss Washington as a political thinker and, similarly, demote Montesquieu's independent philosophic stature. Montesquieu regularly is noted as significant for America's founding principles and constitutional political science, yet his influence does not receive much attention from the historians, political theorists, and religion scholars who survey the intellectual sources of the founding and then debate which one predominates, or whether it is just a hodgepodge of historical accident.[39] Among some advocates of the dominant influence of liberal philosophy there now is recognition that multiple intellectual traditions shaped the American founders, yet insistence that Lockean philosophy still predominated. For this view, Americans interpreted Locke's rationalist philosophy of individual rights and the threat of revolution as able to accommodate to itself, in a subordinate role, Christian belief, Scottish moral sentiment and common sense, and Whig opposition principles. Indeed, the founders were led to this tactic by Locke's deliberate ambiguities

---

[38] See Donald Lutz, "The Relative Influence of European Writers on Late Eighteenth-Century American Political Thought," *American Political Science Review* 78 (1984), 189–97; James Muller, "The American Framers' Debt to Montesquieu," in *The Revival of Constitutionalism*, ed. Muller (University of Nebraska Press, 1988), 87–102; Anne Cohler, *Montesquieu's Comparative Politics and the Spirit of American Constitutionalism* (University Press of Kansas, 1988), 148–69; and Judith Shklar, "A New Constitution for a New Nation," in *Redeeming American Political Thought*, eds. Hoffman and Thompson (University of Chicago Press, 1998), 158–69.

[39] For the founding as an incoherent "plethora of views," see Isaac Kramnick, "The Great National Discussion," *William and Mary Quarterly* (3rd series) 45 (January 1988), 3–32. One of the few surveys that considers Montesquieu on a par with Locke, the Scottish Enlightenment, or Whig opposition thought is Forrest McDonald, *Novus Ordo Seclorum: The Intellectual Origins of the Constitution* (University Press of Kansas, 1985). Gibson's useful survey, *Interpreting the Founding*, emphasizes Locke's liberalism but never discusses Montesquieu.

and slyness.[40] A variation of this approach admits Montesquieu's influence but reduces his philosophy to Lockean liberalism, albeit of a sort that – as in Locke's original – disguised its radical import so as to attract collaborations, thereby to better insinuate its influence.[41] As Chapter 1 argued, this is a debatable view of Montesquieu's philosophy in itself. It has the further disadvantage of explaining away Montesquieu's influence on the American founding, on the range of ideas influencing the founding debates, and on the capacity of American thinkers and statesmen to recapitulate his philosophical blending of seemingly rival ideals into a coherent alloy – or, to use his concept, a complex spirit or mind.

While the American constitutional order is not a mixed regime in the classical sense – blending distinct claims to rule by democracy, aristocracy, and monarchy – it clearly balances constitutional powers or orders against each other within federalism and the separation of powers. This conception should be adapted to explain as well the American capacity to blend classical republicanism, liberal rights, Scottish common sense, Whig opposition thought, the common law, and Christian charity into a new polity.[42] When *The Federalist* explains its own understanding of federalism and of separation of powers – indeed, of political science itself – it turns not to Locke, who is never cited, but to Montesquieu. Moreover, the opening and closing essays invoke moderation as a guiding intellectual as well as a practical principle for politics.[43] Our undue emphasis upon Locke would benefit from the further realization that the Americans did not first discover Montesquieu in the 1780s, and that the extensive influence held by the common-law, amalgamating mind of the American legal profession appreciated *The Spirit of Laws* from its arrival in the 1750s. James Stoner argues that the principled complexity of the American founding arises in substantial part from the influence of the common-law tradition, both the classical conception in Coke and the liberalized version in Blackstone that

---

[40] Michael Zuckert, *The Natural Rights Republic: Studies in the Foundation of the American Political Tradition* (University of Notre Dame Press, 1996), and also Thomas Pangle, *The Spirit of Modern Republicanism: The Moral Vision of the American Founders and the Philosophy of John Locke* (University of Chicago Press, 1988).

[41] Thomas Pangle, "The Philosophic Understandings of Human Nature Informing the Constitution," in *Confronting the Constitution*, ed. Bloom (AEI Press, 1990), 9–76, and Michael Zuckert, "Natural Law, Natural Rights, and Classical Liberalism: On Montesquieu's Critique of Hobbes," *Social Philosophy and Policy* 18 (2001), 227–51.

[42] See my chapter "Hamilton's Common Law Constitutionalism and Judicial Prudence" in *The Cloaking of Power: Montesquieu, Blackstone, and the Rise of Judicial Activism* (University of Chicago Press, 2003), especially the section on "Montesquieu, Common Law, and the Complexity of the American Founding" and the closing discussion of a modern mixed regime; also "The Complexity, and Principles, of the American Founding: A Reply to Alan Gibson," *History of Political Thought* XXI (2000), 711–17.

[43] See *Federalist* nos. 9, 47–51, and 78 for direct reliance upon Montesquieu, and also nos. 1 and 85. As noted in the Prologue, Peter Berkowitz discusses Publius and moderation in *Constitutional Conservatism: Liberty, Self-Government, and Political Moderation* (Hoover Institution Press, 2013).

came to America in the late 1760s.[44] The common law emphasizes assimilation of disparate ideas, rather than the analysis and division that marks the radical Enlightenment and Locke's philosophy. Moreover, Montesquieu was a lawyer and judge who considered the Gothic jurisprudence that he wove into his philosophy to be a cousin of the English common law and its constitutionalism. Jefferson himself indicates that an amalgamating mind informed the Declaration of Independence, since it was intended to reflect "the harmonizing sentiments" that encompassed "the elementary books of public right, as Aristotle, Cicero, Locke, Sydney, etc."[45]

To argue for Jefferson's characterization of the Declaration as a blend of ideas that expressed "the American mind" is not to argue that Lockean liberalism was not centrally important for the Declaration; it is to suggest that, even for Jefferson, it was not necessarily the matrix into which other traditions were absorbed, nor was it the only tradition of central importance. A full reading of the Declaration, with attention to the few but important revisions made to Jefferson's draft by the drafting committee and Congress, reveals the substantial influence of the common law in its title and form. As with the 1774 Declaration and Resolves of the First Continental Congress, the title is a technical term for a legal remonstrance. The bulk of the document lists charges as violations not only of the Laws of Nature and Nature's God but also of a positive law. Indeed, that reference to a divinity is one of four mentions of a deity, which in turn anchor the invocations of natural law and Anglo-American common law. The deity invoked is not a watchmaker but a providential agent of justice. The positive law being invoked is identified in the middle of the list of charges, when declaring that the king "has combined with others" to impose authority and laws "foreign to our constitution." As Stoner argues, this striking invocation of a constitution cannot mean colonial charters or state constitutions (not even drafted), let alone the Articles of Confederation. Perhaps the common-law constitutionalism of Coke and Blackstone, adopted and adapted for centuries in America, is the matrix into which Lockean liberalism is absorbed to make its argument for dissolving the legal bands between Britain and America.[46]

Further consideration would recall the commonplace that the American Revolution is more moderate than the French or later revolutions inspired by radical Enlightenment doctrines or other radical philosophies. One reason is

---

44 James Stoner, *Common Law and Liberal Theory: Coke, Hobbes, and the Origins of American Constitutionalism* (University Press of Kansas, 1992), especially at 176–96.

45 Jefferson also sought to draft not "new principles, or new arguments, never before thought of," but "to place before mankind the common sense of the subject." To Henry Lee, May 8, 1825, in *Writings*, 1500–1501. See also Hans Eicholz, *Harmonizing Sentiments: The Declaration of Independence and the Jeffersonian Idea of Self-Government* (Peter Lang, 2001).

46 Stoner, *Common Law and Liberal Theory*, 188–89, and also "Common Law and Constitution: Original Understanding, Republican Synthesis, and Modern Transformation," in *Common Law Liberty: Rethinking American Constitutionalism* (University Press of Kansas, 2003), 9–29 especially at 15.

the continuity of law, institutions, and thought provided by the common law. Moreover, Americans would have been shaped by Montesquieu's philosophy to associate the "constitution" with liberty ever since the English translation of *The Spirit of Laws* arrived in the early 1750s. Montesquieu boldly claimed that the English constitution alone held liberty for its purpose (*The Spirit of Laws*, Book 11, Chapters 5 and 6). Blackstone celebrates this testimony as his first citation of a modern philosophic authority in the opening of his *Commentaries on the Laws of England* (1765).[47] A thorough study of Montesquieu's presence in American libraries, newspapers, and public debate prior to 1776 argues that his "authority" on liberty and constitutionalism was well established in American thinking, and was broadly "in the air" before the Revolution and "cited in support of their case against England" – especially through repeated citations, in the 1760s and early 1770s, to his analysis of the English constitution.[48] Two Americans especially important for views of rights and revolution, James Otis and Jefferson, cite Montesquieu before 1776, and indeed, Jefferson copied twenty-eight pages worth of passages from *The Spirit of Laws* sometime between 1774 and 1776 in his "Commonplace Book" – extracting passages from twenty-six of the thirty-one books of the work.[49]

Montesquieu's philosophy of moderation informs the Constitution and the explication of it in *The Federalist*, but also the Declaration of Independence. Its increasing presence "in the air" from the 1760s helps to explain the intellectual and political character of the Founding Father. Of course the influence of the founding itself, and of Washington, has declined in American thought and life into its third century. Nonetheless, the Washingtonian, founding conceptions of moderation or balance still pervade American constitutionalism and shape the complexity of life and thought, blending pluralism and principle, individual rights and public purposes. The Epilogue addresses why it is our choice, and not an inexorable fate, that Washington's constitutional children have turned away from the sources of self-understanding and moderation available through serious study of the founding. That said, there also are reasonable concerns raised by those who admire older dimensions of the American polity but view the founding as narrowly Lockean, thus as inevitably producing problems, decay, and amnesia.[50] The Anti-Federalists who opposed ratification of the

---

[47] Discussed in *The Cloaking of Power*, for example, at p. 114, among three chapters on Montesquieu's influence on Blackstone, and Blackstone's influence in turn on American thought and constitutionalism.

[48] See Paul Merrill Spurlin, *Montesquieu in America, 1760–1801* (Louisiana State University Press, 1940), 126–27, 137, 180; see also 116–17, 122–23, 141–53, 157–58, 175–77, 259–60.

[49] Spurlin, *Montesquieu in America*, pp. 153–57, citing Gilbert Chinard, *The Commonplace Book of Thomas Jefferson* (Johns Hopkins University Press, 1926) and Chinard's speculations on Montesquieu's perduring influence even after Jefferson's criticism begun in 1790 (on this, see Spurlin, 240–41); on Otis (also John Adams) before 1776, see 99, 118–21.

[50] See, for example, Wilson Carey McWilliams, "Democracy and the Citizen: Community, Dignity, and the Crisis of Contemporary Politics in America," in *Redeeming Democracy in America*, eds. Deneen and McWilliams (University Press of Kansas, 2011), 9–28.

Washingtonian constitutional order voiced such doubts from the beginning, and the scholar Herbert Storing later redressed our amnesia by recovering and commenting upon their writings. Tocqueville, however, incorporated those Anti-Federalist concerns into his analysis of America and of modern liberal democracy without viewing the foundations as narrowly Lockean. He therefore did not see an inevitable liberal apocalypse of individualism, materialism, social disintegration, and governmental centralization or gigantism.

Tocqueville famously warned, of course, that the latter indeed were possible for America and the modern liberal world. He nonetheless hoped America might choose to avert these dangers because, as an heir to Montesquieu, he discerned the moderation and complexity in America's character and constitutionalism. The balance in its original amalgam, and the example offered in the bright alloy of its founding statesman, might give it a fighting chance – especially with the aid of new philosophic guidance and statesmanship for the new challenges of the mass democratic era.

3

Tocqueville's Deepening of Modern Moderation

Tocqueville analyzed and expressed the philosophy of moderation more profoundly than any other modern mind. Whether compared to Montesquieu, Burke, Constant, Publius, or later thinkers, he best comprehends the three dimensions of moderation examined here: an intellectual virtue that seeks truth by avoiding extremes or single-minded imbalance; a political science featuring a complex constitutionalism and moderate liberalism, to include classical and medieval elements; and due regard for statesmanship and principled prudence by those who study and practice politics. He sought to moderate the radical Enlightenment not only by highlighting its disruptive or damaging effects, such as total revolution and war, but also by discerning its more subtle but still dangerous consequences for culture and thought. Thus he did not declare a principle of moderation as Montesquieu had done, or declare any philosophical doctrine per se. Nor did he state, as his fellow French nobleman had done, that he was a genius akin to classical and modern philosophers. While distancing himself from philosophy, his first and perhaps greatest work, *Democracy in America* (1835, 1840), still borrows substantially from *The Spirit of Laws* in structure and spirit, including its philosophy of moderation. Understanding Tocqueville as this kind of philosopher, seeking to avoid intellectual extremes and find the right middle ground for politics with guidance from natural right, addresses several puzzles about his work. Scholars long have noted the "strange" quality of his liberalism and the elusiveness of the first principles of his thought. There also is debate on whether the two volumes of *Democracy in America* cohere as one work. If Tocqueville is understood as modifying a Montesquieuan conception of philosophy – balancing and reconciling earlier philosophic insights so as to best discern the truth and also respond to the challenges of one's epoch – then the complexity of his philosophy, and of the great work that first presented it, can come to light on their own terms.

Tocqueville deepens Montesquieu's philosophy. He seeks moderation rightly understood. For the good of both the new democratic societies and those who still seek moral or intellectual greatness, modern philosophy needs moderating. Even the moderate Enlightenment philosophy of Montesquieu needs tempering through greater respect for religious belief and for limits of narrowly rational inquiry. However, since Christianity is a source of modern democracy, the proper relationship between philosophy, democracy, and religion is complex. While Tocqueville seeks to restore forgotten wisdom and perspective to the brashly progressive modern world, he affirms the basic truth and justice of the democratic era. It needs guidance from religious faith and metaphysical thinking generally, and he promotes such resources neither on cynically utilitarian grounds nor through devotional theology. A rational, balanced view of human nature indicates that democracy will be its best only by moderating its self-worshiping expectations, avoiding its tendencies toward such extremes as materialism and rationalism, and properly elevating its gaze. Democracy will find its best self in moderation, thus understood.

Democracy in America brought Tocqueville to the forefront of the community of letters in France and beyond.[1] He wrote other philosophical works about France and modern liberal democracy as it undertook, and suffered, the tumultuous transition from the feudal European order, through revolution, to repeated unsuccessful efforts at building a liberal constitutional order. He employed the fame garnered by *Democracy* to secure elected office in the national assembly, forsaking his noble legacy as a lawyer and judge and never using his title of Count. As a French statesman he eventually rose to become foreign minister while continuing literary and philosophical pursuits. He thus had grounds for preparing memoirs, his *Recollections*, published posthumously. *The Old Regime and the Revolution* (1856) extends his philosophy of moderation, counseling avoidance of intellectual and political extremes and affirming the search for a higher middle ground for philosophy and for the new era of mass democracy.[2] The fresh and audacious *Democracy* offers much to consider in itself, and its obvious echoes of *The Spirit of Laws* deserve more

---

[1] Françoise Mélonio illuminates Tocqueville's context in French intellectual culture, including his unusual appreciation for religion, in "Tocqueville and the French," *The Cambridge Companion to Tocqueville*, ed. Welch (Cambridge University Press, 2006), 337–58; while Mélonio glimpses moderation in his thought, and cites Montesquieu's influence, he overemphasizes historical context and indeterminate meanings. Cheryl Welch's introduction to this volume, "Tocqueville in the Twenty-First Century," recounts his intellectual achievements and the scholarly responses; 1–20. In general, see Harvey Mansfield, *Tocqueville: A Very Short Introduction* (Oxford University Press, 2010).

[2] In *The Old Regime* Tocqueville characterizes *Democracy* as arguing that the democratic revolution is "a force which we can hope to moderate," and avers that events since then have not altered his judgment; he adds, in opening Book 3, further critique of the radical intellectuals and *philosophies* of the eighteenth century and their role in shaping the French Revolution. "Preface" and III.1–2 in *The Old Regime and the Revolution*, vol. 1, eds. François Furet and Françoise Mélonio, tr. Alan Kahan (University of Chicago Press, 1998), 87–89, 195–209.

examination. Tocqueville initially develops his philosophy of moderation by explaining how the Americans at once embodied and threatened moderation, and how much Europe and especially France need it. *Democracy* sees in America multiple foundings, or a complex political culture that eventually produces its constitutional founding as a federal republic. First the Puritan republicans balance liberty and religion through mores or culture as much as through laws; then a second founding by thinkers and statesmen, influenced by the common law and the moderate Enlightenment as well as by the Christian-republican blend, declares independence and builds a constitutional republic. As a quietly philosophical work, *Democracy* is conscious of the trauma inflicted on France by the radical Enlightenment and the extreme philosophical claims made by modernity's vanguard. While he notices flaws in America, he therefore sees much to admire, and broadcast to Europe. This includes admiration for statesmanship and prudent judgment, and for Washington above all, praising him particularly for his moderation. He also states that *The Federalist* should be known globally for its contributions to the political science of constitutional republics. Paradoxically, his moderation is more philosophical than Montesquieu's in one sense even while seeming to eschew philosophy, since he more strongly affirms dispositions of premodern philosophy. These include humanity's natural orientation to theology and metaphysical inquiry, the intrinsic goodness of religious belief and communities (not only their social utility), the limits of reason, and the links between morals and politics as well as morals and philosophy or science.[3]

Tocqueville thus affirms Montesquieu's aims to moderate the rationalism and idealism of earlier liberalism, but as he studied and advised the new liberal democracies, he also thought Montesquieu's philosophy needed tempering. He did not affirm reactionary or traditionalist views at the other extreme, but thought the truth about justice was found in a middle ground between claims of modern Enlightenment and traditionalist claims for particularity and hierarchy. The search for truth requires constant wariness of the limits of any particular parties or schools.[4] Nonetheless, some scholars take a dim view of Tocqueville's intellectual capacities and insist he could not transcend his aristocratic class and

---

[3] Beyond other sources cited in this chapter arguing that Tocqueville is a philosopher, see Pierre Manent, "Tocqueville, Political Philosopher," in *The Cambridge Companion to Tocqueville*, 108–20; and his *Tocqueville and the Nature of Democracy*, tr. Waggoner (Rowman & Littlefield, 1996 [1982]).

[4] On these elements of complexity and balance in Tocqueville's philosophy, see, among other works, Peter Lawler, "Tocqueville's Elusive Moderation," *Polity* 22 (1989), 181–89; James Ceaser, "Political Science and the Political Culture of Liberal Democracy," in *Liberal Democracy and Political Science* (Johns Hopkins University Press, 1990), 143–76; "Editors' Introduction" in Tocqueville, *Democracy in America*, eds. Harvey C. Mansfield and Delba Winthrop (University of Chicago Press, 2000), xvii–lxxxi, especially at xxx–xxxix; Cheryl B. Welch, *De Tocqueville* (Oxford University Press, 2001); and L. Joseph Hebert, Jr., *More Than Kings and Less Than Men: Tocqueville on the Promise and Perils of Democratic Individualism* (Lexington Books, 2010).

its baggage; in this view his thinking is extreme – from his support for French colonialism in Algeria to his warnings about potential dangers of democracy and equality.[5] Responses to these charges argue for a recalibrated definition of extremes and middle grounds, as is often the case in arguments about moderation. At the least, the rebuttals provide solid reason for considering Tocqueville's political science in *Democracy in America* as an effort at moderation.[6]

Tocqueville quietly indicates these bearings when closing the Introduction to *Democracy*: "This book is not precisely in anyone's camp; in writing it I did not mean either to serve or to contest any party. I undertook to see, not differently, but further than the parties; and while they are occupied with the next day, I wanted to ponder the future."[7] As argued in the Prologue, Montesquieu and Tocqueville adapt the modified Socratic dialectic of the Aristotelian tradition, also found in Aquinas, which avoids fixation on a single, rationalist conception or method while also avoiding skepticism or relativism. Montesquieu develops the moderate Enlightenment, but Tocqueville suggests that further moderation requires distance from the Enlightenment – through recourse to classical and medieval guidance so as to preserve the good, avoid the bad, and limit the damage bequeathed by radical modern philosophy and the revolutionary European birth of democracy. This last insight reveals, for Tocqueville, the advantage of America. It developed democracy via gradual European change and nonrevolutionary conflict, by exiles who developed their principles in a new political space. Montesquieu tried to temper the radical liberalism of Hobbes and Locke by addressing moral principles and political culture as well as individual rights; Tocqueville believes this philosophical moderation requires further adaptation in a new era. Given the revolutionary demise of aristocracy in Europe, and its foreseeable demise globally, he saw the primary threat to the new democratic era coming from within. The danger was less from traditional despotism, or

---

[5] See Jennifer Pitts, "Introduction," in Tocqueville, *Writings on Empire and Slavery*, ed. and tr. Pitts (Johns Hopkins University Press, 2000), and Sheldon S. Wolin, *Tocqueville Between Two Worlds: The Making of a Political and Theoretical Life* (Princeton University Press, 2001).

[6] See Delba Winthrop's review of the Pitts volume in *Society* (November/December 2002), 110–13, and my essay "Tocqueville's Foreign Policy of Moderation and Democracy Expansion," in *Alexis de Tocqueville and the Art of Democratic Statesmanship*, eds. Danoff and Hebert (Lexington Books, 2011); see also the critical response to Wolin by Seymour Drescher, "Who Needs *Ancienneté*? Tocqueville on Aristocracy and Modernity," *History of Political Thought* xxiv (2003), 624–46.

[7] Tocqueville, *Democracy in America*, eds. and tr. Mansfield and Winthrop, vol. 1, Introduction, 15. I have checked this translation by consulting Tocqueville, *Œuvres complètes*, ed. J. P. Mayer (Gallimard, 1951), Tome I, 2 vols., and *Democracy in America*, ed. J. P. Mayer, tr. George Lawrence (Doubleday, Anchor Books, 1969). Robert Eden provides a distinctive interpretation to this passage in "Tocqueville and the Problem of Natural Right," *Interpretation* 17 (1990), 379–87; Bryan Garsten sees it as a key to Tocqueville's philosophy, especially his complex view of religion and politics, in "Seeing 'Not Differently, but Further, than the Parties'," in *The Arts of Rule: Essays in Honor of Harvey C. Mansfield*, eds. Krause and McGrail (Lexington Books, 2009), 359–75.

rigid hierarchies of class, or religious and intellectual oppression by government. Rather, democracy might do what any society or mode of government is prone to do: fail to check its own excesses.

Tocqueville's insight into the new demands upon moderation lend credence to the claim that *Democracy in America* is still the best book ever written on democracy, and the best book on America.[8] Intellectuals on the left and right, and politicians across the spectrum, still invoke his insights and quote (as well as misquote or invent) passages from this great work. I add the small testimony that *Democracy* travels well – speaking to philosophical vistas beyond America in what is now the era of global liberal democracy, globalization, and modernization – as I experienced while teaching it in a seminar with graduate students in India. It is worth inquiring, then, about the signs of political and intellectual immoderation Tocqueville warned about when he assessed both America and modern liberal democracy generally. We then would have reliable guidance on the deeper causes of these dimensions of immoderation, and a deeper argument for why we should reconsider moderation as both a political and an intellectual virtue.

Tocqueville's Montesquieuan Science of Politics

Tocqueville provides further evidence of his intent to reconcile and balance prior schools of philosophy in his remark to his cousin Kergolay, while writing Volume Two of *Democracy*, that there "are three men with whom I commune a bit every day, Pascal, Montesquieu, and Rousseau."[9] His wariness about modern philosophical doctrines, or perhaps about abstract philosophy simply, makes it difficult to discern which of these predecessors might be more important. As argued here, we should consider that it is characteristic of Montesquieuan moderation to consult and blend prior philosophical views. For Montesquieu, it made sense to revive a broadly Aristotelian approach after the extreme claims of the radical Enlightenment, and after the political turbulence yielded by modern ideas of liberty. One king had been beheaded in England in the prior century, and Cromwell had demonstrated republican despotism. Only a few decades after publication of *The Spirit of Laws* (1748) and Montesquieu's death (1755), a more radical regicide and revolution would engulf France, and its effects would spread across Europe, North America, and beyond. The architect of balance or moderation in liberal constitutionalism thus had grounds for warning of a virulent strain of philosophical dogmatism or fanaticism arising, paradoxically, from the conditions of modern freedom.

---

[8] "Editors' Introduction," in Tocqueville, *Democracy in America*, eds. and tr. Mansfield and Winthrop, xvii.

[9] See James Schleifer, *The Making of Tocqueville's Democracy in America* (University of North Carolina Press, 1980), 25–26, citing letter to Kergolay, November 10, 1836; in *Œuvres complètes*, ed. Mayer, tome 13, vol. 1, 415–18.

Montesquieu's second portrait of England in *The Spirit of Laws* examines how a constitution of liberty shapes the mores and culture of its people, and his biting criticism may have taught Tocqueville to consider what we now would term a "sociology of knowledge." Thinkers betray the truth under the extremes of despotism because deprived of liberty but extremely free politics yields its own betrayals of truth, because thinkers in such conditions do not grasp how liberty always produces factions – and do not notice they tend to be as enslaved to the prejudices of their faction as if living under a despot (*The Spirit of Laws*, Book 19, Chapter 27, end). This does not mean philosophers cannot rise above such conditions, but an awareness of extremes and moderation is necessary.

Once we place *Democracy in America* alongside *The Spirit of Laws*, the philosophical kinship is all the more evident.[10] This is not to say that Tocqueville aims to write only a footnote to a master. After the French Revolution, and given the evident contrast between the relatively successful launch of American liberal democracy and the disastrous launch of the French version, Tocqueville sees that the truth about human nature, and the demands of the new democratic era together require still greater emphasis on classical and medieval themes about the importance of mores, as opposed to institutions, for sustaining a decent political order. Thus, he emphatically advocates the truth and importance of religious belief, not only its utility. Moreover, Tocqueville sees a European world awash in philosophical ambition that is doing more harm than good – a worry raised long before the rise of Nietzsche and the avowed self-destruction of Western philosophy. He further moderates the Enlightenment by hiding his own philosophical ambition and avoiding abstraction, thus adopting the pose of a thinker, a man of letters, a bridge between theory and practice who eschews the pretensions of *philosophes*.[11] He reiterates this philosophical moderation in the opening to Volume Two of *Democracy*, when recapitulating his Montesquieuan stance on the need to rise above parties and fads. Indeed, this is all the more necessary because he senses the winds blowing in favor of liberal democracy: "it is because I was not an adversary of democracy that I wanted to be sincere with it. Men do not receive the truth from their enemies,

---

[10] Paul Rahe analyzes Tocqueville's debt to Montesquieu, and scholarship on this theme, in *Soft Despotism, Democracy's Drift: Montesquieu, Rousseau, Tocqueville, & the Modern Prospect* (Yale University Press, 2009), 154–61, to include Rahe's typically encyclopedic notes; he suggests that *Democracy* is a sequel to *The Spirit of Laws*, especially since Tocqueville would know that Montesquieu's final portrait of England (*Spirit* 19.27) presciently noted the spread of its form of government and prosperity to colonies (Montesquieu noted that "one would see the formation of great peoples, even in the forests to which it had sent inhabitants").

[11] This is a main theme of Mansfield's *Tocqueville*. Other insights about his moderation, albeit seeing it (in varying degrees) as confusion or ambivalence, include Robert Nisbet, "Many Tocquevilles," *The American Scholar* (Winter 1976–77), 59–75; Lawler, "Tocqueville's Elusive Moderation"; and Aurelian Craiutu, "Tocqueville's Paradoxical Moderation," *The Review of Politics* 67 (2005), 599–629.

and their friends scarcely offer it to them; that is why I have spoken it."[12] Both philosophers sought to temper the claims of modern reason to reorder political and moral life on new foundations, and in their most famous works, *Spirit* and *Democracy*, they try to capture the complexity of both philosophy and human life. This broad comparison of the two philosophers, and two works, sheds interesting light on Tocqueville's choice to describe his effort not as philosophy but as political science. He opens *Democracy* with a bold claim that a "new political science is needed for a world altogether new," and that he aims to provide it (I, Introduction, 7).[13] Here is a paradox: Tocqueville's philosophy is deeper and more capacious than Montesquieu's, because more attuned to the human soul and religion amid modern equality and liberty, and therefore more diligent in seeking political and theoretical moderation; yet, to achieve these aims, he forsakes any direct reform of philosophy and instead seeks to revive, and recalibrate, an Aristotelian conception of political science. Perhaps Montesquieu would understand this effort at moderating if he had witnessed modern revolution and modern mass democracy. Awareness of this paradox at least permits consideration of the character and prospects of modern liberal democracy from an unusual vantage, one that sees the challenges to philosophy itself in an egalitarian and materialistic age.

Both *The Spirit of Laws* and *Democracy in America* are complex works not of sociology but of grand political science, blending philosophical rigor with historical and poetic insight. Prominent observers outside the field of political theory have noted that these two thinkers were foremost in the "first wave" of modern democratization by arguing that liberty requires both a complex constitutionalism and attention to the mores it at once reflects and reinforces.[14] Montesquieu's alternative brand of liberal philosophy informs Tocqueville's not-very-Lockean attention, in one comprehensive work, to geography, mores, complex constitutional forms, judicial power, religion, education, commerce, war, and more.[15] The Montesquieuan emphasis in *Democracy* upon political

---

[12] Tocqueville, *Democracy in America*, eds. Mansfield and Winthrop, vol. 2, Author's Notice, 400. Subsequent references are made parenthetically, citing Volume, Part, chapter, and page of this edition (e.g., II.2.1, 479).

[13] Analyses of this claim include Harvey Mansfield and Delba Winthrop, "Tocqueville's New Political Science," and also Seymour Drescher, "Tocqueville's Comparative Perspectives," in *The Cambridge Companion to Tocqueville*, 81–107, 21–48.

[14] See Fareed Zakaria, *The Future of Freedom: Illiberal Democracy at Home and Abroad* (Norton, 2003), and Marc Plattner, "A Skeptical Afterword," *Journal of Democracy* vol. 15, no. 4 (2004), 106–10, at 107.

[15] Further works comparing Montesquieu and Tocqueville include Raymond Aron, *Main Currents in Sociological Thought*, 2 vols., tr. Howard and Weaver (Penguin, 1968 [1965]), I: 188–90, 200–201, 204–5, 210, 230; Melvin Richter, "The Uses of Theory: Tocqueville's Adaptation of Montesquieu," in *Essays in Theory and History*, ed. Richter (Harvard University Press, 1970), 74–102; Anne Cohler, *Montesquieu's Comparative Politics and the Spirit of American Constitutionalism* (University Press of Kansas, 1988), Chapter. 8; James Ceaser, "Political Science, Political Culture, and the Role of the Intellectual," in *Interpreting Tocqueville's Democracy in*

and theoretical complexity also informs the structure and character of the work. Both philosophers descend from abstract theory to offer advice about moderation, statesmanship, and prudence in service to a decent modern politics. Tocqueville's new science of politics ultimately questions, however, whether Montesquieu's largely negative view of politics and liberty can sustain either decent liberty or the human soul in the new age of equality.

Indeed, Tocqueville's remark that he regularly communed with Pascal, Montesquieu, and Rousseau ultimately suggests that he maintained balance and independence in relating to them – a possibility overlooked by many commentators. Recent emphasis on the Augustinian influence of Pascal might be excused for overplaying that element, since most prior studies had reduced Tocqueville's thought to either Montesquieu or Rousseau. Two recent works, however, each from distinct schools in political theory, characterize Tocqueville's philosophical pedigree as a more complex issue. Scholars from a generally Aristotelian perspective, but also from a generally Rousseauan one, concur that Tocqueville is a political theorist of the first order, and that he provokes us to consider the threats to politics posed, paradoxically, by democratic equality.[16] They also agree that liberty is the central principle of Tocqueville's political philosophy; that he is deeply concerned with individualism and apathy in mass democracy, and that he recommends a selective restoration of ancient and medieval principles to remedy this and related modern problems. That said, the one view portrays a Tocqueville who deems human greatness essential to liberty who finds democratic populism a grave threat to both liberty and humanity, and who sees religion and philosophy, properly conceived, as allies in meliorating several tendencies of modernity. This Tocqueville calls upon all three of his French predecessors while transcending a fundamental reliance upon any one, striving to leaven Augustinian and modern influences with a strong dose of Aristotelian ideas about magnanimity, political virtue, and moderation. The Rousseauan, even postmodern portrait emphasizes the biographical core of Tocqueville's "theorizing" and the political elitism permeating *Democracy* and his later works, the *Souvenirs* and *Ancien Régime*. This Tocqueville never leaves the bygone world of hereditary aristocracy for the new world of egalitarian democracy, or never really commits to the new world despite many affirmations of it. Foremost is a Pascalian rejection of modern humanism combined with a heritage of aristocratic prejudice. This religious, elitist distrust of modern equality makes him a not so friendly critic of democracy, even if we grant his insight about our enervated postmodern, and postdemocratic,

---

America, ed. Masugi (Rowman & Littlefield, 1991), pp. 287–325, and Ceaser, *Liberal Democracy and Political Science* (Johns Hopkins University Press, 1990), Chapter 3.

[16] See *Democracy*, eds. Mansfield and Winthrop, Editors' Introduction and Suggested Readings, xvii–lxxxi, especially at xxx–xxxix; and Wolin, *Tocqueville Between Two Worlds*, 38–45, 84–86, 89–90, 177–82.

condition in which capitalist wealth and consumer satisfaction replace participatory citizenship.[17]

If there are stronger grounds, however, to see Tocqueville as adapting Montesquieu's philosophy of moderation, as seems obvious given the spirit and structure of *Democracy in America*, then he emerges as a new kind of guide to both the opportunities and the dangers of modern democracy. In this light, Tocqueville neither subtly nor boldly dismisses modern equality. Rather, his new political science seeks to translate the truths discerned by ancient and medieval philosophy to a new world that those philosophers should have considered more sympathetically. These earlier resources help to instruct the new world on its need for amelioration. Montesquieu's initial attempt to moderate modern philosophy – by blending elements of ancient philosophy and poetry with medieval political practice and belief to form a more complex modern liberalism and constitutionalism – is the basis for the new political science Tocqueville developed in response to new circumstances and insights. *Democracy* further moderates Montesquieuan liberalism by more explicitly warning the liberal democratic mind of the mixed blessings of equality and individual security. On that basis, it prescribes a moderate dose of the Aristotelian and Thomistic concern with the destiny of the soul. Tocqueville leavens liberal individualism and egalitarianism by restoring the higher potentiality of politics and civil society, but he departed from the strict teleology of ancient and medieval political philosophy. A crucial element of his new moderation is his embrace, on the grounds of natural theology rather than faith, of the basic reasonableness as well as utility of Christian faith. Montesquieu's shift beyond the Lockean, radical Enlightenment concern to cabin religion prepared the way, but Tocqueville sees reasons for transcending the skepticism about human nature informing Montesquieu's predominantly liberal conception of liberty.[18]

Tocqueville's Moderation: Liberty, the Soul, and Political Science

Democracy in America offers, like Montesquieu's masterwork, a complex philosophy addressing the dilemmas and possibilities of the era while also seeking enduring insight. The similarities in form, topics, and approach between *The Spirit of Laws* and *Democracy* arise from a largely shared view of philosophy and nature. Tocqueville endorses Montesquieu's balance of ancient and modern

---

[17] Wolin's approach is echoed by Hugh Brogan, *Alexis de Tocqueville: A Life* (Yale University Press, 2007), although Brogan relies on other Tocqueville scholars and his own historical view. A biography in accord with the Mansfield and Winthrop view is André Jardin, *Tocqueville: A Biography* (Farrar, Straus, Giroux, 1988; originally Hachette, 1984).

[18] Ralph Hancock integrates Tocqueville's respect for Christian faith and traditional metaphysics with his commitments to political liberty, rational inquiry, and human greatness – and occasionally notes how he moderates or balances these elements – in "Tocqueville's Responsible Reason," in *The Responsibility of Reason: Theory and Practice in a Liberal-Democratic Age* (Rowman & Littlefield, 2011), 253–81.

elements, blending the classical quest for human honor and prudence in politics with the modern concern for individual dignity and secure liberty. As such, Tocqueville might understand why he is not entirely welcomed by strict advocates of either the ancients or the moderns today.[19] He would not be surprised at criticism for being antidemocratic or elitist, much like the later Jefferson's harsh criticisms of Montesquieu.[20] In addition to his opening aim to see further than the parties, and his claim in opening Volume Two that he speaks "the truth" to democracy as a friend, Tocqueville also notes that Volume One was praised for its "impartiality" – and, he hopes this is true of the sequel (I, Introduction, 15; II, Author's Notice, 400).[21] He might be referring only to literal parties and the partisan contests, especially in France and Europe, but his general consideration of philosophical views standing behind parties undermines such a narrow reading. We also should query a related kind of narrowness about Tocqueville, practiced by recent communitarian and liberal theorists, who mostly use him to carry the standards of their schools – be it civic participation, equality, or individual autonomy and tolerance.[22]

Tocqueville can help us to see farther than we normally do in late-modern liberal discourse if we consider his cryptic statement in introducing *Democracy* about "a mother thought that so to speak links all its parts." This seems to be not a single abstract concept, nor is it a typical variety of liberalism. In the Introduction, and elsewhere, he emphasizes his concern to ensure that the new "equality of conditions" remains a democratic liberty and not a democratic "tyranny," a kind of equality safe for, even nurturing for, the "natural greatness of man" inherent in the soul (I, Introduction, 14, 3, 5; I.2.7, 239ff.). To undertake this analysis, and convey his judgment, *Democracy* follows *The Spirit of Laws* in comprehensiveness and complexity. Volume One examines institutions and laws (Part I) but also political mores (Part II), and then

---

[19] Criticisms from the perspective of classical political philosophy – which portray Tocqueville as indebted to Rousseau, historicism, or both – include Marvin Zetterbaum, *Tocqueville and the Problem of Democracy* (Stanford University Press, 1967), especially at 39, 42ff., and John Koritansky, *Alexis de Tocqueville and the New Science of Politics* (Carolina Academic Press, 1987); see also Wilhelm Hennis, "In Search of the 'New Science of Politics,'" and Thomas West, "Misunderstanding the American Founding," in *Interpreting Tocqueville's Democracy in America*, ed. Masugi (Rowman & Littlefield, 1991), 27–62, 155–77.

[20] Wolin criticizes Tocqueville as anachronistic and antimodern, elitist, a mythmaker, and fixated with control in *Between Two Worlds*, 7, 60–61, 68–75, 94–95, 98–101, 106, 157–61, 171, 129–31, 332–36, 383–406, 558–60; he is useful for spurring us to "retriev[e] a receding democratic present in order to counteract even more novel forms of despotism," 9.

[21] Norma Thompson emphasizes this Aristotelian quest for an intermediary between extremes in "Surveying Tocqueville," in *The Ship of State: Statecraft and Politics from Ancient Greece to Democratic America* (Yale University Press, 2001), 125–36.

[22] See Krause, "Honor and Democracy in America," in *Liberalism With Honor* (Harvard University Press, 2002), pp. 67–96, on this tendency and her view of *Democracy* as a Montesquieuan effort to moderate liberalism. I discuss some of these themes in "Tocqueville's Judicial Statesmanship and Common Law Spirit," in *The Cloaking of Power*, 211–30.

Volume Two explores, in four Parts, the ideas, sentiments, and private mores that both reflect and reinforce the politics of liberal democracy. If moderation is not the mother thought itself – to declare it as such might seem too abstract and rationalist – then it is the spirit moving through the work. Tocqueville focuses upon and educates about moderation by repeatedly warning about excesses, and praising balance or a proper middle ground. A tour through some highlights of Volumes One and Two reveals this spirit.

Democracy opens by noting that in Europe since 1789 democracy was "adored" and then "weakened by its own excesses," and finally some sought to destroy it "instead of seeking to instruct and correct it" (I, Introduction, 7). He sketches a better democratic society marked by moderation about the rule of law, authority, and class relations; by the balance of individual interests and public duties; and by the ability to avoid both tyranny and anarchy. If "less brilliant, less glorious, less strong" than some aristocratic alternatives, this moderate democratic republic is more just to all persons, and thus "would have taken from democracy all the goods it can offer them" (I, Introduction, 9). The "point of departure" for America itself, and "the key to almost the whole work," is a balance, a principle of moderation: the Americans have succeeded in "incorporating somehow into one another and combining marvelously" two elements often in conflict in other polities, "the *spirit of religion* and the *spirit of liberty*" (I.1.2, 29, 43, emphasis in original). America's federal Constitution is much better than those of the states by following "a more just and moderate course," because the federal framers sought to temper or counteract majority tyranny and the dominance of the popular branch (I.1.8, 143–46; see also I.2.7, 239–242, and I.2.8, 250–258). He declares *The Federalist* a "fine book" that, beyond its specific importance for understanding America, "should be familiar to statesmen of every country" – precisely because it moderates the democratic, populist spirit (I.1.8, 108, n. 8).

Indeed, in each Volume, he pronounces on the highest achievement of the legislator-as-framer, and it is to effect moderation. "Each [kind of] government brings with it a natural vice" and "the genius of the legislator consists in discerning it well" so as to counteract it, which the American framers did (I.1.8, 129). Further, the "whole art of the legislator consists in discerning well and in advance the natural inclinations" of a given society to know "when one must aid the efforts of the citizens and when it would rather be necessary to slow them down" (II.2.15, 518).[23] Once the reader is attuned to this strategy of moderation, its pervasiveness appears. Tocqueville thus opens the final Part of the work by invoking it as his method. He notices that the spirit of equality in modern democracy produces "two tendencies" rather than one: an inclination

---

[23] I discuss specific themes of his constitutionalism, including a common-law judiciary and jurisprudence as crucial moderating elements, in "Tocqueville's Judicial Statesmanship," in *The Cloaking of Power*.

for independence, but also one toward concentrating and centralizing authority, the path to servitude. Equality thus gives birth to an extreme or "evil" but also to the "remedy" to address it, and the philosopher as well as the legislator must emphasize independence to prevent the greater danger of servitude. This is true even though independence itself could go toward the extreme of "anarchy." Since any advocate of humanity would cherish the tendency to liberty produced by equality, he declares that "it is on this side that I cling to it" (II.4.1, 640).

The opening argument in *Democracy* for a new political science to guide the democratic revolution arises as the conclusion to a list of ways that statesmen and philosophers must "instruct" democracy to moderate its beliefs, mores, and judgments (I, Introduction, 7). This echoes the spirit of classical and medieval political science, not the radical Enlightenment. During the writing of both Volumes of *Democracy*, and especially after 1835, Tocqueville read extensively in ancient, medieval, and modern political philosophy. If he is offering a new political science not per se, but for a new egalitarian world, he did so amid study ranging from Plato, Aristotle, and Plutarch to Thomas Aquinas, and on to Machiavelli, Montaigne, Bacon, and Descartes.[24] Moreover, most analysis of his report to his cousin Kergolay, while writing *Democracy*, about communing each day with Pascal, Montesquieu, and Rousseau overlooks his final thought: "A fourth is missing: you."[25] This invocation of his friend's importance reflects a spirit of philosophical conversation rather than pursuit of single-minded doctrine. Unlike the radical Enlightenment, Tocqueville will not claim radical foundations for novel philosophical doctrines; nor is he a commentator or disciple in a particular school. He signals his capacity to employ earlier ideas to aid his understanding in new circumstances, and to develop new blends from diverse thinkers, much as Montesquieu had done before him.

Rousseau's influence is present in Tocqueville's philosophy, but *Democracy* largely blends the spirit of Pascal and Montesquieu to understand the spectacle of mass equality, thereby adapting an Aristotelian political science for Christian and liberal aims.[26] Montesquieu obviously informs the complex structure of a comprehensive work, as well as its opening chapter on terrain and climate, its

---

[24] See Schleifer, *Making of* Democracy in America, 26; Tocqueville reveals some of the range of his mature studies in "Speech Given to the Annual Public Meeting of the Academy of Moral and Political Sciences on April 3, 1852," tr. L. Joseph Hebert, in *Alexis de Tocqueville and the Art of Democratic Statesmanship*, 17–29. On his classical, humanist education prior to study of law, see Jardin, "Education and Emancipation," in *Alexis de Tocqueville*, 56–64.

[25] Schleifer, *Making of Democracy in America*, 25–26.

[26] See Peter A. Lawler, "Introduction," in *Tocqueville's Political Science: Classic Essays*, ed. Lawler (Garland Publishing, 1992), especially on the Aristotelianism of his political science and its distinctive "view of greatness" (xi); see also Mansfield and Winthrop, "Tocqueville's New Political Science," and Hancock, "Tocqueville's Responsible Reason." Compare Catherine Zuckert, "Political Sociology versus Speculative Philosophy," in *Interpreting Tocqueville's* Democracy in America, ed. Masugi (Rowman & Littlefield, 1991), 121–52, arguing that Tocqueville's political science consciously repudiates Aristotle.

emphasis on mores or political culture, and an Aristotelian typology of regimes adapted to the democratic era. That said, Tocqueville's emphatic concern with the human soul in modern democracy, and his serious attention to religion and the transcendent, echoes Pascal. The foundation for his analysis of American mores in Volume Two is a Pascalian skepticism about the capacity of Cartesian philosophy and modern secularism to address our most fundamental questions (II.1.1–7).[27] Nevertheless, just as Montesquieu is more confident about reason than is Montaigne, Tocqueville tempers Augustinian doubts with a political science that can aid mankind in this new era, adapting the Aristotelian and Montesquieuan emphasis on constitutional forms and separation of powers. He tempers or balances Montesquieu's revised Aristotelianism with Pascal's larger questions about the soul and the modern project.

One fundamental departure from Aristotle that complicates this complex new science is Tocqueville's insistence that historical change requires consideration of political realities beyond the standard of an unchanging human nature. Is it anti-Aristotelian to argue that the power of mass democracy must be reckoned with if our nature is to survive such novel pressures and commotion? Tocqueville revives the Aristotelian concern with the soul and its higher destiny only as much as is feasible for serving those ends in radically new conditions. These include the kind of discourse his audience can tolerate or comprehend, and his own acceptance of the fundamental justice of human equality. His neo-Aristotelian method combines observation of particulars with prescription in light of philosophic principles of natural right and constitutionalism.[28] This political science is more concerned with the higher potentiality of politics and the soul than is Montesquieu's new science, while nonetheless stating disagreements with ancient philosophy. This yields Tocqueville's twofold stance toward modern liberal democracy – praise for the greater justice of basic equality, yet concern about the fate of human greatness and the soul (I, Introduction, 5; II.4.8, 673–76).[29] Neither Montesquieu nor Rousseau, even given their

[27] See Peter A. Lawler, *The Restless Mind: Alexis de Tocqueville on the Origin and Perpetuation of Human Liberty* (Rowman & Littlefield, 1993), especially 7–10, 73–87. Another Augustinian–Pascalian reading is Joshua Mitchell, *The Fragility of Freedom: Tocqueville on Religion, Democracy, and the American Future* (University of Chicago Press, 1995). Other works that find in Tocqueville a profound and sympathetic view of religion include Patrick Deneen, *Democratic Faith* (Princeton University Press, 2005); Hebert, *More Than Kings and Less Than Men*, and Hancock, "Tocqueville's Responsible Reason." I explore this in Chapter 4.

[28] James Ceaser continues his earlier analyses, and defense, of Tocqueville's complex philosophy on these points in "Political Foundations in Tocqueville's *Democracy in America*," in *Designing a Polity: America's Constitution in Theory and Practice* (Rowman & Littlefield, 2011).

[29] For Raymond Aron and Pierre Manent, Tocqueville's philosophy aims at liberty, animated by concern for the human soul and human dignity, but they do not find him a Christian or Augustinian thinker. See Aron, "Tocqueville," in *Main Currents*, vol. I, and Manent, *Tocqueville and the Nature of Democracy*. See also Aron, "On Tocqueville," *In Defense of Political Reason: Essays by Raymond Aron*, ed. Mahoney (Rowman & Littlefield, 1994), 175–78, and Lawler, "Was Tocqueville a Philosopher?" in *Restless Mind*, 89–108.

concerns with the degradation of man in modernity, could state with Tocqueville that in aristocracies one finds "inequality and misery" but at least "souls were not degraded" as they can be in mass democracy (8). Tocqueville recommends neither the largely negative liberty of Montesquieu, nor the Augustinian detachment from politics of Pascal, nor the collectivist, historicist liberty of Rousseau's participatory republic. Some elements of each philosopher, blended with something more, now are needed in the new political science.

Justice and Moderation in Constitutional Democracy

Tocqueville warns that modern egalitarianism "lends itself almost as readily" to "the sovereignty of all and the absolute power of one alone" as it does to a politics safe for genuine dignity. His main fear is the power of modern equality to homogenize and enervate souls, to produce not citizens but subjects who would "fall below the level of humanity" (I.1.3, 52; I.2.9, 301; see I, Introduction, 3, 6, 12, and II.4.6, 665). Grounded in this mother thought, his political science practices the kind of statesmanship he commends to American federal judges, to "discern the spirit of their times" so as to "confront those obstacles they can defeat" while steering "out of the current when the flood threatens to carry [them] away" (I.1.8, 147). This echoes Aristotle's argument that political science as a practical science must seek to achieve what good it can in light of both philosophic principles and actual circumstances.[30] Tocqueville thought equality was an irreversible fact of "the times" and was more just than hereditary privilege and prejudice, but he also insisted that a choice confronted mankind between equality in liberty and "equality in servitude" (I.1.3, 52). If modern man is to secure liberty and whatever political virtue is possible, then statesmanlike steering is needed. This prudence must be rooted in a philosophic ability to look beyond any current party and to speak stern truths to democracy as a friend. He sprinkles prudential advice amid his philosophic analyses, as did Montesquieu. A striking case is his effort from the very opening of *Democracy in America* to elevate the democratic soul by linking liberty and religion but also to temper the opposing extremes of Christian reactionaries and rationalist atheists: "One still encounters Christians among us, full of zeal, whose religious souls love to nourish themselves from the truths of the other life; doubtless they are going to be moved to favor human liberty, the source of all moral greatness" (I, Introduction, 11).[31]

Tocqueville offers such moderating advice because after defining a point of departure or ground principle for American constitutionalism in Volume One, and another for American mores (to include intellectual currents) in Volume Two, he warns of problems with each. The fundamental principle of our politics and constitutionalism is complex – the "marvelous combination" achieved

---

30 Aristotle, *Nicomachean Ethics*, 1179a33ff (10.9); *Politics*, 1288b10–1289a25 (4.1).
31 See Manent, "Democracy and the Nature of Man," in *Tocqueville and Democracy*, 67–81.

by the Puritans of "the *spirit of religion* and the *spirit of liberty.*" Indeed, it is a principle of balance and moderation: each spirit prevents the other from going to its characteristic extreme, and thus they "advance in accord and seem to lend each other mutual support" (I.1.2, 43, emphasis in original). However, he later notes that in Europe and America "religions are weakening" and "the divine notion of rights is disappearing" (I.2.6, 228; see also I.2.9, 281–88, 299). He diagnoses the main cause for this decline in Volume Two, as the "philosophic method of the Americans," which he links with America's Protestant principle as well as Enlightenment rationalism. In this opening discussion of Volume Two – implying that this is the point of departure for our mores – he identifies Descartes but also Luther and the "sixteenth century reformers" as the root of this radically modern philosophy (II.1.1).[32] A philosophy that eschews authorities or traditions yields a rationalism that isolates individuals and cuts off succeeding generations from traditional reasoning and judgments. This blend of skepticism with progressive, historicist principles was openly embraced in the twentieth century as the American school of Pragmatism – which Tocqueville defined a half-century before it formed under that name. It now takes many forms that collectively dominate American law and higher education and much of our politics, thought, and culture.[33] The paradoxical result of such individualism is that equally weak minds or souls look to the democratic mass, to public opinion, or to a very few elites (who speak in the name of progress) for guidance: "The same equality that makes him independent of each of his fellow citizens in particular leaves him isolated and defenseless against the action of the greatest number" (II.1.2, 409).

Tocqueville suggests no inevitability or Hegelian end of history for this modern drama, for democracy can yield either liberty or tyranny. He grasped, long before Nietzsche, Kojève, or Fukuyama, that any such end-point entailed the eclipse of humanity, the last man. Such a historicist repudiation of natural right and metaphysical truth was neither progressive nor humane. The unintended consequences of America's blend of pragmatism and skepticism include corrosion of the vital link between religion and liberty achieved in its original point of departure, now replaced by a democratic inclination to "pantheism." Tocqueville diagnoses the deeper implications of American Unitarianism and other innovations – foreseeing the rise of Transcendentalism and its erasure of distinctions between the "microcosm" of the individual and the "macrocosm," its celebration of homogeneous man and democratic society, and its merging of humanity and divinity (II.1.7).[34] This humanist tendency to

---

32 Joshua Mitchell discusses this insight in "Tocqueville on Democratic Religious Experience," in *Cambridge Companion to Tocqueville*, 276–302.

33 See James H. Nichols, Jr., "Pragmatism and the U.S. Constitution," in *Confronting the Constitution*, ed. Bloom (AEI Press, 1990), 369–70; Albert Alschuler, *Law Without Values: The Life, Work, and Legacy of Justice Holmes* (University of Chicago Press, 2000).

34 See Lawler, "Democracy and Pantheism," in *Interpreting Democracy*, ed. Masugi, 96–120; revised in *Restless Mind*, 33–50. In contrast, Wolin's critique of Tocqueville includes his own

consecrate our opinions of the moment – a prescient critique of Rawlsian doctrines of liberal public reason and Kantian constructivism – ultimately yields
a democratic "instinct for centralization" and centralized administration to
secure our materialist aims. Volume Two of *Democracy* thus steadily warns
about, and concludes with an exposition of, "what kind of despotism democratic nations have to fear." This new, soft despotism "reduces each nation to
being nothing more than a herd of timid and industrious animals of which the
government is the shepherd" (II.4.5, 659; II.4.6; 661, 663).

When he suggests in the opening of Volume Two that Puritan liberty cannot
counteract the skeptical individualism caused by democratic philosophy, since
Protestantism is one seed of that philosophy, Tocqueville proposes two anti-
dotes – two ways to moderate democracy through his new political science.
Immediately after explaining why Americans are deeply Cartesian but never
read Descartes, he praises both English empiricism and Catholic Christianity
(II.1, Chapters 3, 4, 5, 6). He contrasts the empiricism and attention to particulars of English thinking with the French taste for philosophic abstraction and
generalization, worrying that American thinking is forsaking the former for
the latter. His endorsement of Catholicism in America deepens the point, since
Luther's search for a radically personal foundation for faith also would undermine the tradition and hierarchy implicit in English common law. Tocqueville
praises this traditional Anglo-American jurisprudence in Volume One, especially its American formulation, which blends respect for precedent and legal
custom with concern for equity and natural right (I.1.6, I.1.8, I.2.8). Moreover, his one thematic statement on rights implicitly echoes the classic common
law view of Sir John Fortescue (fifteenth century) and Sir Edward Coke (sev-
enteenth century), thereby excluding the Hobbesian, Lockean notions of self-
preservation or interest. Tocqueville recalls, instead, the terms of classical and
medieval philosophy: "After the general idea of virtue I know of none more
beautiful than that of rights, or rather these two ideas are intermingled. The
idea of rights is nothing other than the idea of virtue introduced into the world
of politics" (I.2.6, 227).[35]

This striking claim is nonsensical or sloppy to many academics, since it seems
to confuse diverse schools, philosophers, eras, and concepts. For Tocqueville,
the balance among classical, medieval, and modern views is deliberate, and

---

praise of the Emersonian "Over-Soul" without noting that this is the very pantheism and pos-
trationalism Tocqueville criticizes; *Tocqueville Between Two Worlds*, 157–58.

[35] On the Platonic and Aristotelian definition of law as virtue, and its influence on the common law,
see Ellis Sandoz, "Fortescue, Coke, and Anglo-American Constitutionalism," in *The Roots of
Liberty: Magna Carta, Ancient Constitution, and the Anglo-American Tradition of Rule of Law*,
ed. Sandoz (University of Missouri Press, 1993), 1–21, at 6–7, and James Stoner, *Common Law
and Liberal Theory: Coke, Hobbes, and the Origins of American Constitutionalism* (University
Press of Kansas, 1992). Fortescue cites Aristotle and Aquinas in defining law as virtue in "In
Praise of the Laws of England," in *On the Laws and Governance of England*, ed. Lockwood
(Cambridge University Press, 1997), Chapters IV, V, IX, XIII, XVI.

crucial to a political science that moderates. His claim arises in a section of *Democracy* discussing "the idea of rights" and "respect for the law" as among the five "real advantages" America derives from democratic government (I.2.6). In one sense, these remarks develop the emphasis upon judicial power early in the first volume (I.1.6, I.1.8), and they prepare for the striking emphasis upon judging, law, and rights that follows (I.2.8). That later emphasis explicitly falls under the principle of moderation, when he devotes a full chapter to assessing "What Tempers the Tyranny of the Majority in the United States." By treating juridical topics in terms of virtue and beauty, and a legal aristocracy in terms of statesmanship guided by integrity, right, and liberty, Tocqueville pulls American law and democracy toward its highest potential so as to buttress the ennobling influence of its first, but now faltering, point of departure.

Tocqueville reinforces these judgments with a further striking claim, when pondering why the ancients could not discern "the equal right to liberty that each [person] bears from birth." The context is his assessment of modes of thinking in democracy, contrasting English empiricism with the abstraction of radical Enlightenment philosophies. It is not modern philosophy, however, that discovered human equality; rather, "it was necessary that Jesus Christ come to earth" to make it understood that all humans are "naturally alike and equal" (II.1.3, 413). If Montesquieu can puncture the pretensions of modern philosophy by noting that English liberty was found in the Germanic forests (*The Spirit of Laws*, 11.6, end), Tocqueville can credit Biblical religion – not the American Declaration or the French Declaration of the Rights of Man – with first teaching about equality.[36] His concern is that modern rationalism and skepticism exacerbate the individual isolation that in turn threatens democratic liberty, human greatness, and dignity. This guides his choices in *Democracy*, prudential and philosophical, about how to both analyze and moderate modern democracy. His concern with rationalism dictates an initial emphasis on the Puritan origin of American liberty, however flawed, at the expense of discussing the doctrines in either Declaration of rights. Since, however, the Puritan foundation needs buttressing, he recommends, in Volume One, a complex constitutional order that balances and moderates democracy. This features a common law spirit and judicial enforcement of individual rights, the latter understood as virtuous and public-spirited. A moderate constitution and conception of rights can support both Christian mores and liberty. Abraham Lincoln strikes similar themes about a "political religion" and civic spirit that reconciles rule of law and religious

---

[36] Among discussions of this mostly overlooked passage, see Paul Rahe, "Tocqueville on Christianity and the Natural Equality of Man," *Catholic Social Science Review* (2012), 7–20. Larry Siedentop adopts this general thesis on Christian roots of liberalism, but does not cite Tocqueville, in *Inventing the Individual: The Origins of Western Liberalism* (Harvard University Press, 2014). Tocqueville notes in *The Old Regime and The Revolution*, vol. 1, that while he thought in *Democracy* the Puritans developed the New England township as a unique form of liberty, he had discovered local self-government long existed in the ancient regime of France and Germany, and vestiges still survived; see Book 2, Chapter 3, p. 129.

devotion – when warning in his 1838 Lyceum Address of threats to American liberty and decency, then in his rhetorical efforts as President to address such threats. This is not a civil religion in Rousseauan terms. Lincoln concludes his Lyceum Address by invoking the Christian Church as a higher authority, not a civil religion he has invented. The Gettysburg Address and Second Inaugural further invoke religion as a higher, corrective, and demanding authority, not a merely useful one. Lincoln and Tocqueville both were lawyers deeply respectful of the classic common-law tradition, marking this as a faith not in democracy per se but in a tradition of law and constitutionalism, medieval in origin and recently reaffirmed in America.[37]

Statesmanship and Metaphysics for America's Mixed Regime

At least since Aristotle chided Plato for claiming to contemplate city and soul while primarily addressing the soul, a concern about philosophical immoderation has confronted political philosophy and political science. Today most political science either indulges reflection on abstract conceptions of justice without attention to the practice of politics and institutions, or, especially since Machiavelli, analyzes institutions and rational calculations of political actors with no reference to the soul and its proper ends. Aristotle, Montesquieu, and Tocqueville claim to moderate this tendency to extremes by dialectically examining the mutual influence between laws and mores, constitutionalism and political culture, statesmanship and political philosophy. This political science seeks to understand human nature and its potentialities in the light of experience and traditional practical wisdom.[38] The temptation to separate inquiry about aims or values from analysis of institutions and political practice also is evident in scholarship on Tocqueville himself. To some scholars he is a philosopher and quasi-theologian seeking eternal verities; to others, a sociologist or historicist bound by his times. Tocqueville seems to view himself as blending or balancing these approaches. He opens the first Volume of *Democracy* with a plea for moderation and call for a new political science, and then discerns a Christian-republican point of departure for the most successful modern democracy. He affirms this approach in the neo-Aristotelian analysis of laws and institutions undertaken throughout Volume I. Tocqueville seeks a moderate political

---

37 "The Perpetuation of Our Political Institutions" (1838) in *The Collected Works of Abraham Lincoln*, ed. Basler (Rutgers University Press, 1953–56), I: 108–15; Gettysburg Address (1863), VII: 22–3; Second Inaugural (1865), VIII: 332–33. For Lincoln's common law pedigree, see, for example, his dissection of Chief Justice Taney's opinion in *Dred Scott* (1854), Speech at Springfield, June 26, 1857, in *Collected Works*, II: 401.

38 Ceaser, in *Liberal Democracy*, argues that Aristotle, Montesquieu, and Tocqueville embody "traditional political science," which better explains and sustains liberty than do the extremes of empiricism or utopian constructivism; he continues this argument in *Designing a Polity*; see also Mansfield and Winthrop, "Tocqueville's New Political Science."

science that connects the particulars of a new mode of politics with the universal and metaphysical dimensions of human life.

After the call for a new political science, the remainder of the Introduction elaborates a concern about the extremes dominating Europe's transition to modern equality and democracy. Tocqueville urges all modern democracies to moderate their morals, politics, and philosophy (I, Introduction, 7–15). Part I of Volume One carefully assesses the laws and institutions of American federalism and separation of powers, but gradually rises toward the theme of Part II, that good laws alone cannot sustain a decent political liberty. The right mores and character in both citizens and rulers also are necessary, indeed, are most indispensable (I.2.9, 292–95). Montesquieu's moderate political science had consciously departed from Hobbesian and Lockean liberalism to capture the full complexity of the physical, moral, and legal elements that, in their interactions, produce a certain political "spirit." This partially restored the Aristotelian concept of regime (*politeia*), that rule involves both moral character and institutions, but largely did so as a means to liberal security and tranquility. Tocqueville's emphatic attention to mores (*mœurs*) – capaciously defined as "the ensemble of moral and intellectual dispositions which men supply to the state of society" and which political scientists today might translate as political culture – marks his deeper turn (I.2.9, 305, n. 8; see also 287). He develops Montesquieu's attention to mores by recovering some Aristotelian and Christian-Aristotelian standards on right and regime.

In American terms, Tocqueville's moderate political science reconciles the Federalist concern about the necessary powers and constitutional order of good government with the Anti-Federalist concern for the moral presuppositions of self-government. Aristotle's Socratic, dialectical political science had embraced both natural right and a regime's division into distinct functions so as to balance inclusive participation with space for merit in select offices. This science of the mixed regime is partially evident in Montesquieu but more fully in Tocqueville.[39] He endorses the American correction of Montesquieu's largely negative liberalism, and *Democracy in America* more fully captures the American spirit by calling liberal democracy to appreciate those dimensions of the Biblical and Western traditions that moderate the quest for ever-greater equality and individual security. Awareness of Tocqueville's philosophy of moderation reveals the troubling paradox of Montesquieu's political science: a fundamental orientation toward individual tranquility and security permits the rise of rival extremes of individualism and majority tyranny; these, in turn, undermine a stable liberal constitutionalism and the mores meant to ensure tranquility. Tocqueville saw the possibility, however, of moderating Montesquieu with

---

[39] Aristotle, *Politics*, 1297b35–1301a18; see also Ceaser, *Liberal Democracy and Political Science*, and Rahe's discussion of Tocqueville's diagnosis of, and proposed remedies for, democratic immoderation and decline in *Soft Despotism*, 155–220.

those resources in the Western tradition that provide balance to his liberal conceptions of philosophy, humanity, and politics.

Tocqueville's adaptation of Montesquieu's philosophy does not echo ancient or modern or Christian philosophy per se, but offers a modern appropriation of a broadly Thomistic harmonizing of philosophy and religion. While Tocqueville is a modern and a liberal, he is, as noted, a strange one. The extremes evident in modern liberal theory and practice provoked him to revive a medieval sensibility recast for modern dilemmas and possibilities, embracing both the justice of human equality and the dangers accompanying it. Montesquieu had prepared the way for this turn by defending the benefits and naturalness of religion, and especially Christianity, against the modern irreligion evident in Hobbes and other philosophers.[40] *Democracy in America* further moderates Montesquieuan liberalism by prescribing a dose of the Aristotelian and Thomistic concern with the destiny of the soul while embracing the natural dignity of politics. Tocqueville sought to leaven liberal individualism and egalitarianism by restoring the higher potentiality of politics and civil society as guided by religious principles and practice, while nonetheless departing from the strict teleology of ancient and medieval philosophy.

Tocqueville especially blends traditional concerns about metaphysics and the democratic penchant for everyday practice through his focus on mores. This marks an Aristotelian development of Montesquieu's attention to mores because for Tocqueville, religion and the soul are primary concerns, not one among several important elements (I.2.9, 275, 292, n. 8; see generally 275–88, 298–302). Here one wonders whether Tocqueville's moderate political science learned to blend the Federalist emphasis on constitutional government with the Anti-Federalist emphasis on its moral presuppositions by reflecting upon the balanced statesmanship embodied in Washington's "Farewell Address" and his influence on the founding more generally (see I.2.5, 217–21; see also, e.g., I.1.8, 107, 129, 160n; I.2.7, 241–42; I.2.10, 320; II.2.15, 518). As argued in Chapter Two , the Montesquieuan spirit of the American founding, especially as embodied in its Founding Father, informed its view of both constitutional complexity and principled statesmanship. Tocqueville may have learned from American practice about a theoretical correction to Montesquieu's liberalism. *Democracy in America* develops Washington's model to capture the American spirit more fully than either a strictly Montesquieuan analysis or the predominantly (though not exclusively) liberal, Montesquieuan analysis of *The Federalist*. Like Washington, Tocqueville urges popular government and equal liberal

---

[40] I address Montesquieu's moderation on religion, and developments of it by Washington and Tocqueville, in Chapter 4; for the moment I will note – against scholars severely skeptical of his stance on religion – Rebecca Kingston, "Montesquieu on Religion and the Question of Toleration," in *Montesquieu's Science of Politics*, eds. Carrithers, Mosher, Rahe (Rowman & Littlefield, 2001), 375–408; Kingston develops (at note 4, 399–400) the mid nineteenth century testimony of the French Dominican priest Lacordaire (*Œuvres*, 1880), and recent scholarship by Robert Shackleton and F. T. H. Fletcher, to argue for Montesquieu's sympathy to Christianity.

rights to accommodate dimensions of the Biblical and Western traditions that can moderate the restless quest for equality and individual security.

Indeed, Tocqueville's discovery that America's first point of departure – the equilibrium of liberty and religion – is eroding leads him to endorse the moderate Catholicism evident in America, as well as more extraordinary remedies. That argument initially unfolds in Volume Two, Part I, on "the influence of democracy on intellectual movements in the United States." Volume Two as a whole addresses the importance of civil society and moral culture – ideas, sentiments, mores, and manners – as distinct from the institutions, laws, and political mores mostly analyzed in Volume One (albeit not exclusively so; see Volume Two, Author's Notice, 399, and the untitled preface to Volume One, Part II, 165). Tocqueville's approach across the two volumes, and especially in Volume Two, follows Montesquieu's method throughout *The Spirit of Laws* and most especially in Book 19. Here Montesquieu investigates the "general spirit" of any nation that is formed by its laws, religion, climate, history, ideas, and other elements; his larger aim, however, is to note what accords with liberty and natural right as well as what does not. Montesquieu is not a determinist about the factors shaping politics and mores, since he knows that philosophers and other legislators can counteract climate, or history, or mores for good or for ill. His second (and less famous) study of England arises at the end of this book for precisely this reason; having investigated in prior Books and earlier in Book 19 what effect climate, history, and other factors have upon laws and politics, the converse now deserves inquiry (19.27). Montesquieu quietly educates founders and more ordinary legislators about what effect laws and institutions can have upon mores, and ultimately he asks philosophers to be more moderate and responsible in their guidance for statesmen (*Spirit* 29.1, 29.19). The English enjoy many advantages from their laws of liberty, but these also produce extremes; both causes and effects need moderating. Tocqueville approaches study of America, and the lessons that both America and Europe could learn from such study, in this spirit. Thus as Volume Two unfolds, each of its four Parts shifts – from initially investigating the influence of democratic laws and political mores upon social mores and civil society to exploring the converse. He notices good effects of democracy and egalitarianism but also bad effects, including those that ultimately could destroy any decent democratic self-government by undermining its foundations. In each Part of Volume Two, he therefore educates "moralists," educators, and statesmen about how they in turn could reform laws, institutions, or practices so as to counteract the effects of mass democracy and egalitarianism, thereby sustaining good mores or counteracting bad ones.

The most striking of such efforts occurs in Part II of Volume Two , to encourage a role for government in indirectly fostering and buttressing religious faith (II.2.15, "How Religious Beliefs at Times Turn the Souls of Americans toward Immaterial Enjoyments," and II.2.17, "How in Times of Equality and Doubt it is Important to Move Back the Object of Human Actions"). The first half of this Part (II.2, Chapters 1–9) sets the stage by diagnosing an excessive attachment to equality in America and modern democracy generally, at the expense of liberty and higher human life (II.2.1), then focuses upon the first of two bad effects that modern egalitarianism produces in social sentiments. This is his famous analysis of the malady of individualism, an excessive turn inward upon the self, at most including one's friends and family but forsaking citizenship in political and civil senses (II.2.2). Tocqueville also notes how Americans combat individualism with civic participation and free associations, and how the doctrine of self-interest well understood also can temper individualism's effects or prevent it altogether. Here we see the grand strategy of democracy in moderation at work, urging democrats to find resources within their tradition so as to be the best of democrats, even to rise toward republicanism and its more fully human life. Tocqueville turns in the second half of this Part (Chapters 10–20) to address the second bad effect of egalitarianism, its materialism. The two chapters on religion near the end of this section constitute one of the peaks of the entire work, and its philosophy of moderation. The chapter in between indirectly announces moderation as the theme; it examines "How Excessive Love of Well-Being Can Be Harmful to Well-Being" (II.2.16). The chapters on religion surrounding it provide the moderating remedy. In the first of these, Tocqueville acknowledges how controversial it is to urge "the politicians" to "act every day" as if they believed in the soul's immortality, "conforming scrupulously to religious morality in great affairs" (II.2.15, 521).

His model for urging this remedy may have been Washington, for earlier he emphatically praises both "this great man" and Marshall's biography of him, and quotes the Farewell Address (I.1.2, 30, n. 1; I.1.8, 107; I.2.5, 217–21; I.2.10, 320; see also I.1.3, 46, 50, 52). Indeed, *Democracy in America* names only two exemplary statesmen guided by ethical principles and governing in moderation, thereby resisting the clamor of majority opinion – Governor John Winthrop, and Washington (I.1.2, 42; I.2.5, 217–21). For both models he draws upon the analysis of these statesmen by another statesman, Marshall's *Life of Washington*. Winthrop, however, embodies the best and worst of America's first epoch – to include the Puritan fusion of church and state and the "bizarre, tyrannical," and shameful excesses in enforcing Biblical morality through penal law, both of which Tocqueville repudiates (I.1.2, 39; I.2.9, 283). What is needed as America continues its experiment is the moderate and indirect, but powerfully sincere, education in religious principle provided by Washington in America's second epoch. Tocqueville warns that such "great characters are disappearing" and that "the race of American statesmen has shrunk" in America's third epoch, Jacksonian democracy (I.1.3, 50; I.1.8, 130; I.2.5, 188; I.2.7, 246–7; I.2.9, 265). His new political science calls for citizens and especially statesmen educated in religious and constitutional principle who can gently inculcate the moderate aims of ordered liberty and of the dignity of the soul's temporal and eternal destiny. As argued in Chapter 4, modern constitutional parlance would suggest that Tocqueville follows Washington in favoring the accomodationist view about religious liberty – that the First Amendment ensures separation of church and state but not of religion and politics – rather than a narrower separationist view.

Tocqueville's moderation thus transcends mushy centrism by weighing in on the side needing support. Still, he seeks to persuade that his emphasis on one element here, or another there, serves the large-minded pursuit of a greater good. He specifically asks readers who may think he has not fully comprehended his vast subject, or failed to maintain the "impartiality" that offers "the truth" to democracy as its friend, nonetheless to "at least do me this justice: I have conceived and pursued my enterprise in the spirit that could make me worthy of success" (II, Preface, 400).[41] Among the most daring yet subtle of such efforts is his steady argument that Enlightenment rationalism overlooks the soul's natural inclination toward religious belief. This is a rational argument, not an appeal from faith or religious authority. It restores an element of natural theology from the classical and medieval traditions. Late-modern theory, in a more anthropocentric era, might term this a philosophical anthropology; Aquinas includes this within a broader "analogy of being" between a divinity known by reason and humans who discern the incompleteness of reason on its own terms.[42]

Tocqueville's liberal and modern disposition precludes any emphatic turn toward Thomism. This partly reflects his own post-Enlightenment concern with excesses of abstract philosophy and rationalism (e.g., II.1, Chapters 3 and 4, on the modern penchant for "general ideas" and abstraction). It also reflects his attention to intellectual mores, since he knows that, in the democratic era, thinking and language "will abandon little by little the terrain of metaphysics and theology" (II.1.16, 454, and II.1.1). Most citizens and statesmen thus would not benefit from argumentation in natural theology even if Tocqueville tried to undertake it. His careful, muted restoration of elements of natural theology thus indicates both philosophical insight and philosophical prudence. The success of the latter is evident partly in the fact that scholars of diverse academic schools or orientations, and both conservative and progressive inclinations, praise Tocqueville's insights about modern democracy – to include his warnings about its need of tempering.[43] His breadth of concerns, including warnings about

---

[41] Hancock places great emphasis upon this passage in "Tocqueville's Responsible Reason."

[42] See, for example, Thomas Aquinas, *Summa Theologiae*. 2nd edn. tr. Fathers of the English Dominican Province. London: Burns, Oates, and Washbourne, 1920, I–II: q. 94, a. 2, in the three concluding points of the *respondio* on the three levels of natural inclinations that constitute precepts of natural law; the third and highest is the human inclination to know the truths about God and to live in society. Since Aristotle is cited rather than any revealed Scripture, this points back to the natural theology of the opening questions of the *Summa* – to include the Five Ways to rationally discern the existence of a divinity (I: q. 2, a. 3). On the broader issues in Aquinas and for philosophy, see Steven A. Long, *Analogia Entis: On the Analogy of Being, Metaphysics, and the Act of Faith* (University of Notre Dame Press, 2011).

[43] Compare Daniel Mahoney, *The Conservative Foundations of the Liberal Order: Defending Democracy against its Modern Enemies and Immoderate Friends* (ISI Books, 2010), and the

materialism and a new industrialist aristocracy (II.2, Chapter 20) but also about a statist, soft despotism (II.4, Chapters 6–8 especially), simultaneously challenge and attract a range of academic and political stances. In part because he declines any systematic metaphysical investigation, he can gain a hearing in our late-modern discourse, which preemptively dismisses thinking about transcendent meaning, laws of our being, or higher natural inclinations. Tocqueville adopts instead an implicitly Aristotelian spirit, adapting Montesquieu's inductive method by adding Pascalian depth. He candidly observes the human costs of modern rationalism, materialism, and rejection of the transcendent sources of truth. These costs range from solipsistic individualism, loss of civic spirit, and technicism or narrowness in education to the prospect of a soft despotism in which a centralized state takes care of us so comfortably that we descend, quietly, from citizens to subjects. Indeed, we could descend further. Such subjects (not anymore citizens) willingly would "renounce the use of their wills" because the provident state "extinguishes their spirits" and "enervates their souls" (II.4.6, 665). Occasional participation, if that, in elections "will not prevent them from losing little by little the faculty of thinking, feeling, and acting by themselves, and thus from gradually falling below the level of humanity." Unlike Nietzsche's apocalyptic diagnosis, however, Tocqueville's warning of a degraded humanity invites us to consider sustainability initiatives before it is too late. He traces the causes of this erosion of freedom, self-government, and liberal democracy to modernity's epistemic closure about an enduring human nature, natural right, natural theology, and religious faith. These principles confront us with limits on our powers and desires, limits beyond human will. If we seek to liberate ourselves from such constraints, natural sanctions arise. There is no free lunch in Tocqueville's cosmological order.[44]

While Tocqueville deepens his emphasis upon such themes as Volume Two unfolds, he stakes his claim to them in the Introduction. Scholarly attention to religion, philosophy, or natural theology in this initial discourse usually concerns his argument that the development of the democratic revolution across centuries of European and North American history is "a providential fact." All human efforts have wittingly or unwittingly been "blind instruments in the hands of God," of "Providence" understood as "sacred" and "the sovereign master's will" (I, Introduction, 6–7). He returns to this view in *Democracy*'s final chapter, striving "to enter into this point of view of God," of the "creator and preserver of men," in which "the greatest well-being of all" is worth the price of lost grandeur and excellence achieved by a few in aristocratic

---

more progressive views in Dana Villa, "Tocqueville and Civil Society," in *The Cambridge Companion to Tocqueville*, 216–44; Villa notes that voices "across the ideological spectrum" invoke Tocqueville, and Mansfield and Winthrop note the same in "Editors' Introduction," *Democracy in America*, xviii.

44 Aristide Tessitore illuminates Tocqueville's quiet appropriation of Aristotelian political science, including a focus on the human soul, in "Aristotle and Tocqueville on Statesmanship," in *Tocqueville and the Art of Democratic Statesmanship*, eds. Danoff and Hebert, 49–72.

ages (II.4.8, 674–75). Tocqueville distinguishes his invocations of Providence from any deterministic – we now might say Hegelian – intention, since in his view, Providence leaves us responsible for deciding whether equality leads "to servitude or freedom, to enlightenment or barbarism, to prosperity or misery" (II.4.8, 676). This insistence upon human responsibility actually is evident from the Introduction, when he invokes a tradition of thinking related to, yet distinct from, philosophy of history or discernment of divine direction in human affairs. While lamenting the European experience of the democratic revolution, with its political and moral upheaval, Tocqueville invokes "the natural bond" that normally unites deeds and beliefs, theories and moral tastes. More particularly, he describes this element of human reality as "the laws of moral analogy" (I, Introduction, 10–11). The echoes of medieval metaphysics and moral philosophy are not immediately apparent, since his focus is the partisan intellectual and political struggles in post-Revolution France between secularist republicans and reactionary Christians. This struggle has broken the natural bond, these laws of analogy between dimensions of our being. Christians should be advocates of democracy, since it is Christianity that "has rendered all men equal before God," while "partisans of freedom" should embrace such a religion since it provides the mores to support moral and social order in the new polities (I, Introduction, 11). Instead, reactionary Christians battle against democracy and freedom, while advocates of philosophy and science, formerly noble pursuits, now are "striving to make man into matter" by developing utilitarian inquiries that eschew justice, and that pit science against religious or moral beliefs. By contrasting material "well-being" and "virtue," the latter supposedly are "champions of modern civilization" but in fact lack "morality." Thus, "virtue is without genius and genius without honor," and an intellectual and moral vertigo ensues in which "nothing seems any longer to be forbidden or permitted, or honest or shameful, or true or false" (I, Introduction, 11–12).

This is not a theological argument invoking revealed Scripture. Tocqueville does conclude by returning to Providence, suggesting that this moral and intellectual chaos – these competing "intellectual miseries that surround us" – is not inevitable: "God prepares a firmer and calmer future for European societies" (I, Introduction, 12). This confusion instead is an anomaly, since the laws of moral analogy have "been noticeable in all times," and surely "all centuries" have not suffered "a world in which nothing is linked." He cannot believe that "the Creator has made man" to endure this; it must be human choice that inflicts this novel condition upon society. If it were otherwise, he would have to "doubt" God's "justice" (I, Introduction, 10–12). His next move, therefore, is inductive – to point to the "one country in the world" that has completed the democratic revolution without suffering its most destructive aspects. America, while not flawless, has retained the laws of moral analogy, the natural bond linking morals and deeds (12). The intellectual and moral chaos of Europe is not destined, and can be corrected or avoided. This quietly metaphysical argument, moving from observed phenomena to logical and transcendent implications, is the first of many such moments in the work. These are philosophically suspect for some scholars given their brevity, but Tocqueville's new political science adapts an old science, and has other aims in mind. Thus, when discussing the tyranny of the majority – indeed, recommending "precautions that ought to be taken to moderate" popular authority – he implicitly invokes the classical and medieval concept of the *ius gentium*, the law of nations, which Aquinas considers a derivation of natural law. "A general law exists that has been made or at least adopted not only by the majority of this or that people, but by the majority of all men. This law is justice. Justice therefore is the boundary of each people's right" (I.2.7, 240).[45] Another such moment is his invocation of virtue as the core principle of rights (I.2.6, 227). These passages provide a path from the modern, democratic mind back toward serious consideration of natural law and metaphysics in relation to politics. To attract the modern and democratic mind, Tocqueville knows he cannot directly invoke classical and medieval authority or metaphysical argument (II.1.1). Nonetheless, he appropriates and adapts these concepts to form the intellectual and moral anchor of his philosophy of moderation. These will guide analysis and judgment about how the legislator, as moralist or statesman, must discern extremes and correct for them. Because, like Aristotle and Montesquieu, he knows that there are no perfect human regimes and all are fragile or mortal, the legislator has a particular duty to consider sustainability both in the ordering and maintenance of a polity. Neither the moralist nor the statesman can take for granted the social and moral capital, or the institutional legitimacy, needed to build and sustain a decent social and political order.

Tocqueville's deepening of modern moderation thus admires the American effort to form not a mixed regime *qua* classical political science but rather a spirit blending classical, medieval, and modern ideals. He explicitly eschews the concept of a "mixed government" that grants legitimacy to the principles of monarchy, aristocracy, and democracy by blending elements of each (I.2.7). America is democratic in spirit, resting on popular sovereignty. Nonetheless, he concludes that discussion by noting the need for constitutional checks against the democratic spirit "that can restrain its advance and give it time to moderate itself" (241). He then sketches the balanced constitutionalism of Montesquieu and Publius, with a bicameral legislature, an independent and capable executive, and an independent judiciary (I.2.7, 242). This is the political science of moderation, and Tocqueville celebrates this complex constitutionalism throughout the work, not only in Part 1 of Volume I. To establish and sustain such a constitutionalism requires, however, moral and intellectual resources in

---

[45] On *ius gentium* in relation to *lex naturalis* in Aquinas, see, for example, *Summa Theologiae*, I–II, q. 95, a. 2, and a. 4; (on keeping agreements as a universally recognized principle of justice) II–II, q. 57, a. 3; and II–II, q. 77, a. 1; see Samuel Gregg, "Natural Law and the Law of Nations," in *Natural Law, Natural Rights, and American Constitutionalism* (Witherspoon Institute). Available http://www.nlnrac.org/earlymodern/law-of-nations. (accessed May 2013).

the people as well as in those who educate and serve in office. This in turn requires openness to the tradition of philosophical moderation, and to the need for modern democracy to find its best self in moderation. Tocqueville does not deem America a flawless attempt to make an amalgam of classical, medieval, and modern ideals. His new political science does help us to make sense of Washington's forging of an alloy that is more than a hodgepodge, and Tocqueville elevates him accordingly. He also explains why that alloy might well strain or fracture in later generations. Still, that result is not inevitable; he concurs with Washington, and Publius, that we have choices.

PART II

MODERATION AND STATESMANSHIP AT HOME AND ABROAD

If moderation means avoiding intellectual extremes, it suggests a wariness of single-mindedness. Montesquieu's concept of the "spirit" of laws thus seeks to comprehend many elements and relations across several domains of reality. As noted, his philosophical moderation also informs the two sets of laws he defines in Book 1 of *The Spirit of Laws* as guiding, first, his background inquiry, and then his focal investigations. The first of these tripartite sets of laws – the basic laws given by God (religion), philosophers (morals), and legislators (political and civil laws) – redress humankind's capacity to deny the laws and aims of our nature, given our intelligence and freedom (*The Spirit of Laws*, Book 1, Chapter 1, end). At the end of Book 1 he specifies that his work primarily examines the last of these three laws, and he then develops a second set of three laws under that category of political and civil laws (1.3). If Part I of this book has explored the first, broader set of laws, these chapters in Part II examine the second set. Montesquieu argues that to secure peace and order, men must develop an interrelated set of three kinds of political and civil law; these should accord with the prior laws of equity in our nature (1.1) and the general laws of our nature (1.2). This second set comprises the right of nations governing international affairs; the political right governing the constitutional order of rulers and ruled, and the civil right that orders civil and criminal laws affecting individuals (*Spirit*, 1.3).

This comprehensive, two-level schema of laws provides a background principle informing the complex structure and scope of *The Spirit of Laws* and also, in a way, *Democracy in America*. To understand, found, reform, and sustain liberal polities in accord with moderation, the political philosopher as legislator obviously must understand the latter set – the principles of law governing international, constitutional, and domestic affairs. However, the first set of laws must inform the second. Montesquieu and Tocqueville argue that earlier modern philosophers and the radical Enlightenment were immoderate for failing to adequately incorporate religion and morality into the theory and practice of a liberal polity. Tocqueville further implies that Montesquieu himself placed this first set of laws too far in the background, or at any rate that the new reality of the democratic revolution requires revision of this first effort at modern moderation. Nonetheless, both philosophers agree that the complexity of human reality indicates significant limits to earlier modern theory. Judgment is needed by both philosophers and statesmen to negotiate the relationship between the two sets of laws – between the religious and moral laws derived from divinity or nature and the more particular laws of humankind. There is further need for judgment regarding how universals and particulars meet within any of the three domains of political law. Tocqueville does not characterize his understanding of laws through this schema, but it is not accidental that he addresses this full range of right and law. This comprehensive approach leads both philosophers to devote serious attention to statesmanship, historical understanding, and culture while also insisting that natural right undergirds international, political, and civil laws – and must guide prudential judgment.

The chapters in Part II try to reflect the range of this political science of moderation, and thus they address this balance between theory and practice, philosophy and statesmanship. The modern tradition of moderation succeeded to a great degree in its aim to teach legislators and citizens, as is evident in its fundamental influence upon the American polity. Perhaps not accidentally that polity has become the globe's dominant political, military, and cultural power. It is paradoxical that our intellectual and policy elites now tend to eschew or overlook the moderate philosophy that still informs the modern liberal democracies to some degree, since that philosophy helps to explain and guide our debates about domestic and foreign policies. In the hopes of inviting renewed acquaintance with this tradition, three chapters explore first a fundamental question of the character of politics and polity as manifested mostly internally, then the principles and character guiding external relations, and finally the question of how a polity should study politics and educate both citizens and statesmen.

Scholars of Leo Strauss's school have recovered the fundamental importance in the Western philosophical tradition of the "theologico-political question." That said, Strauss's school has not been as helpful in understanding Montesquieu's effort to find a higher middle ground regarding the relationship of reason and revelation, or more particularly political liberty and religion. Chapter 4 takes a fresh look at Montesquieu's analysis of religion in *The Spirit of Laws*, then explores its effects on the American polity through Washington's achievement of a high middle ground. Tocqueville's more famous analysis of religion and liberty is indebted to his study of both his French predecessor and the American Founding Father. Chapter 5 argues, in a similar pattern, for a deeper understanding of the foreign policy of liberal democracy through recovery of the connections between Montesquieu's moderate liberalism, Washington's constitutionalist statesmanship, and Tocqueville's philosophy. Chapter 6 turns to an age-old question of political philosophy – who will educate the guardians and the citizens – by assessing how adequately the discipline of political science now studies our liberal constitutional order, and how it prepares citizens and statesmen to understand and sustain that order. A now-overlooked scholar of political science, Herbert Storing, addressed such questions in the mid-twentieth century and developed a constitutionalist political science informed by moderation. That endeavor still is salient for our anxieties about civic and intellectual culture today.

To be clear, the argument is not that Montesquieu, Washington, or Tocqueville foresaw an easy path to a golden mean regarding liberty and religion, or easy guidance regarding war and peace. If moderation can cultivate prudence regarding these fundamental issues of the polity and its internal character, it offers hope that the extremes and errors in the journey of liberal democracy, whether stemming from religion or politics, can be reduced or ameliorated. Tocqueville in particular warns of the likely difficulty, and of a broader problem. He noted happily in *Democracy in America* that the Americans were not as consumed by abstract ideas and doctrines as his own countrymen were, but he also noted a rising appetite in America for such thinking. Alas, American academic study of political science and international relations has become entirely French, in this sense, since he wrote. Only a few academic voices take seriously Washington's principled prudence regarding either domestic or foreign policy. Storing warned that the same sort of doctrinairism had begun to dominate all of political science, and that the new scientism paradoxically provides less guidance for actually governing or making decisions. Study of Washington's efforts to forge both a constitutional order and the principles of moderation to animate it offers a constructive challenge to the predominant intellectual view that rational doctrines are self-executing, or that constitutions and legal regimes are sufficient. These philosophers, a statesman, and a recent scholar renew an older awareness that a distinctive character is needed in citizens and the polity to produce serious or large-minded parties, candidates, and electoral contests, as well as serious office holders to debate how to serve first principles and operate the constitutional system in new circumstances.

Montesquieu, Washington, Tocqueville, and Storing all note in their distinct ways a tendency in modern rationalism for producing polarization, about ideas of philosophy and human nature and also about practical guidance for politics. The audacity to discard all earlier learning does not yield moderation in theory, practice, or civil debate. Of course, all four of these figures are modern minds, but their recommendation is to tack back a bit. They seek not a radical departure from the whole philosophical tradition but a revision or moderating of it. Storing writes more than a century after Tocqueville's observations about what the radical Enlightenment had done in Europe and might do in America, and by the mid-twentieth century, the Progressives dominated the social sciences. Storing argued for blending the proven insights from the political science of Montesquieu and *The Federalist* with reasonable insights from the new approaches, but also warned about the excesses of a rationalist, putatively value-free science of human affairs. This kind of moderation offers valuable resources in our era of partisan contestation about domestic and foreign affairs that, interestingly, is as deep as ever in the second century of Progressive dominance in American life. Of course, we always have had rancorous debate in American politics, even leading toward civil war, but the science of the Progressives has not tamed such rancor through a higher stage of political rationality. We fret about destructive partisanship and polarization, and we crave better leadership and also studies thereof. Storing extends the lineage of Montesquieu, the American founders, and Tocqueville by offering a salient model for inquiry and civil debate, and also a rediscovery of statesmanship and the principles that inform it.

4

Religion and Liberty in America
The Moderate Spirit of Montesquieu and Tocqueville

America still is largely exceptional among modern liberal democracies for the balance it holds in both law and politics between two principles which, Tocqueville noted, are not happily aligned in most polities – liberty and tolerance on the one hand and respect for transcendent sources of truth and morality on the other.[1] It is striking that Tocqueville selects this balance, or moderation, as the defining "point of departure" for America, thus for understanding its political institutions, political culture, and broader social and moral culture. This principle of moderation does not explain everything about America; moreover, he warns that it is threatened by modern philosophy and democratic mores, and paradoxically, by elements of Protestantism itself. He tries to bolster that founding blend, but also to further moderate or elevate it. It is at once a defining feature of America, and a guide for what America and modern liberal democracy must do to be sustainable. This moderation about religion and politics is, in Tocquevillean philosophy, a delicately calibrated insight into a complex phenomenon. Both as an insight and in its practical manifestations, it is an equipoise full of tension. These qualities suggest that Tocqueville drew upon Montesquieu as much or more than upon Pascal in discerning the salutary balance of liberty and religion, and upon these two more than Rousseau.

Tocqueville does not adopt a "civil religion" doctrine in which religion is subservient to, and tolerated only as useful to, the state and politics – a milder version of the Erastianism of Hobbes and Rousseau. Nor does he fully accept Locke's theory of separation of religious and political authority, with its

---

[1] See Alexis de Tocqueville, *Democracy in America*, eds. Harvey Mansfield and Delba Winthrop (University of Chicago Press, 2000 [1835, 1840]), vol. I, Part 1, Chapter 2, "On the Point of Departure," 43. This chapter draws upon a paper delivered at the Oxford Round Table of Oxford University, England, in July 2010 and also upon talks delivered in India in 2007–2008 while a Fulbright Scholar at the University of Delhi in New Delhi.

selective religious toleration. Such views are not as hostile to religion or meta-physical thinking as those of Hobbes, Spinoza, or Rousseau, but they are cold to religion, viewing it as a problem that liberalism must manage.[2] Tocqueville admires America's mutually respectful accommodation between religion and political liberty because it is not a *modus vivendi* or mere pragmatism, but constitutive of the political order. The roots of his admiration and also of the accommodation itself lie in Montesquieu and the openness to religion, and to classical and medieval thought, he provided by moderating the Enlightenment. To understand America and its influence on modern liberal democracy we need to revisit the scholarly rendition of Montesquieu as a subtle but nonetheless radical critic of religion, and also revisit the view of Tocqueville as Lockean, and utilitarian, about religion and politics. Tocqueville's view of a more constructive relationship between religion and liberty, constructive for both the city and the soul, rests in part upon his admiration for Pascal's turn from modern rationalism to metaphysics and religion; however, the larger constitutional form as well as the balanced spirit derive from Montesquieu. Many Montesquieu scholars beg to differ, especially those who highlight the traditionalist Catholic critics of supposedly antitheological views in *The Spirit of Laws*. To this school, his eighteenth-century Catholic critics expose Montesquieu's effort to develop a subtle version of Lockean separationism and anticlericalism. Montesquieu rejected that view in his lifetime, and curiously enough, the Catholic priest who a century later took up Tocqueville's chair in the French Academy in 1861, upon Tocqueville's death, also argued that Montesquieu was sympathetic to religion. The Dominican theologian Lacordaire declared *The Spirit of Laws* "the most beautiful defense of Christianity in the eighteenth century."[3]

As Chapter 2 argued, Montesquieu's presence in the American mind from the 1750s deeply informs its constitutionalism; but it also shapes the Puritan, Anglican, and more broadly Protestant conceptions of how to blend liberty and religious belief in the new order. Tocqueville later draws upon Montesquieu's philosophic principle of balancing and reconciling diverse views, and on the American practice (itself informed by Montesquieu's philosophy) of forging an alloy of views. Tocqueville fashions his own way of praising yet refining the American achievement, while deepening Montesquieu's accommodation of liberty and religion.[4]

[2] Harvey Mansfield surveys the basic issues, and concludes (in a Tocquevillean spirit) that the views of religion and politics developed by Hobbes, Spinoza, and Locke – which teach humans not to care for their souls, certainly not in relation to politics – ultimately "endanger freedom," in "The Religious Issue and the Origin of Modern Constitutionalism," *America's Constitutional Soul* (Johns Hopkins University Press, 1991), 101–14.
[3] Françoise Mélonio discusses Lacordaire's address to the Academy in *Tocqueville and the French*, tr. Beth Raps (University of Virginia Press, 1998), 112–18.
[4] A rich exchange of views on the broader issues, centered upon Michael Zuckert's effort to incorporate Protestant Christianity into a largely Lockean amalgam of American founding principles, is *Protestantism and the American Founding*, eds. Engeman and Zuckert (University of Notre

Recovering Liberal Exceptionalism in Religion

The spirit of Aristotle, Montesquieu, and Tocqueville recommends an initial turn to practice and then an effort to develop theory that accounts for it and guides it. One fact of the twenty-first century world is that the American balance of religion and liberty is less exceptional than when Tocqueville observed it in the 1830s, given changes both in America and globally. Other peoples and states have developed some degree of equilibrium between liberal freedom and the public (as well as private) importance of religious faith, albeit to include continuing controversy and tensions, even occasional violence; examples might include Turkey, Indonesia, and India. On the other hand, America is less religious as a country than it was in Tocqueville's era. Nonetheless, liberal exceptionalism in religion survives: there is more public and cultural prominence for religious belief in America than in any other advanced liberal democracy, while there also is more religious liberty than in states with a deeply religious culture.[5] This balance has been neither static nor tranquil in America, but it is an achievement of moderation in contrast to the extremes prevalent in many governments. Many peoples live under, on the one hand, enforced or cultural secularism, ranging from China's oppression to the privatizing of religion under France's model of laicism, or, on the other, enforced religious orthodoxy. Indeed, the American moderation between these potential extremes in human nature and politics partly is evident in the very dynamism of and debates about this equilibrium, as we alternately surge between moments of secularism and religiosity in politics, the courts, or academic debate. Nor is the American disposition about religion and politics merely "agonistic" as recent political theorists deploy that term – ever constructed out of thin air in a succession of contingent skirmishes. It is, rather, a Socratic dialectic around settled truths and the enduring tensions they comprise. India, now in its seventh decade as a liberal democracy, is perhaps another example of a dialectical, dynamic political culture of religious liberty that is finding a middle ground. In its early decades it implemented policies of secularism and equal status for distinct religious communities that eventually provoked the rival extreme of majoritarian religious reaction in the Hindu nationalist movement. The great critic of Indian secularism, T. N. Madan, warned after several decades of this rationalist model that one extreme begot another: "in truth it is the marginalization of religious faith,

---

Dame Press, 2004). Zuckert and the range of responding scholars occasionally cite Tocqueville's retrospective analysis, but the volume's largely Locke-centric view of the founding leaves no room for Montesquieu's influence.

5 Two recent sources from the voluminous literature are the sociological analysis of Robert Putnam and David Campbell, *American Grace: How Religion Divides and Unites Us* (Simon & Schuster, 2010), and the more political focus of Kenneth D. Wald, *Religion and Politics in the United States*, 4th edn. (Rowman & Littlefield, 2003). A survey of the literature and the phenomena in a generally Tocquevillean spirit is José Cassanova, "The Religious Situation in the United States 175 Years After Tocqueville," in *Crediting God: Sovereignty and Religion in the Age of Global Capitalism*, ed. Vatter (Fordham University Press, 2011).

which is what secularization is, that permits the perversion of religion."[6] In the past two decades a constructive center may have been found and seems to be holding, defined by less secularist rhetoric from governing elites, more open discussion of the political importance of religious beliefs and religious plural-ism, and repudiation of religious bigotry or crude majoritarian nationalism.[7] In contrast, France's recent political violence, terrorist attacks, and rise in hatred toward Jews suggest that its post-Revolution doctrine of *laïcité* faces grave chal-lenges in an era of greater Muslim immigration and assertiveness.[8]

   As with any analysis of ethics or politics that seeks truth by discerning mod-eration between poles, it is crucial to define, and ground, the extremes and the spectrum between them. In this Aristotelian and Montesquieuan spirit, a provi-sional framing of legal and academic debates on religion and politics in America can note the rival sets of philosophers, theologians, and founding statesmen typ-ically cited to buttress two rival poles. At issue here, as well, is the meaning of liberal exceptionalism in religion – as the separation of religion and philosophy demanded by the radical Enlightenment (itself echoing Epicurus, Lucretius, and Machiavelli among earlier philosophers), or as a balance and mutual accom-modation between religion, philosophy, and liberty. In the American debate, one school cites a lineage stemming from Spinoza, Hobbes, and Locke that informs Madison and Jefferson, to support a separationist or secularist view. This defines America as a modern liberal regime with core principles of individ-ual autonomy and security, and a public sphere defined by secular reason and modern science.[9] The opposing school cites a lineage from Luther and Calvin to the Puritans and such founders as Rev. John Witherspoon, teacher of and correspondent with Madison and Washington. This view supports a claim that

---

[6] T. N. Madan, "Secularism in Its Place," *Journal of Asian Studies* 46 (1987), 747–59, at 749; see also "Whither Indian Secularism?," *Modern Asian Studies* 27 (1993), 667–97, at 695.

[7] See *Secularism and Its Critics*, ed. Rajeev Bhargava (Oxford University Press, 1999); Sumit Gan-guly, "The Crisis of Indian Secularism," *Journal of Democracy* 14 (October 2003), 11–25; *Will Secular India Survive?*, ed. Mushirul Hasan (imprintOne, 2004); *The Crisis of Secularism in India*, eds. Anuradha Dingwaney Needham and Rajeshwari Sunder Rajan (Duke University Press, 2006); and the observations and analysis (occasionally hyperbolic) in Martha C. Nuss-baum, *The Clash Within: Democracy, Religious Violence, and India's Future* (Harvard University Press, 2007).

[8] I discuss France's clash of extremes between rigid secularism and Islamism in "America's Neglected Ideal of Moderation," *The American Interest* (online, January 29, 2015); www .the-american-interest.com/2015/01/29/americas-neglected-ideal-of-moderation/ (accessed November 14, 2015).

[9] As noted, see the range of views in *Protestantism and the American Founding*, eds. Engeman and Zuckert; for the Lockeans in that volume, see Zuckert, "Natural Rights and Protestant Politics," and more generally Leonard Levy, *The Establishment Clause: Religion and the First Amendment* (Macmillan Publishing, 1986), Thomas Pangle, *The Spirit of Modern Republicanism: The Moral Vision of the American Founders and the Philosophy of John Locke* (University of Chicago Press, 1988), and Isaac Kramnick and Laurence Moore, *The Godless Constitution: The Case Against Religious Correctness* (W.W. Norton, 1996).

America was founded as a Christian, or Protestant republican, nation.[10] The argument proposed here is that neither pole captures the moderate, balanced view held by most founders from the 1770s to the 1790s, embedded in the complex clauses on religion and politics in America's three main founding documents. This is because neither pole quite explains how its fundamental lens, Lockeanism or Protestantism, would in itself be disposed to develop an amalgam or alloy of these philosophical and religious elements.

If Montesquieu proposed a philosophy that reconciles seemingly rival principles, and this was fundamentally influential for the founders, it makes sense to examine his views of religion as a model for the American project. As noted, certain philosophical schools declare such an approach to be, by *a priori* standards, an incoherent muddle. Such schools would not be inclined to find a coherent equilibrium in the American amalgam on religion and politics, but would reduce the phenomenon to one dominant principle or another. This, however, does not make sense of the consistent complexity and balance of the American mind – ranging from invocations of "the Laws of Nature and Nature's God" and the "protection of Divine Providence" in the Declaration of Independence (1776); to the ban on religious tests for office but also the special status of Sundays in the Constitution (1787); to the religious clauses on nonestablishment and free exercise in the Bill of Rights (1789); and, finally, to the Founding Father's persistent appeals to both rights and biblical Providence as guiding principles, along with more particularly Christian beliefs and virtues. It is more plausible to find a political and philosophical moderation in this complex blend of views than to find either dominance by any one principle or a mere cacophony of ideas forged for the utility of the moment.[11]

The often-neglected lineage that undergirds this principled moderation stems from Montesquieu and shapes the Founder, Washington; it further extends to Montesquieu's nineteenth-century heir Tocqueville, whose *Democracy in America* comprehends *The Federalist* and Anti-Federalist writings in capturing the spirit of America's political founding. Awareness of the serious philosophic and constitutionalist pedigree of the moderate view on religion and politics illuminates some of the legal, political, and academic debates about religion and politics that continue in American life and other liberal democracies today. This is not to say that a philosophical and historical approach easily

---

[10] See, for example, Barry Shain, *The Myth of American Individualism: The Protestant Origins of American Political Thought* (Princeton University Press, 1994); James Hutson, *Religion and the New Republic: Faith in the Founding of America* (Rowman & Littlefield, 2000); Philip Hamburger, *Separation of Church and State* (Harvard University Press, 2002); Daniel Dreisbach, *Thomas Jefferson and the Wall of Separation Between Church and State* (New York University Press, 2002); and Hutson, *Forgotten Features of the Founding: The Recovery of the Role of Religion in the New American Republic* (Lexington Press, 2003).

[11] An excellent statement of this moderate view, suggesting the importance of Washington for studying the founders' project to blend religion and liberty, is Vincent Phillip Muñoz, *God and the Founders: Madison, Washington, and Jefferson* (Cambridge University Press, 2009).

settles subsequent controversies stemming from new facts and circumstances – ranging from the questions recently posed by certain Islamic practices imported to the Western democracies that clash with liberal principles of equality between men and women, or how to accommodate religious liberty of more traditional Christians with the advance of claims for gay rights. Nonetheless, such a recovery can promote a moderate disposition among rival arguments and advocates by revealing that the perpetuation of these disputes itself reflects the balance between extremes sought by America's founders. Apart from the classic common law of England, which was a main source for American political and legal thought, Montesquieu is the clearest source of a principle of moderation that informs America's constitutional reasoning on religion and politics.[12] Explaining this requires grappling with, in the bulk of this chapter, the carefully calibrated balance about religion and liberalism in his complex political philosophy. A coda on the development of his ideas evident in Washington and Tocqueville seeks to illuminate both Montesquieu's philosophy and how it would be helpful for the liberal democracies in a world now increasingly polarized between Enlightenment modernism and religious devotion. That said, as Tocqueville predicted and as Americans would recognize today, the polarization between Enlightenment and religion was nascent in America and could easily threaten its exceptional moderation.

Indeed, our crises have given us reason to see the importance of this topic and Montesquieu's neglected contribution, even though his moderate conception of religion and politics was declared dated, or out of step with the progress of history, during the nineteenth and twentieth centuries. The philosophies of communism, fascism, progressive liberalism, and postmodernism were dominant or ascendant in the West, and despite their many disagreements, all heralded the epoch of humanity's maturity. Religion, understood as superstitious cultural practices of the unscientific and irrationalist ages of human development, would fade and disappear. The principle of separationism or laicism in liberal thought promised to disentangle religion and politics ostensibly to the advantage of both but especially to the advantage of the individual's right to either believe or not – thus allowing the state to develop free of the strictures of traditional religious doctrine. However, as separationism developed in the modern period, its underlying skepticism about religion became evident. The stance toward religion in Rawlsian, analytical liberalism advocated protecting a rational sphere of politics and public discourse from religious irrationality, requiring that the latter be contained in a private sphere. In political cultures with some foundation for respecting individual liberty and equality of rights among citizens, this approach mostly has yielded a gradually secularizing politics. This is especially true in Western Europe, where this secularist, laicist view

---

[12] On the common law dimension, see James Stoner, "Religious Liberty & Common Law: Free Exercise Exemptions & American Courts," *Polity* 26 (1993), 1–24, and more generally, *Common Law Liberty: Rethinking American Constitutionalism* (University Press of Kansas, 2003).

has predominated, and to a lesser degree in America, where such secularism still competes with the older tradition of separation-but-accommodation between religious liberty and political expression of religious views.

The fundamental issue here is whether religious liberty requires, as separationism or secularism believes, a view that political liberty and religious faith are by definition adversaries such that liberty requires protection from faith. Even in America the trend during the twentieth century toward secularism in the federal courts and university elites had provoked a counter-reaction, by century's end, from traditional Christians to reassert their place in public life and discourse. This phenomenon often is studied in terms of a polarization of American politics over religion, and on related issues of culture and social values, caused by the rise of a "Christian right" or religious fundamentalism. Many elites in academia, the press, and politics who adopt secularism do not consider, however, that polarization requires two poles. Traditional religious voices were responding to the new predominance of a pole of secularism or separationism that had departed from a constitutional and philosophical middle ground.[13] Moreover, several scholars have explored in recent decades the phenomenon of a de-secularization of politics in many liberal democracies, and in global affairs. The long-held thesis among elite Western liberals that modernization entails secularization seems to apply only to Western Europe, making it the exception rather than the norm or vanguard of the future. The work of Peter Berger, among others, suggests that we are not at some rationalist, scientific "end of history." We should take seriously the possibility that an enduring human nature, across time and culture, will rightly invest great importance in questions and practices of transcendent meaning.[14]

Montesquieu's Delineation of Moderation, Liberty, and Religion

As noted in Chapter 2, Montesquieu was cited by the American founders more than the philosophers of radical Enlightenment (Spinoza, Hobbes, Locke, Rousseau) during the two decades of founding a new constitution and Bill of Rights, so the relative scholarly neglect of his work is unfortunate. A further complication is that several recent analyses of religion in *The Spirit of Laws* (1748) argue that Montesquieu subtly deepens the anticlerical rationalism of Machiavelli and Locke. Beneath a veneer of accommodation with faith, he

---

[13] One scholar noting this double-pole reality, giving equal credit for friction to the school of separationism or secularism, is Wald, *Religion and Politics in the United States*; see also Cassanova, "The Religious Situation in the United States."

[14] *The Desecularization of the World: Resurgent Religion and World Politics*, ed. Peter Berger (Eerdmans, 1999); Peter Berger, Grace Davie, and Effie Fokas, *Religious America, Secular Europe?: A Theme and Variations* (Ashgate, 2008); *Between Relativism and Fundamentalism: Religious Resources for a Middle Position*, ed. Peter Berger (Eerdmans, 2009); and see also the many resources at the Pew Forum on Religion & Public Life, at http://pewforum.org/, especially under "Publications."

emphasizes not only toleration but also the privatizing of religion.[15] The bold-est version argues that he cunningly advocates a radical Enlightenment vision of a modern world in which religion is set on a path of destruction, with politics guided by only the materialist lights of science and global commerce.[16] An alternative analysis recapitulates a more traditional view of Montesquieu as a liberal Christian or deist who rejects a strict separation of church and state, while nonetheless being a functionalist who subordinates faith to its utility for politics.[17] The strength of this latter view is its awareness of Montesquieu's own appreciation of complexity in human action and thought, even if it places a narrow emphasis on his utilitarian praise for Christianity as a check on power. This range of views highlights a perennial difficulty in approaching Montesquieu's philosophy, that to understand his views on any topic, one must first account for the principle of philosophical moderation or equilibrium informing *The Spirit of Laws* as a whole. Because little scholarship adequately addresses his declaration that moderation is the key to his masterwork (*Spirit*, Book 29, Chapter 1), or even addresses it at all, our understanding of Montesquieu and his influence remains incomplete.[18] Absent this guiding principle, scholars construe passages on religion in *The Spirit of Laws* as antireligious when Montesquieu instead is

---

[15] Diana Schaub, "Of Believers and Barbarians: Montesquieu's Enlightened Toleration," in *Early Modern Skepticism and the Origins of Toleration*, ed. Levine (Lexington Books, 1999), 225–47; and Robert Bartlett, "On the Politics of Faith and Reason: The Project of Enlightenment in Pierre Bayle and Montesquieu," *Journal of Politics* 63 (2001), 1–28. Each draws upon David Lowenthal, "Book I of Montesquieu's *The Spirit of the Laws*," *American Political Science Review* 53 (1959), 485–98, and Thomas L. Pangle, *Montesquieu's Philosophy of Liberalism: A Commentary on The Spirit of the Laws* (University of Chicago Press, 1973). See also Judith Shklar, *Montesquieu*. Past Masters series (Oxford University Press, 1987). A more subtle argument about Montesquieu's subtle irreligion is Clifford Orwin, "'For Which Human Nature Can Never Be Too Grateful': Montesquieu as the Heir of Christianity," in *Recovering Reason: Essays in Honor of Thomas L. Pangle*, ed. Burns (Lexington Books, 2010).

[16] Thomas L. Pangle, *The Theological Basis of Liberal Modernity in Montesquieu's* Spirit of the Laws (University of Chicago Press, 2010).

[17] Rebecca Kingston, "Montesquieu on Religion and the Question of Toleration," in *Montesquieu's Science of Politics: Essays on The Spirit of Laws*, eds. Carrithers, Mosher, and Rahe (Rowman & Littlefield, 2001), 375–408; Kingston cites arguments by the Dominican theologian Lacordaire, and by scholars Robert Shackleton and F. T. H. Fletcher, that Montesquieu was sympathetic toward Christianity; see n. 4, 399–400. Roger Oake disputes that Montesquieu was irreligious, but finds him more Stoic than Christian in praising religion's utility for moral and social order, in "Montesquieu's Religious Ideas," *Journal of the History of Ideas* 14 (1953), 548–60. Dennis Rasmussen echoes these views and argues that Montesquieu seeks to moderate both religion and rationalism in *The Pragmatic Enlightenment: Recovering the Liberalism of Hume, Smith, Montesquieu, and Voltaire* (Cambridge University Press, 2014), 173–78, but still places too much emphasis on themes of skepticism and utility.

[18] Two further exceptions, with Rasmussen, are Ronald Beiner, *Civil Religion: A Dialogue in the History of Political Philosophy* (Cambridge University Press, 2011), 189–204, and the extensive analysis by Keegan Callanan (discovered after drafting this chapter, but very similar in spirit) in "'Une Infinité de Biens': Montesquieu on Religion and Free Government," *History of Political Thought* 35 (2014): 739–67; both criticize Pangle (2010) and Bartlett while arguing that Montesquieu seeks a middle ground between piety and atheism featuring a tempered, useful conception of Christianity for liberal ends, and both emphasize his principle of moderation.

criticizing an extreme and urging a middle ground justified either by religious belief or reason. Passages more supportive of religion are overlooked; for example, no scholars try to make sense of (or even notice) Montesquieu's unqualified praise in *Spirit* for William Penn's project to establish a Christian republic based upon peace and tolerance (4.6). This is not to deny that Montesquieu is a modern and liberal who diminishes the role for metaphysical thought and religious aspiration in his political philosophy, but rather to insist that his distinctive stance against radical Enlightenment and rationalism applies also to his more sympathetic view of religion and especially Christianity.

As argued in the Prologue and Chapter 1, moderation encapsulates the philosophic complexity Montesquieu thought necessary to comprehend reality, as well as his disposition to avoid extremes in politics. Through both a method and substance defined by balance and reconciliation of rival principles, he seeks to advance liberalism by restoring philosophical appreciation for the multifarious reality of humanity and politics. "I say it, and it seems to me I have brought forth this work only to prove it: the spirit of moderation ought to be that of the legislator; the political good, like the moral good, is always found between two limits."[19] A few chapters later he chastises both ancient and modern political philosophers – Aristotle, Plato, More, Machiavelli, and Harrington – as "legislators" who succumbed to their "passions and prejudices" by reducing all political phenomena to one concept (29.19, 882–83/618). The hero of this epic journey of political philosophizing is, therefore, the philosopher-legislator who watches over mankind by inculcating prudence about how to moderate a given political order and make it more humane (Preface; 1.1; 24.10; 29.19). Indeed, while it was moderate to delay his endorsement of a single principle until completing an extended investigation of the world's complexity (including two of the thirty-one Books devoted to religion), *Spirit* inculcates moderation from its opening passages. He warns in the Preface that only those with the "genius" to exhaustively understand a regime can legitimately propose reforms, since some changes might make matters worse – remarks offered four decades before the French Revolution and its ultimately radical stances toward religion and reason (Preface, 230–31/xlv).

When discussing the spirit of religion in American politics and constitutionalism, it is important to note that the philosophically moderate Montesquieu and his disciple Blackstone, not the social-contractarian and analytic philosopher Locke, were the foremost philosophic influences upon the framers of the Declaration, 1787 Constitution, and Bill of Rights taken as a whole. There are,

---

[19] *De l'Esprit des Lois*, Book 29, Chapter 1, in *Œuvres complètes*, Pléiade edition, ed. Caillois, 2 vols. (Gallimard, 1949–51), 2: 865. Subsequent references are parenthetical, citing book and chapter of *Spirit* and page in vol. 2 of this edition, and also page in the widely available translation *The Spirit of the Laws*, eds. Cohler, Miller, and Stone (Cambridge University Press, 1989) (thus here, 865/602). I have checked my translations against Cohler's and Thomas Nugent's translation (Hafner, 1949 [1750]), occasionally using a more literal, precise rendering.

obviously, distinctively Lockean dimensions to American constitutionalism and the minds of the leading founders, and these are most pronounced regarding the Declaration. As argued in Chapter 2, however, this element should not block our view of the larger complexity of principles that characterizes the American founding, which simultaneously draws upon tenets of not only liberalism and modern republicanism but also classical philosophy, Christianity, and classic common law.[20] Such moderation or balancing of diverse principles pervades American constitutionalism and extends beyond institutions to shape the complexity of American life and thought, evident in its perpetual blending of pluralism and principle, individual rights and public purposes. *The Spirit of Laws* informs and reflects this American complexity more than any other book save the Bible; its other rival for this distinction, Blackstone's *Commentaries on the Laws of England*, in fact draws upon Montesquieu heavily.[21]

Given this guiding principle, it makes sense that Montesquieu's analysis of religion and politics endorses the element of political moderation in Lockean toleration, but also endorses spiritual moderation rather than zeal either for or against religion. We should hold a moderate view of the capacity of reason and modern science to guide human thought and politics in complete separation from an inclination toward faith and transcendent meaning. While Montesquieu is indebted to modern and liberal philosophy, his main works – including the philosophical novel *Persian Letters* (1721) and the philosophical history *Considerations on the Romans* (1734) – comprise a single project to temper rationalism, the distortion of reality caused by artificial insistence upon clarity or demonstrability. His novel blending of the spirits of Montaigne and Newton informs his kinder, gentler view that human nature and natural right seek equilibrium and tranquility through a moderation at once individual and communal, practical and theoretical. While he is most famous for his constitutionalism, which utilizes a portrait of liberty in the English constitution, it is rarely noted that in closing that portrait, Montesquieu warns against "extreme" liberty and extremes "even of reason" that accompany modern political thinking (*Spirit*, 11.4, 395/155; 11.6, 407/166). His predominantly negative idea of liberty, as tranquility or freedom from fear (11.6), does echo Hobbes in

---

[20] Among works cited in Chapter 2, on Montesquieu's influence, are Donald Lutz, "The Relative Influence of European Writers on Late Eighteenth-Century American Political Thought," *American Political Science Review* 78 (1984), 189–97; James Muller, "The American Framers' Debt to Montesquieu," in *The Revival of Constitutionalism*, ed. Muller (University of Nebraska Press, 1988), 87–102; Judith Shklar, "A New Constitution for a New Nation," in *Redeeming American Political Thought*, eds. Hoffman and Thompson (University of Chicago Press, 1998), 158–69; and Paul A. Rahe, *Montesquieu and the Logic of Liberty* (Yale University Press, 2009). On the common law, and more generally on principled complexity, see James Stoner, *Common Law and Liberal Theory: Coke, Hobbes, and the Origins of American Constitutionalism* (University Press of Kansas, 1992), and "The Common Law Spirit of the American Revolution" in *Educating the Prince: Essays in Honor of Harvey Mansfield*, eds. Blitz and Kristol (Rowman & Littlefield, 2000), 192–204.

[21] I argue this in *The Cloaking of Power: Montesquieu, Blackstone, and the Rise of Judicial Activism* (University of Chicago Press, 2003).

defining human nature in rationalist and materialist terms – more by aversion to insecurity than orientation to a higher end. This might provide the rationale for Montesquieu to develop an esoteric doctrine of Lockean skepticism about religion and the need to privatize it. However, as argued in Chapter 1, he repudiates Hobbes by insisting that liberty requires political moderation and the further development of our natural sociability, and that our nature is open to higher aims of magnanimity and greatness, even to the divine (1.1–2; 4.2; 5.12; 24.1).[22]

It seems self-evident that we should privilege the views on religion in Montesquieu's masterwork – which, he noted in the Preface to *The Spirit of Laws*, is the product of twenty years of philosophical labor – but it is worth noting that the balanced view in his mature work marks a shift, especially from *Persian Letters* (1721). Here Montesquieu bitingly satirizes not only Islam but much of European politics and culture, perhaps most shockingly Catholicism and the fusion of church and state – even depicting the papacy as despotic, and mocking the doctrine of the Trinity (letters 29, 59).[23] That said, *Letters* is a philosophical satire that points an acid gaze at not only religion but also many secular institutions and modes of thought, exposing their excesses, absurdities, and injustices, to include the acts of philosophizing, writing, and publishing (e.g., letters 45, 72, 73, 109, 128, 134–37, 145). Moreover, a decade later, his views on religion shifted as he turned from satire to philosophical history, noting in *Considerations on the Romans* (1734) that Christianity is one cause of a modern European world that is less brutal and cruel than ancient Rome (Chapter 15). He includes severe criticisms of Christianity, but mostly focused on the theological disputes fomented by Eastern Orthodox monks and bishops which, he avers, hastened the decline of the Eastern empire. Indeed, he notes that Latin clerics and the Papacy were much wiser about how to balance throne and altar (Chapter 22). He even gives the final word to St. Augustine regarding the controversy between pagans and Christians over which religion caused the collapse of the Western empire (Chapter 19).[24] Ultimately, the analysis of religion in *Spirit*

---

[22] See Mark H. Waddicor, *Montesquieu and the Philosophy of Natural Law* (Martinus Nijhoff, 1970), especially 16–21, 36–45, 64, 76–81, 85–86, 132–33, and 177–92; this contrasts with the analyses by Lowenthal and Pangle cited in note 15, *supra*; as noted in Chapter 1, Rahe's *Montesquieu and the Logic of Liberty* is the most recent work to discern moderation, and distinction from Hobbes and Locke, in Montesquieu's philosophy.

[23] The prevailing scholarly view is that *Letters* is deeply, if cagily, skeptical about religion, for example, Pauline Kra, *Religion in Montesquieu's Lettres Persanes* (Institut et Musée Voltaire, 1970); Sanford Kessler, "Religion & Liberalism in Montesquieu's *Persian Letters*," *Polity* 15 (1983), 380–96; and Diana Schaub, *Erotic Liberalism: Women and Revolution in Montesquieu's Persian Letters* (Rowman & Littlefield, 1995). See also Rahe, *Logic of Liberty*, 45–48.

[24] See Roger Oake, "Montesquieu's Analysis of Roman History," *Journal of the History of Ideas* 16 (1955), 44–59; for the more skeptical view of *Considerations*, as assaulting Christianity for entangling church and state, thus distracting rulers from maintaining political power, see, for example, David Lowenthal, "Introduction," in *Considerations on the Causes of the Greatness of the Romans and Their Decline*, tr. Lowenthal (Hackett, 1999 [1965]), 13–17.

of Laws is his most systematic, and the only one arising under his declared principle of moderation. Perhaps his long experience of England (living there from 1729– 31) also persuaded him of the drawbacks of a rationalist culture of individual liberty that had begun to privatize and control religion in accord with Lockean theory; this is evident in his critical remarks at the close of his second portrait of England (*Spirit*, 19.27, end).

Montesquieu's systematic analysis of religion begins with his conception of human nature and its inherent laws in Book 1, arguing that "the law that impresses on us the idea of a creator and thereby leads us toward him is the first of the natural laws in importance, though not first in the order of these laws." This accepts the modern focus on man's material condition and how to improve it, but it also revives an ancient and medieval spirit by recognizing man's higher ends (*Spirit*, 1.2, 235/6). He also transcends the more rationalist conceptions of liberalism, whether of Hobbes, Locke, or John Rawls, by arguing that among the "relations of equity" or natural right that preexist human laws is the principle that "if one intelligent being had created another intelligent being, the created one ought to remain in its original dependency" (1.1, 233/4). It is true that *The Spirit of Laws* pervasively criticizes despotism, since Montesquieu will not have man suffer physical, political, or moral oppression as a patient citizen of the city of God. It also is true that he criticizes the oppressive or despotic practices of religion or of religious influences upon politics, to include severe criticisms of Christian leaders or doctrine. Still, while he condemns the brutality of ambitious princes or factious republics, he also repudiates the yoke of security and tranquility imposed by any kind of Leviathan. His criticisms of philosophers and of extremes of reason suggest that he sees no panacea in the dominance of secularized reason, science, technology, and commerce. He would reform the city of man by emphasizing the natural desire for a tranquil, hospitable abode, but also leaves room for, and marks his respect for, higher aspirations.

Natural Theology and Jurisprudence in *The Spirit of Laws*

The larger philosophical aims evident throughout *The Spirit of Laws* must govern, then, any interpretation of its complex analysis of religion and politics. To interpret Montesquieu as a rhetorically deft irreligionist akin to Machiavelli, Spinoza, Bayle, or Locke places him at an extreme of rationalism and secularism that defies the spirit of the work. Several such analyses are confident he engages in an "audacious" attack on Biblical religion, natural law, and providence, attempting to "rid us of the concern with the next world for the sake of peace and security in this one"; there is no doubt that he views "Christianity as a danger to a sound politics" and adopts several "heretical" views that "convict [him] of irreligion"; his philosophical project is "antitheological" for arguing that "[p]olitical life is to cease to take its bearings by any of the previously dominant claims for the supremacy of revealed, supernatural, and suprarational or contrarational divine authority and law."[25] This school interprets his every utterance or silence about religion in the direction of irreligion, although the only principle justifying this is that his mode of writing is estericism that hides radical philosophizing. There is no mention of his stated goal to moderate the zeal of modern philosophy. Moderation is seen merely as a rhetorical or prudential device and not a principle of his philosophy (further implying that prudence, too, is a device and not a substantive political and ethical principle for Montesquieu). Or, if we should note moderation, it is best understood as an "intransigent moderation" that basically equates to the radical secularizing of a Machiavelli, Locke, or Bayle. Montesquieu's statement on moderation is even said to be a disguised admission of his recognition of the "absurd inadequacy" of modern philosophy compared to the great classical and medieval philosophers, given that he felt "impelled to obfuscate" the true greatness of prior philosophy because of its illiberal, intolerant tendencies.[26]

In these analyses of Montesquieu's most philosophic discussions of religion, human nature, and politics in *Spirit* – Books 1, 24, and 25 – each scholar assumes that true Christian faith entails severe opposition between reason and revelation, philosophy and theology. This yields the paradox that a philosopher must either signal subordination to the Church and thus imperil philosophical integrity, or declare philosophical independence and signal irreligion. A related assumption is that a philosopher is hostile to Christianity, and Biblical religion generally, unless he accepts some degree of theocracy or union of religious and political authority; a corollary is that a philosopher is skeptical or hostile toward Christianity unless adopting a radical separation of nature and divine grace, thus accepting illimitable divine will. The pattern of these assumed premises is irremediable conflict between reason and revelation, philosophy and theology, religious authority and liberty; there can be no middle ground. This leads to much emphasis on the contemporary Jansenist critique of *The Spirit of Laws* by the Abbé de la Roche, as the gravest evidence that Montesquieu very likely was a Spinozist who rejected a supernatural creator, miracles, and Biblical religion. Earlier scholarship was more sober about the precarious status of Jansenist theology in the Catholic tradition, given its severely Augustinian views of the depravity of nature and the illimitable power of divine will; such scholars also noted that Montesquieu had many defenders among clergy, and even bishops, who repudiated the Jansenist attack. A more balanced

---

[25] Bartlett, "Politics of Faith and Reason," 18, 27 (see 16–27 generally); Schaub, "Believers and Barbarians," 233, 235, 238; Pangle, *Theological Basis of Liberal Modernity*, 1. Orwin's "Montesquieu as Heir of Christianity" diverges somewhat by noting praise for Christianity in *Spirit*, and discerning a gentler secularist teaching that the humanism in Christianity "points the way toward post-Christianity" and can be subsumed by liberalism (278, 280).

[26] Bartlett, "Politics of Faith and Reason," 24; Schaub, "Believers and Barbarians," 243; Pangle, *Theological Basis*, 145–46.

view notes, for example, that the "Jansenist abbe's conception of natural law was very narrow, and the same applies to his conception of Christianity."[27]

The charge of Spinozism leveled at Montesquieu is more complicated, and doubtful, if one employs other theological and philosophical benchmarks for compatibility with Christian orthodoxy – beyond strongly Augustinian or Jansenist ones. No scholarship in the "Spinozist" school notes, for example, any consensus between Montesquieu and that venerable source of orthodoxy, St. Thomas Aquinas. Some find antitheism implicit in Montesquieu's distinction between Christian "precepts" and "counsels" of perfection (*Spirit*, 24.6), since this permits a dilution of precepts or commands into mere counsels. This in turn points to the privatizing, or political irrelevance, of religious belief. However, Aquinas deemed this an orthodox distinction rooted in the New Testament, fitting for a revelation that neither condemns the happiness of this world nor demands that all Christians be perfect saints to gain Heaven.[28] The Spinozist view also finds irreligion in Montesquieu's arguments for curtailing penal enforcement of Christian morality in politics, as part of his covert depiction of Christianity *in toto* as despotism (see *Spirit* 12, Chapters 4–6; 25, Chapters 9–15; 26, Chapters 2, 7–13). If this were valid, then Aquinas holds the same antitheological stance. He states that legal regulation of morals should address only the basic requirements of order and security, not enforce Christian perfectionism.[29] According to the hyper-Augustinian standards for Christian or Biblical orthodoxy assumed by the Spinozist view of Montesquieu, Montesquieu and Aquinas are equally antireligious.

There was a time when Aquinas's arguments for compatibility between reason and revelation, politics and salvation led to controversy and, eventually, condemnations by the Bishops of Oxford and Paris. We are on safer ground, however, to note that Aquinas's theologically moderate views about the relationship of nature and grace have a greater claim to Christian orthodoxy than do the extreme standards convicting Montesquieu here. Tertullian's stance that the Church must reject any accommodation between Athens and Jerusalem was declared heretical by the Church Fathers themselves, while Aquinas was canonized not long after condemnation by some. Montesquieu is no Thomist; the point, rather, is that he might reasonably be interpreted as criticizing the irreligion he found in his modern predecessors, most particularly Machiavelli and Bayle, while staking out his own moderate position between rationalist

---

[27] Compare Pangle, *Theological Basis*, 15–19, with the measured view in Waddicor, *Montesquieu and Natural Law*, x, 85. A middle view, noting support for Montesquieu by Archbishop de Beaumont but also the "relativism" and utilitarianism of Montesquieu's view of religion, is Andrew Lynch, "Montesquieu and the Ecclesiastical Critics of *l'Esprit des Lois*," *Journal of the History of Ideas* 38 (1977), 487–500.

[28] *Summa Theologiae*, I–II, q. 108, a. 4, "Whether certain definite counsels are fittingly proposed in the New Law?" (Dominican Fathers translation); see in the New Testament, for example, Matthew 19:21ff and 19:12ff; 1 Corinthians 7:35.

[29] *Summa Theologiae*, I–II, q. 96, a. 2, "Does It Belong to Human Law to Repress All Vices?"

atheism and Christian perfectionism. Nor does this deny that, in comparison to Tocqueville's philosophy, his stance toward religion is more utilitarian, with some degree of deism and skepticism about metaphysics. Examination of a few suggestive passages from *The Spirit of Laws* will have to suffice to discern his moderation, mostly from Books 1, 24, and 25 in which Montesquieu declares his thematic attention to natural theology and religion.

As noted in Chapter 1, Book 1 does open with brief and seemingly rationalist generalities about the metaphysics of law in the created universe. Much scholarly debate has arisen over whether Spinoza, Descartes, Hobbes, or other modern philosophers are the greater influence here. Characteristically balancing the mind of the jurist and that of the philosopher, Montesquieu's topic in Book 1 is not law, but laws. In a discussion of "laws in general," he opens with a few paragraphs on metaphysics and natural theology, "laws in their relation with the various beings," and barely returns to these topics in the remaining 700 pages (in recent English translation). Laws in their "most extended meaning" are the "necessary relations deriving from the nature of things" (1.1, 232/3). All of the five levels of "beings" have laws, and in this "extended" sense, "the divinity has its laws." He immediately rejects, however, either cosmological fatalism or determinism on the grounds that the free and metaphysical dimension of "intelligent beings" could not be the product of "blind fate." By the third brief paragraph he moves a step back toward medieval views, to define laws by reason: the divinity is a "primitive reason," a primary or basic reason of all beings, and laws are the relations between the prime reason and the various beings but also the relations of these beings to each other. In the fourth paragraph he defines the divinity as "creator and preserver" of "the universe," and it is by laws made through "his wisdom and his power" that he creates and preserves. The next three paragraphs adopt a Newtonian tone, emphasizing that the "invariable laws" from the prime reason organize nonintelligent matter in motion, that "the creator" governs and preserves the world through these rules, and that, paradoxically, all the motion and complexity of the world presuppose these laws: "every diversity is *uniformity*, every change is *constancy*" (1.1, 232–33/ 3–4, emphasis in original). Scholars of philosophy and natural theology find these analyses cryptic, or inadequate, or perhaps deliberately misleading; as noted, both theists and nontheists detect Spinoza or other radical rationalist philosophies here, including an implicit denial of miracles.[30] In one of his public responses to theological criticism – the *Defense of the Spirit of Laws* (1750) – Montesquieu persistently identifies himself as a lawyer or jurist as well as a

---

[30] Skeptical views of Book 1 and Montesquieu's conception of philosophy and human nature, developing the analyses of Lowenthal and Pangle (1973) and placing him closer to (or in) the radical Enlightenment and secularism, include Pangle, *Theological Basis*, Michael Zuckert, "Natural Law, Natural Rights, and Classical Liberalism: On Montesquieu's Critique of Hobbes," *Social Philosophy and Policy* 18 (2001), 227–51; and Stuart D. Warner, "Montesquieu's Prelude: An Interpretation of Book I of *The Spirit of the Laws*," in *Enlightening Revolutions: Essays in Honor of Ralph Lerner*, ed. S. Minkov (Lexington Books, 2006).

philosopher, and argues that requiring a work of philosophy, politics, and law to overtly profess theological orthodoxy is an error.[31] This response presumes a degree of philosophical and jurisprudential autonomy from clerical authority less evident in France than in English common law, as in works by Fortescue or Coke that open with brief statements about divine law, natural law, and common law; but it is not evidence of irreligion. Montesquieu offers a weak, hardly Thomistic teleology about human nature, law, and the aims of politics; such rational analysis does not challenge or offend Biblical conceptions of the creator, but barely supports them. On the other hand, few scholars note that, in sharp contrast to Hobbes or Locke, he finds it necessary to define human law in relation to natural theology and metaphysics at all.[32]

Moreover, few if any scholars examine the actual authority cited in 1.1 on the necessary laws binding all of creation: the *Moralia* of the Hellenic biographer and moralist Plutarch. It is an odd choice, but one that seems to emphasize a jurist's concern with connecting cosmic natural law to the moral and political laws governing human affairs. The passage cited from Plutarch's essay "To an Uneducated Ruler" quotes the ancient Greek poet Pindar, that "law is the king of all, mortal and immortal."[33] It is a distinctive choice of an authority to

---

[31] See Montesquieu, "Défense de *l'Esprit des Lois*," in *Œuvres complètes*, 2: 1121–66; for example, Part 1, section I, defining *Spirit* as a work of "pure [or mere] politics and pure jurisprudence" (1121); Part 1, section II, answer to Objection III, that "every sensible man" grasps that 1.1 of *Spirit* is not a "treatise of theology" on sacred doctrine (1130); end of Part I, insisting on the distinction between "natural religion" (seeming to mean natural theology) and Christian "revelation" while declaring his respect not for one or the other but both – indeed, that his arguments from natural theology enable him "to destroy the system of Spinoza" (1135–36); in Part II, he should not be judged as if he sought to write "a Treatise on the Christian religion" or "Treatises on Christian theology" (1139); he sought not to write on Christian virtues but "books of natural philosophy, politics, and jurisprudence" (1145); he insists he should not be judged as a "theologian" when he writes as a "jurist" (1148); in Part III, opening, after again distinguishing theologians and jurists, he defines his Jansenist critic's "manner of reasoning" as flawed because it "confuses the various sciences" and fails to properly distinguish "the ideas of each science" (1160–61).

[32] In Part I of "Defense," section I, answer to objection III, Montesquieu seems to respond about necessary natural laws restricting divine agency and excluding miracles; he insists he reasoned only about "effects" (and infers causes), and about rules established by God, and has "said neither more nor less" (*Œuvres complètes*, 2:1124). He does not cite Aquinas, but reasoning from observable natural effects back to a divine mind as cause is, while not acceptable to the hyper-Augustinian view, the approach of *Summa Theologiae*, I, q. 2 (which includes, in a. 3, the Five Ways), and q. 12, a. 12 (among other passages); and Montesquieu's brief arguments in 1.1 are not obviously incompatible with the Thomistic view of divine omnipotence, eternal and natural law, and miraculous intervention that supersedes but does not violate eternal and natural law, for example, *Summa Theologiae* , I, q. 25, a. 3 and a. 4, q. 105, a. 6. Montesquieu has not foreclosed a personal, moral divinity creating and ordering nature and human nature. Zuckert notes some similarities between the reasoning about divinity and natural law in Montesquieu and Aquinas but also many differences, in "Natural Law, Natural Rights, and Montesquieu's Critique of Hobbes," 230–31.

[33] Plutarch, "To an Uneducated Prince," in *Moralia* 780c, ed. Fowler (Harvard University Press, 1936), X: 56–57. Pindar and Plutarch have "king," but Montesquieu writes "queen."

define the most "extended" meaning of law. Pindar's poem suggests a divine and natural law in which might makes right, and many Sophists, as well as Plato's Callicles in the *Gorgias* and his Athenian Stranger in the *Laws*, so interpret it. Plutarch, however, emphasizes to his young ruler that natural law stands above human power and counsels a benevolent wisdom and justice, and Montesquieu endorses this interpretation.[34] The substance and manner of Book 1 thus suggest an intention to moderate the canonical views of natural law in ancient and medieval philosophy, but also to temper the reductive tendency of modern philosophy. Even in passages bearing the strongest imprint of earlier modern and liberal theorists, he asserts his genius by referring his most abstract conception of law to Plutarch, in a didactic work, quoting a poet. Unlike Descartes, Hobbes, Spinoza, Clarke, or Locke, he is more concerned with educating statesmen than with abstract analysis. The allure of Machiavellism is false, for all rulers ultimately are governed by a higher law (see also 6.5, 21.20). On the other hand, nature and human nature do not support the degree of moralism in classical and medieval natural law.

As argued in Chapter 1, this complex analysis in Book 1 launches a redefinition of natural right in the work, in non-Hobbesian terms of basic individual and social feelings such as sentiments toward family and friends. The first four "natural laws" of prepolitical man are to seek peace, nourishment, sociability, and sexual union with other humans, and finally both knowledge and society (1.2).[35] The first (or fifth) natural law, to seek knowledge of God, has an ambiguous status: it is first "in importance," since nature "impresses on us the idea of a creator and thereby leads us toward him," but we only develop this inclination after experiencing the first four laws (1.2, 235–36/6). For Montesquieu, human nature and natural law ascend higher than earlier moderns had thought, but they stop short of the teleological heights of the ancients and medievals.[36] He confirms this modern, if humane and elevated, anthropology in the next discussion of natural law or natural right (*droit naturel*)

---

[34] See Thomas L. Pangle, ed., *The Laws of Plato* (University of Chicago Press, 1988 [1980]), 690b (III, n. 24, 522–23). The reliance on Plutarch is still more interesting given that Dryden finds Plutarch influenced by the Eclectic school in Hellenic philosophy, "which selected from all the other sects what seemed most probable in their own opinions." *Lives of the Noble Grecians and Romans*, ed. H. Clough, tr. Dryden (Modern Library, 1992), Introduction, xxiv.

[35] Both Bartlett and Schaub claim the natural laws in 1.2 implicitly repudiate the "relations of equity" described in 1.1 as governing all created beings. This reads back into Book 1 the irreligion they find in Books 24 and 25; moreover, the traditional ideas in Western philosophy regarding natural theology and ethics, and also equity and natural law, indicate that these sets of principles are more complementary than contradictory. As for the claim that Montesquieu undermines both equity and natural law by stating that humans regularly violate both, Aquinas accepts that we regularly violate natural law since custom can overwhelm it; see *Summa Theologiae*, I–II, q. 94, a. 4, "Is the Natural Law the Same in All Men?" See also I–II, q. 95, a. 2.

[36] That said, Aquinas accepts a similar distinction about human capacities, that knowledge of God is not the first object of human knowledge – thus, we first would know and think about material things, not metaphysical realities; *Summa Theologiae*, I, q. 88, a. 3.

in the work (3.10).[37] For Montesquieu, natural right primarily involves neither self-preservation nor self-defense, nor even egoistic liberty, each of which reductively privileges isolated, Hobbesian or Cartesian individuals. Rather, it concerns "natural feelings," such as "respect for a father, tenderness for one's children and women, laws of honor, or the state of one's health" – all of which are complementary with religion (3.10, 260/29–30). Of course, near this same passage he equates monarchical honor with self-interest, hardly marking himself a virtue theorist (see 3.7). Nevertheless, these humane dimensions to his anthropology and natural right upset reductionist readings of his philosophy. His political science steers a middle course between the substantive natural right of Aristotle or natural law of Aquinas, and the minimalism of Machiavelli or Hobbes.[38] A human nature oriented to not only security but also sociability and freedom, including the freedom to pursue higher aims, holds a middle ground because we are neither as beleaguered in a hostile cosmos, nor as blessed with intimate affinity for the high, as some have thought. The genius of politics – the proper spirit of laws – is to best preserve our nature in all its complexity and moderation.

Freedom for and Freedom from Religion in Montesquieu's Moderation

This fundamental understanding of *The Spirit of Laws*, and of the views of law, natural theology, and human nature in its early Books, permits a briefer analysis of the subsequent remarks on religion. When viewed from this ground it is harder to interpret Montesquieu's particular remarks as simply hostile to religion or Christianity particularly. Their more natural or obvious meaning is more probably his intended one: a friendlier stance toward religion than held by the radical Enlightenment, but predominantly for utilitarian service to liberal ends. The negative theme of tolerance persists, to moderate the role of religion in public life and its possible threats to tranquility. Still, if Montesquieu's stance is utilitarian and tends to lower the aims of politics, he is the novel modern who persistently praises revealed religion and religious faith as not only useful but instructive for philosophy and politics. One such moment is his praise for William Penn, and also for the Jesuit missionaries in Paraguay, when discussing ancient Greek ideas of republics, their virtues, and the distinctive education needed for demanding ideals (4.6). This remarkable chapter is widely discussed, given its contrast between "extraordinary" republican institutions and "the dregs and corruption of our modern times." He blends

---

[37] Pangle overlooks this passage in *Philosophy*, 309–10, and in "The Philosophic Understandings of Human Nature Informing the Constitution," in *Confronting the Constitution*, ed. Bloom (AEI Press, 1990), 15–18, 24–37; he does discuss it in *Theological Basis*, 34–35, but through the lens of his Spinozistic reading of Montesquieu; Zuckert also omits it in "Natural Law, Natural Rights."

[38] Lowenthal suggests this momentarily in "Book I," 495; see also moments of more moderate interpretations in Pangle's earlier work, *Philosophy*, 20–47.

criticism and praise for legislators from Lycurgus and Plato to the Jesuits, and he does not fairly present all of these philosophers and founders on their own terms. The project of seeking republican virtue, especially on the Greek model, is singular, extraordinary, severe, and domineering, although the Jesuits have made the native people "happier" through their efforts. Still, there is unqualified praise for "Mr. Penn," "a true Lycurgus" and "honorable gentleman" (*honnête homme*) as a legislator or founder. He has "formed a people" according to "integrity" or probity. Unlike Lycurgus, he has persuaded "a free people" to adopt "peace" rather than war as the polity's object (4.6, 268/37). There is no mention that Penn is, famously, a Quaker, nor of the religious toleration in his Pennsylvania colony, but Montesquieu eventually will cultivate these ideas. He praises the Jesuits (and seemingly Penn as well) for demonstrating "the idea of religion joined to that of humanity" – the virtue of gentleness and respect for human dignity that is central to this moderate philosophy and political science (4.6, 268–69/37).

A tour of some highlights from Montesquieu's treatment of religion prior to the two books dedicated to it (Books 24 and 25) reveals his blend of praise and criticism. He offers striking praise of "the religion of the present day" for the mildness it brings to the modern "right of nations" governing war, displacing Roman ferocity (10.3, 378–79/139).[39] He also credits "our modern times," "contemporary reasoning," and modern philosophy and mores. Still, one of the four "sorts of laws" that defines the right of nations itself is "the law of natural enlightenment, which wants us to do to others what we would want to have done to us" (378/139). This duty to treat others as we would wish for ourselves, even in international relations and war, is a striking extension of a Christian principle (discussed in Chapter 5). To be sure, it is one that Christian statesmen or peoples fail to meet, as the sequel declares when castigating the Spaniards in their conquest of Mexico for discarding their "gentle religion" and instead committing "evils," exterminating the conquered, and spreading "a raging superstition" (10.4, 381/142). Then again, his book on slavery in relation to climate credits Christianity for beginning to abolish and curtail slavery, as no other religion or philosophy has done (15.7).

As Montesquieu's analysis begins to transcend the dominance first of classical and medieval political science (Part 1, Books 1–8), then of climate and culture (Part 3, Books 14–18), he explores how enlightened laws can moderate the effects of climate and culture especially. He includes religion in the seven elements comprising the "general spirit" that governs any people (19.4). His discussion of the English mores produced by their constitution of liberty (19.27) thus includes brief remarks on religion, noting the spirit of free thinking and atheism that arises, but also the "evil" and "repressive" laws against the former established religion. This comment on Protestant persecution of Catholics

---

[39] Rahe notes this in *Logic of Liberty*, 93, and also in "Was Montesquieu a Philosopher of History?," in *Cahiers Montesquieu* no. 10 (2013), 71–86.

suggests criticism of Locke's apology for this principle in his *Letter on Toleration* (1690) (19.27, 580/330). Further, king and Parliament do not trust the permitted clergy to be self-governing – perhaps to prevent backsliding toward Catholicism; for this reason, and given the culture of liberty, the clergy must earn any respect they enjoy or flocks they guide. They thus "would seek to persuade," and "very fine works would come from their pens, to prove the revelation and the providence of the great Being" (581–83/331–33). As noted, he also warns of the atomism or individualism of English culture, and its extreme individual and political liberty (582/332). Nonetheless, as he turns to commerce, he notes that the nominally Protestant English have so moderated Christianity that they are "the people in the world who have best known how to take advantage of each of these three great things at the same time: religion, commerce, and liberty" (20.7, 590/343). His largely utilitarian approach continues when criticizing the Scholastics, "infatuated" with Aristotle's criticisms of usury, for banning any lending at interest. This brings economic "misfortunes" as well as a new form of anti-Semitism, since Jews could lend for profit when Christians could not (21.20, 639–41/387–89). Eventually, as the chapter title notes, commerce "made its way through" this "barbarism" of Scholasticism, bigotry, and also the rapacity of princes and their occasional persecution of Jews. Once the Jews invented bills of exchange and international credit, both the theologians and the princes learned to "more wisely" accommodate this new path to "prosperity." Theology lagged behind the virtue of humanity, but was taught a lesson by an exploiting self-interest. The princes especially have "begun to be cured of Machiavellism," learning that there "must be more moderation in councils" (20.21, 641/389).

These occasional remarks in Parts 1–4 of the work remind the reader that religion is one of the elements that comprises "the spirit of laws" itself, and that it must be examined in its turn (1.3, end; see also 19.4). Part 5 of the six Parts is dedicated to religion – exclusively so in Books 24 and 25; Book 26, on the relation of various kinds of laws, features analysis of how "divine right" and "ecclesiastical right" relate to natural right and political right (26.1, 750–51/494). Indeed, the opening theme of Book 24 addresses the predominant, rival tendencies to evangelize either "the next life" or "this one," to elevate either "heaven" or "earth" over the other. Montesquieu's moderate alternative is to "unite them both." This requires his open admission that he will adopt the narrow perspective of the political philosopher, that he is "one who writes on politics" and "not a theologian." He seeks to provide not the best path to "the more sublime truths" of eternal salvation but to balance the aim of heaven and the necessities of earthly politics while damaging neither (24.1, 714/459). "The Christian religion, which orders men to love one another, no doubt wants the best political laws and the best civil laws for each people, because those laws are, after it, the greatest good men can give and receive" (715/459). This effort to harmonize the city of man and the city of God, as directed by the new political science of the general spirit while respecting "the one [religion] whose roots are in heaven" and negotiating the many "false religions," has been immensely influential in subsequent centuries. That said, it earned only tepid public support from clergy and bishops in France at the time, and vociferous criticism from more Augustinian or strictly orthodox voices. As noted, however, if this general approach is antitheist *per se*, then sections of Aquinas's *Summa Theologiae* also are so for adopting the confined horizons of ethics and politics – not to mention Aquinas's commentaries on Aristotle's *Ethics* and *Politics*, or his letter *On Kingship*.

The view that every concern for politics expressed in Books 24 and 25 must be covertly irreligious, rather than seeking a middle ground between atheism and fanatical religiosity, also fits poorly with the opening themes of Book 25. Montesquieu again contrasts rival extremes to be avoided – here as "the pious man" who "always speaks of religion" in terms of "what he loves" versus "the atheist" obsessed with religion in terms of "what he fears." The sequel notes that humans are "exceedingly drawn" to idolatry (object worship) and, at the other extreme, to worship of a purely spiritual divinity; we also are "exceedingly drawn to hope and to fear" (25.1, 735/439; 25.2, 735/439, 737/480). Given his main concern with philosophical, political, and moral moderation, it seems that his criticisms of Pierre Bayle – for advocating categorical separation of church and state, and seeing only Christianity's bad effects on politics – are genuine (24.2, 24.6). Just as Montesquieu earlier criticizes the antipolitical aspects of both Epicureanism and ascetic Christianity as too extreme for human nature (23.21), here he criticizes both an Augustinian fusing of religion and politics that subsumes politics and also the antireligious stance of Epicurean and radical Enlightenment thought. A philosophy that finds no transcendent inclinations in human nature or no room for them in politics, whether propounded by Lucretius, Machiavelli, Hobbes, or Bayle, is too extreme, missing a crucial part of the human phenomena. At the other extreme, he clearly seeks to temper Christian perfectionism as embodied in monks, medieval Inquisitors, and advocates of an "overly contemplative life," given his aims of tranquility, toleration, and moderation (24.11, 722/466; see also 5.2, 25.11).

The Spinozist portrait of Montesquieu as subtly adopting Machiavellian secular ambition and rationalism, to achieve those aims through esoteric writing, also fits ill with other remarks on religion in *The Spirit of Laws*. His respect for Christianity does emphasize its utility in tempering Machiavellian brutality, citing its impetus toward a more humane, moderate domestic politics and international right (10.3, 24.2–3; see 6.13, 12.29 and 19.18 on political moderation that religion, even Islam, can provide). Christianity in particular – in explicit contrast to Islam – inclines politics toward moderate rather than despotic government (title of 24.3). Thus, we moderns "owe to Christianity both a certain political right in government and a certain right of nations in war, for which human nature can never be sufficiently grateful" (24.3, 717/461–62). A concern to moderate fanatical Christian faith and any other religious zealotry is equally vital; this leads him to argue that humane utility is more important than truth when a political philosopher evaluates religion. He thus offers advice on how to "attack" or weaken the attachment to a religion – we might infer, immoderate and illiberal religions most especially (24.1; 24.19, 25.12; see also 26.7–12).[40] As a modern and liberal, he balances his respect for the natural inclination to seek transcendent truth (1.2, 24.1) with concern that religion should not mandate perfection, or place too much emphasis on a contemplative life (24.7, 24.11), or threaten individual or political tranquility. He states that it is not the theological truth or falsity of any dogma that makes it useful or pernicious in politics, but the use or abuse made of it (24.19).

These Enlightenment emphases should not obscure the fact, however, that Montesquieu does not belittle Christianity or man's natural inclination toward transcendent meaning as do Lucretius, Machiavelli, and Rousseau, or as Bayle's radical separationism might tend to do. His moderating of any programmatic atheism also is evident in his recognition that religious faith is "the greatest spring (*ressort*) among men" (24.14, 725/469; see also 20.7). Indeed, two final passages encapsulate his insistence upon the mutual utility of religion and politics properly understood, and the moderation he seeks between them. Since "both religion and the civil laws should aim principally to make good citizens of men," if one of these strays from this aim toward a dangerous extreme, then "the other should aim more toward it." The danger in fact is that a cycle of extremes would subsume a political culture due to a failure in "the harmony and precision of ideas" in either religion or civil law, which then "spreads" from one to the other. Then, "religion condemns things that civil law should permit," while the "civil laws permit on their side what religion should condemn" (24.14, 724/468). Still, his counsels on moderation are not simply utilitarian, for he offers genuine insights about religious belief. Thus, while satirizing the bloodthirsty fanaticism of Inquisitors toward Jews, in the guise of reporting a "humble remonstrance" from a Jew, Montesquieu includes the Jewish view that Christians should not punish "the quite pardonable error of believing that God still loves that which he loved." Having stated that eloquent argument for toleration, he also provides, in a note, an interesting rebuttal that supports toleration but distinguishes it from religious relativism: "This is the source for the Jews' blindness, of their failure to sense that the economy of the Gospel is within the order of God's designs and that thus it is a continuation of his

---

[40] All the scholars who cite 25.12 on penal laws in religion – which argues it is better to weaken attachment to a religion via enticements (such as commerce or prosperity) rather than threats or punishments – mistranslate a crucial phrase, and thus amplify its putative irreligious import; the Cohler translation also errs here. The text shifts between addressing religion generally and the proper approach to "a religion"; the phrase in question states: "it is more certain to attack a religion" – not "religion" generically – "by favors, by the comforts of life," "by what makes one forget" religion, "by what leads one to indifference" (25.12, 746/489; *il est plus sûr d'attaquer une religion par la faveur...*). Given earlier statements in Books 24 and 25 on the special status of Christianity, on avoiding extremes about religion, and about the dangers of Islam in particular to moderate politics, a narrower reading of this passage is warranted.

immutability itself" (25.13, 746–47/490). For a writer on politics who is not a theologian, this discourse advocating tolerance reveals substantial knowledge of Christian theology.

There is much evidence in the modern liberal democracies to confirm Rousseau's warnings about the spiritual hunger left unsatisfied by bourgeois life and about the inadequacy of the Enlightenment secularism that promoted such materialism (*Emile*, Book IV).[41] However, when Rousseau chastises modern reason for failing to appreciate the "great" and powerful "spring" of religious longing, he takes his cue from Montesquieu. Moreover, none of the Spinozist interpretations of Montesquieu accounts for the judgment by the prominent Dominican priest and Catholic apologist Henri-Dominique Lacordaire, who in his address upon reception into the French Academy in 1861 declared the first book on religion in *The Spirit of Laws* (Book 24) "the most beautiful defense of Christianity in the 18th century" and the work of "a great soul."[42] A skeptic might rejoin: this is to damn with faint praise, because there weren't many such books in that century or because Lacordaire was a liberal Catholic advocating rapprochement between certain elements of Enlightenment and Catholicism. Even if granted, neither qualification diminishes the praise; each affirms not the truth of Montesquieu's account of religion but its effort to find a sincere middle ground between religious and atheistic extremes.

Montesquieu's Legacy of Moderation in Washington and the American Founding

Montesquieu's philosophical and political moderation provides a crucial foundation for an American constitutionalism marked by institutional, legal, and philosophical balance – a moderation evident both in the Constitution and Declaration of Independence. As noted in Chapter 2, the Declaration balances its Enlightenment abstractions with appeals to an active Providence, common law legal tradition, duty, and honor. This echoes a Montesquieuan moderation that assimilates moderns and ancients, liberalism and republicanism, and also Christianity and the classic common law. The substitution of "the pursuit of happiness" for the Lockean right of property as a primary natural right also echoes Montesquieu's common-sense philosophy, neither strongly teleological nor starkly reductive about the ends of man and purposes of government. Standing next to the Declaration, Constitution, and Bill of Rights as an embodiment of American moderation is the Founding Father, George

---

[41] Jean-Jacques Rousseau, *Emile, or On Education*, tr. A. Bloom (Basic Books, 1979), Book IV, note 312; cited in Bartlett, "Politics of Faith and Reason," 27.

[42] Lacordaire, "Discours de reception a l'Academie Francaise," 1861, taking up Tocqueville's seat in the Academy. Available at: www.academie-francaise.fr/discours-de-reception-et-reponse-de-francois-guizot-1 (accessed May 2013), fourth paragraph; Book 24 further is praised as "the highest testimony of what truth can do in a great soul who sincerely puts his thought in the service of men."

Washington. Even a brief survey of his views on religion reveals the political and philosophical balance he pursued as leading statesman.[43] As argued in
Chapter 2, his central, unifying presence from the 1770s through the 1790s suggests the value of studying his thought as epitomizing the high middle ground,
and core meaning, of America's founding principles.[44]

Washington's best-known writing, his "Farewell Address" (1796), carefully
reconciles and moderates the tensions between not only the Jeffersonian and
Hamiltonian moments in the founding but its Enlightenment and Christian
principles as well. He opened this long public letter to his "Friends, and Fellow-
Citizens" by offering prayers to Heaven for continued blessings upon his country, which continued the pattern in his career of not only invoking Providence
but praying to the divinity for protection and guidance. After explaining and
justifying his insistence upon retiring from public service, he sought to "offer to
your solemn contemplation, and to recommend to your frequent review" advice
on a sound constitutional politics – to include the importance of religious principles and character in a republic.[45] One source of Washington's thoughtfulness
and his consistent intertwining of religious and political principles is one of his
earliest writings, a handwritten copy of "Rules of Civility and Decent Behavior in Company and in Conversation" – a sixteenth century work by French
Jesuits to educate for private and political life. The Rules instilled both ethical principles and an intellectual trait of clarifying the ultimate principles to
guide one in any stage of life (W, 3–10). The influence of a French Catholic
work on the Anglican American statesman also is a case study of the American tendency to harmonize diverse sources and traditions. Indeed, the first of
Washington's major public writings, his 1783 Circular to the state governors
and legislatures, opens and closes with gratitude for Providence and calls upon
the citizens of the new nation to realize the larger principles at stake in their

---

[43] Among the sources noted in Chapter 2, Muñoz cites the Montesquieuan character of Washington's views on religion and politics in *God and the Founders*, 54–56; Jeffry H. Morrison, *The
Political Philosophy of George Washington* (Johns Hopkins University Press, 2009), emphasizes his efforts to reconcile and balance Protestant Christian, classical republican, and liberal
principles, with attention to Christian principles in his thought.

[44] Washington's personal beliefs, a matter of controversy even in his lifetime, are only indirectly
relevant for his views as statesman, especially given his awareness of his status as *primus inter
pares* among the founders. His reticence to express his private views seems a statement of moderation itself. For investigations of his low-Anglican and Masonic beliefs that deem him an
American Deist, see, for example, Paul F. Boller, Jr., *George Washington & Religion* (Southern
Methodist University Press, 1963), and David L. Holmes, *The Faiths of the Founding Fathers*
(Oxford University Press, 2006); on Washington as a devout Christian, arguing with voluminous
documentary research and single-minded advocacy, see Peter A. Lillback and Jerry Newcombe,
George Washington's Sacred Fire (Providence Forum Press, 2006).

[45] "Farewell Address," in *George Washington: Writings*, ed. John Rhodehamel (Library of
America/Literary Classics of the United States, 1997), 962, 964, hereafter cited parenthetically
as W. I revise spelling in Washington's writings, but retain capitalization, emphases, and other
features. Another useful one-volume edition is *George Washington: A Collection*, ed. William
B. Allen (Indianapolis,: Liberty Fund, 1988), hereafter cited as *GWC*.

endeavor. Given America's success in war despite long odds, and the "natural," "political," and "moral" blessings now enjoyed, the "Citizens of America" should note the providential fact that "our Republic" came to freedom in an era of history providing "a fairer opportunity for political happiness" than any other. Washington boldly harmonizes Enlightenment confidence in human reason with respect for traditional religious belief. Having transcended "the gloomy age of Ignorance and Superstition," America must work to secure the intellectual, philosophical, political, commercial, and moral achievements of the Western tradition precisely by appreciating that "above all" of these developments, "the pure and benign light of Revelation" has meliorated human affairs and "increased the blessings of Society" (*W*, 516–17).

Washington evoked a Montesquieuan blend of virtue and interest, Christianity and Enlightenment, throughout his arguments for constitutional reform in the Circular. Perhaps because it was a retirement address, his closing is the most pointed of his appeals to religious belief as both true and indispensable for the republic, to include a rare reference to Christianity:

I now make it my earnest prayer, that God would have you and the State over which you preside, in his holy protection, that he would incline the hearts of the Citizens to cultivate a spirit of subordination and obedience to Government, to entertain a brotherly affection and love for one another, for their fellow Citizens of the United States at large, and particularly for their brethren who have served in the Field, and finally, that he would most graciously be pleased to dispose us all, to do Justice, to love mercy, and to demean ourselves with that Charity, humility and pacific temper of mind, which were the Characteristics of the Divine Author of our blessed Religion, and without an humble imitation of whose example in these things, we can never hope to be a happy Nation. (*W*, 524–26)[46]

If this is civil religion – the philosopher or statesman invoking vague religious ideas to support the state – then it is not a version that emphasizes utility far above (or at the expense of) piety. While Washington's efforts to harmonize religion and constitutional, republican liberty grew more politic as he returned to public life and became the indisputably central statesman of the founding, he never adopted the merely utilitarian tone of a ceremonial deism. He steadily balanced respect for the diversity of Christian churches and professions of faith in Biblical religion with a liberal, enlightened condemnation of any coercion of belief, evident in his solicitude for religious minorities. His First Inaugural address as President (1789) thus opens with a prayer that is generically monotheistic but genuinely suppliant. It was fitting, he said, to offer "fervent supplications to that Almighty Being who rules over the Universe" that "his benediction may consecrate to the liberties and happiness of the People of the United States, a Government instituted by themselves for these essential purposes" (*W*, 731). "No People can be bound to acknowledge and adore

---

[46] Compare the Book of Micah 6:8, and the Gospel of Matthew 23:23.

the invisible hand, which conducts the Affairs of men" more than Americans; most recently in the "revolution" that brought a new constitution, the "tranquil deliberations, and voluntary consent of so many distinct communities" contrasted with the way "most Governments have been established," suggesting a "providential agency." Further appeals in the Inaugural to moderation and virtue among public officials, and among the citizenry, presuppose these invocations as both the foundation and the aspiration for a free politics. His Thanksgiving Proclamation of October 1789, issued upon Congress's request to declare "a day of public thanksgiving and prayer," edifies the citizenry by harmonizing piety, republicanism, religious liberty, and liberal enlightenment. Americans should pray to "Almighty God" in gratitude for many blessings and benefits enjoyed, including their "religious liberty." We should humbly offer "prayers and supplications" that "the great Lord and Ruler of Nations" will enable them to achieve further political and moral blessings, but also "to promote the knowledge and practice of true religion and virtue" (*GWC*, 534–35). His letters to two minority religions, Jews and Roman Catholics, are meditations on the harmony between Biblical faith and the "natural rights" of peaceful citizens to pursue their own piety. A just government "gives to bigotry no sanction, to persecution no assistance" and thus transcends mere "toleration," but it also should exhort citizens to "the cultivation of manners, morals, and piety."[47]

Across his career Washington echoes not only Montesquieu's argument that free government must shape the morals or manners of its citizenry, but more particularly the view of harmony between Christianity and good citizenship in Book 24 of *The Spirit of Laws*. Government can promote religious belief as necessary for citizens of a free regime, and conversely can tolerate religious beliefs and practices not directly inimical to society and good citizenship. It is no surprise, then, that the Farewell Address opens with Washington's gratitude to Heaven for the country's blessings, and with prayers for continued Providence. Nearer the end he exhorts his countrymen to strike a just balance between religious belief and liberty. In his most famous lines he balances the utility of piety and morals with genuine appreciation: "Of all the dispositions and habits which lead to political prosperity, Religion and morality are indispensable supports"; "A volume could not trace all their connections with private and public felicity"; just policies are "recommended by every sentiment which ennobles human Nature" (*W*, 971, 972–73). Nor can we suppose that "morality can be maintained without religion," for while "a refined education" might serve for exceptional minds, "reason and experience forbid us to expect that National

---

[47] To Hebrew Congregation, August 18, 1790 (*W*, 766–67); to Roman Catholics, March 15, 1790 (*GWC*, 546–47). Muñoz, *God and the Founders*, discusses Washington's correspondence with other minority congregations, including Quakers and Baptists; Robert Faulkner discusses these statements on religious liberty in "Washington and the Founding of Constitutional Democracy," in *Gladly to Learn and Gladly to Teach: Essays on Religion and Political Philosophy in Honor of Ernest L. Fortin*, A. A., eds. Foley and Kries (Lexington Books, 2002).

morality can prevail in exclusion of religious principle." A Montesquieuan spirit obviously informs the immediate sequel, that "virtue or morality is a necessary spring of popular government"; *The Spirit of Laws* identifies a principle or spring of each government, with virtue as the animating principle of republics (see *Spirit*, 3.1, 4.3, 5.1, 11.13, and also 19.27). Washington endorses neither a secularist wall of separation between religion and government nor the sectarian view that America is a Christian nation. Similarly, a republic should neither ignore the mutual influence between governmental and private morality nor have government scrutinize the morals of citizens. His discourse on religion in the Address then shifts seamlessly to education, and a policy he had advocated since his First Annual Message (1790): "Promote then as an object of primary importance, Institutions for the general diffusion of knowledge," since in a republic "it is essential that public opinion should be enlightened" (*W* 972, 750).

As discussed in Chapter 5, Washington's counsels on American foreign policy draw on these statements to balance national interest with religious principle and justice. The guiding spirit of the entire Address is moderation, so that prudence and a balance of principles would guide domestic and foreign affairs, private and public life. He closes with the hope that these "counsels of an old and affectionate friend" would "control the usual current of the passions" and "moderate the fury of party spirit" (*W*, 976; see also 832, 851, 924). Private and public support for religious belief, to include education in schools, is a central element of his moderation. This clearly extends beyond utilitarian civil religion to a robust accommodation between religion and liberty, since religion is praised for ennobling and bringing felicity to private and public life.

Transcending Civil Religion: Tocqueville on the Spirit of American Liberty

Tocqueville draws on Montesquieu's philosophy and Washington's statesmanship to develop his own view of religion and liberal democracy, and to deepen the modern philosophy of moderation. As argued in Chapter 3, his "new science of politics" (*Democracy*, Introduction) ultimately questions whether Montesquieu's somewhat negative liberalism can sustain either decent liberty or the human soul in the new age of equality. Thus, his advocacy of the benefits to liberal democracy of genuinely supporting, and heeding the guidance from, Biblical religion is closer to Washington's advocacy than to Montesquieu's cautious stance.[48] Given this foundation, scholarly debates about Tocqueville's precise orientation toward religion in *Democracy in America* appear in a different light. Tocqueville's distinctive blend of three modern philosophers – Pascal, Montesquieu, and Rousseau – moderates Montesquieuan liberalism with elements

---

[48] The discussion here presupposes the analysis in the final section of Chapter 3, and sources cited therein – "Statesmanship and Metaphysics for America's Mixed Regime."

from Pascal and Rousseau, evident in his deep concern about the dangers to the human soul posed by modern democracy. Montesquieu's attempt to moderate modern liberal philosophy is a beginning: employing elements of ancient philosophy and poetry, and of medieval political practice, to defend the benefits and naturalness of religion against modern irreligion. *Democracy in America* further moderates Montesquieuan liberalism by warning the liberal democratic mind of the mixed blessings of equality, individual security, and material prosperity. It then prescribes a moderate dose of the classical and medieval concern with the destiny of the human soul. Comparing Montesquieu's more modest efforts at philosophical and political moderation with Tocqueville's deeper ideas of constitutionalism, liberty, and religion thus reveals the larger project of *Democracy*. Tocqueville sought to leaven liberal individualism and egalitarianism by restoring higher aims to politics and civil society as guided by religious principles and practice. He cannot adopt the strict teleology of ancient and medieval Christian political philosophy, but proper balance requires a shift toward this view.

Recent debates about the true nature of Tocqueville's view of religion, and of its role in modern democracy, thus might be viewed differently given this conception of moderation informing his thought. One approach suggests that he is a genuine advocate of the true light that Biblical faith and theology shed upon the human condition, regardless of the trials of faith and personal doubt that dogged him personally.[49] An alternate view suggests he is a functionalist advocate of a civil religion, endorsing only utilitarian counsels either because of philosophic skepticism about faith or concern about its zealous, illiberal tendencies.[50] If Tocqueville deepens Montesquieu's philosophy of Montesquieuan moderation, balancing and blending ancient, medieval, and modern elements in a distinctive way, then his endorsement of religion would indeed be moderate but in a way that transcends skepticism, functionalism, or a primary concern with the illiberal potential of faith.[51]

---

[49] See Doris Goldstein, *Trial of Faith: Religion and Politics in Tocqueville's Thought* (Elsevier, 1975); Peter A. Lawler, *The Restless Mind: Alexis de Tocqueville on the Origin and Perpetuation of Human Liberty* (Rowman & Littlefield, 1993); Joshua Mitchell, *The Fragility of Freedom: Tocqueville on Religion, Democracy, and the American Future* (University of Chicago Press, 1995); Patrick Deneen, *Democratic Faith* (Princeton University Press, 2005); L. Joseph Hebert, Jr., *More Than Kings and Less Than Men: Tocqueville on the Promise and Perils of Democratic Individualism* (Lexington Books, 2010); and, to some degree, Ralph Hancock, "Tocqueville's Responsible Reason," in *The Responsibility of Reason: Theory and Practice in a Liberal-Democratic Age* (Rowman & Littlefield, 2011), 253–81.

[50] For example, Catherine Zuckert, "Not by Preaching: Tocqueville on the Role of Religion," *Review of Politics* 42 (1981), 259–80, and "The Role of Religion in Preserving American Liberty – Tocqueville's Analysis 150 Years Later," in *Tocqueville's Defense of Human Liberty: Current Essays*, eds. Lawler and Alulis (Garland, 1993), 223–39; Sanford Kessler, *Tocqueville's Civil Religion* (State University of New York, 1994); and Aristide Tessitore, "Alexis de Tocqueville on the Natural State of Religion in the Age of Democracy," *Journal of Politics* 64 (2002), 1137–52.

[51] Scott Yenor argues that Tocqueville hopes for a return to genuine religious faith after the decline of Protantism at the hands of pantheism and materialism, in "Natural Religion and Human

Scholars who perceive Christian thinking at the core of Tocqueville's philosophy also discern a principle of moderation in his thought. While helpfully noting his concern to moderate or balance democratic tendencies, this approach also can overstate the influence of Pascal and of other neo-Platonic minds, such as Augustine or Rousseau, upon Tocqueville's perception of the dangers to human greatness and the soul in modernity.[52] Moderation as an effort at philosophical balance has roots in Socratic dialectic, but this disposition is not the hallmark of Plato's psychology, ethics, or politics – as best as one can glean from the Socratic skepticism of the dialogues. Plato and neo-Platonism emphasize dualistic antagonisms between the high and the low, and the need for the high to vanquish or dominate the low. This is an important element of Augustinian thought, and particularly Augustine's view of the two cities animated by two diametrically opposed loves, the City of God and the City of Man. In contrast, equilibrium as an aim and the means of achieving moderation to reconcile extremes are hallmarks of the Aristotelian tradition, which broadly includes a range of minds from Thomas Aquinas – who is more philosophically moderate than much Thomism – to Montesquieu. The neo-Platonic, Augustinian interpretation of Tocqueville implies that his anthropology, ethics, and politics, or his basic approach to philosophy, is shaped predominantly by Augustine or Pascal, with some adjustments. The difficulty, however, is to explain how Tocqueville can depart from Pascal (and neo-Platonism generally) by so strongly affirming the dignity of politics if his central focus is said to be the spiritual impoverishment of the city of modern man.[53] This would require one important element in Tocqueville's blending of earlier philosophical sources to displace the moderation or balance of the whole that he develops.

It may be that the example of Washington, and of American practice generally, persuaded Tocqueville to transcend Montesquieu's more cautious version of moderation about religion while stopping short of Pascal's skepticism about politics and human dignity in this life. Tocqueville's famous attention to political culture or sociology – specifically to mores, defined as "the ensemble of moral and intellectual dispositions which men supply to the state of society" – is his Aristotelian development of Montesquieu's attention to mores. He thus declares the beliefs and habits of religion to be the primary component of mores.[54] In American terms, Tocqueville's moderate political science agrees with Washington's blend of the Federalist concern with the necessary powers and order of constitutional government and also the Anti-Federalist and

Perfectibility: Tocqueville's Account of Religion in Modern Democracy," *Perspectives on Political Science* 33, no. 1 (2004), 10–17; see also Deneen, *Democratic Faith*, and Hebert, *More than Kings*.

52 On moderation and religion in Tocqueville, see Lawler, *Restless Mind*, 137–39, 142–43; and Mitchell, *Fragility of Freedom*, x–xi, 78–87, 132–40.

53 See Lawler, *Restless Mind*, 78–87, 141–58; Mitchell, *Fragility of Freedom*, 3–11, 22–28, 78–87.

54 *Democracy*, eds. Mansfield and Winthrop, vol. I, Part 2, Chapter 9, 275, 292, n. 8; see, more generally, 275–95, 298–302. Subsequent citations refer parenthetically to volume, part, chapter, and page of this edition.

Jeffersonian concern with the moral presuppositions of self-government (see, e.g., I.1.8, 129; I.2.7, 241–2; II.2.15, 518). In this synthesis he saw the American correction to Montesquieu's still largely negative liberalism. *Democracy* more fully captures the American spirit by calling liberal democracy to appreciate those dimensions of the Biblical and Western traditions that moderate the quest for ever-greater equality and individual security.

Tocqueville warned of a difficulty, however, with religion's role in guiding democracy away from individualism, materialism, and apathy about politics. He defines America's "point of departure" as the equilibrium or mutually moderating relationship between the spirit of liberty and the spirit of religion (I.2), yet he also detects that this alloy is cracking. It is not only in Europe that the spirit of equality, and the rationalism and materialism it yields, have corroded religious faith and a balanced orientation between the transcendent and the earthly (I.2.6, 228; I.2.9, 281, 299). He deepens this concern in Volume II (II.1, Chapters 1, 2), and proposes extraordinary remedies, the peak being a role for government in indirectly fostering and buttressing religious faith (I.2, Chapters 15, 17). He knows that it will be controversial to ask "the politicians" to "act every day" as if they believed in the soul's immortality, "conforming scrupulously to religious morality in great affairs" (II.2.15, 521). As noted, his model for this remedy may have been Washington, for he emphatically praises both "this great man" and John Marshall's study of America's founder, and he quotes the Farewell Address (I.1.2, 30 n. 1; I.1.8, 107; I.2.5, 217–221; I.2.10, 320; see also I.1.3, 46, 50, 52). Only Governor John Winthrop and Washington exemplify statesmen guided by fundamental ethical principles and resisting majority opinion – as Tocqueville discerns through another statesman's analysis, in Marshall's *Life of Washington* (I.1.2, 42; I.2.6, 217–20). Since Winthrop also embodies some excesses of Puritan zeal (see I.1.2, 39; I.2.9, 283), the better model is Washington's moderate and indirect, but sincere, affirmation of religious principle. This balance of respect for religious tradition and political liberty is one that America and other liberal democracies always will struggle to maintain, but it is a fundamental resource not only for a sound domestic politics but also for their foreign policies with other states, regions, and religious traditions.

Tocqueville thus dissents from currents in modern philosophy and social theory that emphasize the destructive or oppressive power of religion, or its social construction as a tool of elites or interests. He does not see true liberation in the modernizing and secularizing forces of modern reason and modern democracy left unchecked, or simply in increased levels of basic education, urbanization, and material prosperity. He avoids directly spiritual or theological arguments, instead criticizing the modern theories inductively. Social evidence shows the failure to predict and control human affairs through attempts at a rational, postreligious utopia. There are limits in human nature. Still, if nature can't be erased, it can be degraded; many aspects of the modern postreligious society will take shape, but as dystopia. Because he finds modern liberal philosophy to be correct in some elements, especially the defense of human equality and political liberty, he will not restore any Aristotelian, Augustinian, or Thomistic remedies that directly address the soul through the city, with coercive laws. Yet, a philosophy that ignores transcendent inclinations in human nature now is the more dangerous extreme, missing a crucial part of the phenomena, and requires correction. Like Montesquieu, he is "considering religions from a purely human point of view," but in contrast, he not only notices but also emphasizes the inclination to belief as "one of the constituent elements of human nature." Modern rationalism may turn people from traditional religious beliefs, but "faith alone is the permanent state of humanity" (I.2.9, 283–84). His new political science thus partially restores the old one to argue that while laws maintain a democratic republic more than material causes do, mores sustain it most of all. Indeed, this consideration is "a central point" of his thinking; "I perceive it at the end of all my ideas" (I.2.9, 292, 295). He nearly echoes Montesquieu in stating a main aim of his work (compare *The Spirit of Laws*, 29.1): "If, in the course of this work, I have not succeeded in making the reader feel the importance" he attributes to "the mores" of the Americans, then "I have missed the principal goal that I proposed for myself in writing it" (295).

These mores are deeply religious, and moderate. In opening this chapter he invokes his initial insight that America's "point of departure" is a distinctive blending of religion and liberty: the exceptional American moderation (I.2.9, 266–67). He also defines mores capaciously, as "the ancients" did, to include not only "habits of the heart" and manners but also "habits of the mind" and indeed "the whole moral and intellectual state of a people" (275). Religious belief is the crucial element because, if "the human mind" is allowed "to follow its tendency," it "will regulate political society and the divine city" in the same way, seeking "to *harmonize* the earth with Heaven" (275, emphasis in original). This quasi-Thomistic view departs from the Augustinian emphasis on the clash of the two cities, but he also defends traditional metaphysics, natural theology, and religion against attacks by the radical Enlightenment – as if "the freedom and happiness of the human species lack nothing except to believe with Spinoza in the eternity of the world and to assert with Cabanis that the brain secretes thought" (I.2.9, 281). This scorn anticipates his extended critique in Volume II of modern rationalism and materialist philosophy. This transcends any utilitarian case for civil religion, animated by fear of religion and the aim to both control and exploit it. True, religion is for the Americans "the first of their political institutions" since it "facilitates their use" of freedom (280). Perhaps "despotism can do without faith, but freedom cannot," and "religion is much more necessary" in republics: "what makes a people master of itself if it has not submitted to God?" (282). Yet, the ultimate stakes transcend ordinary politics. His final analysis of modern democracy in Volume I anticipates the anxiety that opens Volume II, worry for the higher reaches of the soul and for philosophy itself amid egalitarianism and materialism. Here in this remarkable summary chapter on how to sustain democracy in moderation, while identifying mores and religion as the key, he invokes for the first time the fear that democratic peoples will "fall below the level of humanity" (I.2.9, 301). He uses the same phrase, about the same fate, in the work's closing theme of a new "mild" despotism that degrades democracy from within (II.4.6, 665). While this is not a pious defense of the need for religion, it is not merely utilitarian. The particular teachings of Christianity – more broadly of religions that teach the immortality of the soul and the moral discipline needed to cultivate one's soul – retain a wisdom that modern philosophy mostly has lost (II.2.15).

Ever the moderate, Tocqueville pauses in Volume II to notice extremes in religious beliefs (an echo of his warning in Volume I about Puritanism), but his concern with "exalted spirituality" is not only with Christian faith itself, or the "bizarre sects" that splinter from earlier Protestant splinters. He warns modern rationalism of the extremes it begets by enforcing its radical views on human nature, since "the taste for the infinite" will persist but will take unhealthy forms if not cultivated in sound ways (II.2.12, 510–11). He invokes Pascal as he admires Christians who transcend individualism and also self-interest well understood in their devotion to neighbors and to "love of God," a "magnificent" ideal made all the better by being "freely" chosen (II.2.9, 504–5). When building toward his extraordinary counsel that statesmen must indirectly support religious belief and morality, he invokes moderation as the principle for political philosophers and statesmen: "The whole art of the legislator consists in discerning" the particular "inclinations" of a given society "in order to know when one must aid the efforts of citizens and when it would rather be necessary to slow them down" (II.2.15, 518). Moderation is not mere centrism, and democracy needs more of the "precious inheritance" that gave birth to it, a religion that teaches human equality but not only equality, so as not to lose humanity's "most sublime faculties" and "degrade" itself (519). Still, in moderation, Tocqueville recommends Plato's metaphysical philosophy as much as he commends Christianity. Platonism's "spiritualism" and "sublime spark" accord with the "instinct and taste of the human race" for immortality of the soul (520). "The human heart is vaster than one supposes; it can at once contain a taste for the goods of the earth and a love of those of Heaven; sometimes it seems to give itself over frantically to one of the two; but it is never long before it thinks of the other" (520). He cautions, however, that if it is "easy to see" that "it is particularly important in times of democracy to make spiritualist opinions reign, it is not easy to say what those who govern democratic peoples ought to do to make them reign" (520). Indeed, he invokes his earlier endorsements of "the complete separation of church and state" and only an "indirect influence" of religion on politics as better for both religion and liberty (I.2.9, 283, 278).

Nonetheless, democracy in moderation requires that statesmen and governments must "act every day" as if they believed in "the dogma of the immortality of the soul" by "conforming scrupulously to religious morality in great affairs." This is the only way to ensure "they are teaching citizens to know it, love it, and respect it in small ones" (II.2.15, 521). He suspects that stating so "is indeed going to harm me in the eyes of politicians." Tocqueville had prepared for this tough teaching on moderation by confronting modern philosophy about its limits and its need for openness (at least) to metaphysics and religion. He invokes Pascal to this end, on the grandeur of the highest quest for truth, but also corrects his predecessor's fideist skepticism by affirming a reflective, rational judgment lying between unreflective beliefs, mere skepticism, and theological dogma (II.1.10, 435–46; also I.2.3, 179). He employs philosophy and poetry as well as theology to insist that we are neither beasts nor gods but the beings in between. While we must make space for the higher dimensions of our soul, for "the angel" to teach "the brute" in us, our politics must be free both to protect religion from the deleterious effects of establishment and to allow souls to freely choose beliefs (II.1.17, 462; II.2.16, 521–22). We need reminders that Christianity taught us human equality, before philosophy did (II.1.3, 413) – reminders more pointed than Montesquieu as Enlightened philosopher may believe, or Washington as statesman could safely or constructively emphasize.[55] Still, Washington's alloy has shown such strains and cracks even in the few decades after his passing that Tocqueville must deploy a stronger array of means, from metaphysical argument to endorsement of Christianity specifically, so as "to lead the human race by a long detour back toward faith" (II.2.17, 524).

Tocqueville's moderation thus helps us to see the deeper spirit of the three clauses on religious liberty in Article VI of the Constitution and the First Amendment. As noted in opening this chapter, this moderation helps us to address contentious issues of religion and politics in modern liberal democracy more generally. Because Tocqueville does not equate moderation with centrism he endorses accommodation, not strict separation or secularism, for supporting the principles of the founding and sustaining liberalism.[56] We can affirm Tocqueville's praise for the exceptional achievement of the Americans by noting that the declaration in Article VI that "no religious Test shall ever be required as a Qualification to any Office or public Trust under the United States" was the first such entrenchment of religious liberty in a written national constitution. The clauses in the First Amendment then develop the balance or complexity that generally is evident in the founding (including Article VI), by affirming the negative aim of tolerance but further articulating a positive one. Congress shall not make any "law respecting an establishment of religion," or any law "prohibiting the free exercise" of religion. By encompassing not only the negative aims of no test or establishment, but also the affirmative aim of freedom to pursue

---

[55] Larry Siedentop, *Inventing the Individual: The Origins of Western Liberalism* (Harvard University Press, 2014) argues this general thesis, but does not cite Tocqueville.

[56] In the voluminous literature, two recent works argue for some conception of moderation as embedded in, or required for interpreting, these constitutional issues; see Muñoz, *God and the Founders*, 206–21, especially at 213, and Murray P. Dry, *Civil Peace and the Quest for Truth: The First Amendment Freedoms in Political Philosophy and American Constitutionalism* (Lexington Books, 2004), 10, 288.

religious belief, the framers balanced accommodation of the importance of religion for public and private life with religious toleration, to develop a more complete principle of religious liberty. Accommodation argues that government need not and should not be neutral regarding the importance of religion and metaphysical beliefs for a healthy liberal order, even while it must not act preferentially toward any one religion, nor enforce any particular doctrine. The fundamental conditions and experiences that led Washington and a majority of framers to adopt this view have not changed, even if America in its third century since the founding is more pluralist and more egalitarian. The latter realities would suggest to Tocqueville all the more reason to lean toward accommodating religion. He also would encourage us to embrace the tensions and difficult judgments that come with such moderation, since only misleading or one-sided doctrines would claim a capacity to avoid them.

5

Moderation, American Grand Strategy, and Washington's Statesmanship

The philosophy of moderation developed by Montesquieu and Tocqueville is more attentive to statesmanship, thus the limits of theory, than are other versions of liberal philosophy. Hobbes had translated Thucydides' capacious study of the Peloponnesian war, and studied Machiavelli's historical and philosophical works, but *Leviathan* launched a scientism that largely dominates study of international relations in the modern era. Hobbes (the father of the school of realism) and Kant (the father of liberal internationalism or idealism) studied both history and philosophy, and particular statesmen. They do not feature this balance or breadth, however, in their philosophical works. In contrast, both *The Spirit of Laws* and *Democracy in America* cite Plutarch's *Lives of the Noble Greeks and Romans* for insights on statesmen and statesmanship. Both works seek an equilibrium between historical reflections of human nature and liberal philosophizing about them. Both Montesquieu and Tocqueville wrote philosophical histories and works of political philosophy. Indeed, Tocqueville cites Montesquieu's *Considerations on the Causes of the Greatness of the Romans and their Decline* (1734) as the model for *The Old Regime and the Revolution* (1856).[1] *The Spirit of Laws* cites many exemplars of prudence and moderation, ranging from the Viscount d'Orte's refusal in 1572 to obey King Charles IX's order to kill the Huguenots, to Alexander's restraint as conqueror compared to Caesar and the Romans. His general aim is to educate statesmen by warning that "great souls who are moderate are rare."[2] As noted in

---

[1] Tocqueville to Kergolay, December 15, 1850, cited in François Furet and Françoise Mélonio, "Introduction" to Alexis de Tocqueville, *The Old Regime and the Revolution*, vol. I, eds. Furet and Mélonio, tr. Kahan (University of Chicago Press, 1998), 56.

[2] Charles de Montesquieu, *De l'Esprit des Lois*, Book 4, Chapter 2, also 10.13 and 14, and 28.41, in *Œuvres complètes*, Pléiade edition, ed. Caillois, 2 vols. (Gallimard, 1949–51), 2:264, 387–91, 858. I have checked my translations against *The Spirit of the Laws*, eds. Cohler, Miller, and Stone (Cambridge University Press, 1989) (here, 33, 147–51, 595). Subsequent references are

Chapter 3, Tocqueville writes *Democracy in America* as much for statesmen and citizens as theorists. Hegel just had celebrated Napoleon as a world-historical figure in his philosophy of world history, but Tocqueville dared to praise the more moderate framers of the American Constitution as including "the finest minds and noblest characters that had ever appeared in the New World." He elevated one particularly: "George Washington presided over it." *The Federalist*, inspired by Washington's statesmanship and written by protégés, is "a fine book that, though special to America, ought to be familiar to statesmen of every country." It also is telling that the first use in *Democracy* of his concept of enlightened self-interest arises in commenting upon Washington's foreign policy and "character."[3]

Both philosophers knew that a liberal polity needs statesmanship in domestic as well as foreign affairs, but Tocqueville forecasts his term as French foreign minister by emphasizing Washington's deeds and words regarding foreign policy and war. A statesman's character and judgment are peculiarly exposed when acting as executive for the polity with other polities. Paradoxically for America, our increasing democratization in thought and deed has produced a political culture of the perpetual campaign, which defines the presidency as a domestic office and then is surprised when global affairs dominate every incumbent. This process began early in the nineteenth century, but the Progressive redefinition of the presidency – launched as theory by Woodrow Wilson and practiced by him and other Progressive executives – emphasized this shift by seeking to combine populist support with the new science of administrative expertise. Oddly, this shift occurred precisely as America rose to be a great power, which should have led us to underscore the office's emphasis on foreign affairs and grand strategy. True, Montesquieu noted that "the spirit of republics is peace and moderation" – modern republics, post Christianity, he seems to presume – whereas the spirit of monarchy is "war and expansion." Such republican executives might emphasize domestic affairs (*The Spirit of Laws*, 9.2, 371/132). Still, this is not a proto-Kantian moralism about abolishing war, and he knows all about warlike republics from his *Considerations*. Given his reference therein to Thucydides, he knows about imperial democracy, too. Moreover, he describes the modern polity that he examines most closely, and largely recommends, as a blend of monarchy and republic (19.27, 580/330 on England; see also 5.19, 304/70). While it is a persistent myth that Washington was an isolationist, it is true

parenthetical, citing part of the work and pages in the Pléiade edition (vol. 2) and the Cohler translation (e.g., 4.2, 264/33).

[3] Alexis de Tocqueville, *Democracy in America*, eds. Harvey C. Mansfield and Delba Winthrop (University of Chicago Press, 2000), I.1.8, 107–8; I.2.5, 218, 220. I have checked this translation by consulting *De la Démocratie en Amérique* in Tocqueville, *Œuvres complètes*, ed. J. P. Mayer (Gallimard, 1951), Tome I, 2 vols., and *Democracy in America*, ed. J. P Mayer, tr. George Lawrence (Doubleday, Anchor Books, 1969). Subsequent references will cite Volume, Part, chapter, and page number of the Mansfield and Winthrop edition.

that a republican-pacific element persists in America's character, and flares up occasionally. Jefferson was the first president to endorse such idealism, warning of "entangling alliances" in his First Inaugural, a phrase often mistakenly attributed to Washington. Jefferson, nonetheless, couldn't help being American: he then deployed the U.S. navy and marines to Tripoli to vanquish the Barbary pirates, and doubled the size of the republic by purchasing Louisiana from Napoleon.

The argument pursued here is that our debates about foreign policy and grand strategy thus are hampered by two imbalances that evade deeper realities about human affairs and America. The first is a radical Enlightenment and now social-scientific penchant for scientistic or purely idealist theories, whether realism or liberal idealism. The second, discussed in Chapter 6, is the project to replace statesmanship with a bipolar notion of leadership that encompasses populist favor and scientific administrative expertise – thus eliminating prudence or practical wisdom. The international relations theory that advises American leaders forms around poles that fail to see politics as a liberal-democratic statesman naturally would, as steward for both a distinct state and fundamental ideals. Realism cares not that we are a liberal constitutional democracy, since international affairs concerns only the interests and power of states, and the balances and calculations thereof. Realism presumes we are from anywhere. Liberal internationalism, at the other extreme, deems our liberal character as entailing construction of global institutions and binding international law, and grants only minimum scope for a state. Liberalism presumes we are from everywhere.[4] These dominant poles in academia have not helped the citizenry, or leaders, with serious consideration of global affairs. The realist school contains a subset that is happy if Americans have little regard for such affairs, leaving them to experts, especially if the latter hold the neo-isolationist view that America causes itself more harm than good in many global engagements.[5] Thus, neither school really advises on a foreign policy for America – for a liberal constitutional republic, with both ideals and interests. Even Henry Kissinger, putatively a realist, recently has argued (or admitted) that American foreign policy or strategy must balance power and principle,

---

[4] Amid the voluminous literature, a proponent of liberal internationalism who discusses the interests or incentives that should pull America toward liberalism is G. John Ikenberry, *Liberal Leviathan: The Origins, Crisis, and Transformation of the American World Order* (Princeton University Press, 2011). For Kant's categorical moralism in international affairs, see "Perpetual Peace: A Philosophical Sketch" (1795), in *Kant: Political Writings*, ed. H. S. Reiss, 2nd edn. (Cambridge University Press, 1991), 93–130.

[5] Amid the voluminous literature, an exposition of realism as a neo-isolationist "offshore balancing" is Christopher Layne, *The Peace of Illusions: American Grand Strategy from 1940 to the Present* (Cornell University Press, 2006); a milder version of realism that surveys several grand strategies for twenty-first-century America is Robert J. Art, *A Grand Strategy for America* (Cornell University Press, 2003).

pragmatic concerns and ideals.[6] As to the neo-conservative school, to which few academics ever subscribed, it revived the American tradition of blending principles, but forgot moderation in both aims and rhetoric. Liberal ideals of a democratic peace theory suggested that since democracies don't make war on each other, we spread peace by spreading democracy; a variant of realism known as hegemonic stability theory also suggested that many states recognize the benefits of having one great power provide economic and political order. A strong dose of American exceptionalism would bind the two principles.[7] The academic and intellectual backlash to the brief neoconservative moment in George W. Bush's presidency, and to wars in Iraq and Afghanistan, has reinforced war fatigue, a flare-up of an isolationist mood, and thoughts of American decline.[8] It may be that the public mind also was glutted with contentious debates about doctrines and schools, and thus is happy to avoid settling upon an American grand strategy – as containment and deterrence had defined the Cold War, albeit with much debate about applying these principles.

The dangers of not bothering to have a grand strategy, and of academic discourse so refined and polarized as to repel both officials and citizens, are threefold. The Executive and Congress (and officials serving them, including the military) conduct affairs by crisis response, not larger policy; difficult decisions are evaded because a disengaged citizenry fails to signal support for difficult but necessary policies; the result is a lurching from extreme to extreme – in the past two decades, from overconfidence prompting overextension to self-criticism prompting withdrawal. If our theory doesn't serve our practice, we should question our theory.[9] This is especially true given that however attractive restraint or disengagement seem either for moral aims or interests, America guarantees

---

[6] Henry Kissinger, *World Order* (Penguin Press, 2014), pp. 9–10, 234–36, 268–69, 274–79, 295, 306–13, 327–29, 362–63, 367. Kissinger's shift from realism to balance among principles, and between theory and practice, mirrors a concern among international relations scholars to redress the latter imbalance; see Alexander George, *Bridging the Gap: Theory and Practice in Foreign Policy* (United States Institute of Peace, 1993); many subsequent publications lamenting this gap suggest that its academic or intellectual causes persist.

[7] On hegemonic stability theory, see Robert Gilpin, *The Political Economy of International Relations* (Princeton University Press, 1987); Francis Fukuyama criticizes neoconservatism in *America at the Crossroads: Democracy, Power, and the Neoconservative Legacy* (Yale University Press, 2006); Robert Kagan's neoconservative works include *Of Paradise and Power: America and Europe in the New World Order* (Alfred A. Knopf, 2003) and *The World America Made* (Alfred A. Knopf, 2012).

[8] Kagan discusses these themes in *The World America Made*; see also Fareed Zakaria, *The Post-American World* (W.W. Norton & Company, 2008).

[9] Jack Snyder summarizes realism and liberal idealism in particular, and advocates blending or balancing such views in the practice of policy, in "One World, Rival Theories," *Foreign Policy*, no. 145 (November/December 2004), 53–62; see also Joseph S. Nye, Jr., "Neorealism and Neoliberalism," *World Politics* 40 (1988), 235–51; on the limits of various theories or paradigms, from "the end of history" to "the clash of civilizations," see Stanley Hoffman, "Clash of Globalizations," *Foreign Affairs* 8, no. 1:4 (2002), 104–15.

the current global order.[10] Our interests, ideals, and people span the globe, and the system of independent states tied by law and commerce is largely the fruit of American policies and principles dating to our founding. Publius (Hamilton) called America to oppose European imperial power in 1788: we should "vindicate the honor of the human race" and "teach that assuming brother moderation."[11] We have not left the world alone, and the world is unlikely to leave us alone. Moreover, much of what we find familiar, comfortable, and just – global commerce and relative prosperity at home, cheap energy, the Internet and social media, freedom to travel the globe, great power peace – are provided by a global order sustained by Anglo-American power and influence. Can this be enjoyed without American leadership? Given the global, instantaneous reach of new technologies and threats? A deeper question is whether our citizenry and leaders will forthrightly consider foreign and defense policies, and our larger role, as America confronts problems old and new. Only a section of either national party, and a small set of academics and intellectuals, now seem interested to defend American internationalism as a strong presence in both hard power (military and intelligence capabilities) and soft power (diplomacy, aid, economic and cultural influence) to uphold global order. The few who combine internationalism with advocacy of American responsibility tend to emphasize regions of great importance for our interests and ideals – such as the Middle East and East Asia – but the systemic order also deserves concern.

While every generation of Americans may think it is the first to enter uncharted seas of foreign and security policy, these debates and perplexities date at least to Washington's presidency. Politics usually has not stopped at the water's edge, in good times or crisis.[12] After the Cold War ended a quarter century ago, America was the superpower with unrivaled military, economic, and cultural might but we also saw the dawn (we now realize) of a global struggle with Islamist terrorism. We were the global hegemon, yet beset by shadowy threats and unique burdens. Now we face such new issues as cyber-attacks that could damage our financial, communications, and power systems. The range and perplexity of threats but also opportunities, and the

---

[10] Andrew Bacevich has criticized that status in a series of provocations, first in *American Empire: The Realities and Consequences of U.S. Diplomacy* (Harvard University Press, 2002); his neo-isolationist view blends insight with selective presentation of American history and ideals, for example, by erasing any Hamiltonian elements until the 1890s. More recently, see *Washington Rules: America's Path to Permanent War* (Metropolitan Books, 2010).

[11] Alexander Hamilton, James Madison, and John Jay, *The Federalist Papers*, eds. Rossiter and Kesler (Mentor-Penguin, 1999), no. 11, 59. See generally Walter Russell Mead, *Special Providence: American Foreign Policy and How It Changed the World* (Century/Knopf, 2001).

[12] Henry Kissinger advocated, a decade into America's status as lone superpower, recovery of the study of history and philosophy as essential to a clear national strategy and genuine statesmanship, in *Does America Need a Foreign Policy? Toward a Diplomacy for the 21st Century* (Simon & Schuster, 2001), 283–88; see also Charles Hill, *Grand Strategies: Literature, Statecraft, and World Order* (Yale University Press, 2010), including his striking chapter "America: A New Idea," 134–76; and Kissinger's recent work *World Order*.

possible responses across a range of hard and soft power capabilities, call for debates over grand strategy so that our liberal constitutional republic can clarify the right balance of ends, ways, and means. Otherwise, we have only *ad hoc* responses to crises, and fail to confront challenges and choices on more advantageous terms. That will not sustain an international order. How should we address the persistence of Islamist terrorism, and of authoritarianism in Russia and China? How should we win our wars of the past decade in the Middle East and South Asia, wars that don't end despite our efforts to withdraw? How should we respond to, or shape, events flowing from the Arab "Spring" or revolution, which mostly has yielded chaos given America's cautious, inconsistent response? Should we stop a revolutionary Iranian regime from acquiring nuclear weapons, with military might if necessary? A few scholars will admit that doctrines of realism, liberal internationalism, neo-conservatism, and other schools tend to cut us off from the full balance of our first principles, as well as a fresh view of new developments. Moreover, such doctrines often yield not candid deliberation but contests between armed camps.[13]

A return to first principles, in particular to Washington's statesmanship in founding American foreign and security policy, may help us to chart a grand strategy more consonant with the better angels of our history and national character, and with our just interests. America was the first deliberately founded polity in history; it would be odd if her rise to global dominance in both hard and soft power justifies amnesia about her original aims. Another great statesman, amid terrible crisis, defined America as dedicated to propositions about liberty, equality, pursuit of happiness, and the rule of law – which place in perspective our debates about global empire, global commerce, global democracy, a national security state, or a balance of power. Indeed, much of Lincoln's greatness lay in a strategy of rededication to the founding principles, including care in balancing military power with the higher ends it serves. He knew that novel challenges required him to think and act anew, but also that America was grounded in principles of natural justice and religious truths about the humility yet dignity to which mankind is called – however much we fail to abide by these. Several decades prior, Tocqueville had worried about some of America's tendencies in foreign affairs, fearing we had abandoned Washington's principled prudence. Still, he hoped America could combine liberal principles and power to be the global pillar for liberty, and he predicted it would oppose a sole global rival, Russia, standing for authoritarian rule – with each power holding "the destinies of half the world in its hands" (*Democracy*, I.2.10, 395–96). This prescient insight occurs just after "Some Considerations on the Causes of the Commercial Greatness of the United States" (384) – a signal of

---

[13] In addition to the work by Snyder, Nye, Mead, and Hill already cited, see also Jakub Grygiel, "Educating for National Security," *Orbis* (Spring 2013), 201–16; and Paul Carrese and Michael Doran, "Republican Prudence: The Founders' Foreign Policy School," *The American Interest* (May–June 2014).

Montesquieu's influence on America's character, and on Tocqueville's political philosophy. Brief consideration of Montesquieu's philosophy of moderation about international affairs prepares for a deeper look at Washington's grand strategy for America; I close with Tocqueville's praise for Washington, and the continued salience of these insights for challenges facing both our liberal democratic republic and the world order it built during the twentieth century and, until recently, has sustained.

Montesquieu's Right of Nations and Liberal Moderation

As discussed in Chapters 1 and 4, Montesquieu's philosophy of moderation encompasses several spheres of law. From the first book of *The Spirit of Laws*, international right joins political (constitutional) law and civil (criminal and civil) law as integral to his inquiry (*Spirit*, 1.3). This adapted a legacy gradually developed by Aristotle, Plutarch, and medieval theories of just war and prudence articulated by Augustine and Aquinas. He seems particularly shaped by Grotius, who drew on such sources to expand the first modern jurisprudence of international law in *On The Rights of War and Peace* (1625). Montesquieu's conception argues that statesmen must heed liberal principles while making the necessary judgments about how to actually apply them – or find the least-worst departure from them. A few scholars note his importance in providing fundamental principles for American thought on international relations, but generally his contribution is confined to advocacy of commerce. This view casts him as a forerunner of democratic peace theory, that modern republics or democracies will not make war on other democracies given a mutual concern for peaceful pursuit of prosperity and stability. While Montesquieu's advocacy of commerce is important, marking him as the first philosopher to advocate a liberalized global culture of international affairs, his thinking transcends this element and is not captured by any of today's doctrines or schools.[14]

Montesquieu's philosophy is more comprehensive and sober than liberal idealism, by conceiving a liberal polity that pursues tranquility at home and both commercial expansion and power abroad. His "right of nations" theory has

---

[14] See Michael Doyle, "Liberalism and World Politics," *American Political Science Review* 80 (1986), 1151–69; and Spencer R. Weart, *Never at War: Why Democracies Will Not Fight One Another* (Yale University Press, 1998). Doyle sees Montesquieu's focus as commerce (1152); in fact, Montesquieu discerns limits of liberal rationalism, as does Doyle (1162–63). More discerning analyses include Nicholas G. Onuf, *The Republican Legacy in International Thought* (Cambridge University Press, 1998), 233–46, 262; David C. Hendrickson, *Peace Pact: The Lost World of the American Founding* (University Press of Kansas, 2003), 29, 43–45, 53–54; Daniel Deudney, *Bounding Power: Republican Security Theory from the Polis to the Global Village* (Princeton University Press, 2007), 10–11, 126–28, 269–71; and Michael Mosher, "Montesquieu on Empire and Enlightenment," in *Empire and Modern Political Thought*, ed. Sankar Muthu (Cambridge University Press, 2012), 112–54 – which glimpses Montesquieu's moderation, but often does not give him full credit for adhering to it.

quietly informed America and influenced other liberal democracies, although he gets little credit now. Moderation in international affairs seeks a humane policy toward war, conquest, and commerce that blends realist concerns about power, interest, and security with liberal and Christian principles about natural right and peace as higher aims. His complex blend of liberal principles with realistic necessity borrows a disposition from medieval just war theory, which blended ideals with prudence.[15] He also drew on the modern jurists Grotius and Pufendorf to formulate guidance for statesmen that balanced the necessity of power with limits to war found in rights of individuals and basic international right.[16] The complexity of his blend of classical, modern, and Christian elements echoes Grotius's encyclopedic efforts.[17] Montesquieu obviously is the great authority for the American founders on principles of constitutionalism and the theory of pluralism or competing interests, but his influence upon international relations theory or American foreign policy now is largely neglected. Perhaps his theory was seen as too complex and ambiguous; there is a cleanness to the rational calculations of Machiavelli and Hobbes, and to the liberal doctrines of Rousseau and Kant. His innovation was to argue that principles of domestic constitutionalism and the rule of law point to analogues in international affairs that should govern, as much as is possible, claims of interest and security. Rational efforts to moderate the human tendency to conflict can extend from domestic to international affairs, bolstered by a dose of Christian humanism, while recognizing the anarchy or lack of government to enforce any international law. He found this blend or balance of principles arising from our nature and political condition:

> Considered as inhabitants of a planet so large that different peoples are necessary, they have laws bearing on the relation that these peoples have with one another; and this is the RIGHT OF NATIONS ... The *right of nations* is by nature founded on this principle: that the various nations should do to one another, in peace, the most good possible, and, in war, the least ill that is possible, without harming their true interests. (*Spirit*, 1.3, 236–37/7, emphases in original)

One of the few extensive analyses of Montesquieu's theory of international relations offers important insights but reduces him to the realism of Machiavelli, Hobbes, and Locke, distinguished only by merely prudential counsels to limit power and interest.[18] This overlooks Montesquieu's statement that the right of

---

[15] As noted in the Prologue, several scholars challenge the view of Aquinas's natural law and just war philosophy as categorical; see the discussion and sources at note 18 therein.

[16] See Gerhard von Glahn, *Law Among Nations: An Introduction to Public International Law*, 5th edn. (Macmillan, 1986), 3, 22–25, 27–35; and Hendrickson, "Foundations of the New Diplomacy," in *Peace Pact: The Lost World of the American Founding*, 169–76.

[17] I discuss this in essays on the "Liberty Matters" blog, contributing to discussion of "Hugo Grotius on War and the State," March 2014, at http://oll.libertyfund.org/pages/lm-grotius.

[18] Thomas L. Pangle and Peter J. Ahrensdorf, *Justice Among Nations: On the Moral Basis of Power and Peace* (University Press of Kansas, 1999), 157–61. William C. Martel mentions

nations is "the political law of nations considered in their relation with each other," and that offensive force must be "regulated" by it (*Spirit*, 10.1, 377/138). It also neglects his declaration that conquest and force must follow the "law of natural enlightenment, which wants us to do to others what we would want to have done to us" (10.3, 378/139). His summation of this philosophy is even more striking and pronounced when assessing modern Europe's principles as an improvement over those of the Romans. The right of nations now is marked by a spirit of preservation and justice rather than of subjugation, and for this progress, "homage" is owed to "our modern times, to contemporary reasoning, to the religion of the present day, to our philosophy, and to our mores" (10.3, 378–79, 139).[19] This tribute to Christianity also suggests that his advocacy of commerce as softening international affairs and promoting peace does not aim to undermine religion. Rather, the great theme of his right of nations philosophy, from international law to commerce, is that "it is moderation which governs men, and not excesses" (*Spirit*, 22.22, 682/426; see also 29.1). One of his final remarks on the topic seems idealistic in crediting Christianity for humane principles to moderate politics, "for which human nature can never be sufficiently grateful." Ever the moderate, he also warns of religious fanaticism: the victor now "leaves to the vanquished these great things: life, liberty, laws, goods, and always religion, when one does not blind oneself" (*Spirit*, 24.3, 717/462).

Montesquieu's philosophical commitment to moderation is Aristotelian in some ways, identifying the extremes often present in both the theory and the practice of politics and seeking the right balance between them – even if his ultimate aims are more modern and liberal. Another link to Aristotle often overlooked is that Montesquieu conceives of prudence in pre-Machiavellian, prerealist terms. Prudence is not calculation of self-interest divorced from moral principle but rather the awareness that principle is not self-enacting. Morally astute leaders must exercise judgment in concrete situations. Conversely, Montesquieu affirms recognition of the practical limits facing particular leaders or states, in particular situations, to defend high moral ideals at the expense of other political and moral principles. This prudential spirit directly informs the idea of promoting liberal democracy found in Tocqueville's philosophy and also in American foreign policy, which tries to balance liberal ideals with the limits that come from necessity, circumstances, and the promoter's national interest or other obligations.

Moderation of course informs the principles for which Montesquieu is better known, separation of powers and federalism, prescribing a balance between

Montesquieu and moderation, linked to Washington's Farewell address, but offers no further analysis – in "Grand Strategy of 'Restrainment'," *Orbis* 54 (2010), 356–73.

[19] Grotius invokes "the law of charity" repeatedly in analyzing *ius ad bellum* and *ius in bello*; for example, the law of nature might permit risk of killing innocents for self-preservation, but "the law of charity...does not." In Hugo Grotius, *The Rights of War and Peace*, 3 vols., ed. Richard Tuck (Liberty Fund, 2005 [1625]) II.1, 398; see also, for example, III.2, 1243.

multiple centers of power as best for securing rights, liberty, and stability in politics. Indeed, America's constitutional order is the showcase of such moderation. His less-noted influence on the foreign policy of the founders is most evident, paradoxically, in the most famous foreign policy statement of the era, Washington's Farewell Address of 1796. Tocqueville praised such ideas as still guiding American policy four decades later, and he particularly praised their moderation or balance.

Washington's Principles for an American Grand Strategy

In the mid twentieth century Hans Morgenthau urged America to revive the realism of its founders, especially Washington and Hamilton, to guide our foreign policy in new circumstances and to transcend both isolationism and Wilsonian internationalism.[20] Morgenthau eloquently advocated his favored theory of international affairs, but his reconception of Washington as simply a realist did not stick. The Founder more typically labors under a graver misreading: that his Farewell Address and other writings avow isolationism or passivity. Fortunately, several scholars in the post-Cold War era have explained why uncertain times call for revisiting this statesman who rarely favored "isms" or doctrines, but who offered sound principles on right, might, and diplomacy that long were cited as the guiding ideals of our republic.[21] We should expand our thinking and assess our current options by recovering the practical wisdom and distinctive American principles found in the Declaration of Independence, *The Federalist*, and the Constitution – all of which both reflect and inform Washington's statecraft.

As discussed in Chapter 2, Washington's Farewell to "Friends, and Fellow-Citizens" offered principles he thought "important to the permanency of your felicity as a people."[22] Leading statesmen and thinkers did consult it up

---

[20] Hans Morgenthau, "The Mainsprings of American Foreign Policy: The National Interest vs. Moral Abstractions," *American Political Science Review* 44 (1950), 833–54. See also Joseph Cropsey, "The Moral Basis of International Action," in *America Armed*, ed. Robert Goldwin (Rand McNally, 1963), 71–91, and more recently, Dmitri Simes, "Realism: It's Highminded…and It Works," *The National Interest* 74 (Winter 2003/2004), 168–72.

[21] See especially David Hendrickson, "The Renovation of American Foreign Policy," *Foreign Affairs* 71, no. 2 (1992), 48–63; Patrick Garrity, "Warnings of a Parting Friend," *The National Interest* 45 (Fall 1996), 14–26; Matthew Spalding and Patrick Garrity, "Our Interest, Guided by Our Justice," in *A Sacred Union of Citizens: George Washington's Farewell Address and the American Character* (Rowman & Littlefield, 1996), 91–139; Walter McDougall, *Promised Land, Crusader State: America's Encounter with the World since 1776* (Houghton Mifflin, 1997), and "Back to Bedrock," *Foreign Affairs* 76, no. 2 (1997), 134–46; and Hill's insightful praise of the Farewell Address in *Grand Strategies*, 148–50.

[22] "Farewell Address," in *George Washington: Writings*, ed. John Rhodehamel (Library of America/Literary Classics of the United States, 1997), 962, 964; hereafter cited parenthetically as *W*. I revise spelling only. Another useful one-volume edition is *George Washington: A Collection*, ed. William B. Allen (Liberty Fund, 1988). This section presupposes the analysis of Washington, and the Farewell, in Chapter 2.

through Henry Cabot Lodge during the First World War and Morgenthau in the Cold War. President Eisenhower decided to deliver a farewell address in 1961 modeled upon Washington's, to offer similar counsel about the equipoise needed between military capability and protection of liberty in an era of new challenges.[23] In recent decades, however, a dominant consensus largely deems the Farewell irrelevant, as isolationist or outdated. Some also consider Washington just a figurehead for his bright aides Madison and Hamilton. Even brief engagement with the Address, however, sheds light on current dilemmas; deeper study shows that he revised every argument, hoping, as if a latter-day Thucydides, to distill counsel for the ages. His deeds and words are no cookbook of recipes for today, since the main lessons of the Address and the career informing it are architectonic, not specific: America must base its security policy on principle and prudence rather than on power or popularity, and prize a decent republican politics over conquest or glory. The Address marked the second time Washington had relinquished near-absolute power. When his countrymen ranked him with a disinterested Roman statesman, Cincinnatus, this recalled the best of the Republic – not the Empire. While he rose to fame through military command, he appraised power and security as means to higher ends. Like many statesmen of his era, Washington held an edition of Grotius's *On the Rights of War and Peace* (1625) in his personal library. Principles of personal and civic virtue guided his policies and counsel, to a degree that Americans alternately admire and find hard to believe, but the enlightened liberal-republicanism of Grotius, Montesquieu, and other leading lights demanded nothing less.

Familiarity with Washington's career reveals service to the republic's principles before himself, demonstrated in decades of deeds and words devoted to liberty, constitutionalism, and moderation. The Address encapsulates a comprehensive approach to foreign policy, security, and war, but his words and deeds are best understood when viewed in light of each other. Indeed, as befits a statesman, one can glean from the Address and the career informing it a handy set of guidelines – five broad, overlapping principles for strategic thinking: *first*, the priority of a decent republic, rooted in natural justice and guided by transcendent truths about humankind; *second*, the subordination of military to civil authority, and avoidance of either militarism or weakness; *third*, balancing liberty and security through a complex, moderate constitution that divides responsibility for foreign and defense policy; *fourth*, the need for statesmanship within such an order, especially an executive balancing deliberation, prudence, and flexibility in both grand strategy and tactics; and, *fifth*, balancing interest, independence, and justice in foreign affairs through prudent recourse to just-war principles and the classic right of nations. Washington was a

---

[23] See Jean Edward Smith, *Eisenhower in War and Peace* (Random House, 2012), 759, and documents in the Eisenhower Presidential Library at www.eisenhower.archives.gov/research/online_documents/farewell_address.html.

practical man, but he insisted policies and action be guided by basic principles and informed judgment. Those seeking concrete plans on pressing issues may think these principles vague or useless. He knew, however, that republics typically falter on strategic thinking – the effort to find systematic conceptions of the sustainable ways to connect ends with means. We seize on short-term problems, adopt favored doctrines of the day, or follow popular impulses. For Washington, sound policy judgments require candid deliberation guided by fundamental principles. He doubtlessly would admit that we face massive, new problems today, with new technologies and threats in a globalized and inter-connected life, not to mention the envy and mistrust attending our extraordinary political and military might. He might remind us, however, that across three decades, he defeated a superpower and managed an international coalition, forged trust within his own republic, and navigated ruthless great power politics – all with vastly fewer resources at his disposal than America can marshal today.

Washington's principles on republicanism and constitutional complexity, and on balancing interest and justice, transcend the doctrines and quarrels of the moment to restore an enduring horizon. He has been caricatured as incompetent at strategy, while his example actually recalls a Clausewitzian grand strategy that links security policy with larger moral and political aims.[24] We now obscure this perspective given our faith in technology and analytical thinking. We are distracted by the dynamism and drive for novelty in policy, the media, and academia. At its peak Washington's moderation recalls the sober, humane, and complex republicanism of Thucydides, equally aware of the necessity of war and of imperial temptations to which democracies, and ambitious leaders, are prone.[25] After surveying the principles evident in specific episodes and writings of his statesmanship, I offer some more particular lessons that his republicanism and principled prudence might suggest for current challenges and debates.

A Decent Republic, Natural Rights, and Providence – Washington's career proved that his deeds and words rested on principles. As noted in Chapter 2, his writings and actions prior to attending the First Continental Congress in 1774 invoke rights to liberty and self-government, and "natural justice." In protesting British policies he connected "natural Right" with England's "Laws &

---

[24] On Washington and Clausewitzean grand strategy, see Donald Higginbotham, *George Washington and the American Military Tradition* (University of Georgia Press, 1985), 5, 114, 117, and Mackubin Owens, "General Washington and the Military Strategy of the Revolution," in *Patriot Sage: George Washington and the American Political Tradition*, eds. Gregg and Spalding (ISI Books, 1999), 61–98. In general, see Paul Kennedy, *Grand Strategies in War and Peace* (Yale University Press, 1991), and John Lewis Gaddis, *Strategies of Containment: A Critical Appraisal of Postwar American National Security Policy* (Oxford University Press, 1982).

[25] Among other readings, see W. Robert Connor, *Thucydides* (Princeton University Press, 1984); Paul A. Rahe, "Thucydides' Critique of Realpolitik," *Security Studies* 5, no. 2 (1995), 105–41; and Nancy Kokaz, "Moderating Power: A Thucydidean Perspective," *Review of International Studies* 27 (2001), 27–49.

Constitution" (1774; W, 157). He supported strong measures in Congress, and after the battles at Lexington and Concord in 1775, he attended the Second Congress in carefully chosen attire: his Virginia uniform. Several principles forged in that crisis directly address our twenty-first century concerns. The founders did not know of terrorism, but they knew of pirates and other outlaws. They justified their separation with legal and philosophical principles publicly stated, and formed a professional military force reporting to an elected civilian government. The Declaration of Independence justifies a war to protect basic natural rights and constitutional government, as a last resort; it also specifies unacceptable forms of warfare concerning civilians, property, and prisoners. This spirit of constitutional republicanism informed Washington's General Orders of July 9, 1776, which ordered the Declaration to be read to the troops so that they might understand "the grounds & reasons" of the war (W, 228).

The same General Orders provide for chaplains and religious services, and call upon the "blessing and protection of Heaven"; indeed, Washington hoped every officer and enlisted would live "as becomes a Christian Soldier defending the dearest Rights and Liberties of his country" (W, 228). As noted in Chapter 4, after the war, his major writings always cite the guidance of transcendent ideals but in more careful, nonsectarian language, broadened to embrace the rights to religious liberty for which the war also had been fought. He did not separate republicanism, justifiable and limited force, and divine guidance about decency and honorable conduct. The radical direction of the French Revolution by the mid 1790s – replacing Christianity with a religion of reason, progress, and ferocious republicanism – unintentionally affirmed the moderation of Montesquieu's law of natural enlightenment. The famous exhortations in the Farewell Address to instill religious faith as well as moral and intellectual virtue thus defy the categories of recent American disputes about church and state: "Of all the dispositions and habits which lead to political prosperity, Religion and morality are indispensable supports"; "A volume could not trace all their connections with private and public felicity"; just policies are "recommended by every sentiment which ennobles human Nature" (W 971, 972–73). As is evident from his 1783 Circular, and his extraordinary letters to religious minorities, he steadily balanced respect for Christian churches and Biblical religion with an enlightened view of religious liberty. These were ideals worth dying for, but military and security measures were neither ends in themselves nor a replacement for a decent republican politics at home and abroad.

Civil–Military Relations, and Necessary Defenses, for a Republic – Throughout his decades in public life, from colonial Virginia to establishing a sound national constitution, Washington noted the dangers of either militarism or weakness. He established the republican principle of civil–military relations, which many nations still do not enjoy. He drew upon British practice, but both America and the world chiefly should thank Washington for demonstrating that a professional military is both necessary to protect liberty and can be safe for it through subordination to laws and civil authority. This reflected his political moderation: real liberty is ordered liberty, securing self-government and political decency under law. Indeed, John Marshall, the great Chief Justice of the United States, having served as a young officer under Washington, argued that without his character and principles, the American cause would have failed in the war's darkest hours.[26] Washington resisted temptations of power when the war's prospects brightened, and when President under the Constitution. After the victory at Yorktown in 1781, an American colonel suggested he should be king, perhaps a tempting offer for a general admired by his army. The temptation might strengthen given the great disorder in Congress: Washington long had proposed reforms about supplies, equipment, and pay for his men. Still, he immediately expressed "abhorrence" and "astonishment" to learn of "such ideas" in the army: "Let me conjure you then, if you have any regard for your Country, concern for yourself or posterity, or respect for me, to banish these thoughts from your Mind" (W, 468–69).

After long enjoying this principle, Americans tend to forget that our civil–military relations have not been trouble-free, and that Washington's high standard is difficult. A concern in post-Cold War America is that the military is isolated from civilians, and is too conservative. The deeper issue, clarified by Washington's perspective of, is that many liberal democracies now conceive of citizenship as requiring neither military nor any other service. Many analyses of a civil–military gap, or demands that the military adopt the egalitarian, individualistic trends of wider society, similarly misunderstand the need for a distinct military character, professionalism, and education, both for military efficacy and to inculcate an ethic of the rule of law. His example also sheds light on debates about the strictly professional versus professional–political models of officership offered by Samuel Huntington and Morris Janowitz. Some now argue that the military and its distinct services are semiautonomous interests pressing elected officials for money, personnel, capabilities, and security policies; others argue that elected civilians have a constitutional duty to challenge and manage top officers and the armed services – on everything from tactics to force structure – to ensure that larger objectives are served.[27] The perspective of Washington reminds us of the stakes involved for our constitutional republic, and recommends a balance between the functional and the political models of officership. He was no wall-flower as General, but he always respected civilian authority; conversely, as President, he selected and then closely supervised the

---

[26] John Marshall, *The Life of George Washington: Special Edition for Schools*, eds. Faulkner and Carrese (Liberty Fund, 2000 [1838]), 75. Hereinafter cited parenthetically as *LGW*.

[27] Compare Peter Feaver, *Armed Servants: Agency, Oversight, and Civil-Military Relations* (Harvard University Press, 2003), with Eliot Cohen, *Supreme Command: Soldiers, Statesmen, and Leadership in Wartime* (Free Press, 2002). For Higginbotham the model of Washington and George C. Marshall blends professionalism and republicanism, and transcends Huntington's categories; *Washington and the Military Tradition*, 114–38. I discuss these issues in "For Constitution and Profession: Paradoxes of Military Service in a Liberal Democracy," in *NOMOS LIV: Loyalty*, eds. Levinson, Parker, and Woodruff (New York University Press, 2013).

generals fighting Indian tribes in the Northwest Territory (replacing St. Clair with Wayne) and the army that suppressed the Whiskey Rebellion (see *LGW*, Chapters 29, 32).[28]

Washington eventually persuaded Congress to establish executive offices, and procedures to supply the army and manage revenue; this supported the success of the Yorktown campaign of 1781 (*LGW*, 259–60). He upheld discipline and civil authority during two troop mutinies in 1781 over pay and supplies, dealing moderately with the first, severely with the second (*LGW*, 245–48). In 1783 when the peace process threatened to disband the army before being paid, a letter at headquarters in Newburgh, New York, summoned officers to discuss mutiny against Congress. Washington denounced such ideas in an extraordinary speech that deplored "discord and separation between the Civil and Military powers" as violating American principles (W 495–500). After appealing to both reason and emotion he ultimately invoked virtues of duty and honor. He then stumbled in reading a letter from Congress, saying: "Gentlemen, you will permit me to put on my spectacles, for I have not only grown gray, but almost blind, in the service of my country" (W 498–500, 1109; see note 496.12). The once-rebellious officers, some in tears, unanimously reaffirmed allegiance to civil authority. Today the main doctrine manual of the U.S. Army opens with "Washington at Newburgh: Establishing the Role of the Military in a Democracy," finding in these deeds and words "a fundamental tenet of the American military profession."[29] Principled to the end, he disbanded the army once peace was official. After his final Circular to the states recommending reforms, he resigned before Congress in December 1783 (W, 547–48). Jefferson praised "the moderation & virtue of a single character" as having saved the revolution from the typical problem of military victor turning dictator.[30]

A Constitutional and Moderate Path to Foreign and Defense Policy – The Clausewitzian character of Washington's grand strategy, placing forces and policies in a frame of larger political aims, is evident in his commitment to a constitutional order.[31] As argued in Chapter 2, he was the crucial leader in the constitutional reform effort from 1783 to 1789, both in public acts and by

---

[28] See Ryan Barilleaux, "Foreign Policy and the First Commander in Chief," in *Patriot Sage*, 141–64, at 144–50.

[29] Department of the Army, *The Army, Field Manual 1* (Department of the Army, 2005), ch. 1 sec.4 and ch. 1 sec.15. See also Douglas V. Johnson and Steven Metz, "Civil-Military Relations in the United States," in *American Defense Policy*, eds. Hays, Vallance, and Van Tassel, 7th ed. (Johns Hopkins University Press, 1997), 495–96.

[30] Jefferson to Washington, April 16, 1784, in *The Life and Selected Writings of Thomas Jefferson*, ed. Koch (Modern Library, 1972), 791. See Marshall's tribute, *LGW*, 301.

[31] See Peter Paret, "Clausewitz," in *Makers of Modern Strategy: from Machiavelli to the Nuclear Age*, ed. Paret (Princeton University Press, 1986), 187–213, arguing that Clausewitz adopted Montesquieu's theory of the complexity, or spirit, of politics. Gordon Craig and Felix Gilbert, "Reflections on Strategy in the Present and Future," *ibid.* 869–70, praise Washington and *The Federalist* for grand strategic thinking akin to Clausewitz's formulation that "War is the continuation of politics by other means."

encouraging Madison, Hamilton, and other framers. His 1783 Circular noted that a general should abstain from politics, but it was "a duty incumbent upon me" to address constitutional reform since, in "the present Crisis" of affairs, "silence in me would be a crime" (W 516–18). The third of four "pillars" he proposed was "adoption of a proper Peace Establishment," which included "placing the Militia of the Union upon a regular and respectable footing." The common good required that state militias have "absolutely uniform" organization, equipment, and training – a complex system of defense that prevented militarism through citizen engagement, while providing an effective national capability (W 524).[32]

From 1787 to 1789 Washington risked his reputation to establish a complex, effective constitutional order, by serving as president of the Philadelphia Convention; helping to reprint *The Federalist* in Virginia; letting his name be used in state ratification debates; and serving as the first President under the new Constitution. Still, even with the Electoral College's unanimous support, he returned to office reluctantly. The great themes of his presidency were that executive power was safe for republicanism, and that constitutional government, not populism or parties, should guide the way through domestic and foreign trials. He recruited the best talents and characters for offices, from a range of viewpoints: Hamilton and Jefferson were in the cabinet; his ambassadors included John Jay, Gouverneur Morris, and John Quincy Adams; he replaced General St. Clair after the disastrous campaign in the Northwest Territory. His adherence to separation of powers dictated respect for the legislative dominance of Congress, with the President recommending few measures, mostly concerning core Article II powers of foreign and security policy. The executive and Senate should collaborate on treaties while maintaining separate roles and judgments; the House had no role, given "the plain letter of the Constitution" and his knowledge of "the principles on which the Constitution was formed" (W 930–32). The President should represent all the American citizenry, its common principles and highest ideals, and especially so regarding war and foreign affairs.

Moderation is Washington's general principle guiding foreign and defense policy, understood as the sober balance among ideas or actions, and the avoidance of political or intellectual extremes. The intellectual confidence he had worked to develop allowed him to consult a wide range of intelligent advisers, and then to rely upon one over another as he saw fit.[33] He tried to perpetuate this ideal of wide consultations and balanced judgment among a new

---

[32] In May 1783 he had sent Congress "Sentiments on a Peace Establishment," which mixed a small professional army with larger state militias; recommended forts, arsenals, a navy, coastal defenses, and a military academy; but noted political and economic limits to defense requests. See *Writings of George Washington*, ed. Fitzpatrick, 39 vols. (U.S. Government Printing Office, 1931–44), vol. 26: 374–98; Higginbotham, *Washington and the Military Tradition*, 124–25, 129–30; Barilleaux, "Foreign Policy," 156–57.

[33] Higginbotham notes that Washington and George C. Marshall shared the unusual quality of seeking out diverse views from aides, in *Washington and the Military Tradition*, 76–78, 121–22;

generation of military and civilian leaders. Fashioning sound foreign and defense policies requires proper deliberation and judgment, within and across constitutional branches, about particular situations – a complex, messy process in a constitutional republic, but a path of political moderation and sobriety that avoids extremes of doctrine or of momentary passion.

Executive Power, Prudence, and Flexibility in Statecraft and Tactics – Washington's complex, political approach to formulating foreign and defense policy included an executive who balanced consultation, prudential judgment, secrecy, speed, and flexibility in both grand strategy and tactics. The arguments in *The Federalist* (nos. 67–77) on the necessity of such an office to secure republican liberty employ the theories of Locke and Montesquieu, but they draw shape from Washington as General and citizen-founder. Indeed, many scholars and statesmen have admired his balance of executive toughness and republican principle as embodying an ideal of the prudent statesman traceable to Thucydides, Plato, Aristotle, Cicero, and Plutarch. A recent analysis of his strategic sense as general and field commander – marrying long-term objectives with constant short-term adjustments – could describe his later record as a civilian executive:

He always kept the political object foremost in his considerations. He always seemed to examine his alternatives in terms of the whole strategic picture. Learning from his early mistakes, he constantly adapted his strategy to the circumstances. Recognizing the defects of his tactical instrument [a citizen army], he never asked too much of it.[34]

Several scholars applaud Washington for avoiding any restriction of "strategy" to Napoleonic annihilation, or Upton's bureaucratic war machine; instead, his "military career provides a model of leadership and [both] strategic and tactical expertise."[35] As General he eventually discerned the blend of tactics, campaigns, and geopolitical alliances that could deny victory to his superpower opponent, while ensuring that victory would provide geographic and political independence. He had to keep an army in the field amid dire need, and forge a French alliance without succumbing to their ambitions, until he could maneuver the British into fatigue or a major defeat. His judgment of the enemy, potential allies, and resources in America's character and materiel dictated that he control his passion for reputation and honor, so as to retreat or fight as strategy required. Marshall, drawing on Plutarch, praised his balance by comparing

---

see also Richard Brookhiser, *Founding Father: Rediscovering George Washington* (Free Press, 1996), 39, and generally, 121–56.

[34] Mackubin Owens, "Washington and the Strategy of the Revolution," in *Patriot Sage*, 98.

[35] Albert T. McJoynt, "Washington, George (1732–99)," in *International Military and Defense Encyclopedia*, ed. Dupuy (Brassey's U.S./Maxwell Macmillan, 1993), 6: 2932–34; see also Dave Palmer, *The Way of the Fox: American Strategy in the War for America, 1775–1783* (Greenwood Press, 1975). Compare the treatment in Russell Weigley, "American Strategy from Its Beginnings through the First World War," in *Makers of Modern Strategy*, ed. Paret, 408–43, at 410–13.

him to two Romans who fought the great Carthaginian Hannibal – Fabius, who harassed and retreated, and Marcellus, who attacked: "He has been called the American Fabius; but those who compare his actions with his means, will perceive as much of Marcellus as of Fabius in his character" (*LGW*, 467). A. T. Mahan, founder of American strategy studies, credits Washington with seeing the importance of naval power; he also should have included him when analyzing grand strategy or praising such exemplars of strategic sense as Lord Nelson.[36]

Washington's development of practical judgment would be merely Machiavellian if the aims were immoral or amoral, or if low ends justified any means. The pattern of his career, however, was to avoid either amoral expedience or impractical moralism. Rediscovery in the past century of Aristotelian ethics has restored such ideas as statesman and prudence, which are reserved for those "who have exercised the art of ruling with sufficient excellence to earn the gratitude of their contemporaries and posterity." Figures like Washington, Lincoln, and Churchill exhibit "moral wisdom" in political crises, guided not by abstract morals alone but by prudence understood as "the mediating process and personal virtue through which they connected the moral ends they pursued with their everyday actions and policies."[37] Thus, as general and President, Washington employed realistic arts of intelligence and covert operations while avoiding ruthlessness.[38] On larger matters Tocqueville praised his ability to discern a sound policy in the 1790s when the French Revolution and Europe's great power contest unleashed a storm of ideas and passions upon American politics. The same spirit informed Washington's policy on the popular protests to a federal tax on liquor that became the Whiskey Rebellion of 1794.[39] Still, his highest achievements of prudence and principled power involved the crises of foreign affairs and war. Voices on all sides, including Hamilton and Jefferson, saw these clouds on the horizon in 1792 and pleaded that he delay his wish to retire. He shelved that initial farewell address he had asked Madison to draft; but after navigating a stormy second term, he asked Hamilton to redraft such an address. Ever moderate, he insisted that his increasingly partisan aide include ideas from the draft by Hamilton's once partner, now bitter rival, Madison.

---

[36] Alfred Thayer Mahan, *The Influence of Sea Power Upon History, 1660–1783*, 12th edn. (Little, Brown, 1944 [1890]); on Washington, 342–43, 364–65, 387–89, 397–400; on grand strategy, 7–10, 22–23; on Nelson, 23–24.

[37] Alberto Coll, "Normative Prudence as a Tradition of Statecraft," in *Ethics & International Affairs: A Reader*, ed. Joel Rosenthal (Georgetown University Press, 1995), 58–77, at 75. On Lincoln and Churchill, see Cohen, *Supreme Command*; on Washington, see especially *LGW*, 465–69, and Brookhiser, *Founding Father, passim*.

[38] Stephen Knott, "George Washington and the Founding of American Clandestine Activity," in *Secret and Sanctioned: Covert Operations and the American Presidency* (Oxford University Press, 1996), 13–26; see also 27–57.

[39] See Brookhiser, *Founding Father*, 84–91, 97–100; W, 789, 829, 870–73, 882–84, 887–93, 922.

Balancing Interest, Independence, and Justice: Just War and International Law – Washington wanted rival views joined in his Farewell Address to affirm the balanced thinking and shared principles nearly eclipsed in the partisan 1790s. Tocqueville praises this "admirable letter addressed to his fellow citizens, which forms the political testament of that great man" as the basic charter of American foreign policy (*Democracy*, I.1.5, 217). As President, his main policies sought an adequate federal army and navy; peace with Indian nations and defense of existing American settlements by force as needed, but not expansion; and protection from European great powers but also from two rival doctrines of international relations. In light of today's academic disputes, it is telling that he adopted neither the realism of Hamilton nor the liberal idealism advocated by Madison and Jefferson in germ, later by Woodrow Wilson fully. Washington did not face globalization, or the prospect of Pax Americana, or postmodern relativism and pacifism; still, amid the crises of his day, he neither embraced nor overreacted to doctrines of *realpolitik* and perpetual peace on offer.[40] Interpretations of his Farewell Address find anything from proto-Jeffersonian insularism and pacific ideals to an ambition for American empire, but the likely intent is what Washington actually stated and long had endorsed: America should stand for a reasonable balance of interest and justice in its relations with other states, and provide a confident new example in international affairs.[41]

The two great crises of Washington's presidency stemmed from the upheaval of the French Revolution and the radical democratic theory it sought to impress upon the world. He tried to shield America from such storms with his 1793 Neutrality Proclamation and 1795 treaty with Britain (the Jay Treaty). He knew these policies would offend the revolutionary French republic and its zealous supporters in America. Amid charges of monarchism and groveling to Britain, he defended his "system" or grand strategy as maintaining America's true independence and a just peace. His Seventh Annual Message (1795), and letter to the House rejecting its demand for Jay Treaty documents (1796), defended the Framers' principle that foreign policy should bow neither to popular passions nor to abstract creeds but should be debated by the branches insulated from popular opinion – the Senate and President. Indeed, despite reservations about

---

40 Compare Karl-Friedrich Walling, *Republican Empire: Alexander Hamilton on War and Free Government* (University Press of Kansas, 1999), with Robert Tucker and David Hendrickson, *Empire of Liberty: The Statecraft of Thomas Jefferson* (Oxford University Press, 1990); see also Madison's "Universal Peace" (1792) in *James Madison: Writings*, ed. Rakove (Library of America/Literary Classics of the United States, 1999), 505–8. Edmund S. Morgan praises Washington's grasp of strategy and power as surpassing that of his counselors, in *The Genius of George Washington* (W.W. Norton & Co., 1980), 6, 22–25.

41 Compare the insularist, Jeffersonian reading in Edward Pessen, "George Washington's Farewell Address, the Cold War, and the Timeless National Interest," *Journal of the Early Republic* 7 (Spring 1987), 1–25, with criticism of Washington in Burton Ira Kaufman, "Washington's Farewell Address: A Statement of Empire," in *Washington's Farewell Address: The View from the 20th Century*, ed. Kaufman (University of Chicago Press, 1969), 169–87.

the Treaty, he ratified it in part to quell disorder from the kinds of partisan clubs that had stoked civil and international war in France, and the Whiskey Rebellion in America. The "prudence and moderation" that obtained and ratified the Treaty sought an honorable peace as the basis for America's prosperity and strength. These "genuine principles of rational liberty" would serve our "national happiness;" having been "[f]aithful to ourselves, we have violated no obligation to others" (*W*, 920–22, 930–32; *LGW*, Chapters 30–32).

The Farewell Address encapsulates and elevates the principles Washington had endorsed his entire career. The counsels on foreign policy, read in the Address's larger spirit, outline a grand strategy befitting America's characteristic ends, ways, and means.[42] He postpones advice on grand strategy until he has affirmed the American principles to guide foreign and security policy. The Address thus opens by invoking republican virtue and civic duty; patriotic devotion to the common good; gratitude to Heaven for America's blessings, and prayers for continued Providence; and the need for prudence and moderation to sustain such goods amid furious partisanship. He pledges "unceasing vows" that his country and the world would enjoy the further blessings of Heaven's beneficence, the Union and brotherly affection, perpetuation of a free constitution, and wisdom and virtue in government. He further prayed that the happiness of a free people would be so wisely used as to gain for them "the glory of recommending it to the applause, the affection, and adoption of every nation which is yet a stranger to it" – invoking the widely held view that America was exceptional among nations and in history (*W*, 963–64). Only after further advice on perpetuating the Union and constitutional rule, on moderating partisan politics, and on ensuring both religion and education in the citizenry (*W* 964–72) does he raise his final counsel – that America should seek both independence and justice in foreign affairs.

Washington's maxim "to steer clear of permanent Alliances" is among the best-known ideas of the Address (*W*, 975). That said, many accounts of his foreign policy mistakenly substitute Jefferson's maxim from his First Inaugural (1801) about "entangling alliances," perpetuating the error that the Farewell Address espouses isolationism.[43] His main principle, rather, was that a secure,

---

[42] Classic studies are Samuel Bemis, "Washington's Farewell Address: A Foreign Policy of Independence" (1934), in *American Foreign Policy and the Blessings of Liberty*, ed. Samuel Bemis (Yale University Press, 1962), 240–58, and Felix Gilbert, *To the Farewell Address: Ideas of Early American Foreign Policy* (Princeton University Press, 1961), 115–36, esp. 124–36. I also am indebted to studies by Garrity, Spalding and Garrity, McDougall, and Hill cited in note 21 *supra*; see also confirmations of these views in Bradford Perkins, *The Cambridge History of American Foreign Relations*, vol. I, *The Creation of A Republican Empire, 1776–1865* (Cambridge University Press, 1993), 109–10, and John Lewis Gaddis, *Surprise, Security, and the American Experience* (Harvard University Press, 2004), 22–24.

[43] Joshua Muravchik contrasts "Washingtonian" isolationism and "Wilsonian" internationalism in *The Imperative of American Leadership: A Challenge to Neo-Isolationism* (AEI Press, 1996), 20–21, 210; see Patrick Buchanan's similar misreading in *A Republic, Not an Empire: Reclaiming America's Destiny* (Regnery, 1999; 2nd edn., 2002).

independent nation should surrender to neither interest nor abstract justice, neither passions nor fixed doctrines, but must find a balance among these human propensities. If we did so, he is confident America will be "at no distant period, a great Nation" (W, 972). His main concern was that a nation be independent enough to act wisely and justly: to be able to "choose peace or war, as our interest guided by justice shall Counsel" (W, 975). To steer America toward such moderation he obliquely refers to the circumstances of the 1790s, in which American policy risked being subservient to either Britain or France, but he names neither state – presumably to avoid offense and to focus on general principles:

Observe good faith and justice towards all Nations; cultivate peace and harmony with all. Religion and morality enjoin this conduct; and can it be that good policy does not equally enjoin it? It will be worthy of a free, enlightened, and at no distant period, a great Nation, to give to mankind the magnanimous and too novel example of a People always guided by an exalted justice and benevolence. (W, 972)

Having stated these aims, he tackles the immediate challenge of being overwhelmed by the great power conflicts of Europe:

In the execution of such a plan, nothing is more essential than that permanent, inveterate antipathies against particular Nations, and passionate attachments for others, should be excluded; and that, in place of them, just and amicable feelings towards all should be cultivated. The Nation which indulges towards another a habitual hatred or a habitual fondness is in some degree a slave. It is a slave to its animosity or to its affection, either of which is sufficient to lead it astray from its duty and its interest. (W, 973)

Washington thus formulates the further counsel that citizens must remain vigilant "[a]gainst the insidious wiles of foreign influence," since "history and experience prove that foreign influence is one of the most baneful foes of Republican Government" (W, 974). He then offers his strongest counsel about independence from or neutrality toward great power controversies and wars, balanced with advocacy of commercial relations:

The Great rule of conduct for us in regard to foreign Nations is in extending our commercial relations, to have with them as little *political* connection as possible. So far as we have already formed engagements, let them be fulfilled with perfect good faith. Here let us stop. Europe has a set of primary interests, which to us have none, or a very remote relation…Our detached and distant situation invites and enables us to pursue a different course. If we remain one People under an efficient government, the period is not far off when we may defy material injury from external annoyance; when we may take such an attitude as will cause the neutrality we may at any time resolve upon to be scrupulously respected…Why forego the advantages of so peculiar a situation? Why quit our own to stand upon foreign ground? Why, by interweaving our destiny with that of any part of Europe, entangle our peace and prosperity…?. (W, 974–75)

Those who read a doctrine of disengagement in the Address must ignore the larger moderation informing Washington's statesmanship, thus overlook the balance he holds between these admonitions and an overriding concern with independent capacity, whether to engage or refrain. He elevates that concern as his final word on grand strategy, in a closing discussion of his 1793 Neutrality Proclamation: "With me a predominant motive has been to endeavor to gain time to our country to settle and mature its yet recent institutions, and to progress without interruption, to that degree of strength and consistency, which is necessary to give it, humanly speaking, command of its own fortunes" (W, 977).

Washington sees in America the potential not only for exemplary greatness, but also for great power simply. Thus, amid his admonitions about avoiding Europe's petty and unjust conflicts, he calibrates his advice about avoiding ties that would make the young republic subservient:

'Tis our true policy to steer clear of permanent Alliances with any portion of the foreign world. So far, I mean, as we are now at liberty to do it; for let me not be understood as capable of patronizing infidelity to existing engagements (I hold the maxim no less applicable to public than to private affairs, that honesty is always the best policy). (W, 975)

To serve this grand strategy of independence and a path to great power status, Washington repeats policies he long had advocated, to include provision for "the national security." Theodore Roosevelt later praised the maxim from Washington's First Annual Message that "[t]o be prepared for war is one of the most effectual means of preserving peace" (W, 749, 791–92, 848).[44] Roosevelt did not observe, however, Washington's balance, for the Address also reiterates his maxim that America must avoid "those overgrown Military establishments, which under any form of Government are inauspicious to liberty, and which are to be regarded as particularly hostile to Republican Liberty" (W, 966). Such moderation further counsels that even "a respectably defensive posture" will not always deter aggressors, so "we may safely trust to temporary alliances for extraordinary emergencies." Further emphasizing the importance of international engagement, he reiterates the idea that "[h]armony, [and] liberal intercourse with all Nations, are recommended by policy, humanity, and interest" (W, 975).

Washington's alloy of realistic concern with moral ideals adapts the just war tradition of classical philosophy, Christianity, and modern natural law and international law. Enlightenment jurists such as Grotius developed specific principles of war and diplomacy, while granting that prudent judgment must govern particular decisions. As noted, Montesquieu was an influential source as Americans developed policies that accorded with a right of nations

---

44 See Theodore Roosevelt, "Washington's Forgotten Maxim" (address at Naval War College, 1897), in *The Works of Theodore Roosevelt* (New York: Charles Scribner's Sons, 1926), 13:182–99.

balancing the necessity of military power with limits to war grounded in natural rights of individuals and basic international right. The grand strategy of the Address thus reflects the great theme of Washington's career: intellectual, moral, and political moderation. Prudence and decency should guide private and public life, domestic and international; he hoped such "counsels of an old and affectionate friend" would "control the usual current of the passions" and "moderate the fury of party spirit" in domestic and foreign affairs (W, 976; see also 832, 851, 924).

Liberal-Republican Prudence for a Globalized World: Enlightened Self-Interest

Our pitched battles in academia and public discourse today between schools of international relations, and the rhetoric volleyed between parties and pundits about our foreign policy since the 2001 terrorist attacks, suggest the salience of moderation and of recourse to bedrock principles. Washington steered American foreign and defense policy through such polarization and warned against it. The authority on moderate republicanism, Montesquieu, warned that a free people and especially its intellectuals could be as blinkered or irrational as if under despotism: " ...in extremely free states, [historians] betray the truth because of their very liberty, for, as it always produces divisions, every one becomes as much the slave of the prejudices of his faction as he would be of a despot" (*The Spirit of Laws*, 19.27, 583/333).

Tocqueville's analysis of Washington's grand strategy, which informed his own ideas of liberal moderation in international affairs, is useful preparation for speculating on how these principles of grand strategy can guide our debates today. As argued in Chapter 3, Tocqueville studied and advised the new liberal democracies by drawing upon Montesquieu's effort to moderate the rationalist extremes of earlier liberalism. The focus on statesmanship in *Democracy in America* flows from this liberal moderation and its elevation of prudence. He first cites Marshall's *Life of Washington* early in *Democracy*, and praises the constitutional founder. His emphatic attention to Washington arises in addressing "The Manner in Which American Democracy Conducts External Affairs of State" (*Democracy*, I.2.5, 217). He observes that the Farewell Address still guided American policy in the 1830s, and he endorses its maxims as "beautiful and just." These maxims also "succeeded in keeping his country at peace when all the rest of the universe was at war." Moreover, Tocqueville coins here one of his signature concepts about modern democracy, while assessing the proper balance of justice and interest in foreign affairs. He praises Washington for "establishing as a point of doctrine that the self-interest well understood of Americans" was to avoid Europe's great power quarrels in a spirit of moderation (*Democracy*, I.2.5, 217–220; compare II.2.8, 500–502). He also noted, more generally, America's difficulties in holding to enlightened self-interest given temptations from two opposing extremes, idealism or imperial conquest. Idealism led many Americans in the 1790s to favor war against Britain to support republican France, however unprepared America was, or how unjust such a war would be in light of broader principles. A statesman's hand at the wheel was needed:

> The sympathies of the people in favor of France were...declared with so much violence that nothing less than the inflexible character of Washington and the immense popularity that he enjoyed were needed to prevent war from being declared on England. And still, the efforts that the austere reason of this great man made to struggle against the generous but unreflective passions of his fellow citizens almost took from him the sole recompense that he had ever reserved for himself, the love of his country. The majority pronounced against his policy; now the entire people approves it. If the Constitution and public favor had not given the direction of the external affairs of the state to Washington, it is certain that the nation would have done then precisely what it condemns today. (*Democracy*, I.2.5, 220)

This analysis is striking both for what it states and omits. Perhaps in deference to Jefferson (praised elsewhere in *Democracy* and noted earlier in this chapter), and to Madison, Tocqueville omits the fact that in the interval this very temptation led America into the disastrous War of 1812. America declared war against a superpower to defend its rights – but per the very popular Jefferson-Madison strategy, it had eschewed a national bank and failed to invest in military forces, the crucial means for deterring, or coping with, such a power. The predictable British invasion burned America's capital city in 1814.[45] Tocqueville's fundamental point is that if the Constitution had not given firm powers to an executive, and if not for the right statesman in office, American policy in the 1790s would have been precisely what it wisely condemns in hindsight. Democracies thus should candidly recognize that in international affairs they will be "decidedly inferior" to nondemocratic states regarding war and foreign policy unless they incorporate sufficient constitutional balance to compensate. The "everyday practical wisdom" of individuals and groups fostered by "democratic freedom" is good in domestic politics, but international policy requires capacities to "coordinate the details of a great undertaking, fix on a design, and afterwards follow it with determination through obstacles." Democracies also must be able to formulate measures "in secret" and "patiently await their result," as all states must. He warns, however, of the democratic tendency "to obey sentiment rather than reasoning in politics, and to abandon a long matured design to satisfy a momentary passion" (*Democracy*, I.2.5, 219). In the 1790s and War of 1812, this extreme of idealism or naiveté yielded a reckless rush to war. In the second volume of *Democracy* he warns of the converse – an idealistic pacifism that dictates isolationism. This view dismisses war as a wasteful diversion

---

[45] Tocqueville earlier criticizes American conduct of the war, in *Democracy in America*, I.1.8, 159–61.

from pursuit of prosperity. Tocqueville discerns a refusal to recognize what may be necessary (II.3.19 on "So Few Great Ambitions," 601, 604; II.3.22, "Why Democratic Peoples Naturally Desire Peace," 617, 620–21).

Tocqueville discerns another extreme, opposite to these versions of naïve idealism, that tempts America to eschew Washington's moderate policy for other reasons. This extreme arises when indicting the cold-blooded realism behind the brutal treatment of African slaves and Amerindians. He attributes this ruthless expediency to America's restless desire for prosperity and power. In both volumes of *Democracy* he analyzes great power politics and America's rise to global prominence as a natural consequence of its geographic position, its political principles, and its economic dynamism.[46] He is ambivalent about America's nationalism and power politics of continental expansion, and foresees America amplifying these. He respects the realities of "great states" and "force" in world affairs, for happiness requires freedom and conquered peoples are miserable (I.1.8, 151–54). On the other hand, he pointedly notes that Americans have not followed Washington's "noble and virtuous policy" of benign treatment of the Amerindians and a halt to westward expansion, instead constantly invading Indian territory and violating treaties (I.2.10, 320; see 320–35).[47] Nonetheless, he does not shrink from forecasting the role he sees America called to play as a great power, even while warning of the slide from republic to imperial republic to empire, much as Montesquieu warned in *Considerations on the Romans*. His dramatic juxtaposition of America and Russia, in closing this chapter, foresees a global struggle in which the enlightened self-interest of the Americans – their effort to balance justice and interest – will make democratic expansion the better alternative to autocratic expansion. This strategic judgment would explain why, as the volume closes, he tempers his earlier criticism of America's power politics and its injustice toward slaves and Amerindians.[48]

Whatever the differences in the scope and technology of America's power today, or in the complexity of our global threats or opportunities, Washington and Tocqueville remind us of essential challenges for liberal democracy. While hoping to avoid the platitudes of a latter-day Polonius, I close with suggestions of policy advice informed by this legacy and the enlightened self-interest Tocqueville discerns in it. Given the overlap in Washington's five principles, any effort to apply them to situations finds that each informs and presupposes

---

[46] See I.1.8, 149–61; I.2.5, 217–20; and in the long chapter on "The Three Races" in America, I.2.10, at 319–22, 368, 391–96. In Volume Two , see the discussion at the close of III.1 on "the right of nations" (539), and III.22–26 on war and armies (617–35).

[47] For criticism that Tocqueville mistakenly viewed American racism and imperialism as alien to liberalism, see Rogers Smith, "Beyond Tocqueville, Myrdal, and Hartz: The Multiple Traditions in America," *American Political Science Review* 87 (1993), 549–66.

[48] I discuss this further, including criticism of his policy on Algiers as illiberal, in "Tocqueville's Foreign Policy of Moderation and Democracy Expansion," in *Alexis de Tocqueville and the Art of Democratic Statesmanship*, eds. Danoff and Hebert (Lexington Books, 2011).

the others. Moreover, such broad counsels of liberal moderation are difficult to practice because they presuppose capacities for prudence that defy abstract description, and require long cultivation.

First, we should observe the great success achieved by placing principle above power, by sticking to moderate policies amid partisan claims, and by carefully matching means to ends. America should note that her Founder, in his moment of dominance, resisted both the hubris of power and the thrill of partisanship, instead sticking to the virtues and aims that got him there and made power legitimate. A Kantian may detect Machiavelli in the advice that honesty is the best policy, while realists may find it either naiveté or duplicitous cunning. This maxim, however, stems from the prime principle of adherence to republicanism, natural justice, and transcendent truths about humankind. America would be "a great Nation" only if holding to a blend of Aristotelian teleology and Biblical Providence: power and goodness ultimately coincide; power only endures if founded on virtuous aims and decent conduct; greater power brings temptation to diversion from true aims. Washington's other principles, and his policies, rest on this base. If such discipline secured the founding of America, and was at least partially followed by his successors as we became a world power, on what grounds should we ignore it now? Our grand strategy must have this moral–political principle as its lodestar, lest like most cases in history ours, too, loses its grandeur. We should consider what this means not only for our use of military power, but also for our national desire for wealth, easy prosperity, and global economic dominance, or for how we deliberate about any means to these larger ends. Are compromises with this principle – and Washington knew that human affairs always require compromises to some degree – justified by larger support for this principle itself?

Second, his insistence upon civil authority, and avoidance of either militarism or weakness, implicates a range of issues from force structure to public and private diplomacy. Washington's advice to balance republican liberty and national defense suggests restoration of some national service, military or civilian, for all young citizens – a policy long debated, but never engaged, by political leaders.[49] More generally we should recall, as the global power with vast superiority in everything from training to weaponry and technology, that the Romans lost a republic to empire and that the British gave up empire to preserve liberty under constitutional monarchy. In the post-Cold War era voices such as George Kennan and Henry Kissinger invoked Washingtonian warnings against power and a militarized foreign policy that were echoed shortly after the founding by John Quincy Adams. Adams worried, in 1821, not about the temptation of sheer power but that moral aims might pull us to pursue power projection. America "goes not abroad in search of monsters to destroy," he warned, for efforts to right all wrongs in world affairs would change her focus "from *liberty* to *force*"; she "might become the dictatress of the world," but would no longer

---

[49] See William Galston, "Thinking About the Draft," *The Public Interest* 154 (2004), 61–73.

be "ruler of her own spirit."[50] That said, within two years, Quincy Adams formulated the Monroe Doctrine, declaring America the hegemon of the Western hemisphere. A strategy of enlightened self-interest requires armed forces with a distinct professional culture and national support to navigate such enduring tensions, but we must not mistake a noble instrument for an end in itself, letting it displace other means of policy – such as political debate at home, and forthright diplomacy and cultivation of good relations abroad. Thucydides's analysis of the Athenian decline from hubris to disaster supports Washington's advice that patient diplomacy always must balance, or supersede, claims of pride and power. This is not to say Washington would place a primary trust in international institutions or law, or in utopias of perpetual or democratic peace. We should recall Eisenhower's decision, in the era of truly global war and nuclear terror, to model his farewell address on Washington's and that – contrary to widespread misinterpretation – Eisenhower endorsed the new military–industrial complex while calling for balance and vigilance about its scope and influence.[51]

Third, Washington's constitutional ideals touch policy at home and abroad. We should affirm a complex structure for making foreign and security policy so as to best balance liberty and security, and vet policies through multiple institutions – seeking not the lowest common denominator but the highest possible consensus on means and aims. Recent decades have emphasized the natural tendency of executive offices to dominate policy debates and decisions on use of force, and of Congress to reluctantly insist upon full deliberation about war and deployment of force – then to snipe about problems or setbacks. Washington hoped his moderate principles would "prevent our Nation from running the course which has hitherto marked the Destiny of Nations" (*W*, 976), but this presupposed widespread vigilance about both necessary defenses and the perils of war. Abroad, if necessity truly demands that we engage in regime building, then we should underwrite not democracy but liberal constitutionalism – extending to new regimes the complexity and moderation we enjoy (or should) at home.[52]

Fourth, Washington's counsel that executives should employ consultations, prudence, and flexibility in both grand strategy and tactics is difficult to achieve

---

[50] George Kennan, "On American Principles," *Foreign Affairs* 74 (1995), 116–26, and Kissinger, *Does America Need a Foreign Policy?*, 237–40; see John Quincy Adams, "Address of July 4, 1821" in *John Quincy Adams and American Continental Empire*, ed. LaFeber (Quadrangle Books, 1965), 45 (emphasis in original); see also Hendrickson, "Renovation of American Foreign Policy."

[51] See Carrese and Doran, "Republican Prudence"; I explore these themes in "The Grand Strategy of Washington and Eisenhower: Recovering the American Consensus," *Orbis* (Spring 2015), 1–18.

[52] Fareed Zakaria, *The Future of Freedom: Illiberal Democracy at Home and Abroad* (W.W. Norton & Company, 2003), advocates liberal constitutionalism, citing Montesquieu, the American framers, and Tocqueville.

today, since we embrace populism, partisanship, and permanent campaigning more than the founders ever could. Still, those in elected office, and both the temporary and the more permanent officials advising them, can strive to emulate the balanced thinking of the first administration. Such moderation also implicates the last Washingtonian principle, on balancing interest and justice – but the aim of Clausewitzean grand strategy to assess the entire moral and political complexity of war has special relevance for the executive. One counsel both Thucydides and Washington offer is to resist the temptation to let current dominance and superior technology narrow our thinking about when to wage war, and about the consequences or complications when the battle is over.[53]

The fifth Washington principle, to balance interest and justice, was a difficult ideal for a weak power, and now taxes a superpower. The great dissensus about post–Cold War American grand strategy, especially our global role, might be constructively resolved if we consulted bedrock principle. If we now think the grand strategy and international regimes America built for the Cold War and as leader of the free world are irrelevant, what policies will satisfy both Washingtonian standards and the threats or opportunities of our era?[54] His counsels do not neatly fit our rival doctrines in realism and liberal idealism, and the neoconservative blend of Wilsonian zeal and realism would need to moderate its tone and emphasize prudence. Does Washington no longer fit our character and purposes, or do our discrete doctrines fail to comprehend America? For example, aren't globally engaged policies on nonproliferation of weapons of mass destruction and serious opposition to Islamist terrorism animated by both interest and benevolent justice – an enlightened self-interest? Such a blend is characteristically American, and we should revise our theories to recognize the wisdom of such balancing in given situations, rather than depicting ourselves as polarized or confused. Doesn't enlightened self-interest also justify continued leadership of NATO, and commitments to lead other multilateral efforts to maintain a liberal global order?[55] Another example of American

[53] For Clausewitzean strategy as alert to the limits of "total war" and technology, see Andreas Herberg-Rothe, "Primacy of 'Politics' or 'Culture' Over War in a Modern World: Clausewitz Needs a Sophisticated Interpretation," *Defense Analysis* 17, no. 2 (2001), 175–86, and Frederick Kagan, "War and Aftermath," *Policy Review* 120 (August 2003), 3–27.

[54] An analysis of the Bush 2002 National Security Strategy from this larger perspective is John Lewis Gaddis, "A Grand Strategy," *Foreign Policy* (November/December 2002), 50–57, and also *Surprise, Security, and the American Experience*. Even sympathetic assessments of the Obama presidency sense an absence of grand strategy; see Daniel W. Drezner, "Does Obama Have a Grand Strategy?," *Foreign Affairs* (July/August 2011), and Anne-Marie Slaughter, "Why a Grand Strategy is Needed for Obama's Second Term," *The Washington Post*, January 23, 2013. Criticisms include Robert Kagan, "Superpowers Don't Get to Retire," *The New Republic*, May 26, 2014, and, obliquely, Kissinger, *World Order*, for example, 168–71, 326–29, 361–74.

[55] Studies supporting such thinking include Samuel Huntington, "American Ideals versus American Institutions," *Political Science Quarterly* 97 (1982), 1–37; Jonathan Monten, "The Roots of the Bush Doctrine: Power, Nationalism, and Democracy Promotion in U.S. Strategy," *International Security* 29 (2005), 112–56; and Mead, *Special Providence*, on the perpetual need to balance and blend distinct strands of American thinking.

prudence rising above recent doctrine is the liberal-democratic partnership with India pursued by recent presidents of both parties. Better relations between the world's leading liberal democracy and its largest one serve both principle and prudence. The specific policy problem was India's nuclear weapon status and addressing it through a mature conception of the nonproliferation treaty, which India had candidly resisted from its inception. To note only American opposition, neither the liberal nor the realist schools could break from doctrine to see a middle way to a higher good. Prudent statesmanship from both states eventually secured the foundations for a nascent partnership.[56]

Our challenges indeed are new in many ways, but the highest consensus of the founders still is the aim proclaimed by all American presidents and parties – to benefit mankind and ourselves by respecting "the obligation[s] which justice and humanity impose on every Nation" (W, 977). Each of the doctrinal alternatives of the past century asks us to place either too much faith in ourselves alone, or international institutions alone, or the rational calculations of other states or actors. Some schools suggest we now lead largely by force, others that we lead only by example and principle, still others that we should withdraw into our interests and a "do-no-harm" crouch. The genius of Washington's counsel is to ever seek the proper equilibrium among these tendencies in any given situation and for the long haul, so as to abide by republican principles of natural justice. He knew that international affairs always requires "temporary alliances" and engagement with foreign nations, while trying to "cultivate peace and harmony" with all (W, 975, 972). He might well accept that the complexities of our age and our power now compel this to a great degree, such as our enduring leadership of the NATO alliance – but that America could retain independent judgment if leading alliances, not dominated by them. His advice on "permanent alliances" concerned the blinkered thinking and "permanent, inveterate" antipathies or attachments that could entangle a weak power, not the "great Nation" he foresaw (W, 973).

While his basic moderation tells us to avoid either isolationism or unilateralism, it also counsels that America would mark a *Novus Ordo Saeclorum* (new order of the ages) only if we heeded the classic just war prudence that balances power with right, necessity with decency.[57] Specific debates on a preemptive strike or regime change, on a humanitarian or political intervention, on a war or a new partnership, on how to sustain the liberal global order – all

---

[56] I address this in "The Ideal of Liberal-Democratic Partnership: Philosophies of International Affairs and the Indo-US Nuclear Accord," in *Nuclear Synergy: Indo-US Strategic Cooperation and Beyond*, ed. N. K. Jha (Pentagon Press, 2009).

[57] Efforts to blend just war thinking with realism, or articulate it anew, include Reinhold Niebuhr, *The Irony of American History* (Charles Scribner's Sons, 1952); Michael Walzer, *Just and Unjust Wars: A Moral Argument with Historical Illustrations* (Basic Books, 1977; 4th edn., 2006); Jean Bethke Elshtain, *Just War Against Terror: The Burden of American Power in a Violent World* (Basic Books, 2003); and George Weigel, "The Development of Just War Thinking in the Post-Cold War World: An American Perspective," in *The Price of Peace: Just War in the Twenty-First Century*, eds. Reed and Ryall (Cambridge University Press, 2007), 19–36.

such situations must be pulled up toward the principle of enlightened self-interest. Washington's counsels thus are difficult and resist precise formulas, but are worthy of our efforts. His grand strategy exemplifies both the moral principle to stand up to evil and the humility to check one's power, to lead alone if necessary but with allies and by law or persuasion when possible.

It is precisely the gravity of the threats and prospects facing America today, and the global order it has built, that justifies recurrence to such statesmen as Washington and Lincoln, even if our conditions require new applications of their principles and prudence to our problems.

6

Constitutionalist Political Science

Storing's Moderation and Our Polarization

This study of moderation features two philosophers who extensively discuss education within their complex works of political philosophy. Montesquieu devotes an entire book of *The Spirit of Laws* to it, and Tocqueville dedicates an entire Part of *Democracy in America* to intellectual formation in a democracy.[1] This reflects the age-old interest of philosophers in proper education for a regime, and more particularly reflects the Montesquieuan focus on the complex "spirit" of laws, politics, and culture that collectively shapes a people. That approach helps us to address the current concerns about political polarization in America by considering the study of politics, and how we teach the citizenry. If we are concerned about a self-destructive partisanship, and a consequent failure to develop serious policies about social, economic, or international problems, we might consider how the social sciences and especially political science educate the citizenry about politics itself. If, for example, this discipline neither studies nor appreciates moderation very much, as an intellectual and political virtue, this surely would affect political thinking and action. A philosophy of moderation also is more concerned, as noted, with connecting theory and practice in a way attentive to their mutual influence, because theory must appreciate the constraints human nature places upon realistic activity.

---

[1] See Montesquieu, *The Spirit of Laws*, eds. Cohler, Miller, and Stone (Cambridge University Press, 1989), Book 4, "That the Laws of Education Should be Relative to the Government," and Alexis de Tocqueville, *Democracy in America*, eds. Harvey Mansfield and Delba Winthrop (University of Chicago Press, 2000), vol. 2, Part I, "On the Influence of Democracy on Intellectual Movements in the United States"; see, for example, chapter 15, "Why the Study of Greek and Latin Literature is Particularly Useful in Democratic Societies." This chapter adapts my essay "Constitutionalist Political Science: Rediscovering Storing's Philosophical Moderation," *American Political Thought*, Vol. 4, No. 2 (Spring 2015), pp. 259–88; © 2015 by The Jack Miller Center.

As it turns out, it is a hallmark of American discourse – perhaps since our founding – to worry that our forms of government are dysfunctional, that we are at a crisis, and that our civic culture and education are crucial reasons why. The present discontent about our discourse itself being too polarized and acrimonious perhaps adds a new dimension. The opening and closing essays of *The Federalist* call all the contending sides to moderation, and Lincoln sought recourse to "the better angels of our nature" to promote moderation amid acrimony and dysfunction. Today, however, there is a further concern about polarization that is a refrain among the professional students of politics, the political scientists: that the discipline needs fundamental reorientation so as to better address the crisis or dysfunction currently diagnosed. One reason to take seriously such concerns is that the opening argument of *Democracy in America* emphasizes just these fixtures of American political and intellectual discourse – that the newly born democratic republics of America and Europe face a crisis of self-understanding about how to stabilize and perpetuate politics, and that a new political science is needed to assist them.[2]

To better understand what these challenges mean in our day, we can call upon another American trait – our propensity to mark anniversaries – as an occasion to rediscover the controversy over American political science sparked by Herbert Storing fifty years ago. Known today mostly as a scholar of Anti-Federalist thought and the founding era, his contribution to political science and study of American political thought is much broader. Storing's trenchant critique of the vogue political science of his era informed, in turn, his practice of what he considered a better version. Both of his contributions offer lessons for how we think today about perpetual issues of political crisis and polarization, academic irrelevance, and leadership.

Neither Mere Politics nor Rigid Science: Toward More Balanced Study

In 1962 Herbert Storing edited *Essays on the Scientific Study of Politics*, a collection that criticized the behavioralist and positivist revolution in social science and particularly political science – the view that politics should be studied more strictly on the model of the natural sciences.[3] Two preliminary observations about this mostly forgotten work and its quiet legacy are obvious a half-century later. First, while it was among the earliest critiques of behavioralism and a value-neutral scientism in political science, it has received little credit for anticipating more widely noted critiques. The latter include Theodore Lowi's call for a reformed political science in *The End of Liberalism* (1969), providing moral-juridical criticism of interest-group liberalism or pluralism. More recently, the

---

[2] Tocqueville, *Democracy in America*, vol. 1, Introduction, 1, 6–9, 12–15.
[3] Herbert J. Storing, ed., *Essays on the Scientific Study of Politics* (Holt, Rinehart, and Winston, 1962). Storing contributed a preface and a long chapter, and the senior contributor, Leo Strauss, contributed an epilogue (305–27); hereinafter cited parenthetically as *Essays*.

Perestroika movement has argued for methodological pluralism to break the dominance of rational choice and mathematical methods or models.[4] As discussed in the next section, "Perestroika" began as one anonymous political scientist issuing a manifesto in 2000 but spawned a movement of sympathetic discussion and scholarship that urges greater space for qualitative approaches in the discipline. A second observation helps to explain why these later critiques were more favorably received, while little credit has been given to Storing and the fellow protégés of Leo Strauss who in 1962 criticized the behavioralism and scientism of Herbert Simon, Arthur Bentley, Harold Laswell, and the new field of voter studies. The characteristic reaction by prominent political scientists to this Straussian critique of scientism has been either denunciation or silence. Denunciation arrived immediately, in the excoriating review by political theorists John Schaar and Sheldon Wolin in *The American Political Science Review (APSR)* in 1963.[5] Schaar and Wolin condemned the Storing collection, *inter alia*, as "fanatical," informed by a darkly medieval Manichaeism of "stark dualisms and doctrinal zeal," as polemical and passionate rather than philosophical, as implicitly calling for the "*auto-da-fé*" treatment for behavioralists, as the work of a sect of extremists, and as marked by invective, innuendo, bald pronouncement, and tautology rather than reasoned argument.[6] Schaar and Wolin were not concerned, apparently, that their condemnation evinced the fanaticism they claimed to denounce (as Storing noted in his reply in *APSR*). More importantly, a half-century later, we can lament a lost opportunity. The review did nothing to advance serious discussion in political science of the scientistic revolution, although the reviewers had admitted that such a revolution was a problem.[7]

Three larger points follow from this rediscovery of Storing's prescient critique of the new scientism and also the dismal reaction to it. First, that a

---

[4] Harvey Mansfield argues that Lowi's *The End of Liberalism: Ideology, Policy, and the Crisis of Public Authority* (Norton, 1969) launched the "postbehavioral revolution" criticizing behavioralism; see Harvey C. Mansfield "Introduction: Political Science and the Constitution," in *America's Constitutional Soul* (Johns Hopkins University Press, 1991), 1, 4. Mansfield notes that the "institutionalists" did not defend themselves against the behavioralists, rather the "political theorists" did so, presumably Strauss's school; however, he does not note Storing's *Essays* here.

[5] John H. Schaar and Sheldon S. Wolin, "Review Essay: Essays on the Scientific Study of Politics: A Critique," *American Political Science Review* 57 (1963), 125–50. One prominent exception is Benjamin Barber; I examine this below. For context, and why Strauss's professional reception (as distinct from Storing's) was so controversial – to include analysis that Strauss's intentionally polemical tone provoked like responses – see Nasser Behnegar, *Leo Strauss, Max Weber, and the Scientific Study of Politics* (University of Chicago Press, 2003), 141–49, and Rafael Major, "Thinking through Strauss's Legacy," in *Leo Strauss's Defense of the Philosophic Life: Reading What Is Political Philosophy?*, ed. Rafael Major (University of Chicago Press, 2013), 1–21, at 5–11. See also David Kettler, "The Political Theory Question in Political Science, 1956–1967," *American Political Science Review* 100 (2006), 531–37, at 535–36.

[6] Schaar and Wolin, "Review Essay," predominantly at 125–29, but *passim*.

[7] Herbert J. Storing, Leo Strauss, Walter Berns, Leo Weinstein, and Robert Horwitz, "Replies to Schaar and Wolin: I – VI," *American Political Science Review* 57 (1963), 151–60.

recent development in political science – the launching of an American Political Thought group affiliated with the American Political Science Association (APSA), and also of the *American Political Thought* journal published by University of Chicago Press – is indebted to Storing, both for his path-clearing critique of scientism and for the subsequent range and depth of his scholarship. His brief career helped to launch a constitutionalist political science that appreciated how America's founding principles and first political science persist in American political life and thought. Their percolating presence is visible given his understanding of the founding as marked by debates, thus as promising or entailing further argument. For Storing, a serious understanding of the founding political science and the constitutionalism it supported, to include weaknesses and strengths, was indispensable for any serious study of American politics or liberal democracy generally. This was as true for those who would improve upon or displace the original approach. His critique of narrow scientism cleared space for his own contributions to what he deemed a more adequate, post-Progressive and postscientistic political science. His later scholarship endures into a new era both for its reasonableness and its insights about politics and particularly American politics, and it provides a much-needed diversity in political science. Moreover, while the breadth and moderation of Storing's political science shares something with the calls for methodological pluralism of the recent Perestroika movement, his approach would disagree with the overtly value-neutral but *de facto* progressivism, and thus academic activism, of the Perestroika view.

A second larger point is that Storing's constitutionalist political science sought to reinvigorate the political science of the founding as a whole and not the narrower views of Federalists, or Anti-Federalists and Jeffersonians. This was a consequence of his overriding intellectual moderation or balance. This model and legacy of tough-minded, Socratic moderation in Storing's scholarship is something that self-identified Straussians, as well as those who vociferously criticize or silently shun them, profitably could recognize and ponder.[8] Several of his students emphasize the dialectical fairness and care, and aversion to intellectual or polemical extremes – what I term "intellectual moderation" – that marked his teaching and scholarship.[9] The fact that Storing studied and

---

[8] Harry Clor identifies Storing's intellectual moderation in contributing to "A Symposium on Herbert Storing"; see "Our Problem of Moral Community: Lessons from the Teachings of Herbert Storing," *Political Science Reviewer* 29 (2000), 94–120. Clor praises his "spirit of sobriety," and dialectical or "balanced reflectiveness" about the study of politics: in reviewing his work as "a scholar, political educator, a teacher," the "general idea that comes most frequently to mind is…moderation" (95). Clor also acknowledges Storing's broad influence in *On Moderation: Defending an Ancient Virtue in a Modern World* (Baylor University Press, 2008), x.

[9] See Murray Dry, "Herbert Storing: The American Founding and the American Regime," in *Leo Strauss, the Straussians, and the American Regime*, eds. Kenneth L. Deutsch and John A. Murley (Rowman & Littlefield, 1999), 305–28. Dry particularly notes that Storing's "dialectical" method in teaching, which also informed his scholarship, was to "contrast two different approaches to a

published in a range of subfields in his discipline further indicates his intellectual balance, qualities of a scholarly moderation that resists monomania or stridency. Indeed, his particular contributions to understanding American political thought, American constitutionalism, and American statesmanship or leadership evince the careful sobriety and avoidance of bias in a moderate mind. For political scientists (perhaps more broadly for social scientists) today, the map of extreme poles is not simply of right and left, but includes versions of dogmatism and skepticism. The landscape is perplexing because some scholars or schools tend to be at once skeptical and activist. Progressivism, the American philosophical school of Pragmatism, behavioralism, methodological scientism, and postmodernism are skeptical about any objective, universal truth regarding the moral ends of politics – then are liberated (wittingly or not) to be more or less dogmatic and polemical in their advocacy, left or right. More concretely, the dominant pole of American political thought and scholarship within academia and beyond (in think tanks and popular journals) seems to be versions of Deweyan pragmatism and constructivism. This stance both includes and in turn provokes partisan advocacy and polemic thinly veiled as academic inquiry and scholarly relevance, left or right. One reaction to such contestation is a mere pragmatism (not avowedly Deweyan) that seeks intellectual compromise or peace at the expense of arguing about or seeking the truth, yielding a mushy kind of pluralism. Storing's moderation recognized the earlier versions of these alternatives, and consciously sought a higher middle ground that was not dogmatic in its appreciation of the founding political science and its search for reasonable, substantive ends and means for a free politics. Thus, he did not think it reasonable or useful to encase that first political science in amber for filio-pietistic study. Instead, he sought to understand the claims of that view in its full breadth, evaluate them, and develop them for application to new phenomena. His studies of American political thought prominently featured the critics of or dissenters from the constitutional order, ranging from the Anti-Federalists to African-American voices on slavery, race, and equal rights. He also affirmed the need for study of American political development since the founding, through his scholarship on public administration and the new conception of the presidency.

A third larger point – here returning to his prescient critique of the presumption that newer intellectual views must be better – is that Storing's political science addresses concerns about the relevance of academic work in a deeper, less partisan manner than is true of many reflections on "the state of the discipline." One kind of disciplinary self-critique, as noted, is Lowi's neo-Progressive assessment of interest-group pluralism. This is one among several forms of what James Ceaser terms "the new normativism," to include the postbehavioralist work by Robert Dahl or the neo-Jeffersonian arguments of Benjamin Barber.

given problem of government" and then pursue "reasoned argument" while featuring discussion, questions, and disagreement from students (305–306).

Another kind is the Perestroika movement's neo-Progressive, seemingly post-modernist call for a methodological pluralism that should emphasize relevance and academic activism.[10] A comparison of Storing's constitutionalist political science with these postconstitutionalist alternatives suggests why a wider, fairer hearing should be given to his emphasis on moderation, basic civic education, and liberal education for statesmanlike leadership. To assess this argument for greater balance, we should put aside, for the moment, larger debates about the Progressive and neo-Progressive critiques of the founders' constitutionalism and political science, or calls for a new constitutional convention to fix the errors of the founders' system. Also beyond the scope of this article is any claim to demonstrate that Storing's conception of political science is simply correct, or undoubtedly superior to alternative conceptions. The suggestion, instead, is that political science and the study of American political thought would benefit from considering two more manageable topics that neo-Progressives today, both within political science and in wider discourse, emphasize when arguing that American politics is dysfunctional – but considering them anew, in light of Storing's alternative view. His more balanced, broad-minded approach to American politics and political science, especially his inclusion of a central role for American political thought, arguably offers a better understanding of these two phenomena.

The first issue is the widely voiced concern about polarization and hyper-partisanship in politics, today most often blamed upon the extremism of conservative intellectuals, partisans, or office holders. A prominent argument in this vein by two political scientists is Mann and Ornstein's *It's Even Worse Than It Looks*. These professed moderates, and established figures in the culture of Washington, D.C., decry "the new politics of extremism" stemming almost wholly from the post-Gingrich Republican Party.[11] In response, a more complete consideration of causes or blame would recall that the political science of Woodrow Wilson and its various neo-Progressive progeny – all of which reject the broad constitutionalist principles of America's first political science or any attempts to revise them – have held the commanding heights of the discipline for a century. Indeed, a major effort of the discipline during the twentieth

---

[10] In addition to Mansfield's arguments for reform of the discipline in *America's Constitutional Soul* and other works, James Ceaser has repeatedly addressed these themes, first in *Liberal Democracy and Political Science* (Johns Hopkins University Press, 1990), particularly on "the new normativism" (114–42). While Storing's work anticipates several concerns shared by Mansfield and Ceaser, Storing's distinctive substance and tone merit separate consideration.

[11] Thomas E. Mann and Norman J. Ornstein, *It's Even Worse Than It Looks: How the American Constitutional System Collided With the New Politics of Extremism* (Basic Books, 2012). They argue that recent Republican extremism is so revolutionary (an "asymmetric polarization") that journalists and other leading voices should abandon neutrality or balance, since "a balanced treatment of an unbalanced phenomenon is a distortion of reality and a disservice" to the culture and citizenry (102–103, 194–96). To their credit, they state that their imbalance about Republicans informs the entire analysis (184–87); yet this raises a question about the accuracy or sobriety of their diagnosis of asymmetry, especially how they arrived at it.

century was to achieve ideological purity in the parties as a way to promote "responsible party government," a project directly descended from Wilson and other Progressive minds.[12] Are not these postconstitutionalist schools somewhat implicated in the failure to produce a more civil discourse or a better kind of partisanship? To their credit, Mann and Ornstein cite the APSA's call in the 1950s for an ideologically clear and (it was expected) more responsible party system as being a source of the current hyperpolarization. This view has produced "a mismatch" between the new "vehemently adversarial" parties characteristic of a parliamentary system and our "governing system" of a complex constitutionalism that frustrates the easy achievement of majoritarian action. However, they do not trace this call for neo-parliamentary reform, and the consequent mismatch and hyper-partisanship, to Progressive political science.[13] Storing's political science would help to explain why the various postconstitutionalist approaches arguably produce as much polarization, whether intentional or not, as any conservative voices do. Storing's emphasis that the American founding embodies both principles and reasoned debate about them, and his advocacy of a political science appreciative of reasonable judgments and disagreements among politicians and public servants, are valuable resources for addressing the causes of our excessive partisanship. This is because his political science first understands the principles of our constitutional order, what its reasonable aims are, and what reasonable debate about ends and means has been and could be. In that last vein, Storing was a complex sort of Hamiltonian who saw the founding principles as open to "big government" while also seeking to sustain minority voices who warned (as from the beginning) about the not-immediately-obvious costs to political and social order of centralized, and ever bigger, government and administration.[14]

The second contemporary issue that Storing can help us address comprises the widely voiced complaint among academics and beyond about a leadership crisis in American political culture; related to this is the angst of political scientists about the seeming irrelevance of their discipline to actual problems of politics and leadership. Storing's political science offers a rich understanding of statesmanship provided by a constitutionalist view rooted in the value of competing institutions, which in turn demands adaptation of deeper principles amid continual debate. His careful study of Blackstone, who along with Montesquieu was a primary guide for America's framers, reflects his appreciation

---

[12] See, for example, Austin Ranney, *The Doctrine of Responsible Party Government: Its Origins and Present State* (University of Illinois Press, 1954); and the American Political Science Association's 1950 report advocating reforms, "Toward a More Responsible Two-Party System," 44 *American Political Science Review* 3, Part 2 (September 1950).

[13] Mann and Ornstein, *It's Even Worse Than It Looks*, xiii–xiv, 163–65, 198.

[14] Storing's 1974 essay "The Problem of Big Government," reprinted in Joseph Bessette's fine collection of his writings, captures this complex conception of American federalism and political development; see *Toward a More Perfect Union: Writings of Herbert J. Storing*, ed. Joseph M. Bessette (AEI Press, 1995), 287–306.

that constitutionalism calls forth reasonable and diverse judgments by both office holders and citizens in a complex order. Openness to including Storing's moderate science in our academic culture thus would provide more academic substance to the proliferating "leadership studies" programs in higher education and beyond.

What follows is not a comprehensive study of Storing's scholarship; nor does it aim to prove that Storing was simply correct on all points. Rather, analysis of some elements of his understanding of political science, of American constitutionalism and political thought, and of intellectual moderation suggests why his discipline should make room to consider a now-marginal perspective in order to better grapple with its professed concerns.[15]

Storing's Critique of Scientism: Not Your Typical Methodological Pluralism

Neither Storing's brief preface to *Essays on the Scientific Study of Politics* nor his chapter in it made a complete argument for a constitutional or (as the volume termed it) neo-Aristotelian political science; nor did Storing intend them to do so. His preface noted that the essays were "largely critical and 'negative'" about the new social science; while "[t]he criticisms have positive implications" partially delineated in the essays and epilogue, those points were "incidental to the primary intention" of appraising the new science (*Essays*, vi).[16] The positive case was made in his later scholarship, and even there he develops it subtly. The emphasis of Storing's own chapter on Herbert Simon's science of administration was analytical exposition of the illogic and unfulfilled promises of the new scientism. This largely negative task characterizes even Leo Strauss's "Epilogue" to the collection, which addressed the fundamental stakes for political science and constitutional, liberal democracy of a putatively value-neutral scientism. Strauss's essay closes with a provocation: the new science, by definition neutral on the value-based struggle between communism and liberal democracy, "fiddles while Rome burns." Strauss excuses it from being diabolical or Neronian, however, since "it does not know that it fiddles, and it does not know

---

[15] Limitations of space prevent consideration of Storing's courageous and moderate scholarship on African-American political thought – including his (unfortunately) out-of-print anthology *What Country Have I? Political Writings by Black Americans* (St. Martin's Press, 1970). A more comprehensive assessment is in the 2000 symposium in *Political Science Reviewer* and in Bessette's collection, to include Bessette's introduction. That collection includes four Storing selections on slavery and race in American thought, including his striking introduction to the 1970 anthology and "The Case against Civil Disobedience" (1969).

[16] For a more explicit argument in defense of a political science informed by Aristotle, Montesquieu, and Tocqueville, see, in addition to the preceding chapters, Ceaser, *Liberal Democracy and Political Science*, especially "Traditional Political Science" (41–69). Ceaser has pursued this argument in subsequent works, most recently *Designing a Polity: America's Constitution in Theory and Practice* (Rowman & Littlefield, 2011).

that Rome burns" ("Epilogue," *Essays*, 327). A half-century later, it seems clear that Storing's contributions to political science in part have been lost amid the polemics and controversies that engulfed Strauss and the Straussians. Strauss's closing provocation aside, his epilogue emphasizes the inadequacies and dangers of the new science while offering only an outline of a restored constitutional science. His brief defense of Aristotelian and even of Montesquieuan political science (see *Essays*, 311) suggests that the older, constitutional political science of the ancients and early moderns would more adequately explain and defend liberal constitutionalism given the threats it faced in the Cold War.[17] Nonetheless, the predominant aim of the Storing collection was to clear the space for regeneration of the older science. That work unfolded in the subsequent decades, and Storing was a leader in that effort. The alternating denunciation and silence that the *Essays* received in turn indicated the headwinds that this constitutionalist school would face.[18]

To explain the significance of Storing's renewal of a constitutionalist political science – shaped by his study of Blackstone as well as the American founders – it is helpful to compare his critique of scientism with calls for methodological pluralism in the recent Perestroika movement that has percolated in political science since 2000. Storing's ninety-page chapter on Herbert Simon in *Essays* painstakingly reviews the latter's works on a science of administration, organization theory, a new theory of decision-making, and the broader views about a new science of politics that inform Simon's prolific writings. While Storing as editor had reserved for Strauss a discussion of the larger implications of the new scientism, he quietly addresses these in his own chapter as well. These distinctly nonpolemical analyses are still salient for anyone interested in the role of "methods" in political science and its curricula, and also for the related question of the relevance – or aid to citizenship and governing – of a discipline dominated by scientism.

Simon's project, says Storing, is to replace the old-fashioned, prescientific study of administration and government with a precise, empirically verifiable, and neutral method. That new method claimed to focus upon actual behavior and a value-neutral analysis that would bring greater predictability and guidance than mushy, proverb-laden talk about ends and means or good governance. The critique by Schaar and Wolin concedes that Storing finds many flaws in Simon's work, but they censure Storing for scoring easy points against an inconsistent, second-rate thinker while neglecting a serious analysis of behavioralism and scientism. His chapter is "substantively empty."[19] It is odd that

---

[17] I discuss in the next section below what Storing meant by moderation and constitutionalism, and the influence of Blackstone and Montesquieu for American understandings of these terms.

[18] Michael Zuckert's essay in the Storing symposium is one of the few analyses to defend the *Essays* and Storing's approach; moreover, it emphasizes his moderation (as I term it) in both understanding the American regime and criticizing it. See Zuckert, "Herbert J. Storing's Turn to the American Founding," *Political Science Reviewer* 29 (2000), 9–38, at 9–13, 29–32.

[19] Schaar and Wolin, "Review Essay," 133–37; quotation at 136.

the reviewers dismiss Simon, given his public stature and influence within academia. Simon would receive the Nobel Prize in Economics a decade later precisely for his achievements in the scientific study of organizations, and his theoretical assumptions continue to influence the social sciences. Moreover, Schaar and Wolin overlook Storing's deeper analysis of why the new science, in Simon's version and more broadly, cannot make sense of its own reasoning and theorizing. Given its dogmatic insistence upon finding value-neutral, narrowly precise definitions of terms to replace the vague thinking of "common sense," the new science cannot explain why its view is important, why its judgments should be trusted, or why one should take it seriously – for these are value judgments. As Storing notes, the "behavior of the scientist as such – the activity, that is to say, of the search for truth – is beyond the [new] science of human behavior. What purports to be a vocabulary for the description of human behavior cannot describe the highest form of it" (*Essays*, 128).

Storing concludes his chapter by returning to this self-undermining character of a scientistic view of human affairs, a concern salient for today's advocates of "methods" who struggle to explain its worth to those who don't presuppose the value of mathematizing and quantifying human phenomena. Indeed, Storing notes, scientism cannot even explain the principle of "efficiency" and maximization of utility so central to Simon's studies of administration – a concern salient for today's advocates of rational choice analysis. Storing's insight is that the new science is the less useful the closer it gets to the practically important question of offering guidance about choosing the ends or aims of human conduct:

Ultimately a commitment to rationality or to any value providing the basis for rational behavior (such as consistency) is a value commitment like any other. The inevitable, if paradoxical consequence of Simon's theory is that a man is no less rational if he spurns rationality altogether. It is wholly within a man's province to decide whether or to what extent to commit himself to the sober, efficient pursuit of stable and consistent preferences rather than to the excitement or the ease of doing what seems pleasant at this moment with no thought for the next. (*Essays*, 148)

Storing quips that the supposedly less scientific scholar Luther Gulick, a target of Simon's work, was more subtle in understanding the difficulty of a narrow science of human affairs when he offered the "sly paradox" that (to quote Gulick) "'should' is a word political scientists should not use in scientific discussions!" (*Essays*, 149). The result, in Storing's judgment, is that scientism fails in its central claim: "Science remains dependent both for its definition and for its standards of significance and relevance, on a common sense grasp of the phenomena to be investigated." A political scientist instead should seek to clarify the assumptions of common sense, and pursue their implications and consequences, but not discard that perspective.

As noted, the *Essays* mostly have been ignored or denounced, but an exception is Benjamin Barber's "The Politics of Political Science" in a centennial commemoration of *The American Political Science Review* in 2006. Barber grants that a worthy issue was raised by Storing and the Straussian critique of scientism. Still, he largely excuses the denunciation by Wolin and Schaar, whom he identifies as "unapologetically leftist" and "radical in the best sense." The exchange between Storing-Strauss and Schaar-Wolin was less a dialogue between theorists than a clash of right and left. He identifies himself as advocating "strong democracy" and Progressive politics, thus as agreeing with the "politics" of the denouncers.[20] His view of "the politics of political science" apparently holds the constructivist view that all meanings are invented and all discourse ultimately is "politics" akin to partisanship. He is torn, therefore, between admiring this denunciation of conservatives and warning that an open shouting match between theorists had harmed the field in the eyes of the broader discipline. Indeed, he admits that the Schaar-Wolin polemic distracted from the serious issue of the rise of scientism, thereby losing an opportunity to help political science. On the other hand, Barber's own constructivism, which endorses academic partisanship and activism, presumes that not only Strauss but Storing and the other authors in the *Essays* were polemicists. Therefore, the "political" denunciation by the academic left in 1963 was legitimate.[21] Barber's mixed verdict on the 1962–63 exchanges is thus, in one sense, an advance over the hyperbole of Schaar and Wolin. However, it never engages the deeper critique by Storing (or the substance amid Strauss's polemic) of a political science that cannot investigate the question of fundamental truths or objective meanings regarding the ends of politics, since constructivism repudiates such efforts.

A serious confrontation with Storing's critique of scientism also would contrast his political science with the Perestroika movement launched in political science, first in America and then worldwide, in 2000.[22] The initial statement by "Perestroika Glasnost" emphasized the narrowness of quantitative methodologies; the irrelevance of this dominant approach and thus of the discipline to real-world developments and problems; and grievances about not only diversity of viewpoint but equal status and diversity regarding race, gender, and the pecking order of leading institutions or departments. We can note an irony of this call for methodological pluralism, both by "Mr. Perestroika" and the subsequent movement amplifying his concerns, in that it does not welcome Storing's brand

---

[20] Benjamin Barber, "The Politics of Political Science: 'Value-free' Theory and the Wolin-Strauss Dust-Up of 1963," *American Political Science Review* 100 (2006), 539–45, at 544, 543.

[21] Barber, "Politics of Political Science," 541–42, also 544. What I refer to as constructivism is termed the "new normativism" by Ceaser, in *Liberal Democracy* (114–42); more recently, he critiques this as "the doctrine of nonfoundationalism" in *Designing a Polity*, 3–21.

[22] This movement was launched with an email message from "Perestroika Glasnost" to the editors of *The American Political Science Review* and PS: *Political Science and Politics*, October 15, 2000, entitled "On Globalization of the APSA and *APSR*: A Political Science Manifesto"; available in *Perestroika! The Raucous Revolution in Political Science*, ed. K. R. Monroe (Yale University Press, 2005).

of constitutional political science. This is evident from the Perestroikan silence on Storing's main argument – that a science of human affairs cannot renounce evaluation of and debate about values, that is, ultimate moral and ontological standards of truth and justice. Perhaps supporters of the Perestroika approach are more pluralistic or tolerant in practice than its founding documents and subsequent main voices; and there may be more tolerance for Strauss's school and more broadly for Storing's kind of constitutionalist, post-Progressive political science since 1963. Nonetheless, the headwinds still faced by constitutionalist political science appear in the Perestroikan emphasis upon a pluralism of qualitative as well as quantitative approaches, whatever they might be. Storing's call for reorientation of the discipline was broader and deeper, because basically Socratic. It insisted that we know enough about human affairs and government to know of fixed standards for truth and right, but not enough to be closed to reasonable debate and to further development of our understanding, let alone closed to engagement with common sense and traditional reasoning. This is the broad, moderate approach shared by the political science of Aristotle, Montesquieu, and Tocqueville, which is not to deny serious tensions or disagreements among them. Subsequent statements in and about the Perestroikan view emphasize space for qualitative studies in various subfields, but also echo the theme that method diversity is a means toward relevance understood as serving political progress, progressive action, and democratic change.[23]

Thus, while this recent call for methodological balance aligns with elements of Storing's political science, his view ultimately suggests that the Perestroikan criticism exchanges one kind of narrowness for a deeper one. The Perestroikans have no qualms with the generally postmodernist turn in the discipline, broadly shared between scientism and a range of constructivist views. The disciplinary consensus is not just open to but insists upon *de jure* relativism about moral ends or highest aims, even if *de facto* its aims are progressive and egalitarian.[24] Storing might wonder how much was gained in subsequent decades, since two strands of hypermodern thought now dominate the discipline, scientism and versions of postmodernism. This is true even in fields such as American Political Development and American Political Thought that harbor some space for considering permanent ends or ultimate principles in

---

[23] See, for example, the essays in Monroe, ed., *Perestroika!* and also "Symposium: Perestroika in Political Science: Past, Present, and Future," in *PS: Political Science and Politics* 43 (2010), ed. Patrick J. McGovern, 725–54.

[24] Recent examples that embody this broadly postmodernist and neo-Progressive approach, in introductory or advanced surveys of the discipline, include Sanford S. Schram and Brian Caterino, eds., *Making Political Science Matter: Debating Knowledge, Research, and Method* (New York University Press, 2006), and David Marsh and Gerry Stoker, eds., *Theory and Methods in Political Science*, 3rd edn. (Palgrave Macmillan, 2010).

politics.[25] We can gain a sense of what he might think through Joseph Bessette's anthology of his writings, which includes Storing's broader remarks about political science. His reflections anticipate problems with a pluralistic, relativistic stance toward methods and the discipline.[26] Storing emphasized that the "Chicago School" of his era was not dominated by any one methodological or philosophical view about political science. Instead, the department was marked by serious, occasionally contentious debate about these primary questions. He endorsed this contentiousness in search of truth as "a good thing" (*Writings*, 440). That said, he also eschewed a model that is "no doubt the worst (and unfortunately probably the most common) picture of all" – a "department where everyone agrees a little and disagrees a little, where everything is very gentle and dull, and no one says (or learns) much about anything" (*Writings*, 441).

Storing argued that the better model is a scholarly community in which "political theory" presses such primary questions and holds "the central place," but not a monopoly. This nonrelativist but still Socratic approach – one could call it philosophical moderation with a spine – ensures that professors and students always must account for "the wide variety of approaches to the study of political phenomena" (*Writings*, 442, 443). Further, in a 1973 essay on Strauss, he insisted (seemingly for himself and Strauss) that methodological pluralism and the debate about it "need to be informed and guided – as political life itself is informed and guided – by a concern with the ends of political life" (*Writings*, 445). This meant a constitutionalist political science, which "pointed the student of politics back to the principles of the regime – to those rules and ends and standards of the human good that constitute the life of the community" (*Writings*, 446). He criticized a political science so immoderate in its scientism or its postmodernist commitment to democratic progress and new values that it had forgotten fundamental questions of importance to citizens, statesmanlike leaders, and open-minded theorists and political scientists.

Because Storing died suddenly in 1977, only two decades into his career, we do not have his mature reflections connecting his theory of political science with his scholarship. Political science, and the self-identified Straussians, lost a distinctively moderate, nonpolemical voice for this school and for a broader approach to the study of American politics and political thought.

---

[25] For a recent critique along these lines, see George Thomas, "What Is Political Development? A Constitutional Perspective," and the subsequent debate – Karen Orren and Stephen Skowronek, "Have We Abandoned a 'Constitutional Perspective' on American Political Development?," then Thomas, "A Reply to Orren and Skowronek" – in *The Review of Politics* 73 (2011), 275–95, 295–99, 301–304.

[26] See Storing on "The 'Chicago School' of Political Science," in *Toward a More Perfect Union* (hereafter cited in this chapter as *Writings*), 440–43; note also his 1973 statements on political science in selections that Bessette entitles "The Achievement of Leo Strauss," *Writings*, 444–49.

Reinvigorating a Moderate, Constitutionalist Political Science

Storing's analysis of scientism's failure to provide either more logical or more relevant insights into politics intimated that there were not sound reasons for discarding America's first political science. That science, in his view, largely was the work of the Federalists, but not exclusively so. This complex stance is a further sign of his philosophical moderation or balance. He explicitly invokes moderation on occasion, and protégés identify this as a mark of his political science. A clear root of this outlook is his essay "William Blackstone," an exposition of *Commentaries on the Laws of England* (1765); it also reveals Storing's views on the limits of pure science and the reasonableness of complex institutions that avoid political extremes.[27] Storing observes Blackstone connection of "first principles" of law with the practice of a legal-political order, and he defines the main theme of the *Commentaries* with a quotation about ascending from positive laws to arguments drawn "from the spirit of the laws and the natural foundations of justice" (*Writings*, 234). Storing sees a "philosophical intention" in Blackstone's effort to refocus both study of law and "civic education" on "examination of the laws of the land, their natural foundations, and the intervening 'spirit of the laws'." He notes debts to both Locke and Montesquieu, but sees Blackstone's contrast to Locke given an emphasis on ordered liberty: "Blackstone says, following Montesquieu, that in England as perhaps nowhere else, 'political or civil liberty is the very end and scope of the constitution'" (*Writings*, 226).

Storing notes a further distance from abstract liberal theory given that Blackstone insists liberty should be practically defined as what the laws permit. Thus, regarding a natural right of self-defense, he quotes Blackstone's statement that "we must not carry this doctrine to the same visionary length that Mr. Locke does" since no "well-regulated community" could sustain peace on such individualistic, contentious terms (*Writings*, 227; see 223–229 generally). He next emphasizes Blackstone's repeated praise of a complex constitutionalism of separated powers, and explains that the *Commentaries'* views on a right of revolution and parliamentary sovereignty are more subtle than appears at first. Blackstone discerns "the extremes" of tyranny and anarchy and endorses a constitutionalism that can resist both, since "either is fatal to liberty"

---

[27] Originally published in *History of Political Philosophy*, eds. Leo Strauss and Joseph Cropsey (University of Chicago Press, 1963), and retained in later editions (1972, 1987); it is reprinted in Bessette's collection, and I cite pages from that source (*Writings*, 223–35). On Montesquieu's deep influence on Blackstone, see James Stoner, *Common Law and Liberal Theory: Coke, Hobbes, and the Origins of American Constitutionalism* (University Press of Kansas, 1992), 162–75, and my *The Cloaking of Power: Montesquieu, Blackstone, and the Rise of Judicial Activism* (University of Chicago Press, 2003), 124–49, with sources cited therein. On Montesquieu's pervasive influence upon America's constitutionalism and founding, see Chapter 2 (final section); on his philosophy of moderation, see Chapter 1.

(*Writings*, 228–29). This complex approach, says Storing, informs Blackstone's great emphasis on the courts, within the structure of king-in-parliament, for holding a middle ground between extremes. Rights of individuals can be protected, and reforms to law advanced, without discarding communal order and tradition. Blackstone thus takes a middle view on the Glorious Revolution of 1688, which (as Storing quotes) avoided "the wild extremes into which the visionary theories of some zealous republicans would have led them," but also avoided acquiescence to James II's anticonstitutional tyranny. Blackstone teaches, he argues, that anything like a right of revolution should "be exercised as wisely and moderately as it was" in 1688, to sustain both liberty and the constitutional fabric upon which it depends (*Writings*, 231–32). Storing closes by featuring Blackstone's themes of the balance needed between "science" and "art" for a proper understanding of the common law, and the need to reform while preserving the larger forms of a constitution. Thus, he twice discusses the "Gothic castle" metaphor of the *Commentaries*: for Blackstone, legal reform should appreciate the sturdy walls of the constitutional fabric while modernizing the interior details (*Writings*, 232–235).[28]

Storing's appreciation of Blackstone's political and intellectual moderation led him to emphasize the pluralism or complexity in America's first political science. This is a deeper sense of pluralism, beyond a focus on diversity of interests or values as in the science of David Truman or David Easton. For Storing, it was an expression of the essential moderation or balance that informed the consensus view of the founders. Such moderation in part stemmed from the dialogical character of American constitutionalism, produced not by a Solon or Lycurgus but by deliberation among thinkers and statesmen. As argued in Chapter 2, Washington was the Founding Father, the embodiment and forger of a consensus on founding principles, yet his mode was not dictation but moderation. The founding alloy, and its political science, also was marked by substantively moderate views of politics and thought; this is the conception of moderation invoked in the opening and closing essays of *The Federalist*. Storing noted that while the founders' constitutionalism sought to improve upon the ancient and medieval views of a free politics, it held a modest estimation of how rational, and precise, its analysis could be. This is especially true if one assessed, as he took the lead in doing, both the Anti-Federalist and Federalist views in that science. His work does not often cite Tocqueville, but does so often enough to prompt suspicion that he may have adopted from Tocqueville this capacious, balanced view of America's first political science. Nonetheless, Storing

---

[28] Clor's *On Moderation* cites Storing's general influence and then analyzes moderation in three dimensions that (just happen to) fit the legal and moral spirit of the *Commentaries*, and Storing's explication – moral, political (constitutional), and intellectual. In the Prologue, I discuss recent books by Aurelian Craiutu and Peter Berkowitz that explore similar themes about modern constitutionalism and moderation.

knew that in the complex amalgam of the founders' thought, the Federalists dominated.[29]

Hamilton had argued in *Federalist* no. 9 that "the science of politics" had improved in recent centuries, citing Montesquieu. Madison's sequel boldly claimed that new conceptions of federalism, and of a pluralism of interests in an extended republic, provided the republican solution to republican faction (no. 10). These were not modest claims about their political science. Nor is it timid to declare that enlightened statesmen would not always be at the helm in this new constitutionalism, thereby recommending a complex and balanced order that presumed the interest of the various office holders (*Federalist* nos. 10 and 51). On the other hand, Storing saw that these views did not entail exclusion of such Aristotelian and Montesquieuan categories as moral judgment, prudence, statesmanship, and regard for ultimate ends of justice. To take only the institutional dimensions, he noted Madison's defense in *The Federalist* of a Senate guided by these high republican standards and aims (e.g., nos. 62–63). This not-so-democratic body would correct a tendency toward narrow interests and short-term concerns among factions or a popular majority. He also noted Hamilton's similar defense of the high-toned republicanism and constitutional balance provided by a single executive and independent courts. Storing identified the American founders's careful calibration of such competing principles and forces as an effort "to steer a course between these extremes." Indeed, this complex constitutionalism, especially distribution of powers with checks and balances, was "an attempt to institutionalize moderation" ("The Problem of Big Government" and "Political Parties and the Bureaucracy," *Writings*, 299, 320).

That said, Storing's own moderation insisted that a constitutionalist political science must look beyond the Federalists to see their flaws. If at mid-century such scholars as Douglas Adair and Martin Diamond were transcending Progressivism by reviving study of *The Federalist*, Storing's dialectical, Socratic approach sought other voices needing amplification. A main path to such balance – and to viewing the heirs of the founders as continually self-governing, not filio-pietists – was to recall the vital contributions of the Federalists's critics. Indeed, he saw that Anti-Federalist insights percolated throughout American thought and conduct. True, his introduction to his collection of Anti-Federalist writings – completed posthumously by Murray Dry – stated that "the Anti-Federalists lost the debate over the Constitution" not for forensic or tactical

---

[29] See Storing's essays on "The Constitution and the Bill of Rights" and "Federalists and Anti-Federalists: The Ratification Debate" in *Writings*. This theme of the complex constitutionalism and republicanism of the founders' political science is addressed in Clor, "Our Problem of Moral Community," and is the focus of Bessette's contribution to the Storing symposium, "Herbert Storing and the Problem of Democracy," *Political Science Reviewer* 29 (2000), 70–93. I address this in Chapter 2, and in "The Complexity, and Principles, of the American Founding: A Reply to Alan Gibson," *History of Political Thought* xxi (2000), 711–17.

reasons but "because they had the weaker argument."[30] His moderation nonetheless led Storing to do more than any political scientist of his era to restore the Anti-Federalist viewpoint and their essential ideas. He took seriously and indeed endorsed several of their criticisms of the Federalist political science, including their concern with a tendency to overemphasize interests and individual interest.[31] He thus seems to echo the complex approach of Montesquieu and Tocqueville, which adopts a deeper kind of pluralism about method and inquiry. Theory should clarify ultimate principles of natural justice and decent morality, but, guided by these, political science also demands empirical observation and sound method. The moderate Enlightenment (especially Montesquieu), then its heirs among the American founders, and finally Tocqueville all insisted upon only as much rigor or method as the phenomena can bear. This is the generally Aristotelian view that method is a means, not an end, and shouldn't obscure the reality of the phenomena or displace discussion of ends.[32] One of Storing's prominent successors, James Q. Wilson, adopted this balanced approach in his widely used text on American government, defining political science as inquiring about who governs and how – and also, to what ends.[33]

Here an important dimension of Storing's moderation is his view that the founding was complex, the product of debate as well as a consensus on first principles. Several studies quote his insight that while the Constitution "established a lasting structure of rules and principles," nonetheless "the political life of the community continues to be dialogue." Indeed, the founders grasped how unique their constitution was for "the extent to which it was the product of deliberation."[34] Only a balanced, moderate science could understand

---

[30] From Storing's *What the Anti-Federalists Were FOR*, posthumously edited by Murray Dry (University of Chicago Press, 1981), which also was the first volume of Storing's *The Complete Anti-Federalist*, seven volumes, eds. Storing and Dry (University of Chicago Press, 1981); quotation is also at *Writings*, 68. See also Walter Nicgorski's review, "The Anti-Federalists: Collected and Interpreted," *The Review of Politics* 46 (1984), 113–25.

[31] One essay with such pointed criticisms is the posthumously published "American Statesmanship: Old and New," *Writings*, 403–28; Bessette emphasizes this in his symposium contribution, "The Problem of Democracy"; see also Zuckert, "Storing's Turn," 29–32.

[32] The *locus classicus* is Aristotle, that a science of human affairs should seek only "the clarity that accords with the subject matter"; thus, "one should not seek precision in all arguments alike." See Aristotle, *Nicomachean Ethics*, eds. and trs. Bartlett and Collins (University of Chicago Press, 2011), Book I, Chapter 3 (1094b12–28), 3–4. I deploy the distinction of moderate versus radical strands of Enlightenment implicit in the scholarship of Jonathan Israel; see the Prologue.

[33] Shep Melnick argues this when reviewing Wilson's legacy in "Political Science as a Vocation: An Appreciation of the Life and the Work of James Q. Wilson," *The Forum* 10, no. 1 (May 2012); see also his review of J. Q. Wilson, *American Politics, Then and Now*, in "Balance Is All" (a phrase from Wilson), *The Claremont Review of Books*, vol. x, no. 4 (Fall 2010).

[34] Storing, *What the Anti-Federalists Were FOR*, 3; also cited in Dry, "Herbert Storing" 321, and by Ralph Rossum, "Herbert Storing's Constitutionalism," *Political Science Reviewer* 29 (2000), 39–69, at 59. Elsewhere in *What the Anti-Federalists Were FOR*, Storing noted: "If, however, the foundation of the American polity was laid by the Federalists, the Anti-Federalist reservations

such a founding and help its citizens – or those of any liberal democracy – to improve upon and govern under those principles and perspectives. He was critical of both Federalists and Anti-Federalists at points, especially on slavery, but insisted that the best thinking of both schools should be studied. His judgment was that the principles of natural rights and constitutionalism in the founding political science, and the debate about them, were perhaps incomplete in theory and surely incomplete in practice but had not been obviously bettered by rival views of politics, political science, and constitutionalism. Thus, they had to be seriously studied and debated, no matter how much time had passed, or the defects discerned, or what circumstances had changed. Developing new means to address old and new problems echoed the confidence in progress evinced by Publius and other founders. It is unfortunate that Gordon Wood, in a career of great intellectual moderation among historians of the founding, in one essay included Storing among Straussian "fundamentalist" scholars.[35] This lapse misses the spirit of Storing's political science. Perhaps Wood sensed he had painted with too broad a stroke, for he was less critical of Storing in particular. A more productive assessment by a non-Straussian of Strauss's influence on scholarship of American political thought is Wilson Carey McWilliams's argument that this school elevated the study of America, its debates, and the sources of its thought and character.[36]

The moderation that Storing valued in Blackstone, the Founders, and Montesquieu evokes the moderate Enlightenment. Relevant here is Montesquieu's critique of the scientism in such Enlightenment minds as Hobbes (and, he also may have thought, Locke).[37] The radical Enlightenment (especially Hobbes) is the precursor to twentieth-century behavioralism. The early conception of scientism insisted upon a narrowly foundationalist view of politics, defined by individual claims and interests. In contrast, Montesquieu's science sought both

---

echo through American history; and it is in the dialogue, not merely in the Federalist victory, that the country's principles are to be discovered," 73 (also in *Writings*, 69).

[35] Gordon Wood, "The Fundamentalists and the Constitution," *New York Review of Books* (February 18, 1988), 33–40. Among the scholars assessed, Wood shows more grudging respect toward Storing's Anti-Federalist scholarship, and he admits of insights gained by the Straussian approach – amid the greater part he disdains. Wood serves on the board of the new *American Political Thought* journal, edited by a Storing student (Michael Zuckert). I praise Wood's intellectual moderation in reviewing his recent book *The Idea of America: Reflections on the Birth of the United States* (2001), *American Political Thought* 1 (2012), 158–61.

[36] Wilson Carey McWilliams, "Leo Strauss and the Dignity of American Political Thought" (1988), in *The Democratic Soul: A Wilson Carey McWilliams Reader*, eds. P. Deneen and S. J. McWilliams (University Press of Kentucky, 2011), 192–206. A sign of Storing's moderation arises in the criticism of Jeremy Rabkin, "An American Scholar," *The Public Interest* 123 (1996), 118–23, reviewing Bessette, *Writings*. Amid praise, Rabkin regrets Storing's lack of a bolder, provocative political science and view of the founding; his "habitually lofty" view made him remote from "the great political debates" about the New Deal and scope of government.

[37] See the Prologue and Chapter 1, including sources cited therein; I also argue this in "Montesquieu, Charles de," in *The Encyclopedia of Political Thought*, ed. Michael Gibbons (Wiley-Blackwell, 2014).

intellectual and political moderation, evident in his criticism of ancient and modern philosophers who fall prey to intellectual extremes, and also his formulation of a "spirit" of laws and nations that captures the multifariousness of political reality (*The Spirit of Laws*, Book 29, Chapters 1 and 19; Book 1, Chapter 3). It is telling that Publius cites in *The Federalist* such figures of the moderate Enlightenment as Montesquieu, Hume, and Blackstone but never Hobbes or Locke. A political science that would reduce politics to one idea, or to only those elements that can be quantified with mathematical precision – as both Hobbes and Herbert Simon sought (in their own ways) – would not understand laws, politics, or the spirit of laws. This kind of philosophical moderation informs the first American political science achieved by Federalists and Anti-Federalists jointly. It is a kind of science that sought to institutionalize moderation, as Storing put it, and it deserved a second look. Nonetheless, he reinvigorated this spirit by addressing his own scholarship not only to the founding debates but also to their current relevance, to adaptations of their constitutionalism, and to recent manifestations of the enduring questions facing a free politics.

Deeper Relevance and Higher Utility: Lessons for Moderation and Leadership in Politics

A brief discussion of two dimensions of Storing's scholarly practice further suggests the value of his contributions regarding political science and America's founding constitutionalism, especially their salience for current expressions of our persistent anxieties. One idea addresses worries about polarization; the other addresses academic angst about relevance, particularly political science's contribution to the study and practice of political and civic leadership.

The first observation is that Storing's moderate approach to liberal democratic politics likely would yield more moderate rhetoric and conduct over time than any alternative, especially versions of neo-Progressive thinking and, at the opposite pole, conservative arguments for strict return to the founding constitutional order. At least since Ronald Reagan's rise to the presidency, then the conservative activism of Newt Gingrich, many political scientists have warned of excessive partisanship or polarization. This is a variant of the critiques by Walter Bagehot and Woodrow Wilson of the dysfunctions of America's Montesquieuan constitutionalism, although each critic preferred a different version of a parliamentary government and party unity in mass democracy.[38] In the spirit of Storing's political science, one can reply that these critiques overlook

---

[38] While Mann and Ornstein, in *Worse Than It Looks*, criticize the parliamentary party proposal of the 1950 APSA report, they in fact echo the Progressive critique of the founding by calling for reforms that keep the outlines of separation-of-powers constitutionalism while boosting majoritarianism in Congress and shifting authority to the executive and administrative agencies (163–78); this echoes Woodrow Wilson's approach to transforming the constitutional order.

the awareness of partisanship in the founding political science, thus neglect its attempt to moderate both lower and higher kinds of faction. Since we now largely ignore the framers and their sources, we cannot benefit from their sober views on how to ameliorate the partisanship endemic to constitutional politics. This is the perspective informing, among other arguments, *Federalist* no. 10. *The Spirit of Laws* (cited in *Federalist* no. 9) not only diagnosed high and low partisanship in liberal constitutions, it also argued that even intellectuals would fall into blinkered thinking. A culture devoted to liberty would warp even "historians" in a paradoxical way. Montesquieu himself was a historian (publishing *Considerations on the Romans* in 1734), so he includes a range of thinkers here. Under despotisms, he warned, historians betray the truth because they don't have liberty, but "in extremely free states," they betray it because of the factions arising from liberty, with each becoming "the slave of the prejudices of his faction" (*Spirit* 19.27, at end). To be aware of this pull was, for Montesquieu and the American founders, to arm oneself against it. Today, in contrast, the main voices of the social sciences urge us to embrace our inner partisan through various constructivisms, and our outer partisan through academic activism.

The cost of our amnesia about the framers' moderation is evident in contrasting the Progressive and behavioralist critique of the founding with Storing's more measured view. The former is typified by John Roche's widely read essay on the 1787 Constitutional Convention as a reform caucus featuring bargaining among interests, and this contrasts nicely with a neglected Storing essay on the founders' political science and statesmanship.[39] Roche's essay (and general approach) is vastly more influential upon journalists, politicians, and opinion leaders today. It therefore probably does as much, however unintended, to provoke harsh polarization as an equal dose of Storing's view would do to moderate and elevate our partisanship. Storing's essay on the 1787 Convention cites Roche's essay and thus invites the comparison.[40]

Storing finds Roche's focus on the rivalry of narrow interests among the delegates to be "flat, lacking in perspective." He admits that as practical men they held interests, but his careful review of the months of debate reveals that "they also saw beyond" the "clash of interests." For the higher consensus view among the founders, such narrow interests were "defensible only insofar as they were carriers of certain broad principles of free government" (*Writings*, 21). Storing emphasized the deliberation and debate, alternately reasonable and heated, that led to deeper compromises and in turn produced the Constitution. These were conciliations on how to implement shared but also divergent

---

39 John P. Roche, "The Founding Fathers: A Reform Caucus in Action," *American Political Science Review* 55 (1961), 799–816.

40 In the Bessette collection, it is "The Constitutional Convention: Toward a More Perfect Union" (*Writings*, 17–36), but Bessette notes that Storing's original title reveals his broader perspective – "The Federal Convention of 1787: Politics, Principles, and Statesmanship" (*Writings*, 17, 452).

principles about representation, a federal republic, and free government. The first grand one, the so-called Connecticut compromise on different principles of representation in the House and Senate, led to others. Storing's broader point is that such debate shows a rise from mere political activity, among mere leaders, to statesmanship. The moderation, intellectual and political, shown in these debates over principles yielded "an example of how such questions are properly approached in political life" (*Writings*, 36). One might call such statesmanlike effort the difficult practice of principled moderation – moderation with backbone, not a mushy search for mushy compromise, but pursuit of a broader view of ends and means in a higher middle ground. Indeed, Storing observes that Benjamin Franklin perhaps saved the convention when small-state delegates made threats about sundering the Union. The elder statesman reminded all sides of the need to (in Storing's words) "moderate their different demands." This helped contending views to realize that "unyielding pursuit of their principle would, almost certainly, have resulted in the irretrievable loss of that very principle" (*Writings*, 33, 36). The question for political science today is whether the view that reduces leadership to manipulating mass opinion – or to charismatic mobilization, or interest-seeking by politicians – exacerbates rather than ameliorates the interests and parties inherent in a free politics, with their attendant intellectual schools or sects. Mention of Franklin reminds of the other elder statesman in Philadelphia among the many young delegates, Washington. Storing might have noted, as argued in Chapter 2, Washington's embodiment of intellectual and practical moderation, to include obvious commitment to natural right and fundamental principle; that moderation led him to endorse the final compromise on the final day of the Convention, in an effort to limit the number of nonsigners and thereby hold together the Union.

The concern about a reductionist political science that eschews statesmanship applies to the legacy of Woodrow Wilson, who as political scientist called for fusing party leadership and a new kind of presidency as a neo-parliamentary path to evade the separation of powers. His new science would unite mass parties and democratic will under administrative leadership provided by party elites.[41] Nothing like Storing's careful study of the founding political science is found in Wilson's writings. He is confident of his superior views – indeed to a degree that lacks the spirit of science, since his scholarship hardly undertakes the close analysis of the founders' political science that would establish the need for his innovations. A century later the dominant approaches range from Wilson's science of the administrative state and mass party discipline to other postconstitutionalist views, as noted above, that share a dismissal of the founding political science while favoring liberal-progressive aims. At the least we have grounds for asking these schools why they, as dominant in teaching and

---

[41] Storing criticizes Wilson's theory in "Political Parties and the Bureaucracy" (*Writings*, 312–16), and also in "American Statesmanship."

scholarship about politics, share no burden for causing (intentionally or unintentionally) the polarization and fierce partisanship they lament.[42] A political science that educates citizens and opinion leaders to think alternately of narrow behaviors and interests, or of revolutionary visions of progress, likely would fail to inculcate understanding of the complex, balanced political order of America's constitutional liberal democracy. Nor would such an education inculcate the political spirit that prepares citizens and opinion leaders to constructively debate, and compromise, about how to achieve the ends of such a constitutional order, or how to implement means toward them. Indeed, the predominance of such an education and elite political culture paradoxically radicalizes the small-government and social conservatives who, as a substantial plurality of the electorate, reject the Progressive view of progressively larger government. We tend to point only at a conservative reaction against the Progressive state and the New Deal as the main culprit rather than considering, as well, what role the revolutions within political science might play in producing, or failing to redress, destructive polarization. Political science and the study of American political thought should make space for an alternate view within departmental faculty and curricula – namely, the constitutional political science of the American founders and the sources informing it, especially in Storing's capacious and critical recounting. That view at least anticipated partisanship, and called upon constitutional and moral resources for elevating or moderating it.

A related issue here, one that Storing might particularly lament, is the steep decline of constitutional law within political science, displaced by a narrow behavioralism and realism about law, judges, and lawyers.[43] If, as even these scholars of "judicial politics" occasionally lament, there is destructive partisanship on the bench or a declining public approval for judges and especially the Supreme Court, we should wonder whether legal-realist and attitudinal studies distort and erode the distinctive, constitutional character of judging and public law both for judges and citizens. The stakes ultimately involve the independence of the judiciary, since this behavioral, realist analysis finds no essential distinction between judges and politicians. The corrosiveness of this new approach is evident in the increasing polarization around Supreme Court and especially federal appellate court nominations since at least the Reagan era – leading to vacancies on the bench, withdrawal of highly qualified candidates of all

---

[42] Melnick's review of James Q. Wilson's scholarship, "Political Science as a Vocation," supports the argument of Alan Abramowitz, *The Disappearing Center: Engaged Citizens, Polarization, and American Democracy* (Yale University Press, 2010) that deeper causes of polarization need to be assessed, and that it is not only elites who are polarized – the latter view argued by Morris Fiorina, with Samuel J. Abrams and Jeremy C. Pope, *Culture War? The Myth of Polarized America*, 3rd edn. (Longman, 2011 [2004]).

[43] Further resources for Storing's views about constitutionalism, law, and constitutional moderation include his essays "The Constitution and the Bill of Rights" and "William Blackstone," in *Writings*. See also Dry, "Storing"; Zuckert, "Storing's Turn"; and Rossum, "Storing's Constitutionalism."

persuasions, and a highly polarized Senate.[44] If lamentation about destructive polarization means more than a concern that one's party or school is not winning, it must mean a concern for the breakdown of political legitimacy and institutional order. A more balanced academic debate would inquire about which approaches to political science provide resources for understanding the deeper causes of polarization, and for perpetuating or ameliorating the political order of a liberal democracy. Storing's political science frames these issues as centrally important – in contrast to many alternatives in the discipline, which tend to take for granted the perpetuation of the constitutional order and instead emphasize public opinion, or narrow interests, or projects for progress that we should envision in light of our power to construct all meanings.

A second and final example of the salience of Storing's political science is its insight about our recent and diminished conceptions of "leadership." Having taught for two decades at a military academy that takes seriously the officer's oath to the Constitution (rather than to any commander or official) and that also expends great efforts in thinking and teaching about leadership, I am struck by the superior discernment in his posthumous essay "American Statesmanship: Old and New" relative to much current literature.[45] Wider appreciation of Storing's approach would illuminate concerns about the relevance of political science raised by Lowi, then the Perestroika movement, and regularly since. In contrast to many leadership studies within and beyond political science departments – and also to the analysis of leadership in most studies of American foreign policy and international relations – Storing offers a refreshing focus on the questions of ends, and practical judgment, that always confront leaders in a constitutional liberal democracy.

"American Statesmanship" argues that there were flaws in the original theory of statesmanship held by the founders, especially the Federalists, but that the attempts by Progressives and behavioralists to supersede it are detrimental. Characteristically for Storing, he discerns two extreme views, then argues that a search is needed for a balance or higher middle ground. These are, first, a theory of statesmanship regarding interests (the Federalist theory, as distinct from their best practice), and then a theory of mass leadership (first by Jacksonians, then by the Progressives and scientism). Moreover, after the Progressive and behavioralist revolutions in political science, Storing finds that American thinking about statesmanship, or now leadership, is dominated by two Progressive extremes – of populism or mass mobilization, and of scientific

---

44 A general assessment is Brian Tamanaha, *Law as a Means to an End: Threat to the Rule of Law* (Cambridge University Press, 2006). Mann and Ornstein, in *Worse Than It Looks*, note the problem but trace the cause only to the "asymmetric polarization" of conservative Republicans, not (as Tamanaha does) to its roots in legal realism and its cousins, Progressivism and behavioralism. I address this in *The Cloaking of Power*.

45 Storing served in the US Army, enlisted ranks, from 1946–48 (*Writings*, 467); this was not unusual for professors of his generation, but – as a civilian with no prior service myself – it is noteworthy how extraordinarily rare such experience is today in civilian academia.

administration. What is lost is the middle ground the founders practiced but didn't fully theorize, given that their theory emphasized interests and the institutional mechanisms for channeling them (_Writings_, 403–6). Storing thus argues for rediscovery of traditional conceptions of prudence, which the founders practiced at a level better than their political science (especially its Federalist side). He defines prudence as the practical judgment of statesmen who act in service of higher principles; one example is his praise for "leaders trying to deal with problems justly and prudently on their merits." That view of leadership rising to statesmanship required, he notes, both an understanding of and commitment to the complex constitutionalism that the founders learned "from Blackstone and Montesquieu," which encompassed principles about both ends and means (_Writings_, 403, 407). This constitutionalist view therefore pointed to, or called for, principled judgment about how to balance various principles and realities in a free politics. These include popular consent and justice, particular interests and a higher public spirit, and both short-term concerns and long-term requirements of the political order (_Writings_, 407–411). Neither the populism rooted in Jacksonian thought, nor the coupling of mass democracy with scientific administration embodied in Wilson's Progressive science, captures this balance or moderation between high and low that can provide deeper guidance to a political culture and to particular leaders.

The value of Storing's insight about this lowering, and narrowing, of perspective is evident when considering the endless campaign of the American presidential (not to mention congressional) election cycles. Our politics of constant electioneering and posturing emphasizes the mobilizing of popular opinion through appeal to narrow interests, biases, or fears. It disproportionately emphasizes short-term tactics and domestic affairs (barring a foreign crisis imposed upon our attention). Neither tendency was bequeathed to us by the founders' political science, which conceived of the single executive as balanced between concerns of foreign affairs and domestic administration but with the former as predominant; nor did the founders conceive of the office as essentially popular.[46] Even students of international relations and American foreign policy, whose scholarship might seem remote from Storing's concerns, could benefit from reflection upon the extremes to which its dominant schools pull our thinking about policy. The realist school, as a version of reductive behavioralism (thus sharing a root in Hobbes), overemphasizes interests and narrow conceptions of rational calculations by states and leaders. The liberal-internationalist school overemphasizes ideals and progress in international order that require

---

[46] A recent work in the spirit of Storing's approach is Marc Landy and Sidney M. Milkis, _Presidential Greatness_ (University Press of Kansas, 2000), which studies Washington, Jefferson, Jackson, Lincoln, and Franklin Roosevelt. Works on statesmanlike leadership that are more focused on strategic thinking in war and international affairs include Daniel J. Mahoney, _De Gaulle: Statesmanship, Grandeur, and Modern Democracy_ (Transaction Publishers, 2000); Eliot A. Cohen, _Supreme Command: Soldiers, Statesmen, and Leadership in Wartime_ (Free Press, 2002), and Charles Hill, _Grand Strategies: Literature, Statecraft, and World Order_ (Yale University Press, 2010).

transcending any state's particular constitutional order in favor of international institutions and norms. Each school fails to comprehend the complex phenomena of world affairs as one must view it from our kind of constitutional liberal order – which requires attention to both interests and justice, thus recommending some blend of less-dogmatic versions of realism and liberalism. Each school, *qua* school, eschews the complex tradition of American thought and practice about international affairs from George Washington onward. American foreign policy predominantly has emphasized, and still mostly does, a search for moderation in the shifting affairs of America and the world, seeking the right balance between our ideals and interests.[47] A report from the frontlines of professional military education attests that the tendencies toward these stark intellectual extremes of realism and liberal idealism, each with their peculiar vocabularies and refined variants, often provokes military leaders to ignore these important issues and to focus instead on tactics and operations. Many senior officers view the highly refined theories of political science and international relations studies as an intellectual parlor game, and they forsake the dimension of deeper or higher strategic thinking. That is not a sound or sustainable condition for the American military profession or the constitutional order it serves. Political science might think about the role it plays in leading to such a state of affairs.[48]

These considerations point to the related issue of the marginal relevance of political science for America's burgeoning programs in and studies of leadership (of course with some exceptions). Putting aside the perpetual concerns in American political discourse about a crisis of leadership, or failures of ideals of leadership, those who study American political thought in particular should wonder whether a dose of Storing's political science might provide a deeper relevance and higher utility in this domain as well. A constitutionalist science of ends, principles, and reasonable debate might simultaneously elevate and deepen the alternately tactical and platitudinous theories of leadership that dominate in schools of management, business, psychology, and most of the new leadership programs themselves. Political science might then reflect upon why it largely is marginal among such studies, thus why – again, a report from the front – scholars of hotel management or interpersonal psychology are more regularly featured in seminars for officers than are political scientists.[49]

---

[47] This is the argument of Chapter 5; see sources cited therein.

[48] Some international relations scholars have sought to redress an imbalance in their field toward theory to the neglect of practice; see Alexander George, *Bridging the Gap: Theory and Practice in Foreign Policy* (United States Institute of Peace, 1993) and many subsequent publications lamenting this gap – which suggests that its academic or intellectual causes persist.

[49] More general views on statesmanlike leadership that accord with Storing's approach include Timothy Fuller, ed., *Leading and Leadership*. Ethics of Everyday Life series (University of Notre Dame Press, 2000), and Robert K. Faulkner, *The Case for Greatness: Honorable Ambition and its Critics* (Yale University Press, 2007). See also the examples cited in n. 46, *supra*. My friend Daniel Mahoney notes that of all the organized sections in the APSA (55 at present), not a single one is devoted to leadership or statesmanship per se.

I have my own arguments with Storing's scholarship – that he tends to overlook the salience of religion in American politics, and that his conception of federalism leans toward one-dimensional Hamiltonianism, overlooking Montesquieu's more complex theory of compound order and its echoes in American thought (especially in Madison's writings). Nonetheless, how many academics could warn a school or party generally sympathetic to one's scholarship – as Storing did to conservative critics of "big government" – to observe "the sound maxim of moderation" about politics, "that criticism and reform based on a blind determination to wipe away all the evils of the world...are likely to do more harm than good, whatever the ideological underpinnings" (*Writings*, 303). His kind of balance, breadth, and moderation can help political scientists with the unbiased thinking about current and enduring anxieties of American politics that we should expect of scholars as distinct from pundits. This suggests a difficult self-examination about how much progress the discipline actually has achieved in perpetuating and ameliorating constitutional liberal democracy since the scientistic and behavioral revolution, then the postbehavioral calls for immediate relevance, and more recently the postmodernist turn toward constructing reality. Such candid reflection in turn might open us to consider whether alternative conceptions of political science merit space in our departmental faculty, curricula, and leading presses and journals as a matter of balance and intellectual rigor. Rediscovery of Storing and his legacy is a genuinely constructive place to start.

Epilogue

Moderation and Sustainability

What is bad for the republic is good for reviving attention to moderation, if in fact our sharp anxieties about polarization and destructive partisanship, and failures of leadership, are at root pleas to avoid extremes and find a better balance in thoughts and deeds. There is a gap between our current theory – which enforces amnesia about America's constitutional origins in a philosophy of moderation – and our persistent distress over extreme practices, or single-mindedness in theory and curricula. Environmentalist thinking proves that arguments about limits and balance can appeal to modern liberal democracies, despite calling for sacrifices and a tempered faith in technological progress, to achieve a sustainable, healthy system. Our scholars, across disciplines, should hear the similar appeal to recall ideas about balance and extremes, and tempering of faith in progress, to sustain our intellectual, social, and political orders – and for Socratic openness to truth. Montesquieu's philosophy of moderation was adopted by America's founders and especially Washington, was deepened in Tocqueville's philosophy, and renewed in the twentieth century by scholars like Storing. These figures argued for balance and sustainability in thought and practice if we are to enjoy liberty and equality for ourselves and our posterity. Our continuing laments about intellectual and political polarization indicate the absence of just such a broader liberal education that can promote moderation.

In the spirit of Tocqueville's goal to respect the parties but see beyond them – intellectual parties and political ones – we should ask our party of progress and equality, and also our party of cultural preservation and local liberty, to consider that their shared aim for a better liberal democracy would be better served by attention to moderation as a replenishing resource. Progressives might consider that Tocqueville observed in America both patriotic satisfaction and conflicts about slavery, inequality, and revolutions in economics and thought. Great strides have been made toward justice since the 1830s on slavery and discrimination, on other extensions of equal rights, and in spreading economic prosperity or security. We long have been the globe's dominant and most prosperous power. Yet, our party of equality channels what Tocqueville deemed the modern democratic demand for perfectibility of society and humanity. That party often dominated in the past century – certainly among elites, if not always in electoral politics. Nonetheless, America now is discontented about many basic issues, beyond the typical ruckus of electoral politics. One broad indicator of this is the failure during the past half-century of either national party to forge a governing majority on a durable national consensus in either domestic or foreign affairs. Some political scientists argue that periods of party dominance are unusual given our complex constitutional order, but, we also can consider broader discontents. Social and moral conservatives are not alone now in their anxiety about the health of families, marriages, and religious communities; indeed, there also are widespread worries about the safety and solvency of cities, the character of mass entertainment and social media, and the quality or balance within public education, higher education, and journalism.

Daniel Patrick Moynihan warned over two decades ago that we had become inured to "defining deviancy down" – and that we shouldn't accept such moral and social decline.[1] We still worry about the trends that the Democratic US Senator and neoconservative intellectual cited, ranging from mental health and suicides, to family breakdown (especially of "intact biological families"), to dependency on entitlements rather than self-sufficiency, to failures in public education, to substance addiction and crime. Moynihan worried that "we are getting used to a lot of behavior that is not good for us," and warned that "societies under stress, much like individuals, will turn to pain killers of various kinds that end up concealing real damage." As a Democrat he prized equality, and social programs (funded by progressive taxation) to ameliorate such problems and redress the causes of great disparity in wealth and opportunity. Nonetheless, he understood that social and especially family disorder are primary causes of poverty and other poor outcomes in life. He bluntly urged that we stop diluting deviancy, or explaining it away. We should confront "the manifest decline of the American civic order."

Perhaps the intervening decades have brought improvement of our social and moral fabric, and we might note progress in some areas, but many citizens and even academics don't sense improvement. In our intellectual culture, Moynihan already was a peculiar liberal (thus the label neoconservative) for invoking fixed standards of the good, and traditional measures of social and civic health. It is telling that his discomforting essay opens by citing the nineteenth century sociologist Durkheim, whose sociological analysis is indebted to Montesquieu.[2]

---

[1] Daniel Patrick Moynihan, "Defining Deviancy Down," *The American Scholar* (Winter 1993), 17–30.

[2] See Raymond Aron, *Main Currents in Sociological Thought*, vol. 2, *Durkheim, Pareto, Weber*, tr. Howard and Weaver (Penguin, 1968[1965]). As noted in Chapter 1, in Volume One Aron

Our concerns with decline in civic culture and constructive political debate, if paired with concerns about our social fabric, might suggest a pause in our confident journey of intellectual and social progress in which newer approaches or paradigms always predominate. We might then be open to consider that a more reasonable path is to broaden our thinking – in our curricula and public discourse – to also include sources from the tradition of moderation.

To conservatives anxious for cultural preservation and local liberty, rediscovery of the modern tradition of moderation might permit reconsideration of the view that our social decline is the result of flaws in America's founding. Not all conservatives hold this view. Some students of Leo Strauss, and some traditionalists, do share a concern about the corrosive effects of John Locke's individualistic version of social contract philosophy, which is deemed the dominant guide for the founding. This atomistic notion of human nature and politics, we are warned, leads to materialism and inevitable decay of religious, communal, and natural standards of what is right or good. One such voice is the political scientist Wilson Carey McWilliams, who argued that the largely Lockean principles of the American founding established a flawed regime that could not provide for democracy, because it did not properly support "community, civic dignity, and religion."[3] McWilliams, however, does not discuss Montesquieu, and such a mono-chrome reading cannot account for – to cite just one large issue – the dominance of Washington's alloy of several traditions of political thought, taking Lockean rights as but one element. Moreover, Tocqueville is not so single-minded in his view of America's founding, even though he warns of the need to redress both original and subsequent problems in the polity. A reengagement with the tradition of moderation would remind us of the complex resources within the American experience, to include the classical and medieval sources upon which the founders drew, that can help to redress current imbalances in theory and practice.

McWilliams's broader scholarship contributed to renewed study of the founding and earlier American thought, including neglected voices such as the Anti-Federalists – thus bringing moderation or balance to our understanding of America. The Prologue noted a few other studies that sustain the embers of philosophical moderation, by questioning our excessive faith in democracy and the self-worship inherent in our confidence about reason and progress. We need spaces for voices reminding us of the complexity in Western thought given its diverse searches for balance and an even keel in thoughts and deeds. Whether classic or more recent, such studies offer divergent interpretations of philosophers and the human phenomena, but all are, like Tocqueville, friends of

---

addresses Montesquieu as the root of modern sociological analysis, together with Comte, Marx, and Tocqueville.

3 Wilson Carey McWilliams, "Democracy and the Citizen: Community, Dignity, and the Crisis of Contemporary Politics in America," [1980], in *Redeeming Democracy in America*, eds. Deneen and S. McWilliams (University Press of Kansas, 2011), 9–28.

modern liberal democracy who warn about its excessive tendencies. The particular legacy explored here sees moderation as not merely positional but as holding a core concern with natural right, thus with limits to human will and political power. Still, these are minority voices in an intellectual culture committed, wittingly or not, to deficit spending of the intellectual and moral capital that sustains liberal democracy. Moderation once was considered "the silken string running through the pearl-chain of all virtues."[4] This is not mythology; there once was an appreciation of an intellectual, political, and moral virtue that was the underlying disposition connecting the virtues, and supporting the distinct functions of each. It was normal to see the greatness of statesmen such as Washington and Lincoln as demanding both political and intellectual respect, a Plutarchan appreciation of their greatness of soul and prudence. Our predominant trends in academic and public discourse now eclipse consideration of such sources, leaving us more likely to rest in our separate, narrow intellectual or political parties rather than be able to see farther. This spirit dominates not only in thinking about domestic affairs, but also informs the shift in America toward disengagement or isolation from global affairs and commitments.

As I discovered when teaching *Democracy in America* in India, Tocqueville's moderation and his effort to see in America more than America – to see the spirit of modern liberal democracy – travels well. Efforts to rediscover the tradition of moderation in political thought also should appeal widely, to intellectual and political cultures in various parts of the world and at various stages of the journey of liberal democracy. That said, it would be immoderate to imply that Tocquevillean philosophy, and considerations on its insights for theory and practice, are the final word about modern liberal democracy, let alone political philosophy simply. Moderation deserves rediscovery because our current condition of both theory and practice suggests that the old reasons behind the principles and forms of moderate liberal constitutionalism can appear cogent once again – in comparison to the extreme alternatives proposed and tested in recent centuries, and to the cycles of intellectual and political polarization these innovations have spawned. Montesquieu's philosophy provides particular insights given that it both predicted and shaped our world today, the world of complex constitutional democracies rising to prosperity and global power but troubled by moral confusion, spiritual decay, and decline in social order. Tocqueville further explains America's likely preeminence in the era of equality given its exceptional attachment to religion and constitutional complexity, yet he also warns about the need for philosophical and religious resources to cope with the challenges posed to the soul, and to societies, by a dynamic, materialistic, and globalized life. Still, these strengths do not entail any claim to be

---

[4] Aurelian Craiutu, *A Virtue for Courageous Minds: Moderation in French Political Thought, 1748–1830* (Princeton University Press, 2012), 241, quoting an English Bishop, Joseph Hall, writing a century before Montesquieu.

a complete theory of human affairs. It is not immoderate to suggest that such an approach is necessary while not sufficient. The spirit of moderation is not that of a single-minded theory of justice but rather the spirit of Socratic conversation, held together by certain principles and stances about justice, but not reduced to the quarrels of sects or schools.

Bibliography

Abbot, W. W. "An Uncommon Awareness of Self: The Papers of George Washington." In *George Washington Reconsidered*. Ed. Don Higginbotham. Charlottesville, VA: University of Virginia Press, 2001.

Abramowitz, Alan. *The Disappearing Center: Engaged Citizens, Polarization, and American Democracy*. New Haven, CT: Yale University Press, 2010.

Adams, John Quincy. "Address of July 4, 1821." In *John Quincy Adams and American Continental Empire*. Ed. LaFeber. Chicago, IL: Quadrangle Books, 1965.

Adler, Eve. *Vergil's Empire: Political Thought in The Aeneid*. Lanham, MD: Rowman & Littlefield, 2003.

_____. "Vergil on World Empire." Unpublished essay.

Alschuler, Albert W. *Law Without Values: The Life, Work, and Legacy of Justice Holmes*. Chicago, IL: University of Chicago Press, 2000.

American Political Science Association. "Toward a More Responsible Two-Party System." *American Political Science Review* 44:3, Part 2 (September 1950).

Aquinas, St. Thomas. *Summa Theologiae*. 2nd edn. Tr. Fathers of the English Dominican Province. London: Burns, Oates, and Washbourne, 1920.

Arendt, Hannah. *The Human Condition*. Chicago, IL: University of Chicago Press, 1958.

_____. *The Life of the Mind, Volume Two: Willing*. San Diego, CA: Harcourt Brace Jovanovich, 1978.

Aristotle. *Nicomachean Ethics*. Ed. and Tr. Martin Ostwald. Indianapolis, IN: Library of the Liberal Arts, Bobbs-Merrill, 1962.

_____. *Nicomachean Ethics*. Eds. and Tr. Robert C. Bartlett and Susan D. Collins. Chicago, IL: University of Chicago Press, 2011.

_____. *Politics*. In *The Politics of Aristotle*. Ed. and Tr. Peter Simpson. Chapel Hill: University of North Carolina Press, 1997.

Aron, Raymond. *Les Étapes de la pensée sociologique: Montesquieu, Comte, Marx, Tocqueville, Durkheim, Pareto, Weber*. Paris: Gallimard, 1967.

_____. *Main Currents in Sociological Thought. Volume 1: Montesquieu, Comte, Marx, Tocqueville. Volume 2: Durkheim, Pareto, Weber*. Tr. R. Howard and H. Weaver. New York: Penguin, 1968 [1965].

_____. "On Tocqueville." In *In Defense of Political Reason: Essays by Raymond Aron.* Ed. Daniel Mahoney. Lanham, MD: Rowman & Littlefield, 1994.

Art, Robert J. *A Grand Strategy for America.* Ithaca, NY: Cornell University Press, 2003.

Bacevich, Andrew. *American Empire: The Realities and Consequences of U.S. Diplomacy.* Cambridge, MA: Harvard University Press, 2002.

_____. *Washington Rules: America's Path to Permanent War.* New York: Metropolitan Books, 2010.

Barber, Benjamin. "The Politics of Political Science: 'Value-free' Theory and the Wolin-Strauss Dust-Up of 1963." *American Political Science Review* 100 (2006) 539–45.

Barilleaux, Ryan. "Foreign Policy and the First Commander in Chief." In *Patriot Sage: George Washington and the American Political Tradition.* Eds. Gregg and Spalding. Wilmington, DE: ISI Books, 1999, 141–64.

Bartlett, Robert. "On the Politics of Faith and Reason: The Project of Enlightenment in Pierre Bayle and Montesquieu." *Journal of Politics* 63 (2001) 1–28.

Behnegar, Nasser. *Leo Strauss, Max Weber, and the Scientific Study of Politics.* Chicago, IL: University of Chicago Press, 2003.

Beiner, Ronald. *Civil Religion: A Dialogue in the History of Political Philosophy.* New York: Cambridge University Press, 2011.

Bemis, Samuel. "Washington's Farewell Address: A Foreign Policy of Independence" (1934). In *American Foreign Policy and the Blessings of Liberty.* Ed. Samuel Bemis. New Haven, CT: Yale University Press, 1962, 240–58.

Berger, Peter, Grace Davie, and Effie Fokas. *Religious America, Secular Europe?: A Theme and Variations.* London: Ashgate, 2008.

Berger, Peter, Ed. *The Desecularization of the World: Resurgent Religion and World Politics.* Grand Rapids, MI: Eerdmans, 1999.

_____. *Between Relativism and Fundamentalism: Religious Resources for a Middle Position.* Grand Rapids, MI: Eerdmans, 2009.

Berkowitz, Peter. *Virtue and the Making of Modern Liberalism.* Princeton, NJ: Princeton University Press, 1999.

_____. *Constitutional Conservatism: Liberty, Self-Government, and Political Moderation.* Stanford, CA: Hoover Institution Press, 2013.

Berlin, Isaiah. "Montesquieu." In *Against the Current.* Ed. Hardy. New York: Viking Press, 1980, 130–61.

Bessette, Joseph. "Herbert Storing and the Problem of Democracy." *Political Science Reviewer* 29 (2000) 70–93.

Beyer, Charles-Jacques. "Montesquieu et l'esprit cartésian." In *Actes du Congrès Montesquieu.* Bordeaux: Imprimerie Delmas, 1956.

Bhargava, Rajeev, Ed. *Secularism and Its Critics.* New Delhi: Oxford University Press, 1999.

Boller, Paul F., Jr. *George Washington & Religion.* Dallas, TX: Southern Methodist University Press, 1963.

Brogan, Hugh. *Alexis de Tocqueville: A Life.* New Haven, CT: Yale University Press, 2007.

Brookhiser, Richard. *Founding Father: Rediscovering George Washington.* New York: Free Press, 1996.

_____. *Rules of Civility: The 110 Precepts that Guided Our First President in War and Peace.* New York: Free Press, 1997.

Brooks, David. "A Moderate Manifesto." *The New York Times*, March 3, 2009.

———. "What Moderation Means." *The New York Times*, October 25, 2012.

Buchanan, Patrick. *A Republic, Not an Empire: Reclaiming America's Destiny.* Washington, DC: Regnery, 1999; 2nd edn., 2002.

Callanan, Keegan. "'Une Infinité de Biens': Montesquieu on Religion and Free Government." *History of Political Thought* 35 (2014) 739–67.

Carrese, Paul. "The Complexity, and Principles, of the American Founding: A Reply to Alan Gibson." *History of Political Thought* 21 (2000) 711–17.

———. "Liberty, Constitutionalism, and Moderation: The Political Thought of George Washington." In *History of American Political Thought.* Eds. Frost and Sikkenga. Lexington Press, 2003.

———. *The Cloaking of Power: Montesquieu, Blackstone, and the Rise of Judicial Activism.* Chicago, IL: University of Chicago Press, 2003.

———. "Montesquieu's Complex Natural Right and Moderate Liberalism: The Roots of American Moderation." *Polity* 36 (2004) 227–50.

———. "The Machiavellian Spirit of Montesquieu's Liberal Republic." In *Machiavelli's Republican Legacy.* Ed. Rahe. New York: Cambridge University Press, 2006, 121–42.

———. "George Washington's Greatness and Aristotelian Virtue: Enduring Lessons for Constitutional Democracy." In *Magnanimity and Statesmanship.* Ed. Holloway. Lanham, MD: Rowman & Littlefield Publishers, 2008.

———. "The Ideal of Liberal-Democratic Partnership: Philosophies of International Affairs and the Indo-US Nuclear Accord." In *Nuclear Synergy: Indo-US Strategic Cooperation and Beyond.* Ed. N. K. Jha. New Delhi: Pentagon Press, 2009.

———. "Tocqueville's Foreign Policy of Moderation and Democracy Expansion." In *Alexis de Tocqueville and the Art of Democratic Statesmanship.* Eds. Brian Danoff and L. Joseph Hebert. Lanham, MD: Lexington Books, 2011.

———. (Review of Gordon Wood, *The Idea of America: Reflections on the Birth of the United States*) (2001). *American Political Thought* 1 (2012) 158–61.

———. Review of Aurelian Craiutu, *A Virtue for Courageous Minds: Moderation in French Political Thought, 1748–1830* (2012). *Society* 50 (May 2013) 324–27.

———. "Dear Prudence" (review of Berkowitz, *Constitutional Conservatism*). *Commentary* 135 (May 2013) 41–42.

———. "For Constitution and Profession: Paradoxes of Military Service in a Liberal Democracy." In *NOMOS LIV: Loyalty.* Eds. Levinson, Parker, and Woodruff. New York University Press, 2013.

———. Essay contributions to "Liberty Matters" discussion of Fernando Tesón, "Hugo Grotius on War and the State." March 2014. http://oll.libertyfund.org/pages/lm-grotius. Accessed November 15, 2015.

———. "Montesquieu, Charles de." In *The Encyclopedia of Political Thought.* Ed. Michael Gibbons. Hoboken, NJ: Wiley-Blackwell, 2014.

———. "America's Neglected Ideal of Moderation." *The American Interest online,* (January 29, 2015). www.the-american-interest.com/2015/01/29/americas-neglected-ideal-of-moderation/. Accessed November 14, 2015.

———. "Constitutionalist Political Science: Rediscovering Storing's Philosophical Moderation." *American Political Thought* 4(2) (Spring 2015) 259–88.

———. "The Grand Strategy of Washington and Eisenhower: Recovering the American Consensus." *Orbis* (Spring 2015), 1–18.

Carrese, Paul and Michael Doran. "Republican Prudence: The Founders' Foreign Policy School." *The American Interest* (May–June 2014) 50–59.

Carrithers, David. "Introduction." In *Montesquieu's Science of Politics: Essays on The Spirit of the Laws*. Eds. Carrithers, Mosher, and Rahe. Lanham, MD: Rowman & Littlefield, 2000.

Casabianca, Denis de. "Dérèglements mécaniques et dynamiques des fluides dans *L'Esprit des* lois." *Revue Montesquieu* 4 (2000) 43–70.

Cassanova, José. "The Religious Situation in the United States 175 Years After Tocqueville." In *Crediting God: Sovereignty and Religion in the Age of Global Capitalism*. Ed. Vatter. New York: Fordham University Press, 2011.

Catto, Jeremy. "Ideas and Experience in the Political Thought of Aquinas." *Past and Present* 71 (1976) 3–21.

Ceaser, James. *Liberal Democracy and Political Science*. Baltimore, MD: Johns Hopkins University Press, 1990.

———. *Designing a Polity: America's Constitution in Theory and Practice*. Lanham, MD: Rowman & Littlefield, 2011.

———. "Political Science, Political Culture, and the Role of the Intellectual." In *Interpreting Tocqueville's Democracy in America*. Ed. Ken Masugi. Savage, MD: Rowman & Littlefield, 1991.

Cherry, Kevin M. "The Problem of Polity: Political Participation and Aristotle's Best Regime." *Journal of Politics* 71 (2009) 1406–21.

Chinard, Gilbert. *The Commonplace Book of Thomas Jefferson*. Baltimore, MD: Johns Hopkins University Press, 1926.

Clor, Harry. *On Moderation: Defending an Ancient Virtue in a Modern World*. Waco, TX: Baylor University Press, 2008.

———. "Our Problem of Moral Community: Lessons from the Teachings of Herbert Storing." *Political Science Reviewer* 29 (2000) 94–120.

Cohen, Eliot. *Supreme Command: Soldiers, Statesmen, and Leadership in Wartime*. New York: Free Press, 2002.

Cohler, Anne. *Montesquieu's Comparative Politics and the Spirit of American Constitutionalism*. Lawrence: University Press of Kansas, 1988.

Coll, Alberto. "Normative Prudence as a Tradition of Statecraft." In *Ethics & International Affairs: A Reader*. Ed. Joel Rosenthal. Washington, D.C.: Georgetown University Press, 1995, 58–77.

Connor, W. Robert. *Thucydides*. Princeton, NJ: Princeton University Press, 1984.

Courtney, C. P. "Montesquieu and Natural Law." In *Montesquieu's Science of Politics*. Eds. Carrithers, Mosher, and Rahe. Lanham, MD: Rowman & Littlefield, 2000.

Craig, Gordon and Felix Gilbert. "Reflections on Strategy in the Present and Future." In *Makers of Modern Strategy: From Machiavelli to the Nuclear Age*. Ed. Peter Paret. Princeton, NJ: Princeton University Press, 1986.

Craiutu, Aurelian. "Tocqueville's Paradoxical Moderation." *Review of Politics* 67 (2005) 599–629.

———. "Tocqueville's Paradoxical Moderation." *The Review of Politics* 67 (2005) 599–629.

———. *A Virtue for Courageous Minds: Moderation in French Political Thought, 1748–1830*. Princeton, NJ: Princeton University Press, 2012.

Cropsey, Joseph. "The Moral Basis of International Action." In *America Armed*. Ed. Robert Goldwin. Chicago, IL: Rand McNally, 1963, 71–91.

D'Alembert, Jean. "Éloge de Montesquieu." In *Œuvres complètes de Montesquieu*. Ed. Masson xvii–xviii.

Danford, John. *David Hume and the Problem of Reason*. New Haven, CT: Yale University Press, 1990.

Danoff, Brian and L. Joseph Hebert, Eds. *Alexis de Tocqueville and the Art of Democratic Statesmanship*. Lanham, MD: Lexington Books, 2011.

Deneen, Patrick. *Democratic Faith*. Princeton, NJ: Princeton University Press, 2005.

Department of the Army. *The Army, Field Manual 1*. Washington, DC: Department of the Army, 2005.

Deudney, Daniel. *Bounding Power: Republican Security Theory From the Polis to the Global Village*. Princeton, NJ: Princeton University Press, 2007.

Dijn, Annelien de. "Was Montesquieu a Liberal Republican?" *Review of Politics* 76 (2014) 21–41.

Doyle, Michael. "Liberalism and World Politics." *American Political Science Review* 80 (1986) 1151–69.

Dreisbach, Daniel. *Thomas Jefferson and the Wall of Separation Between Church and State*. New York University Press, 2002.

Drescher, Seymour. "Who Needs Ancienneté? Tocqueville on Aristocracy and Modernity." *History of Political Thought* xxiv (2003) 624–46.

_____. "Tocqueville's Comparative Perspectives." In *The Cambridge Companion to Tocqueville*, Ed. C. B. Welch. New York: Cambridge University Press, 2006.

Drezner, Daniel W. "Does Obama Have a Grand Strategy?" *Foreign Affairs* (July/August 2011).

Dry, Murray P. "Herbert Storing: The American Founding and the American Regime." In *Leo Strauss, the Straussians, and the American Regime*. Ed. Kenneth L. Deutsch and John A. Murley. Lanham, MD: Rowman & Littlefield, 1999, 305–28.

_____. *Civil Peace and the Quest for Truth: The First Amendment Freedoms in Political Philosophy and American Constitutionalism*. Lanham, MD: Lexington Books, 2004.

Eden, Robert. "Tocqueville and the Problem of Natural Right." *Interpretation* 17 (1990) 379–87.

Eicholz, Hans. *Harmonizing Sentiments: The Declaration of Independence and the Jeffersonian Idea of Self-Government*. New York: Peter Lang, 2001.

Eisenhower, Dwight. Documents on 1961 "Farewell Address." Eisenhower Presidential Library. www.eisenhower.archives.gov/research/online_documents/farewell_address.html. Accessed November 14, 2015.

Elshtain, Jean Bethke. *Just War Against Terror: The Burden of American Power in a Violent World*. New York: Basic Books, 2003.

Engeman, Thomas S. and Michael P. Zuckert, Eds. *Protestantism and the American Founding*. University of Notre Dame Press, 2004.

Farrelly, Colin. "Justice in Ideal Theory: A Refutation." *Political Studies* 55 (2007) 844–64.

Faulkner, Robert. "Foreword." In John Marshall, *The Life of George Washington: Special Edition for Schools*. Eds. Robert Faulkner and Paul Carrese. Indianapolis, IN: Liberty Fund, 2000 [1838].

_____. "Washington and the Founding of Constitutional Democracy." In *Gladly to Learn and Gladly to Teach: Essays on Religion and Political Philosophy in Honor of Ernest L. Fortin, A. A.* Eds. Foley and Kries. Lanham, MD: Lexington Books, 2002.

_____. "Obscuring the Truly Great: Washington and Modern Theories of Fame." In R. Faulkner, *The Case for Greatness: Honorable Ambition and Its Critics*. New Haven, CT: Yale University Press, 2007.

Feaver, Peter. *Armed Servants: Agency, Oversight, and Civil-Military Relations*. Cambridge, MA: Harvard University Press, 2003.

Finnis, John. *Aquinas: Moral, Political, and Legal Theory*. New York: Oxford University Press, 1998.

Fiorina, Morris, with Samuel J. Abrams and Jeremy C. Pope. *Culture War? The Myth of Polarized America*. 3rd edn. Boston, MA: Longman, 2011 [2004].

Flexner, James T. "George Washington and Slavery." In *George Washington, Anguish and Farewell*. Boston: Little, Brown, 1972.

Foley, Michael P. "Thomas Aquinas' Novel Modesty." *History of Political Thought* xxv (2004) 402–23.

Fortescue, John. "In Praise of the Laws of England." In *On the Laws and Governance of England*. Ed. Lockwood. New York: Cambridge University Press, 1997 [c. 1471].

Fortin, Ernest L. "The Political Thought of Thomas Aquinas." In *Classical Christianity and the Political Order: Reflections on the Theologico-Political Problem* (Collected Essays, vol. 2). Ed. Benestad. Lanham, MD: Rowman & Littlefield, 1996.

Fukuyama, Francis. *America at the Crossroads: Democracy, Power, and the Neoconservative Legacy*. New Haven, CT: Yale University Press, 2006.

Fuller, Timothy, Ed. *Leading and Leadership*. Ethics of Everyday Life series. University of Notre Dame Press, 2000.

Fumurescu, Alin. *Compromise: A Political and Philosophical History*. New York: Cambridge University Press, 2013.

Gaddis, John Lewis. *Strategies of Containment: A Critical Appraisal of Postwar American National Security Policy*. New York: Oxford University Press, 1982.

_____. "A Grand Strategy." *Foreign Policy* (November/December 2002) 50–57.

_____. *Surprise, Security, and the American Experience*. Cambridge, MA: Harvard University Press, 2004.

Galston, William. "Thinking About the Draft," *The Public Interest* 154 (2004) 61–73.

_____. "The Good, Bad, and Ugly of Brooks's 'Moderate Manifesto'." *The New Republic*, March 4, 2009.

_____. "Realism in Political Theory." *European Journal of Political Theory* 9 (2010) 385–411.

Ganguly, Sumit. "The Crisis of Indian Secularism." *Journal of Democracy* 14 (October 2003) 11–25.

Garrity, Patrick. "Warnings of a Parting Friend." *The National Interest* 45 (Fall 1996) 14–26.

Garsten, Bryan. *Saving Persuasion: A Defense of Rhetoric and Judgment*. Cambridge, MA: Harvard University Press, 2006.

_____. "Seeing 'Not Differently, but Further, than the Parties'." In *The Arts of Rule: Essays in Honor of Harvey C. Mansfield*. Eds. Krause and McGrail. Lanham, MD: Lexington Books, 2009.

Gay, Peter. *The Enlightenment*. 2 vols. New York: Knopf, 1966.

George, Alexander. *Bridging the Gap: Theory and Practice in Foreign Policy*. Washington, D.C.: United States Institute of Peace, 1993.

George, Robert P. "Law, Democracy, and Moral Disagreement." *Harvard Law Review* 110 (1997) 1388–1406.

———. *In Defense of Natural Law*. New York: Oxford University Press, 2001.

Gibson, Alan. "Ancient, Moderns, and Americans: The Republicanism-Liberalism Debate Revisited." *History of Political Thought* 21 (2000) 260–307.

———. *Interpreting the Founding: Guide to the Enduring Debates over the Origins and Foundations of the American Republic*. Lawrence: University Press of Kansas, 2006.

Gilbert, Alan. "'Internal Restlessness': Individuality and Community in Montesquieu." *Political Theory* 22 (1994) 45–70.

Gilbert, Felix. *To the Farewell Address: Ideas of Early American Foreign Policy*. Princeton, NJ: Princeton University Press, 1961.

Gilpin, Robert. *The Political Economy of International Relations*. Princeton, NJ: Princeton University Press, 1987.

Glahn, Gerhard von. *Law Among Nations: An Introduction to Public International Law*. 5th edn. New York: Macmillan, 1986.

Goldstein, Doris. *Trial of Faith: Religion and Politics in Tocqueville's Thought*. New York: Elsevier, 1975.

Goyard-Fabre, Simone. *La philosophie du droit de Montesquieu*. Paris: Librarie C. Klincksieck, 1973.

———. "L'idée de Représentation dans *l'Esprit des Lois*." *Dialogue: Revue Canadienne de philosophie* 20: 1 (1981) 1–22.

———. "Le Réformisme de Montesquieu: Progrès Juridique et Histoire." In *La penseé politique de Montesquieu*. Université de Caen, 1985, 47–68.

———. *Montesquieu: La Nature, les Lois, la Liberte*. Paris: Presses Universitaires de France, 1993.

Gregg, Samuel. "Natural Law and the Law of Nations." In *Natural Law, Natural Rights, and American Constitutionalism*. Witherspoon Institute. Available at: www.nlnrac .org/earlymodern/law-of-nations (accessed May 2013).

Griswold, Charles L., Jr. *Adam Smith and the Virtue of Enlightenment*. Cambridge University Press, 1999.

Grotius, Hugo. *The Rights of War and Peace*. 3 vols. Ed. Richard Tuck. Indianapolis, IN: Liberty Fund, 2005 [1625].

Grygiel, Jakub. "Educating for National Security." *Orbis* (Spring 2013) 201–16.

Guerra, Marc D. "Beyond Natural Law Talk: Politics and Prudence in St. Thomas Aquinas's On Kingship." *Perspectives on Political Science* 31 (2002).

Gutmann, Amy and Dennis Thompson. *Democracy and Disagreement: Why Moral Conflict Cannot Be Avoided in Politics, and What Should Be Done About It*. Harvard University Press, 1996.

———. *Why Deliberative Democracy?* Princeton University Press, 2004.

———. *The Spirit of Compromise: Why Governing Demands It and Campaigning Undermines It*. Princeton University Press, 2012.

Hamburger, Philip. *Separation of Church and State*. Harvard University Press, 2002.

Hamilton, Alexander. *Selected Writings and Speeches of Alexander Hamilton*. Ed. Morton Frisch. Washington, DC: AEI Press, 1985.

Hamilton, Alexander, John Jay, and James Madison. *The Federalist Papers*. Eds. Rossiter and Kesler. New York: Signet Classic/Penguin, 2003 [1999, 1961].

Hancock, Ralph. "Tocqueville's Responsible Reason." In *The Responsibility of Reason: Theory and Practice in a Liberal-Democratic Age*. Lanham, MD: Rowman & Littlefield, 2011.

Hasan, Mushirul, Ed. *Will Secular India Survive?* New Delhi: imprintOne, 2004.

Hebert, L. Joseph, Jr. *More Than Kings and Less Than Men: Tocqueville on the Promise and Perils of Democratic Individualism*. Lanham, MD: Lexington Books, 2010.

Hegel, Georg W. F. *Philosophy of Right*. Ed. Wood, Tr. Nisbet. New York: Cambridge University Press, 1991 [1821].

Hendrickson, David C. "The Renovation of American Foreign Policy." *Foreign Affairs* 71: 2 (1992) 48–63.

_____. "Foundations of the New Diplomacy." In *Peace Pact: The Lost World of the American Founding*. University Press of Kansas, 2003.

Hennis, Wilhelm. "In Search of the 'New Science of Politics." In *Interpreting Tocqueville's Democracy in America*. Ed. Ken Masugi. Savage, MD: Rowman & Littlefield, 1991.

Herberg-Rothe, Andreas. "Primacy of 'Politics' or 'Culture' Over War in a Modern World: Clausewitz Needs a Sophisticated Interpretation." *Defense Analysis* 17: 2 (2001), 175–86.

Higginbotham, Donald. *George Washington and the American Military Tradition*. Athens, GA: University of Georgia Press, 1985.

_____. "Introduction." In *George Washington Reconsidered*. Ed. Don Higginbotham. University of Virginia Press, 2001.

Hill, Charles. *Grand Strategies: Literature, Statecraft, and World Order*. Yale University Press, 2010.

Himmelfarb, Gertrude. *Roads to Modernity: The British, French, and American Enlightenments*. New York: Knopf Publishing, 2004.

Hobbes, Thomas. *Leviathan, or the Matter, Forme, & Power of a Common-wealth Ecclesiastical and Civill*. Ed. C. B. Macpherson. New York: Penguin, 1968 [1651].

Hoffman, Stanley. "Clash of Globalizations." *Foreign Affairs* 81: 4 (2002), 104–15.

Holmes, David L. *The Faiths of the Founding Fathers*. New York: Oxford University Press, 2006.

Hulliung, Mark. *Montesquieu and the Old Regime*. University of California Press, 1976.

Huntington, Samuel. "American Ideals versus American Institutions." *Political Science Quarterly* 97 (1982) 1–37.

Hutson, James. *Religion and the New Republic: Faith in the Founding of America*. Lanham, MD: Rowman & Littlefield, 2000.

_____. *Forgotten Features of the Founding: The Recovery of the Role of Religion in the New American Republic*. Lanham, MD: Lexington Press, 2003.

Ikenberry, G. John. *Liberal Leviathan: The Origins, Crisis, and Transformation of the American World Order*. Princeton University Press, 2011.

Israel, Jonathan. *Radical Enlightenment: Philosophy and the Making of Modernity 1650–1750*. New York: Oxford University Press, 2001.

_____. *A Revolution of the Mind: Radical Enlightenment and the Intellectual Origins of Modern Democracy*. Princeton University Press, 2009.

Jardin, André. *Tocqueville: A Biography*. New York: Farrar, Straus, Giroux, 1988 [Paris: Hachette, 1984].

Jefferson, Thomas. *The Papers of Thomas Jefferson*. Eds. Boyd, Cullen, McClure, and Oberg. Princeton, NJ: Princeton University Press, 1950.

——. *The Life and Selected Writings of Thomas Jefferson*. Ed. Koch. New York: Modern Library, 1972.

——. *Thomas Jefferson: Writings*. Ed. Merrill D. Peterson. New York: Library of America/Literary Classics of the United States, 1984.

Johnson, Douglas V. and Steven Metz. "Civil-Military Relations in the United States." In *American Defense Policy*. 7th edn. Eds. Hays, Vallance, and Van Tassel. Johns Hopkins University Press, 1997.

Kagan, Frederick. "War and Aftermath." *Policy Review* 120 (August 2003) 3–27.

Kagan, Robert. *Of Paradise and Power: America and Europe in the New World Order*. New York: Alfred A. Knopf, 2003.

——. *The World America Made*. New York: Alfred A. Knopf, 2012.

——. "Superpowers Don't Get to Retire." *The New Republic*, May 26, 2014.

Kant, Immanuel. "Perpetual Peace: A Philosophical Sketch" (1795). In *Kant: Political Writings*. 2nd edn. Ed. H. S. Reiss. New York: Cambridge University Press, 1991.

Kaufman, Burton Ira. "Washington's Farewell Address: A Statement of Empire." In *Washington's Farewell Address: The View from the 20th Century*. Chicago, IL: University of Chicago Press, 1969.

Kautz, Steven. "Abraham Lincoln: The Moderation of a Democratic Statesman." In *History of American Political Thought*. Eds. Frost and Sikkenga. Lexington Press, 2003.

Kennan, George. "On American Principles." *Foreign Affairs* 74 (1995) 116–26.

Kennedy, Paul. *Grand Strategies in War and Peace*. New Haven, CT: Yale University Press, 1991.

Kenny, Anthony. *Aquinas*. New York: Oxford University Press, 1980.

Kessler, Sanford. "Religion & Liberalism in Montesquieu's *Persian Letters*." *Polity* 15 (1983) 380–96.

——. *Tocqueville's Civil Religion*. State University of New York, 1994.

Kettler, David. "The Political Theory Question in Political Science, 1956–1967." *American Political Science Review* 100 (2006) 531–37.

Keys, Mary. *Aquinas, Aristotle, and the Promise of the Common Good*. New York: Cambridge University Press, 2006.

Kingston, Rebecca. "Montesquieu on Religion and the Question of Toleration." In *Montesquieu's Science of Politics*. Eds. Carrithers, Mosher, and Rahe. Lanham, MD: Rowman & Littlefield, 2000, 375–408.

——, Ed. *Montesquieu and His Legacy*. Albany, NY: SUNY Press, 2009.

Kissinger, Henry. *Does America Need a Foreign Policy? Toward a Diplomacy for the 21st Century*. New York: Simon & Schuster, 2001.

——. *World Order*. New York: Penguin Press, 2014.

Knott, Stephen. "George Washington and the Founding of American Clandestine Activity." In *Secret and Sanctioned: Covert Operations and the American Presidency*. New York: Oxford University Press, 1996.

Kokaz, Nancy. "Moderating Power: A Thucydidean Perspective." *Review of International Studies* 27 (2001) 27–49.

Koritansky, John. *Alexis de Tocqueville and the New Science of Politics*. Durhan, NC: Carolina Academic Press, 1987.

Kra, Pauline. *Religion in Montesquieu's Lettres Persanes*. Geneva: Institut et Musée Voltaire, 1970.

Kramnick, Isaac. "The Great National Discussion." *William and Mary Quarterly* (3rd series) 45 (January 1988) 3–32.

Kramnic, Isaac and Laurence Moore. *The Godless Constitution: The Case Against Religious Correctness*. New York: W.W. Norton, 1996.

Krause, Sharon. "The Politics of Distinction and Disobedience: Honor and the Defense of Liberty in Montesquieu." *Polity* 31 (1999) 469–99.

———. "Despotism in *The Spirit of Laws*." In *Montesquieu's Science of Politics*. Eds. Carrithers, Mosher, and Rahe. Lanham, MD: Rowman & Littlefield, 2000.

———. "The Spirit of Separate Powers in Montesquieu." *Review of Politics* 62 (2000) 231–65.

———. *Liberalism With Honor*. Harvard University Press, 2002.

———. *Civil Passions: Moral Sentiment and Democratic Deliberation*. Princeton, NJ: Princeton University Press, 2008.

Kries, Douglas. "Thomas Aquinas and the Politics of Moses." 52 *Review of Politics* (1990) 84–104.

Lacordaire, Henri-Dominique. "Discours de reception a l'Academie Francaise." 1861. www.academie-francaise.fr/discours-de-reception-et-reponse-de-francois-guizot-1. Accessed May 2013.

Landy, Marc and Sidney M. Milkis. *Presidential Greatness*. Lawrence, KS: University Press of Kansas, 2000.

Lawler, Peter Augustine. "Tocqueville's Elusive Moderation." *Polity* 22 (1989) 181–89.

———. "Introduction." In *Tocqueville's Political Science: Classic Essays*. Ed. Peter Augustine Lawler. New York: Garland Publishing, 1992.

———. *The Restless Mind: Alexis de Tocqueville on the Origin and Perpetuation of Human Liberty*. Lanham, MD: Rowman & Littlefield, 1993.

Lawler, Peter Augustine and Jennifer D. Siebels. "The Anti-Federalist View of Judicial Review." In *The American Experiment*. Eds. P. A. Lawler and R. M. Schaefer. Lanham, MD: Rowman & Littlefield, 1994.

Layne, Christopher. *The Peace of Illusions: American Grand Strategy from 1940 to the Present*. Cornell University Press, 2006.

Leibiger, Stuart. *Founding Friendship: George Washington, James Madison, and the Creation of the American Republic*. University Press of Virginia, 1999.

Lerner, Ralph. "The Supreme Court as Republican Schoolmaster." *The Supreme Court Review* (1967), 127–80.

Levine, Alan. *Sensual Philosophy: Toleration, Skepticism, and Montaigne's Politics of the Self*. Lanham, MD: Lexington Books, 2001.

Levy, Leonard. *The Establishment Clause: Religion and the First Amendment*. New York: Macmillan Publishing, 1986.

———. *Original Intent and the Framers' Constitution*. New York: Macmillan, 1988.

Lillback, Peter A. and Jerry Newcombe. *George Washington's Sacred Fire*. King of Prussia, PA: Providence Forum Press, 2006.

Lincoln, Abraham. *The Collected Works of Abraham Lincoln*. Ed. R. Basler. New Brunswick, NJ: Rutgers University Press, 1953–56.

Liebert, Hugh. "Plutarch's Critique of Plato's Best Regime." *History of Political Thought* 30 (2009) 251–71.

Locke, John. *An Essay Concerning the True Original, Extent, and End of Civil Govern-ment (Second Treatise). Two Treatises of Government.* Ed. Peter Laslett. Cambridge: Cambridge University Press, 1988 [1690].

Long, Steven A. *Analogia Entis: On the Analogy of Being, Metaphysics, and the Act of Faith.* University of Notre Dame Press, 2011.

Lowenthal, David. "Book I of Montesquieu's The Spirit of the Laws." *American Political Science Review.* 53 (1959) 485–98.

———. "Montesquieu and the Classics: Republican Government in *The Spirit of the Laws.*" In *Ancients and Moderns: Essays in Honor of Leo Strauss.* Ed. Joseph Cropsey. New York: Basic Books, 1964.

———. "Montesquieu, 1689–1755." In *History of Political Philosophy.* 3rd edn. Eds. Strauss and Cropsey. University of Chicago Press, 1987 [1963].

———. "Introduction." In *Montesquieu, Considerations on the Causes of the Greatness of the Romans and their Decline.* Ed. and Tr. David Lowenthal. Indianapolis, IN: Hackett Publishing, 1999 [1965].

Lowi, Theodore. *The End of Liberalism: Ideology, Policy, and the Crisis of Public Authority.* New York: Norton, 1969.

Lutz, Donald. "The Relative Influence of European Writers on Late Eighteenth-Century American Political Thought." *American Political Science Review* 78 (1984) 189–97.

———. *Origins of American Constitutionalism.* Baton Rouge: Louisiana State University Press, 1988.

Lynch, Andrew. "Montesquieu and the Ecclesiastical Critics of *l'Esprit des Lois.*" *Journal of the History of Ideas* 38 (1977) 487–500.

Machiavelli, Niccolò. *The Prince.* Ed. and Tr. Harvey Mansfield. Chicago, IL: University of Chicago Press, 1985.

———. *Discourses on Livy.* Eds. and Tr. Harvey Mansfield and Nathan Tarcov. Chicago, IL: University of Chicago Press, 1996.

Madan, T. N. "Secularism in Its Place." *Journal of Asian Studies* 46 (1987) 747–59.

———. "Whither Indian Secularism?" *Modern Asian Studies* 27 (1993) 667–97.

Madison, James. *The Mind of the Founder: Sources of the Political Thought of James Madison.* Ed. Marvin Myers. Revised edition. Hanover, NH: University Press of New England, 1981.

———. *Notes of Debates in the Federal Convention of 1787 Reported by James Madi-son.* Ed. Adrienne Koch. Athens, OH: Ohio University Press, 1984 [1966].

———. "Universal Peace" (1792). In *James Madison: Writings.* Ed. Rakove. New York: Library of America/Literary Classics of the United States, 1999.

Mahan, Alfred Thayer. *The Influence of Sea Power Upon History, 1660–1783.* 12th edn. Boston: Little, Brown, 1944 [1890].

Mahoney, Daniel J. *De Gaulle: Statesmanship, Grandeur, and Modern Democracy.* New Brunswick, NJ: Transaction Publishers, 2000.

———. *The Conservative Foundations of the Liberal Order: Defending Democracy against Its Modern Enemies and Immoderate Friends.* Wilmington, DE: ISI Books, 2010.

Major, Rafael. "Thinking Through Strauss's Legacy." In *Leo Strauss's Defense of the Philosophic Life: Reading What Is Political Philosophy?* Ed. Rafael Major. University of Chicago Press, 2013, 1–21.

Manent, Pierre. *Tocqueville and the Nature of Democracy*. Tr. John Waggoner. Lanham, MD: Rowman & Littlefield, 1996 [1982].

_____. *The City of Man*. Tr. Marc LePain. Princeton, NJPrinceton: Princeton University Press, 1998 [1994].

_____. "Tocqueville, Political Philosopher." In *The Cambridge Companion to Tocqueville*. Ed. C. B. Welch. New York: Cambridge University Press, 2006.

Mann, Thomas E. and Norman J. Ornstein. *It's Even Worse Than It Looks: How the American Constitutional System Collided With the New Politics of Extremism*. New York: Basic Books, 2012.

Mansfield, Harvey C. *Taming the Prince: The Ambivalence of Modern Executive Power*. New York: Free Press, 1989.

_____. *America's Constitutional Soul*. Baltimore, MD: Johns Hopkins University Press, 1991.

_____. *Tocqueville: A Very Short Introduction*. New York: Oxford University Press, 2010.

Mansfield, Harvey and Delba Winthrop. "Editors' Introduction." In *Tocqueville, Democracy in America*. Eds. and Tr. Harvey Mansfield and Delba Winthrop. Chicago, IL: University of Chicago Press, 2000.

_____. "Tocqueville's New Political Science." In *The Cambridge Companion to Tocqueville*. Ed. C. B. Welch.New York: Cambridge University Press, 2006.

Markowitz, Arthur A. "Washington's Farewell and the Historians: A Critical Review." *Pennsylvania Magazine of History and Biography* 94 (April 1970) 173–91.

Marsh, David and Gerry Stoker, Eds. *Theory and Methods in Political Science*. 3rd edn. New York: Palgrave Macmillan, 2010.

Marshall, John. *The Life of George Washington: Special Edition for Schools*. Eds. Robert Faulkner and Paul Carrese. Indianapolis: Liberty Fund, 2000 [1838].

Martel, William C. "Grand Strategy of 'Restrainment'." *Orbis* 54 (2010) 356–73.

Masugi, Ken, Ed. *Interpreting Tocqueville's Democracy in America*. Savage, MD: Rowman & Littlefield, 1991.

McDonald, Forrest. *Novus Ordo Seclorum: The Intellectual Origins of the Constitution*. University Press of Kansas, 1985.

McDougall, Walter. "Back to Bedrock." *Foreign Affairs* 76, no. 2 (1997) 134–46.

_____. *Promised Land, Crusader State: America's Encounter with the World since 1776*. Boston: Houghton Mifflin, 1997.

McGovern, Patrick J., Ed. "Symposium: Perestroika in Political Science: Past, Present, and Future." *PS: Political Science and Politics* 43 (2010) 725–54.

McJoynt, Albert T. "Washington, George (1732–99)." In *International Military and Defense Encyclopedia*. Ed. Dupuy. Washington, DC: Brassey's U.S./Maxwell Macmillan, 1993, vol. 6: 2932–34.

McWilliams, Wilson Carey. "Democracy and the Citizen: Community, Dignity, and the Crisis of Contemporary Politics in America." In *Redeeming Democracy in America*. Eds. P. Deneen and S. McWilliams. Lawrence, KS: University Press of Kansas, 2011.

_____. "Leo Strauss and the Dignity of American Political Thought" (1988). In *The Democratic Soul: A Wilson Carey McWilliams Reader*. Eds. P. Deneen and S. McWilliams. Lexington: University Press of Kentucky, 2011, 192–206.

Mead, Walter Russell. *Special Providence: American Foreign Policy and How It Changed the World*. New York: Century/Knopf, 2001.

Melnick, Shep. "Balance Is All" (review of J. Q. Wilson, American Politics, Then and Now). *The Claremont Review of Books* 10: 4 (Fall 2010).

———. "Political Science as a Vocation: An Appreciation of the Life and the Work of James Q. Wilson." *The Forum* 10: 1 (May 2012).

Mélonio, Françoise. *Tocqueville and the French*. Tr. Beth Raps. University of Virginia Press, 1998.

———. "Tocqueville and the French." In *The Cambridge Companion to Tocqueville*. Ed. C. B. Welch. New York: Cambridge University Press, 2006.

Milkis, Sidney M. and Michael Nelson. *The American Presidency: Origins and Development, 1776–2011*. 6th edn. Washington, D.C.: CQ Press, 2011.

Mill, John Stuart. *On Liberty*. Ed. Stefan Collini. New York: Cambridge University Press, 1989 [1859].

Minogue, Kenneth. *Citizenship and Monarchy: A Hidden Fault Line in Our Civilisation*. The Institute of United States Studies, University of London, 1998, 10–22.

Mitchell, Joshua. *The Fragility of Freedom: Tocqueville on Religion, Democracy, and the American Future*. University of Chicago Press, 1995.

Montaigne, Michel de. "Of Friendship." In *The Complete Essays of Montaigne*. Ed and Tr. Frame. Stanford, CA: Stanford University Press, 1958.

———. "De l'amitié" (In *Essais*). In *Œuvres complètes*. Eds. Thibaudet and Rat. Paris: Gallimard, 1962.

Monten, Jonathan. "The Roots of the Bush Doctrine: Power, Nationalism, and Democracy Promotion in U.S. Strategy." *International Security* 29 (2005) 112–56.

Montesquieu, Charles-Louis de Secondat, Baron de. *The Spirit of the Laws*. Tr. Thomas Nugent. New York: Hafner, 1949 [1750].

———. *Œuvres complètes*, Pléiade edition. 2 vols. Ed. Roger Caillois. Paris: Gallimard, 1949–51.

———. *Œuvres complètes de Montesquieu*. Ed. André Masson. Nagel, 1950–55.

———. *De l'Esprit des Lois*. Ed. Jean Brethe de la Gressaye. 4 vols. Paris: Belles-Lettres, 1950–61.

———. *Considerations on the Causes of the Greatness of the Romans and their Decline*. Ed. and Tr. David Lowenthal. Ithaca, NY: Cornell University Press, 1968 [1965].

———. *De l'Esprit des Lois*. Ed. Robert Derathé. 2 vols. Paris: Classiques Garnier, 1973.

———. *The Spirit of the Laws*. Eds. and Tr. Anne Cohler, Basia Miller, and Harold Stone. Cambridge: Cambridge University Press, 1989.

———. *The Persian Letters*. Ed. and Tr. George Healy. Indianapolis: Hackett, 1999 [1964].

Morgan, Edmund S. *The Genius of George Washington*. New York: Norton, 1980.

Morgenthau, Hans. "The Mainsprings of American Foreign Policy: The National Interest vs. Moral Abstractions." *American Political Science Review* 44 (1950) 833–54.

Morrison, Jeffry H. *The Political Philosophy of George Washington*. Johns Hopkins University Press, 2009.

Mosher, Michael. "The Particulars of a Universal Politics: Hegel's Adaptation of Montesquieu's Typology." *American Political Science Review* 78 (1984) 178–88.

———. "Monarchy's Paradox: Honor in the Face of Sovereign Power." In *Montesquieu's Science of Politics*. Eds. Carrithers, Mosher, and Rahe. Lanham, MD: Rowman & Littlefield, 2000.

———. "Montesquieu on Empire and Enlightenment." In *Empire and Modern Political Thought*. Ed. Sankar Muthu. New York: Cambridge University Press, 2012, 112–54.

Moynihan, Daniel Patrick. "Defining Deviancy Down." *The American Scholar* 62 (1993) 17–30.

Muller, James W. "The American Framers' Debt to Montesquieu." In *The Revival of Constitutionalism*. Ed. James W. Muller. Lincoln, NE: University of Nebraska Press, 1988.

Muñoz, Vincent Phillip. *God and the Founders: Madison, Washington, and Jefferson*. New York, Cambridge University Press, 2009.

Muravchik, Joshua. *The Imperative of American Leadership: A Challenge to Neo-Isolationism*. Washington, DC: AEI Press, 1996.

Murphy, Walter. *Constitutional Democracy: Creating and Maintaining a Just Political Order*. Baltimore, MD: Johns Hopkins University Press, 2007.

Needham, Anuradha Dingwaney and Rajeshwari Sunder Rajan, Eds. *The Crisis of Secularism in India*. Durham, NC: Duke University Press, 2006.

Nelson, Daniel. *The Priority of Prudence: Virtue and Natural Law in Thomas Aquinas and the Implications for Modern Ethics*. Pennsylvania State University Press, 1992.

Neumann, Franz. "Editor's Introduction." *The Spirit of the Laws*. New York: Hafner, 1949.

Nicgorski, Walter. "The Anti-Federalists: Collected and Interpreted." *The Review of Politics* 46 (1984) 113–25.

Nichols, James. *Epicurean Political Philosophy*. Ithaca, NY: Cornell University Press, 1976.

———. "Pragmatism and the U.S. Constitution." In *Confronting the Constitution*. Ed. Bloom. Washington, DC: AEI Press, 1990.

Nichols, Mary. *Citizens and Statesmen: A Study of Aristotle's Politics*. Savage, MD: Rowman & Littlefield, 1991.

Niebuhr, Reinhold. *The Irony of American History*. New York: Charles Scribner's Sons, 1952.

Nisbet, Robert. "Many Tocquevilles." *The American Scholar* (Winter 1976–77) 59–75.

Nussbaum, Martha C. *The Clash Within: Democracy, Religious Violence, and India's Future*. Cambridge, MA: Harvard University Press, 2007.

Nye, Joseph S., Jr. "Neorealism and Neoliberalism." *World Politics* 40 (1988) 235–51.

———. "Soft Power." *Foreign Policy* 80 (1990) 153–71.

———. *Bound To Lead: The Changing Nature of American Power*. New York: Basic Books, 1991.

Oake, Roger B. "*De l'Esprit des Lois*, Books XXVI-XXXI." *Modern Language Notes* LXIII (1948) 167–71.

———. "Montesquieu's Religious Ideas." *Journal of the History of Ideas* 14 (1953) 548–60.

———. "Montesquieu's Analysis of Roman History." *Journal of the History of Ideas* 16 (1955) 44–59.

Oakeshott, Michael. "Introduction to Leviathan." In *Rationalism in Politics and Other Essays*. Expanded edition. Indianapolis, IN: Liberty Fund, 1991 [1962], 221–94.

———. "The Investigation of the 'Character' of Modern Politics: Montesquieu." In *Morality and Politics in Modern Europe*. Ed. Letwin. Yale University Press, 1993, 29–43.

————. "The Rule of Law." In *On History and Other Essays*. Ed. Timothy Fuller. Indianapolis, IN: Liberty Fund, 1999 [1983]), 129–78.

Onuf, Nicholas G. *The Republican Legacy in International Thought*. New York: Cambridge University Press, 1998.

Orren, Karen and Stephen Skowronek. "Have We Abandoned a 'Constitutional Perspective' on American Political Development?" *The Review of Politics* 73 (2011) 295–99.

Orwin, Clifford. "'For Which Human Nature Can Never Be Too Grateful': Montesquieu as the Heir of Christianity." In *Recovering Reason: Essays in Honor of Thomas L. Pangle*. Ed. Burns. Lanham, MD: Lexington Books, 2010.

Ovid. *Metamorphoses*. Vol. 1. Eds. and Tr. Miller and Goold. Harvard University Press, 1977.

Owens, Mackubin. "General Washington and the Military Strategy of the Revolution." In *Patriot Sage: George Washington and the American Political Tradition*. Eds. Gregg and Spalding. ISI Books, 1999, 61–98.

Palmer, Dave. *The Way of the Fox: American Strategy in the War for America, 1775–1783*. Westport, CT: Greenwood Press, 1975.

Paltsits, Victor H., Ed. *Washington's Farewell Address*. New York: The New York Public Library, 1935.

Pangle, Thomas L. *Montesquieu's Philosophy of Liberalism: A Commentary on The Spirit of the Laws*. Chicago, IL: University of Chicago Press, 1973.

————. *The Spirit of Modern Republicanism: The Moral Vision of the American Founders and the Philosophy of John Locke*. Chicago, IL: University of Chicago Press, 1988.

————. "The Philosophic Understandings of Human Nature Informing the Constitution." In *Confronting the Constitution*. Ed. A. Bloom. Washington, DC: AEI Press, 1990.

————. *Leo Strauss: An Introduction to His Thought and Intellectual Legacy*. Johns Hopkins University Press, 2006.

————. *The Theological Basis of Liberal Modernity in Montesquieu's The Spirit of the Laws*. University of Chicago Press, 2010.

Pangle, Thomas L. and Peter J. Ahrensdorf. *Justice Among Nations: On the Moral Basis of Power and Peace*. Lawrence: University Press of Kansas, 1999.

Paret, Peter. "Clausewitz." In *Makers of Modern Strategy: From Machiavelli to the Nuclear Age*. Ed. Peter Paret. Princeton University Press, 1986, 187–213.

Perestroika Glasnost, "On Globalization of the APSA and *APSR*: A Political Science Manifesto" (October 15, 2000). In *Perestroika! The Raucous Revolution in Political Science*. Ed. K. R. Monroe. Yale University Press, 2005.

Perkins, Bradford. *The Cambridge History of American Foreign Relations, Volume 1, The Creation of A Republican Empire, 1776–1865*. New York: Cambridge University Press, 1993.

Pessen, Edward. "George Washington's Farewell Address, the Cold War, and the Timeless National Interest." *Journal of the Early Republic* 7 (Spring 1987), 1–25.

Pettit, Phillip. *Republicanism: A Theory of Freedom and Government*. New York: Oxford University Press, 1999 [1997].

Pew Forum on Religion & Public Life. http://pewforum.org/

Phelps, Glenn. *George Washington and American Constitutionalism*. Lawrence: University Press of Kansas, 1993.

Pieper, Josef. *The Silence of St. Thomas: Three Essays.* Tr. John Murray and Daniel O'Connor. New York: Pantheon, 1957.

_____. *The Four Cardinal Virtues.* University of Notre Dame Press, 1966.

Pierson, George Wilson. *Tocqueville and Beaumont in America.* Oxford: Oxford University Press, 1938.

Pitts, Jennifer. "Introduction." In Tocqueville, *Writings on Empire and Slavery.* Ed. and Tr. Jennifer Pitts. Johns Hopkins University Press, 2000.

Plato. *The Laws of Plato.* Ed. and Tr. Thomas L. Pangle. University of Chicago Press, 1988 [1980].

Plattner, Marc. "A Skeptical Afterword." *Journal of Democracy* 15: 4 (2004) 106–10.

Plutarch. "To an Uneducated Prince." In *Moralia.* Vol. 10. Ed. Fowler. Harvard University Press, 1936.

_____. *Lives of the Noble Grecians and Romans.* Ed. Clough, Tr. Dryden. 2 vols. New York: Modern Library, 1992.

Putnam, Robert and David Campbell. *American Grace: How Religion Divides and Unites Us.* New York: Simon & Schuster, 2010.

Rabkin, Jeremy. "An American Scholar" (review of Storing, *Toward A More Perfect Union.* Ed. Bessette). *The Public Interest* 123 (1996) 118–23.

Radasanu, Andrea. "Montesquieu on Moderation, Monarchy, and Reform." *History of Political Thought* 31 (Summer 2010) 283–307.

Rahe, Paul A. *Republics Ancient & Modern.* Vol. 2, *New Modes and Orders in Early Modern Political Thought.* Vol. 3, *Inventions of Prudence: Constituting the American Regime.* Chapel Hill, NC: University of North Carolina Press, 1994.

_____. "Thucydides' Critique of Realpolitik." *Security Studies* 5: 2 (1995) 105–41.

_____. "Forms of Government." In *Montesquieu's Science of Politics.* Eds. Carrithers, Mosher, and Rahe. Lanham, MD: Rowman & Littlefield, 2000.

_____. *Montesquieu and the Logic of Liberty.* New Haven, CT: Yale University Press, 2009.

_____. *Soft Despotism, Democracy's Drift: Montesquieu, Rousseau, Tocqueville, & The Modern Prospect.* Yale University Press, 2009.

_____. "Montesquieu's Natural Rights Constitutionalism." *Social Policy and Philosophy* 29 (2012) 51–81.

_____. "Tocqueville on Christianity and the Natural Equality of Man." *Catholic Social Science Review* (2012) 7–20.

_____. "Montesquieu, Natural Law, and Natural Right." In *Natural Law, Natural Rights, and American Constitutionalism.* Ed. Bradford P. Wilson. Witherspoon Institute.www.nlnrac.org/earlymodern/montesquieu (Accessed May 2013).

_____. "Was Montesquieu a Philosopher of History?" *Cahiers Montesquieu* 10 (2013) 71–86.

Ranney, Austin. *The Doctrine of Responsible Party Government: Its Origins and Present State.* University of Illinois Press, 1954.

Rasmussen, Dennis. *The Pragmatic Enlightenment: Recovering the Liberalism of Smith, Hume, Montesquieu, and Voltaire.* New York: Cambridge University Press, 2014.

Rawls, John. *A Theory of Justice.* Cambridge, MA: Harvard University Press, 1971.

_____. *Political Liberalism.* New York: Columbia University Press, 1993.

Ray, John. "George Washington's Pre-Presidential Statesmanship." *Presidential Studies Quarterly* 27 (1997) 207–20.

Richter, Melvin. "The Uses of Theory: Tocqueville's Adaptation of Montesquieu." In *Essays in Theory and History*. Ed. Melvin Richter. Harvard University Press, 1970.

———. *The Political Theory of Montesquieu*. New York: Cambridge University Press, 1977.

Roche, John P. "The Founding Fathers: A Reform Caucus in Action." *American Political Science Review* 55 (1961) 799–816.

Roosevelt, Theodore. "Washington's Forgotten Maxim" (1897). In *The Works of Theodore Roosevelt*. New York: Charles Scribner's Sons, 1926, vol. 13:182–99.

Rossiter, Clinton. *Alexander Hamilton and the Constitution*. New York: Harcourt, Brace & World, 1964.

Rossum, Ralph. "Herbert Storing's Constitutionalism." *Political Science Reviewer* 29 (2000) 39–69.

Rousseau, Jean-Jacques. *Emile, or On Education*. Tr. A. Bloom. New York: Basic Books, 1979.

Ryan, Alan. *On Politics: A History of Political Thought – Book Two: Hobbes to the Present*. W.W. Norton, 2012.

Salkever, Stephen. *Finding the Mean: Theory and Practice in Aristotelian Political Philosophy*. Princeton University Press, 1990.

Samuel, Ana. "The Design of Montesquieu's *The Spirit of the Laws*: The Triumph of Freedom over Determinism." *American Political Science Review* 103 (2009) 305–21.

Sandel, Michael. *Democracy's Discontent: America in Search of a Public Philosophy*. Cambridge, MA: Harvard University Press, 1996.

Sandoz, Ellis. *A Government of Laws: Political Theory, Religion, and the American Founding*. Baton Rouge, LA: Louisiana State University Press, 1990.

———. "Fortescue, Coke, and Anglo-American Constitutionalism." In *The Roots of Liberty: Magna Carta, Ancient Constitution, and the Anglo-American Tradition of Rule of Law*. Ed. Sandoz. Columbia, MO: University of Missouri Press, 1993.

Schaar, John H. and Sheldon S. Wolin. "Review Essay: Essays on the Scientific Study of Politics: A Critique." *American Political Science Review* 57 (1963) 125–50.

Schaefer, David L. *The Political Philosophy of Montaigne*. Ithaca, NY: Cornell University Press, 1990.

Schall, James V. "A Latitude for Statesmanship? Strauss on St. Thomas." *Review of Politics* 53 (1991) 126–45.

———. "The Right Order of Polity and Economy: Reflections on St. Thomas and the 'Old Law'." *Cultural Dynamics* 7 (1995) 427–40.

Schaub, Diana. *Erotic Liberalism: Women and Revolution in Montesquieu's Persian Letters*. Lanham, MD: Rowman & Littlefield, 1995.

———. "Of Believers and Barbarians: Montesquieu's Enlightened Toleration." In *Early Modern Skepticism and the Origins of Toleration*. Ed. Alan Levine. Lanham, MD: Lexington Books, 1999, 225–47.

Schleifer, James. *The Making of Tocqueville's Democracy in America*. Chapel Hill, NC: University of North Carolina Press, 1980.

Schram, Sanford S. and Brian Caterino, Eds. *Making Political Science Matter: Debating Knowledge, Research, and Method*. New York: New York University Press, 2006.

Shackleton, Robert. *Montesquieu: A Critical Biography.* Oxford: Oxford University Press, 1961.

Shain, Barry. *The Myth of American Individualism: The Protestant Origins of American Political Thought.* Princeton, NJ: Princeton University Press, 1994.

Shklar, Judith. *Montesquieu.* Past Masters series. Oxford: Oxford University Press, 1987.

_____. "A New Constitution for a New Nation." In *Redeeming American Political Thought.* Eds. S. Hoffman and D. Thompson. Chicago, IL: University of Chicago Press, 1998.

Siedentop, Larry. *Inventing the Individual: The Origins of Western Liberalism.* Cambridge, MA: Harvard University Press, 2014.

Simes, Dmitri. "Realism: It's High-minded…and It Works." *The National Interest* 74 (Winter 2003–2004), 168–72.

Slaughter, Anne-Marie. "Why a Grand Strategy Is Needed for Obama's Second Term." *The Washington Post,* January 23, 2013.

Smith, Jean Edward. *Eisenhower in War and Peace.* New York: Random House, 2012.

Smith, Rogers. "Beyond Tocqueville, Myrdal, and Hartz: The Multiple Traditions in America." *American Political Science Review* 87 (1993) 549–66.

Snyder, Jack. "One World, Rival Theories." *Foreign Policy* 145 (November/December 2004) 53–62.

Sorel, Albert. *Montesquieu.* deuxième edition. Paris: Librarie Hachette, 1889.

Spalding, Matthew and Patrick Garrity. *A Sacred Union of Citizens: George Washington's Farewell Address and the American Character.* Lanham, MD: Rowman & Littlefield, 1996.

Sparks, Christopher. *Montesquieu's Vision of Uncertainty and Modernity in Political Philosophy.* New York: Edwin Mellen, 1999.

Spector, Céline. "Quelle justice? quelle rationalité? La mesure du droit dans *L'Esprit des lois.*" In *Montesquieu en 2005.* Ed. Catherine Volpilhac-Auger. Oxford: Voltaire Foundation, 2005, 219–42.

_____. "Was Montesquieu Liberal? *The Spirit of the Laws* in the History of Liberalism." In *French Liberalism from Montesquieu to the Present Day.* Eds. Geenens and Rosenblatt. New York: Cambridge University Press, 2012, 57–72.

Spurlin, Paul Merrill. *Montesquieu in America, 1760–1801.* Baton Rouge, LA: Louisiana State University Press, 1940.

_____. *The French Enlightenment in America.* Athens, GA: University of Georgia Press, 1984.

Stoner, James R. *Common Law and Liberal Theory: Coke, Hobbes, and the Origins of American Constitutionalism.* Lawrence, KS: University Press of Kansas, 1992.

_____. "Common Law and Constitutionalism in the Abortion Case." *Review of Politics* 55 (1993), 421–41.

_____. "Common Law and Natural Law." *Benchmark* 5 (1993) 93–102.

_____. "Religious Liberty & Common Law: Free Exercise Exemptions & American Courts." *Polity* 26 (1993), 1–24.

_____. "Sound Whigs or Honeyed Tories? Jefferson and the Common Law Tradition." In *Reason and Republicanism: Thomas Jefferson's Legacy of Liberty.* Eds. G. McDowell and S. Noble. Lanham, MD: Rowman & Littlefield, 1997.

————. "Property, the Common Law, and John Locke." In *Natural Law and Public Policy*. Ed. David Forte. Washington, D.C.: Georgetown University Press, 1998.

————. "The Common Law Spirit of the American Revolution." In *Educating the Prince: Essays in Honor of Harvey Mansfield*. Eds. Blitz and Kristol. Lanham, MD: Rowman & Littlefield, 2000, 192–204.

————. *Common Law Liberty: Rethinking American Constitutionalism*. University Press of Kansas, 2003.

————. "The Passion and Prejudice of Legislators: Book XXIX of The Spirit of the Laws." Unpublished paper, 1995 American Political Science Association meeting.

Storing, Herbert J. *What the Anti-Federalists Were FOR*. Ed. Murray Dry. Chicago, IL: University of Chicago Press, 1981.

————. "William Blackstone." In *History of Political Philosophy*. 3rd edn. Eds. Strauss and Cropsey. Chicago, IL: University of Chicago Press, 1987 [1963].

————. *Toward a More Perfect Union: Writings of Herbert J. Storing*. Ed. Joseph M. Bessette. Washington, D.C.: AEI Press, 1995.

Storing, Herbert J., Ed. *Essays on the Scientific Study of Politics*. New York: Holt, Rinehart, and Winston, 1962.

————. *What Country Have I? Political Writings by Black Americans*. New York: St. Martin's Press, 1970.

————. *The Anti-Federalist*. Selected by Murray Dry. Chicago, IL: University of Chicago Press, 1985.

Storing, Herbert J., Leo Strauss, Walter Berns, Leo Weinstein, and Robert Horwitz. "Replies to Schaar and Wolin: I–VI." *American Political Science Review* 57 (1963) 151–60.

Strauss, Leo. *Natural Right and History*. Chicago, IL: University of Chicago Press, 1953.

————. "What Is Political Philosophy?" In *What Is Political Philosophy? And Other Studies*. University of Chicago Press, 1959.

Tamanaha, Brian. *Law as a Means to an End: Threat to the Rule of Law*. Cambridge University Press, 2006.

Tarcov, Nathan. "A 'Non-Lockean' Locke and the Character of Liberalism." In Eds. MacLean and Mills. *Liberalism Reconsidered*. New Jersey: Rowman & Allanheld, 1983, 130–40.

Tessitore, Aristide. "Alexis de Tocqueville on the Natural State of Religion in the Age of Democracy." *Journal of Politics* 64 (2002) 1137–52.

————. "Aristotle and Tocqueville on Statesmanship." In *Alexis de Tocqueville and the Art of Democratic Statesmanship*. Eds. Brian Danoff and L. Joseph Hebert. Lanham, MD: Lexington Books, 2011, 49–72.

Thomas, George. "The Tensions of Constitutional Democracy." *Constitutional Commentary* 24 (2007) 793–806.

————. "A Reply to Orren and Skowronek." *Review of Politics* 73 (2011), 301–304.

————. "What Is Political Development? A Constitutional Perspective." *The Review of Politics* 73 (2011), 275–95.

Thompson, Norma. *The Ship of State: Statecraft and Politics from Ancient Greece to Democratic America*. Yale University Press, 2001.

Tocqueville, Alexis de. "*De la Démocratie en Amérique*." In *Oeuvres Complètes*. Ed. J. P. Mayer. Paris: Gallimard, 1951.

_____. *Democracy in America*. Ed. J. P. Mayer, Tr. George Lawrence. Garden City, NY: Doubleday, Anchor, 1969 [1835–40].

_____. "The Art and Science of Politics." Tr. J. P. Mayer. *Encounter* 36 (1971) 27–35.

_____. *The Old Regime and the French Revolution, Volume 1*. Eds. François Furet and Françoise Mélonio, Tr. Alan Kahan. University of Chicago Press, 1998 [1856].

_____. *Democracy in America*. Eds. and Tr. Harvey Mansfield and Delba Winthrop. Chicago, IL: University of Chicago Press, 2000.

_____. "Speech Given to the Annual Public Meeting of the Academy of Moral and Political Sciences on April 3, 1852." In *Alexis de Tocqueville and the Art of Democratic Statesmanship*. Eds. Brian Danoff and L. Joseph Hebert, Tr. L. Joseph Hebert. Lanham, MD: Lexington Books, 2011.

Tuck, Richard. *Natural Rights Theories*. New York: Cambridge University Press, 1979.

Tucker, Robert and David Hendrickson. *Empire of Liberty: The Statecraft of Thomas Jefferson*. New York: Oxford University Press, 1990.

Villa, Dana. "Tocqueville and Civil Society." In *The Cambridge Companion to Tocqueville*. Ed. C. B. Welch. New York: Cambridge University Press, 2006, 216–44.

Volpilhac-Auger, Catherine. "Une nouvelle 'Chaîne secrète' de *L'Esprit des lois*: L'Histoire de texte." In *Montesquieu en 2005*. Ed. Catherine Volpilhac-Auger. Oxford, UK: Voltaire Foundation, 2005.

Waddicor, Mark. *Montesquieu and the Philosophy of Natural Law*. The Hague: Martinus Nijhoff, 1970.

Wald, Kenneth D. *Religion and Politics in the United States*. 4th edn. Lanham, MD: Rowman & Littlefield, 2003.

Walling, Karl-Friedrich. *Republican Empire: Alexander Hamilton on War and Free Government*. Lawrence, KS: University Press of Kansas, 1999.

Walzer, Michael. *Just and Unjust Wars: A Moral Argument with Historical Illustrations*. New York: Basic Books, 1977; 4th edn., 2006.

Warner, Stuart D. "Montesquieu's Prelude: An Interpretation of Book I of *The Spirit of the Laws*." In *Enlightening Revolutions: Essays in Honor of Ralph Lerner*. Ed. S. Minkov. Lanham, MD: Lexington Books, 2006.

Washington, George. *Writings of George Washington*. 39 vols. Ed. Fitzpatrick. Washington, DC: U.S. Government Printing Office, 1931–44.

_____. *George Washington: A Collection*. Ed. William B. Allen. Indianapolis, IN: Liberty Fund, 1988.

_____. *George Washington: Writings*. Ed. John Rhodehamel. New York: Library of America/Literary Classics of the United States, 1997.

_____. *George Washington's Rules of Civility: Complete with the Original French Text and New French-to-English Translations*. 2nd edn., Ed. John T. Phillips, II. Leesburg, VA.: Goose Creek Productions, 2000.

Weart, Spencer R. *Never at War: Why Democracies Will Not Fight One Another*. New Haven, CT: Yale University Press, 1998.

Weigel, George. "The Development of Just War Thinking in the Post-Cold War World: An American Perspective." In *The Price of Peace: Just War in the Twenty-First Century*. Eds. Reed and Ryall. New York: Cambridge University Press, 2007, 19–36.

Weigley, Russell. "American Strategy from Its Beginnings through the First World War." In *Makers of Modern Strategy*. Ed. Peter Paret. Princeton University Press, 1986, 408–43.

Welch, Cheryl B. *De Tocqueville*. New York: Oxford University Press, 2001.

———, Ed. *The Cambridge Companion to Tocqueville*. New York: Cambridge University Press, 2006.

West, Thomas. "Misunderstanding the American Founding." In *Interpreting Tocqueville's Democracy in America*. Ed. Ken Masugi. Savage, MD: Rowman & Littlefield, 1991.

Westberg, Daniel *Right Practical Reason: Aristotle, Action, and Prudence in Aquinas*. Oxford: Clarendon Press, 1994.

Wilson, Woodrow. *Constitutional Government in the United States*. New York: Columbia University Press, 1908.

Winthrop, Delba. "Aristotle and Theories of Justice." *American Political Science Review* 72 (1978).

———. Review of Tocqueville *Writings on Empire and Slavery*, ed. Pitts. In *Society*, (November/December 2002), 110–13.

Wolfe, Christopher. *Natural Law Liberalism*. New York: Cambridge University Press, 2006.

Wolin, Sheldon S. *Tocqueville Between Two Worlds: The Making of a Political and Theoretical Life*. Princeton, NJ: Princeton University Press, 2001.

Wood, Gordon. "The Fundamentalists and the Constitution." *New York Review of Books* (February 18, 1988) 33–40.

———. "The Greatness of George Washington." In *Revolutionary Characters: What Made the Founders Different*. New York: Penguin, 2006.

Yenor, Scott. "Natural Religion and Human Perfectibility: Tocqueville's Account of Religion in Modern Democracy." *Perspectives on Political Science* 33: 1 (2004) 10–17.

Zakaria, Fareed. *The Future of Freedom: Illiberal Democracy at Home and Abroad*. New York: Norton, 2003.

———. *The Post-American World*. New York: Norton, 2008.

Zetterbaum, Marvin. *Tocqueville and the Problem of Democracy*. Stanford, CA: Stanford University Press, 1967.

Zuckert, Catherine. "Not by Preaching: Tocqueville on the Role of Religion." *Review of Politics* 42 (1981) 259–80.

———. "Political Sociology versus Speculative Philosophy." In *Interpreting Tocqueville's Democracy in America*. Ed. Ken Masugi. Savage, MD: Rowman & Littlefield, 1991.

———. "The Role of Religion in Preserving American Liberty – Tocqueville's Analysis 150 Years Later." In *Tocqueville's Defense of Human Liberty: Current Essays*. Eds. Lawler and Alulis. New York: Garland, 1993, 223–39.

Zuckert, Michael. *Natural Rights and the New Republicanism*. Princeton, NJ: Princeton University Press, 1994.

———. *The Natural Rights Republic: Studies in the Foundation of the American Political Tradition*. Notre Dame, IN: University of Notre Dame Press, 1996.

———. "Herbert J. Storing's Turn to the American Founding." *Political Science Reviewer* 29 (2000) 9–38.

———. "Natural Law, Natural Rights, and Classical Liberalism: On Montesquieu's Critique of Hobbes." *Social Philosophy and Policy* 18 (2001) 227–51.

Index

Made in the USA
Las Vegas, NV
16 September 2021

30443314R00146